CITY DEVELOPMENT

PATRICK GEDDES

CITY DEVELOPMENT
A Report to the Carnegie Dunfermline Trust

with an introduction by
PETER GREEN

RUTGERS UNIVERSITY PRESS *New Brunswick, New Jersey*

First edition
Edinburgh, Westminster, and Birmingham 1904

This reprint is a complete and unabridged
photolithographic facsimile of the first edition.

© 1973 Carnegie Dunfermline Trust (original text
and illustrations) and Irish University Press
(introduction)

ISBN 0–8135–0748–0

Rutgers University Press, New Brunswick, New Jersey

PRINTED IN THE REPUBLIC OF IRELAND AT SHANNON

INTRODUCTION

PATRICK GEDDES 1854–1932

PATRICK GEDDES, the Scottish biologist, educationalist, and planner, was already a well-known figure in late nineteenth-century Edinburgh. He lived in a dingy close in the Old Town, and organised a series of summer schools, civic exhibitions, and discussions in a building near the Castle. This was the "Outlook Tower", a civic museum which he founded and which became the centre for the work of rehabilitating the slums of Edinburgh.

Geddes was an ebullient scientist who became a social philosopher, a social reformer, and the father of modern town-planning. He was a polymath who never took a degree but came to hold professorships in botany, civics, and sociology. Geddes was a classic wandering Scot—he planned towns and cities in India and the Near East, lectured on education in three continents, and seemed to appear at almost every conference held in the Universities of Europe. Geddes had something stimulating to say on almost every subject—he was a man who provoked response—he could never be avoided.

Ranging so very widely in his theoretical and practical activities, Geddes is a difficult subject on which to pin labels. His very diversity appears to place him in the tradition of a series of polymaths who were notable in the Age of Enlightenment: his objection to overt specialisation as an end in itself and his search for some means of integrating specialist knowledge within a handy scheme of reference aligns him with Bacon and Descartes. At whatever level one analyses this man, it is clear that he bridges the fields of study and philosophies of his day—links the teaching of the Le Play school of social science with Booth and the study of towns; Spencer and Comte with Huxley and Darwin; Robert Owen with Joseph Chamberlain (most strange bed-fellows). He also appears as a figure who bridges time.

Geddes's concern with the problem of the nineteenth-century slum resulted in his advocacy of new towns and of urban rehabilitation; of regional planning and rural conservation as a means to control the spread of towns at a time when towns scarcely showed signs of a massive distillation into the countryside. Perhaps most notably, Geddes placed an emphasis on the right of the individual to shape his environment at a period dominated by mechanistic ways of thought.

Others far better known than Geddes were concerned with the question of the place of the individual within the social and economic system. This had been a preoccupation of philosophers in the Age of Enlightenment and was to be given point and momentum by the Evolutionist school of thought. Geddes embraced, in his own work, many of these mainstream ideas. With Darwin and Huxley, he accepted the notion of an upward progress of humanity; with Rousseau, a belief in man's power and right to change his institutions;

and with Adam Smith, a conviction that wealth may best be created through
co-operative action.

In no way did Geddes inaugurate a new philosophy. He accepted ideas from
any source, used them freely, but in turn took out no patents for his own
interpretation and synthesis of them. He contributed to the advance of ideas
mainly by applying other people's ideas to his own purposes.

Geddes was in no position, in an academic sense, to be severely critical of the
rigorous thinker and researcher. Like Spencer, Geddes was largely self-taught.
He came to work over again the essential bases of each philosophy, reassessing
its findings, not against other philosophies, but against what he saw as the
ultimate test—the living world. His was, in fact, an intuitive philosophy
largely derived from experience.

It is not surprising that Geddes was no purist and not committed to any one
belief. Temperamentally, he found it difficult to subject himself to any one
rigorous academic boundary and the methodology of any one special field of
study. His own writing and thinking show indefinite boundaries. He was
convinced that life had to be lived in the real world, and his deep concern for
contemporary problems, as he defined them, goes some way to explain why he
stressed that interconnexions had to be made between the world of learning and
the world of living.

Patrick Geddes had a strong mind coupled with an extravert personality
and seemed, to many of his contemporaries, a character larger than life. He
met issues head-on, could be dogmatic, self-assertive and absolutely convinced
of the validity of his ideas in spite of constant setbacks and rebuffs. He never
lost a sense of purpose, and elements of the "utopist mentality" in his make-up
made him confident that others would accept his ideas and act accordingly.

Geddes followed a number of careers, and, partly by chance, he only bit
hard into his main life's work in middle age. The fortuitous, in his careers,
generally took the form of some person, family friend, or collaborator, who
took care of his petty problems and gave him moral support. This was most
essential, for Geddes would burst upon a problem, attack it with full vigour,
and leave a shower of secondary and often detailed proposals to be worked out
—a life's work for others. Lewis Mumford, the American writer on the history
and evolution of the city, has spent a lifetime elaborating upon and moving
from many guidelines offered by Geddes.

Many people outside Geddes's family circle gave willingly of their time and
effort, and this testified to his capacity to inspire. Doubtless some of the
devotion sprang from a belief that Geddes was a prophet, but, in spite of all
his foibles, he had many lifelong friends.

Men of great energy can pose problems for others. Geddes was certainly no
easy man to work with, for he was often in a hurry. There was little leisure in his
long and active lifetime. When he was not working, he was thinking, and
generally he was both thinking and working. Thought and action were linked

together in a single and simultaneous process. This often led to situations in which he had too many thought-laden vehicles on the road, and since the road was not wide enough, one after another could not get through. Geddes needed every possible moment to work out his many ideas. In India, for instance, when he was over sixty years of age, he would wake at five in the morning and spend two or three hours elaborating upon the previous day's work or planning ahead. One lifelong friend, Edward McGeegan, has given one aspect of Geddes's vitality: "Pat would break off a discussion sharp at ten o'clock and go to bed and sought to resume the conversation at breakfast next morning, not at the point where he had interrupted it the previous evening, but at a point he had reached after developing the idea. I remember one particular occasion at Lasswade. The Professor and I had sat up to an hour unusually late for him and at last he had gone to bed, leaving a certain problem unsolved. I was awakened next morning by the sound of a pattering upon my bedroom window. I looked at my watch and found that the hour was five o'clock. I looked out of the window and saw the professor, fully dressed, standing on the garden path below. He called softly, but clearly, 'Problem solved. Do come down and discuss where the solution leads to.'"

The vitality of Geddes was also expressed through his power as a conversationalist. According to many of his contemporaries, he was a brilliant talker. His capacity to communicate was at its best in the small group. Like Albert Schweitzer, Geddes drew students to him. His conversation had ease, depth, and breadth of thought, and an extraordinary wealth of image, metaphor, and simile drawn from all the arts, sciences, religions, and philosophies. He revelled in talking and used the long conversation as a medium for exercising his own thinking faculties and carrying his own thoughts on a subject a stage further. In old age Geddes took this to excess, and a conversation with him became less a dialogue and more a monologue by Geddes. This tendency to dominate an audience often accompanies the old age of strong minds.

Unfortunately, Geddes found fluent expression of his thought less easy in writing than he did in conversation, so his writings were often laboured and awkward. One reason for this difference between his written and spoken word, which he acknowledged, was that he required the presence of a group of friends or students to stimulate him towards spontaneous expression. His manuscripts and typescripts are so written and re-written over that often scarcely a word of the original text remains. His attention to editorial work was outstanding, and the efforts he made to revise and further revise were enormous. Geddes's collaborator and friend, Professor J. A. Thomson, a biologist, once commented that Geddes's output of books "was cramped by a strange fastidiousness which led him, like many an artist, to throw away one brilliant sketch after another till the opportunity passed altogether, or else to over-elaborate the canvas till intelligibility was obscured".

It seemed to be the case that by the time Geddes had written drafts of articles his thoughts on the subject had developed several stages further, and the task of revision to incorporate these new ideas often proved too laborious and was left unfinished. Geddes was frequently expressing and developing notions which were, in their essentials, new. He had to find convenient terms for these ideas—words which could explain them adequately in themselves and in relation to the subjects to which they belonged. He came to invent compound words or nomenclatures. Typical of these are terms like "bio-technics", "geotechnics", "ethopolity". The introduction of these into the written text served more to confuse rather than clarify the issue under discussion for the untutored reader.

Another and vital cause of the laboriousness of Geddes's writing was the habit of using what he called his "thinking machines"—a form of intellectual shorthand. These were blank sheets of paper which Geddes folded horizontally and vertically into a number of squares—the number and size varying according to the purpose for which they were to be used. In the divisions or squares Geddes wrote single words expressing ideas or fields of study. At a glance any one of these ideas could be seen in relation to others in squares adjacent to or away from the original square. Thus linkage between ideas, between fields of study, or simply the relation of one fact to another, could be seen. An analogy would be a pictorial cartoon in which two persons exist within a given environment. The relationship between the persons and their setting can be quickly grasped by the reader. He is able to trace a multi-linear relation-ship—relationship of person A to B and to environment C with reverse relationships between B and AC, C and AB superimposed.

Geddes had devised this system of thought in order to pass the time during a period of temporary blindness which afflicted him during a visit to Mexico in 1879. His system was a form of mechanical computing which enabled him to work out intellectual problems with the maximum rapidity and with the minimum amount of secondary mental exertion normally needed for trans-lating ideas into descriptive sentences. Unfortunately these diagrams became ends in themselves as well as intellectual toys. Geddes tended to postpone the task of reproducing them in ordinary syntax and, over time, came to lose the intellectual impetus that had produced them. The difficulty of translating these "thinking machines" is evident when it is realised that the basic schemata on which hundreds of such diagrams were produced was a simple Place, Work, and Folk interrelationship which could be elaborated into over five hundred sub-divisions. "To those who find such notations useful", wrote J. A. Thomson, "they appear as the most remarkable organa which the mind of man has devised for disclosing all the possible relations of any subject."

Nevertheless, in spite of all these difficulties, Geddes alone or in collaboration with others published over two hundred and fifty articles and papers which ranged widely across the sciences and social sciences. A number of these papers explored a field of study in some depth. With J. A. Thomson, for instance,

Geddes produced, at the age of seventy-seven, a fifteen-hundred-page study of biology; with the same collaborator in 1914, an outspoken and learned work on the evolution of sex. Most of Geddes's papers, however, illuminated the connexion between different areas of study. Amongst these was a classificatory system for the sciences, a book on the evolution of the city, and many papers on the need for university and educational reform.

The key to understanding Geddes lies in his search for a universal synthesis, and it was in this search that he pushed back the frontiers of learning. His eclecticism was deliberate—he borrowed with purpose, never indiscriminately. The roots of his ideas came from many studies: in biology from Lamarck, Darwin, Huxley, and Lacaze Duthier; in sociology from Comte, Le Play, and Spencer; in psychology from William James and Stanley Hall; and in philosophy from Rousseau, Bentham, Kropotkin, and a host of others. The fact that Geddes publicised his interpretations so freely and encouraged others to take off from them partly helps to explain why his contributions to scholarship are largely undocumented. Indeed, Geddes saw his role as being catalytic; pointing out to an audience on one occasion that he had no use for the claims of priority, "I am", he said, "like the cuckoo who lays her eggs in other birds' nests—the main thing is that the eggs should develop, not that the cuckoo's ego should be gratified."

The very diversity of Geddes's activities provides scope for research by students of many fields of study. There is a possibility that one's view might be coloured by a sense that here was a man of so many parts that random chance or innate superficiality had created the structure, which thus loses in interest. Few men of stature and high intellectual calibre embark upon a career characterised by omniscience without some ulterior motive. Geddes made distinct contributions to science and could count Darwin and Huxley as referees. He became a professional generalist by choice. He was not unique in following this path and there are close parallels in the lives of Sir Walter Scott, Frederick Le Play, and Herbert Spencer, to name but a few; men of his epoch who moved from the security of professional recognition into chancier futures in general studies. Over a period of time Geddes became convinced that environmental and social planning must come to the forefront if society was to progress. This required integrative studies in order to attain a high level of generality. His work falls into a pattern intended to accomplish this aim. Geddes became a planner of environment and started a process which was to enable the acceptance of planning, within his own lifetime, as a proper field of intellectual activity and one which was created through a co-ordination of the findings emanating from other studies.

Of the four knighted pioneers of British planning—Geddes, Unwin, Howard, and Abercrombie—Geddes ranged the most widely. He was wide-ranging not only in his studies, but also in his practical work. He became involved in education, exhibitions, publicity, and publishing, the encourage-

ment of art and regional language. He was prepared to use any means in order
to enlarge human opportunity and to teach awareness of the components of
the environment. As a result of these far-ranging activities it was inevitable
that Geddes would clash with specialists who were only defining, in his day
and age, what they saw as legitimate subject boundaries beyond which the
practitioner must not venture.

Geddes's unorthodox views brought him into association with many anti-
establishment figures, most notable amongst whom were Kropotkin and
Reclus. Notwithstanding, it is relevant to recall that Geddes collaborated
closely and drew many commissions from governments, princes, private
trusts, and municipal authorities, in two continents. Of his major planning
commissions (comprising over sixty major reports), only two were forth-
coming in his native Scotland—one for the Edinburgh Zoological Gardens,
the other for the Carnegie Dunfermline Trust. The Dunfermline report,
produced in 1904, merits special study as an expression of Geddesian philosophy
and as a crucial step in Geddes's development as a publicist.

Few men of lively intelligence and imagination can live untouched by their
age and its currents. As a country boy brought up near Perth, Geddes absorbed
deeply a sense not only of the organic relationship which exists within nature,
but also of that between market-town and its rural hinterland. Later, he
became impressed by the economic efficiency and modernity of late nineteenth-century Germany, and yet his belief in real progress for man was
founded upon a humane philosophy of the dignity of man. Geddes fell heir
to the late Victorian search for values and for the meaning of progress.

Characteristically, Geddes approached these great problems as an educationalist. In this his attitude was marked by a disdain of formal and rigid academic
systems and awards. He searched constantly for a living education, forged and
created by the learner, rather than for one imposed upon him. Geddes used
his own experience as the measure. He had been given an opportunity to
become aware of the many possible ways of living and experiencing life, had
been privately educated, had then experienced formal schooling, and had been
in a position to reject one university course (Edinburgh) in favour of another
taught by Huxley at the London School of Mines. In this he had been fortunate,
for few others in his day had the opportunity to do more than take advantage
of compulsory primary education, introduced in England in 1870. His experience as a late developer convinced him that a flexible educational system,
permitting a student to develop along lines created by his own interest, was
necessary. With Huxley and Birkbeck, Geddes worked towards the achievement of widespread adult education and the translation of the results of
scientific discovery to a level of a general understanding by the man in the
street. He pressed for an imaginative and lively school curriculum which drew
into its orbit art, aesthetics, practical surveys, and voluntary community
service.

In Geddes's approach to education one can trace clearly the influence of Morris, Ruskin, and Mackintosh, who, through their own work, had tried to restore a symbiotic relationship between art and life. Education, in the Geddesian sense, was to lead to a situation whereby the learner became fully aware of all aspects of his own experience, and to ensure that this experience was as widely based as possible. Geddes campaigned for the view that a general education is necessary to underpin and give meaning to specialised learning. He went further than many of his contemporaries and carried the message into the largely unexplored territory of the dark streets and the slums. He had the good sense to modify his methods according to his audience. He chose to live and work in a slum environment in Edinburgh in order to be an example of his own precept that people must give of themselves in order to advance the cause of education and urban and environmental improvement.

In many respects Geddes's system came to be erected on self-confirming evidence. He was fully prepared to learn from others, but he selected those whose general attitude to life and education mirrored his own. He deliberately sought out Huxley, for instance, a radical thinker from whom he accepted a rigorous scientific discipline and training and who confirmed his intuitive belief in the evolutionary process. It was Huxley who encouraged Geddes and helped in his search for a central philosophy by introducing him to contemporary French intellectual life.

Paris in the 1870s was the centre of an intense re-appraisal of values which followed the disasters of the Franco-Prussian war. In the past Paris had seen its ideas echoed in Scotland, and Geddes was to be yet another Scottish pupil. From the French school of social science, pioneered by Le Play, Geddes absorbed the idea of Place, Work, and Family as a unit of analysis. This fitted closely with his own biological approach of relating organism to environment. By combining the two, Geddes was to produce a broadly-based methodological framework for community studies which added a dimension to the approach then current in Britain.

In Britain at this period the state of towns had begun to attract the attention of individual reformers and governments. Numerous Royal Commissions recorded a mass of data relating to the health and living conditions of town-dwellers. These investigations paid scant attention to vital questions of how towns worked, to the nature of the action and interaction of processes and functions existing within towns and between them and the countryside, and to what is the nature of a community. It was in this area of analytical thinking that Geddes made his mark.

It was in Edinburgh in the late 1880s and early 1890s that Geddes's ideas finally fused into a coherent pattern. The city had many lessons to teach, and Geddes viewed it as an example of what was both desirable and undesirable in urban development. In the eighteenth-century New Town designed by Craig, the Adam Brothers, and Playfair, Geddes saw the gracefulness that could arise from sound spatial and aesthetic planning. Nevertheless, he turned his back upon it after his marriage, gave up a flat in Princes Street, and moved to a tenement block near to the Castle in the Old Town. Here, in the Old Town, was the real planning problem. The building of the New Town had produced many adverse effects upon the Old. The New Town had attracted the well-to-do, and the Old Town had been left to degenerate, to become overbuilt and overpopulated. Nineteenth-century Old Edinburgh was the test-bed of medical science, and the Edinburgh Medical School found every variety of disease richly available there for the training of its students. Town organism malfunctioned in an environment of utter squalor.

The Old Town became Geddes's own laboratory in his search for methods to rehabilitate, conserve, and enhance the stage for living. All his subsequent work as a social planner showed this deep concern for the conditions under which people lived, and the first priority, and indeed precondition of progress, had to be the introduction of rigorous standards of health and hygiene.

Edinburgh provided Geddes with another precept, namely that urban planning is not the same as good architectural design. It confirmed his view that in Paris an excellent architectural style (Renaissance motifs of the primary straight street, the *rond point* and vista) had been created at the expense of a concern for the wider implications of sweeping architectural changes. His experience of Paris had convinced him that those whose homes had been demolished to create space for massive urban works crowded into other areas which became overcrowded, overbuilt, and, in their turn, slums. Edinburgh had become divided into two communities, and loss of interest in civic design in the Old Town had followed. Geddes wanted to build communities, not destroy them. To this end he was to show a greater concern for cities than many of his contemporaries, who either agreed with Haussmann that evils and eyesores must be removed by means of sweeping clearances, or embraced, with Clarence Stein and Robert Owen, a philosophy of retreat from the town to create model communities elsewhere, thereby leaving the essential problem of the slum unresolved.

Geddes's approach to the problem was by way of advocating the practice of comprehensive regional planning. He applauded the work of Ebenezer Howard, the pioneer of the Garden City Movement, and adopted the view that by building new communities the densities in the existing towns could be reduced and the physical fabric improved. Howard went ahead and built his garden city at Letchworth in 1901 and assumed that over time the spin-off effect of this development would result in a general amelioration of conditions in older towns: Geddes, on the other hand, saw the immediate task as an attack on the visible and major problem, the existing slum, and through time to educate society to a regional approach to new town-building. He personally painted the stairways in tenements as an example of what could be achieved with little cost and began to buy up property in order to create gardens and open spaces. His efforts in Edinburgh Old Town resulted in the reconditioning of eighty-five flats and four houses. Over half a century later this form of urban rehabilitation was to be proclaimed as one means of saving the essential character of the centres of historic towns and retaining community structure in cities.

Geddes's idea of organism functioning within environment had special point in Edinburgh in relation to town and country. Edinburgh dominates the lower Forth valley, and its historic and economic links seawards and landwards could not be overlooked. The history, economics, politics, and physical setting of the city reinforced Geddes's viewpoint that town-planning cannot be divorced from rural planning and led him logically to the concept of the city region. He was to develop this concept into a wider view of regionalisation. Geddes pinpointed the process in urban development by which higher functions become concentrated in metropolitan centres. Edinburgh was overshadowed by London, just as many other Scottish towns fell behind Edinburgh. The regional approach seemed to offer a method of overcoming many of the problems arising from the polarisation of functions and, in particular, the resultant regional imbalances—cultural, social, and economic. In this area of his thinking Geddes takes the debate about regionalism far ahead of his contemporaries. Many thinkers and writers of the time stressed distinctive regional culture and the need to recapture a pre-industrial regionalism. Nostalgia for the rural never figures in Geddes's thinking. He accepts the fact of the urban situation and focuses upon the city and its region as the new unit for meaningful social and political reference and allegiance.

Geddes applied to Scotland the regional-survey methods of the French school of human geography pioneered by Vidal de la Blache. He mounted surveys of the geographical, historical, social and economic situation of Edinburgh and its region. This data was gathered together in the Outlook Tower, set alongside material gathered from other sources, and formed the nucleus of a town-planning exhibition which Geddes later exhibited in towns in Europe and the Near East. The Outlook Tower also was the focus of summer schools and housed photographic and other indexed material of towns and their regions. Meetings and exhibitions were aimed at teaching regional and civic understanding.

Patrick Geddes wanted every town to have its Outlook Tower housing a civic exhibition, to promote a public awareness of what could be achieved by sensible civic planning and co-operative action. He anticipated by some fifty years the idea that the average citizen has something positive to contribute towards the improvement of his environment. Geddes was convinced that each generation had the right to inbuild their own aspirations into the fabric of their town. In order to achieve this a basis of civic understanding had to be created through education. Geddes canvassed schools, societies, and associations and attempted to draw them into making surveys and plans of their locality; creating play-spaces, planting trees, and painting buildings. He seized on any vehicle to expose people to situations in which they had to make judgements.

Geddes also took advantage of every opportunity to enhance local culture. He became associated with a Celtic revival of the late nineteenth-century. Its roots were in a mid-nineteenth-century Scottish nationalist movement, and its expression was through a flowering of Scottish letters. Geddes worked closely with William Sharp and Mrs Kennedy Fraser, leaders of the revival movement, and gave it a platform in his own magazine, *The Evergreen*. Like the *Edinburgh Review* and *Blackwoods*, *The Evergreen* carried all forms of literary propaganda. It was not a platform for Geddes alone, but one for a movement of ideas. Geddes had little to say on the specific issue of Scottish nationalism. He encouraged the traditional, took a considerable pride in the achievements of Scots in the sciences and the arts: but his regionalism had wider connotations than the narrow separatist ideal. Scotland, for Geddes, was an entity made up of differing regional units and set within a British and European framework. Nationalism without internationalism was unthinkable, just as was specialism without comprehensiveness.

The Outlook Tower, summer meetings, publishing, and urban rehabilitation were all Edinburgh ventures. Geddes's ability to carry on so many activities at one time was as much due to his wife as to himself. His wife, Anna Morton, was not only talented, having studied music in Dresden, but was a devotee of Octavia Hill, and had herself founded a girls' club. She came to bear the brunt of Geddes's social work, and her support freed his mind and energies for wider and changing horizons, of which there were many. One of these was Cyprus.

In 1897 Geddes sailed from Marseilles to study at first hand the problem of displaced Armenian refugees from Turkey. Cyprus, where the refugees were to be rehoused, provided a testing-ground for a now mature philosophy of social and economic planning. In Scotland, Geddes's immediate problem had been housing; in Cyprus it was one of revitalising a whole regional economy. Geddes came to show a marked talent for topographical and resource-analysis and man-management. Seizing on the relationship between water and agriculture, Geddes created a series of irrigation schemes to ensure an enlarged economic base and employed specialist agronomists and sericulture experts after scouring Europe and the Near East for the right men. He developed a number of small settlements, processing industries, new roads, and experimental agricultural colleges. His intention was to use experts to set up and supervise agricultural schools, processing and craft industries, and to train the Armenian refugees to a point where they could take over management of the venture. He begged plots of land from monasteries, finance from philanthropic associations, and created an agricultural credit bank and marketing organisation. The scheme worked well as long as Geddes remained in Cyprus to supervise its overall management. It floundered after he left, partly through a lack of continuing finance. Cyprus confirmed Geddes's idea that co-operative action could be effective, and he came to commit himself to this ideal.

By the beginning of the twentieth century Geddes had laid the foundations for his career as a social planner. The guidelines emanated from his definition of planning as an activity requiring a special expertise derived from correlative studies and a comprehensive approach to life systems. Planning, in the Geddesian sense, could never be narrowly defined. It was concerned with interconnexions—the uses of land and the activities resulting from land-use; a balance between local, urban, and regional scales of activity—a management system which applied special skills to resolving demands made upon resources in the interest of posterity. Geddes was sufficiently pragmatic to accept that his ideal system could not be achieved overnight, for, in effect, he was attempting to change the direction taken and the priorities of a whole society. He waged his campaign at different levels.

Geddes became a passionate advocate of planning as a new type of professional career. As a founder-member of the Institute of Town Planning he pressed for a recognition of the special skills required in this new and testing discipline. He accepted planning commissions from widely varying sources and used these commissions as vehicles for education of the sponsors (governments, local authorities, and private organisations), the then leaders of society. Above all, he became a publicist in order to influence the mass of the public towards critical standards of judgement. His attempt to persuade teachers to introduce into curricula a broadly-based study of civic affairs was especially important. In this way Geddes hoped to bring an influence to bear on the young and the future leaders of society.

Geddes was asking a great deal of his listener—a sense of social and public purpose emanating from a capacity to relate a problem of the moment to a whole background of thought. Others before Geddes had tried to teach the synoptic view; Bacon, Descartes, and Comte failed in this purpose, but left a legacy of ideas for their intellectual heirs. Geddes was no more and no less successful. Perhaps, for a listener, the real difficulty was in an apparent deficit of prescribed courses of action to follow. It was all too clear what Geddes was against, but often very difficult to derive any clearcut prescriptions for action in concrete circumstances from his advice. Geddes was always prepared to start a discussion by reference to the situation then current, but his analyses and syntheses seemed to offer an infinite variety of alternative answers. To a certain extent this was inevitable, for Geddes believed in the infinite possibilities of human change, and that the answers of one day may not suffice for the next. Geddes's acceptance of the fact that each generation should reshape its institutions according to its needs did not stop him from speculating on the form that changes were likely to take. As an evolutionist he pinned his hopes on prediction of trends and on the definition of alternative goals. Although

Geddes's methods of prediction were often suspect, he brought into perspective and debate many weighty issues relating to social goals. That he could not bring about a widespread change of attitudes during his lifetime in no way detracts from the perspicacity of his observations of the social scene or from the validity of many of the goals which he pointed out.

THE DUNFERMLINE REPORT

The commission which Geddes received from the Carnegie Dunfermline Trustees in 1903 gave him the first opportunity of propounding his whole philosophy of planning. His study of Dunfermline was printed in 1904, and was the only major planning report which he produced in Britain.

Andrew Carnegie had been born in Dunfermline in 1835, the son of a hand-loom weaver. By the time he was fourteen, the family had emigrated to America, where over the next fifty years enterprise and judgement earned him a huge fortune in the expanding railway and steel industries. Carnegie was an optimist who, like Geddes, accepted the idea of "an upward progress of humanity": he also had some remarkable ideas of his own, one of which appeared in print at the end of the nineteenth-century as the "Gospel of Wealth" —the rich man, after providing moderately for himself and his dependants, should consider all surplus funds as held in trust for his poorer fellows. Now, in 1903, thirty years after his first gift of a Swimming Bath to his native town, Carnegie set up for its citizens a Trust Fund consisting of $2,500,000 and the Estate of Pittencrieff—the mansion house, gardens, and grounds which in his youth he had thought Paradise. The Lairds of Pittencrieff had allowed the people of Dunfermline to visit the Park now and then, but young Andrew had himself been excluded because of his relatives' radical politics, and it was one of his life's ambitions to buy the Estate and give it to Dunfermline. The whole Trust endowment was to be used in an experiment—to attempt to solve the problem "What can be done in towns for the benefit of the masses by money in the hands of the most public-spirited citizens?".

The first meeting of the Trustees took place on 28 August 1903, and within a month the Trustees commissioned two Reports on the laying out of the Park, one from Geddes and the other from a well-known landscape architect, T. H. Mawson. Within a year, Geddes produced his study, which contained 230 pages of detailed information and argument supplemented by well over 100 photographs.

The report came at a significant point in the history of modern British planning. A growing nineteenth-century awareness of the adverse effects of unrestricted urban growth on human welfare had found its expression in major public health legislation which gave local authorities power to acquire and demolish slum property. Standards of hygiene could be imposed through sanitary regulations. Joseph Chamberlain had used these powers to some effect in Birmingham and thus had set a model for selective urban improvements.

Ebenezer Howard had produced his blueprint for garden cities, and the Letchworth model had been launched in 1901.

Chamberlain and Howard exemplified two mainstreams of nineteenth-century thought. Chamberlain took the view that the urban problem could be solved by selective public works—street-widening, clearance of eyesores, and improved sanitation. Howard, on the other hand, maintained that only a fresh start in a new environment could improve the urban situation. The time was ripe for the introduction of a third approach—a comprehensive treatment of an existing town. Geddes's report offered just this. He brought to Dunfermline the experience he had gained in Cyprus and Edinburgh, and his 1904 study marks his coming-of-age as a planner. This report forcefully stated the principles on which planning had to be based in order to achieve a complementary balance of working parts within a town.

Dunfermline appealed to Geddes's sense of history. It stands on a hill-top, and its western approaches are dominated by two buildings of historical and architectural interest: an abbey and a monastery. They are buildings to catch the imagination, and Geddes seized on the opportunities they offered as the nucleus of a planning scheme and also as a platform on which to erect Dunfermline's future as a town of note.

Geddes based his appraisal of Dunfermline's role in the future on a sound understanding of the currents of urban development at that time. He saw that an accelerated rate of urbanisation would increasingly confirm and enhance the magnetic attraction of big cities. Already a hierarchy of Scottish towns existed, dominated by the administrative and commercial centres of Glasgow and Edinburgh, so that the vital functions promoting economic growth were being abstracted from lesser towns and increasingly becoming centralised in the major cities. Geddes feared that in the long run this trend would erode regional culture, and his answer was to search for a special and continuing role for the smaller town of Dunfermline. There had to be created a physical and social environment which would act as a magnet and reverse the current trend. Towards this end Geddes stressed the cultural heritage of Dunfermline and tried to confirm and deepen its individuality.

One of the most characteristic features of his scheme was its insistence that each generation of inhabitants of the town must achieve a sense of place and a sense of belonging. Hasty, restrictive, and inflexible planning could be inimical to a civic spirit—each generation must have the opportunity to inbuild their own traditions without losing sight and sense of what had gone before. A successful planning venture, he noted, is "an exercise in some form of the imaginative powers not with a view to leaving nothing to future developments, but with the aim of creating circumstances for progressive improvement whereby public interest and co-operation will be continually available. This alone can achieve lasting success".

What was required for Dunfermline, and indeed for many other towns, was confidence and a sense of purpose; the opportunities needed to be spelt out and a basis established for civic leaders and the public to make choices. Town-planning, in this Geddesian sense, meant the creation of a launching pad, not of a once-for-all finished product.

Geddes was supposed only to advise on the laying-out of one part of Dunfermline: the Pittencrieff Park, which forms the town's western green boundary. His remit from the Carnegie Trust was specific on this point. Nevertheless, he strayed well beyond his brief. He believed that a town, like an organism, was made up of numerous interlocking systems, so that change in any one part could reverberate throughout the whole. Thus, any proposals for Pittencrieff Park had to be related to its wider background. He evolved the notion of the park as a cultural core for the entire town; not simply a place of beauty, but a focus for a scheme embracing purposive community-development.

Geddes saw his initial task as one of breaking down barriers: first, the confining brief; and, second, the general assumption that there were town activities and park activities which were quite independent of each other. "The problem", he wrote, "compels its own restatement as that of the culture policy of a small but fairly typical city as far as park and associated buildings are concerned." Buildings large and small, he added, "must be fitted within an overall concept of civic needs both present and future, and there must be a degree of organic unity in the final design". He anticipated opposition and tried to forestall it. His scheme was to be practical, but would, at the same time, be unconventional in many of its recommendations. There was to be no fetish made of preservation, only a careful appraisal for constructive conservation, no "keep off the grass" philosophy, only the provision of opportunities. In essence the proposals were to "appeal to each level of age and culture and meet the many requirements of recreative and educative use, of individual taste and social culture neither too radically destroying the past in the supposed interest of the present, nor too conservatively allowing the past to limit this, but incorporating the best results of the past with the best we can do in the present, towards the bettering of the opening future".

Having nailed up his thesis against all comers, Geddes invited an objective and unprejudiced appraisal, and pleaded "that since the problem has been set from the first not only upon the best usual level, that of utilising and adapting the best that has been thought and done in the world, but beyond this, where it is practicable, upon the most ambitious height, that of pioneers always ahead", the "unconventional nature" of his proposals "must in fairness be set to their credit, at any rate not used as an argument against them".

Geddes's characteristic claim to bring to bear on this problem the "best" reveals how much confidence he had in his own ability. It arose from his belief that he could synthesise and apply all the results from other fields of study into a workable scheme. Nevertheless, his method of presentation shows that he foresaw the difficulty which others might have in following his path.

Dunfermline is surveyed and analysed, step by step, in order "to produce a clear observation of the thing as it is and the design of it as it may be". His report shows no break between the sections relating to survey and those concerned with recommendation; the two aspects are treated together. Not that Geddes believed that this would be invariably the best method of presentation. Indeed, as the pioneer of the precept "survey before plan", Geddes influenced many of his contemporaries and successors in planning towards such a division of substance in reports—a practice which is still common. His own way of working tended, however, to fuse survey data and proposal together. The complex thinking process achieved through his thinking-machines permitted and encouraged a consideration of actual and possible in one mental process. It would have been time-consuming and untypical for Geddes to translate such synoptic thinking back into the separate components of survey, analysis, and recommendation.

The original survey notes for the Dunfermline study include many instances of "ideagrams" leading to definite proposals at the time of survey. To overcome the need for elaborate explanations for many of his proposals, Geddes adopted the judicious use of photographs, juxtaposing one photograph of a feature, as he had seen it, with one showing how it might be improved or modified. He adopted a conversational style of presenting information; took his reader on a conducted tour of the town and tried to convey, by terse comment supported by illustration, how planning could improve the fabric of Dunfermline. He reserved for lengthy treatment in words only those aspects of the report which bore on questions of principle. It is in these sections that Geddes incorporates a wide background of comparative town-studies and his knowledge of past experiments in town-planning.

In one further aspect, Geddes's report shows an interesting and novel approach. He worked in great detail, especially in connexion with site-planning and landscaping, but one seldom has the impression that Geddes is swamped by detail. He appears to shift the object of his attention, moving from a discussion of a detailed matter or particular feature to a general principle and back again to the particular. This grasshopper technique is a recurring feature and has its own logic. Geddes uses detail as a focus to argue a general case and not as an end in itself, to relate, for instance, the need for specific remedial action to a longer-term strategy of overall environmental improvement.

One would normally expect, in a work of this sort, that the argument would progress along logical lines with each section fully documented, but, whilst avoiding over-elaboration of detail, Geddes's deft presentation enforces a consideration of the general principle at all stages. His insistence, from the very first page, that priorities can only be chosen with longer-term goals in mind comes through very clearly and makes the report a major educative document as well as a contribution to planning thought far greater than any mere set of random proposals designed to solve the problem of the moment.

One instance of the approach adopted in this study is the case of Pittencrieff Glen, defined as an area for comprehensive treatment. The subject is raised early in Chapter I, where the point is made that any improvement to the Glen would be jeopardised owing to the polluted state of one stream. Clearly stream-purification measures and catchment-area-control are required. Geddes avoids stating this radical and costly inference, but moves on to discuss less costly and controversial subjects for improvement. He does not lose sight of his point of departure, for in Chapter XI he returns to a consideration of the Glen, having shown that the sum of minor improvements can bring about the required comprehensive improvement. At this point, however, he has moved somewhat further along the line of his original argument and is able to show that the Glen, with its beauty thus enhanced, could be linked into a green-belt scheme for Dunfermline and provide a much-needed recreational facility for all the inhabitants to enjoy. This case, besides being an example of Geddes's method of presentation, illustrates his view of the planner's role—a critical topic in the early days of the planning profession. Although Geddes operated under a brief from a client, he was concerned also that the client should be persuaded to consider taking action in areas hitherto unconsidered. This approach inevitably aroused opposition. Geddes's Dunfermline report was the first of many similar reports in which he strayed beyond his brief, thus provoking controversy over the planner's responsibilities and his client's wider role, and clouding the real value of his professional advice.

The Dunfermline report was based upon a thorough analysis of the geography, economy, and social constitution of the town. In the introduction Geddes argues that planning must, *a priori,* be based on the view that improvement is always possible in any human situation. Planning is a social service, and in the preparation of any plan, "human and social uses must dominate our constructive tasks; theirs the demand which must determine the supply". The start-point in this planning approach is elemental but vital. Geddes starts by posing fundamental questions about the requirements for a full life. Amongst other things he pinpoints: a need for safety to walk, talk, and meet; contact with growing things in nature; a stimulating visual environment; a wide range of educational and recreational facilities; and, above all, he believes, a sense of community pride and a sharing by the citizen in the creation of the built environment. These were the main aims of the plan.

In one important area of human well-being Geddes had little to offer; and although he was well aware that to live one must have an income, he scarcely made reference to any economic plan for Dunfermline. He stressed that the growth of employment lay outside his control, but assumed that industrial development along the shores of the River Forth (a few miles from the town) and the role of Dunfermline as a provincial regional centre would ensure a continuing source of employment. His only significant contribution to the question of economic growth was in his argument that one sure means of bringing about the decline of any town was to avoid or defer investment in urban improvements.

Geddes introduces his study by directing attention to the initial impact the town has upon a visitor arriving at the railway station. Arguing from this, Geddes draws the conclusion that Dunfermline has suffered in the past from piecemeal and unplanned development. "The disastrous loss to the improvement of a city", he notes, "through looking at each of its public parks as a well defined 'property' enclosed within its own boundaries is here at once realised." He goes on to point out that, "we may readily see how its present beauty might have been doubled had the approaches and interconnections of its parks been adequately studied, instead of independently conducted, on the one side by a Parks Committee, and on the other by a Streets and Buildings Committee, and so practically by unlucky chance." What is required, according to Geddes, is an organisational change in the town administration to effect a close co-ordination of the work of different departments within an overall design conception. An immediate remedial measure would be to plant trees and forge connexions visually between the separate areas of open space. Geddes goes on to draw a further lesson. Tree-planting involves patience, whereas planning, to be successful, must operate quickly and be seen to be beneficial. His image of a tree-lined walkway indicates a goal to work towards—an enhanced visual environment over time—but there are other areas in which planning must operate with speed.

Geddes makes a close analysis of the possibilities offered by Pittencrieff Park for the creation of various ecological associations (trees, shrubs, animals); as an area safe for children; and as one suitable for all-year-round recreation. He suggests that it may, in future, be possible to link this open space to new suburban housing areas, but warns that without a comprehensive approach to planning these possibilities may never be realised. This point is driven home in Chapter II. Abutting on Pittencrieff Park were "the uninteresting backs" of tenement houses. Geddes pleads for an integration of park and neighbouring properties—a natural link between folk, their residences, and open-space amenity. A sound scheme of improvement in the Park should not be framed by unsightly views, and he suggests that the Dunfermline Trust should invite the co-operation of adjacent property owners in a scheme to give the area a face-lift. The Trust, he believes, could initiate the process by offering to create pleasing views into the Park by lowering a high wall, in return for improvements, by the individual house-owners, of the appearance of those buildings visible from the Park.

Geddes goes a great deal further in suggesting a catalytic role for the Trust based on its position of influence in Dunfermline, where it could take the responsibility of setting an example of well-designed housing. As a first stage the Trust could build on vacant land adjacent to the Park. As part of this wider social responsibility he recommended that the Trust should undertake a comprehensive social survey of the whole town. Geddes felt that, in the long run, the Trust would be judged by the improvements it achieved for Dunfermline as a community, and he offered specific suggestions for neighbourhood-planning designed to create areas with a sense of community.

Geddes's ideas relating to the need for social contact and enjoyment of the landscape are outlined in Chapter IV, entitled "Park and Gardens". "This portion of the Park", he records, "the most accessible and convenient, should, therefore, be especially laid out for the young children and for old folks who do not care to ramble far; this contrast of ages is also one of the happiest combinations of human life—the old finding their keenest pleasures in watching the activities of the young." Geddes is well aware of the problems which may arise out of the possible clash between children's play—noisy and space-demanding—and the old people's desire to sit and view. He overcomes possible difficulties by producing conditions for the uninhibited expression of continuous play in a series of interconnected play areas, which are relegated to a secondary place in the visible environment, and special play areas for the very young. Geddes adds, characteristically, that these playgrounds could provide an opportunity to encourage the training of play-teachers. The play areas themselves could contain additional educational elements, such as miniature museums housing geological or palæontological collections. Here again, the basic notion is that the Trust could provide a launching pad for social and educational advancement.

Another feature of civic leadership is spotlighted in a discussion relating to the preservation of buildings. During the survey stage of his study Geddes had noted that "popular sentiment is frequently expressed in a desire to remove the aged and decrepit structure." He sees a need for caution, with each case being studied on its merits and measured against the longer view. In Chapter VII, for instance, he recommends the renovation of a monument, the reorganisation of one garden as a botanical laboratory and of another as a tennis court, and insists that changes such as these, or, indeed, recommendations for preservation, must follow a careful review of all factors. These decisions must never arise from either dogmatic preservationism or popular whim.

Geddes returns to this theme in Chapter XVIII. He suggests that those who advocate indiscriminate removal of buildings may well overlook their tourist appeal. Equally, claims for retention could well rest on a mistaken view of the importance of a building. "Fortunately for old architecture", he observes, "the many houses in which Queen Mary happens to have slept in her peregrinations seem partly thereby preserved; yet such an incident is not, of course, a serious historical reason at all. . . . History is primarily social: it is by their place and part in social changes that places, buildings, individuals have historical importance at all." The smithy under discussion has to go. It is a "blot upon a great architectural composition", namely the Palace. A mill is also to be removed, but for a different reason—it is outdated. Nevertheless,

Geddes pleads for a form of preservation on educational grounds. He advocates minute documentation of both buildings as an appropriate study in industrial archæology and the construction of a new smithy within a new craft centre.

A detailed statement of the Geddesian philosophy of urban change is set out in Chapter XII. The heading, "Parks and Buildings in their Bearing on City Improvements", is a clear indication of the importance of the synoptic view. Geddes pleads for great care to be exercised in the planning of Dunfermline. The plan must emerge from an appraisal of the distinctive character of the town.

Geddes cites London as an example of a chaos of *ad hoc* developments— "a mass of routes, indiscriminate dissection of an urban area—isolated buildings without a master conception or integrated areal composition". There could have been something better, for Wren's plan for the City, prepared after the Great Fire, with its emphasis on symmetry of layout and architectural composition, could have provided the correct discipline and framework for future building. This comprehensive plan was never realised, much to Geddes's regret. Not that he advocated a similar design for Dunfermline: its situation, morphology, size, and traditions called for planning, no less comprehensive, but of a different order. "Here is a place for the conservative treatment, the naturalistic, in the sense of making the best of things as we find them—this does not prevent the formation of open spaces wherever possible, in fact it encourages them—but it does not enter upon any regular plan of improvement comparable to that which should be designed for the new city which is to come." As in Edinburgh, gradual modification can produce "a far better result . . . than could the greater schemes of clearance and widening which have been from time to time proposed for it".

Geddes synthesises what he regarded as the two main contemporary schools of thought in planning, naturalism and formalism. His own approach includes both; where appropriate, the Renaissance motif; selective clearance of blight; the linking of green spaces; adoption of a unified transportation plan; and the integration within a unified plan of old and new residential areas. In essence, he is working towards a blueprint of, and a philosophical approach to, an "old hill city preserved in all essential characters, even renewed".

A picture is drawn for the client of what could be achieved in Dunfermline: "its group of culture buildings around the Abbey Church and Monastery, its stately Palace and venerable Tower—its two Parks brought together by their verdant parkways and this splendid central group spreading out its radiating avenues to suburbs, country and coast towns, ancient and modern. Here then", Geddes contends, "we should have a complete city, Old and New, which would be in its way the first in Scotland; in fact, an example and encouragement to city progress throughout the United Kingdom and even beyond."

Of the many innovatory ideas in Geddes's report, one which was to be emulated a generation after his death, is the juxtaposition of recreational and educational facilities within a connected open-space system. Geddes had noted the possibility of extending Dunfermline's green belt by linking the Pittencrieff Park to other green spaces. Here could be located field-study centres and fun-palaces, buildings provided solely for spontaneous creative recreation. In Chapters XX and XXI, which discuss improvement to the Abbey-Palace complex, Geddes was to offer an opportunity to initiate yet another educational experiment, a proposed centre of historic studies. The whole valley scheme, embracing Abbey, Park, and Glen, was the first major attempt to plan a walkway system within which were a variety of facilities to satisfy the leisure needs of all ages. To achieve this system required joint action by the Trust, the Town, and its citizens. Perhaps Geddes goes too far in offering such a variety of possible buildings and educational ventures; and in one self-critical paragraph he confesses that "the richness of detail and variety of appeal may readily obscure the underlying unity of conception. The principle here adopted carries with it the corresponding risk of seeming to overload the design." This was valid criticism, for Geddes certainly came to overstress his case and, through enthusiasm, to over-elaborate his plan.

The conclusions (Chapters XXXII-IV) form in themselves a notable essay which bears directly upon the nature of the city and its future. Geddes contends that the time has arrived when the techniques and knowledge gained during the Industrial Revolution must be applied to "the completest social art of city building". The contemporary city constitutes the central problem of the day, and a sound understanding of the urban process is long overdue. Science must be directed towards solving this problem. Each town must be analysed in all its different components, and town-planning must become a continuing process.

Geddes saw a tendency for city-improvement to operate for a short period and then come to a halt. He recommended a role for planning far-reaching in its implications. Apart from plan-preparation, there was the task of plan-monitoring and a need for a continuous reassessment of goals, for the great objective must be a satisfaction of the needs of man at all life stages. The collorary of that is the need for the involvement of citizens in planning. "Since our park and gardens and buildings are but a stage on which men and women are the players, what is to be their part? Mere passive receptivity, whether of immaterial or material dole, is of no value." Geddes is convinced that a continuing partnership is necessary—a joint action between citizens and administrators—in fact, a "civic union". He places the responsibility squarely upon the administrator and planner to bring this about. Eventually, they must make decisions relating to change, but this decision-making process must take note of the views of those most affected by it. The citizens must be educated to understand the importance of planning for the future so that they can gradually become capable of widening their area of decision-making. Planning and education are linked. Planning schemes should, therefore, incorporate possibilities for direct action by citizens, such as creating playgrounds and planting trees, youth organisations could be invited to make local plans, and the schools to extend their teaching of civic affairs. Geddes was original in seeing the relation between politics, education, and urban renewal.

Geddes's discussion of Dunfermline as a town also introduces some new perspectives. For the first time a town-planner had stated the case for urban rehabilitation and renewal as a means of attracting industry. He described as the Neotechnic Age that phase in history when the transition from coal to electricity began to release industry from being tied to sources of raw materials. He saw here a force for planned dispersal and an opportunity for the creation of visually more attractive landscape. The Neotechnic Age would also bring a demand for higher standards of design of the residential environment. For a town to possess an environment of a high order would give it a decided advantage in this new age. Geddes stressed that quality of environment embraced many elements. It would only be found where there was a combination of sound and imaginative design with a wide range of civic facilities. Half a century later it became widely accepted that this combination of elements had to be achieved in the economically depressed areas of Britain in order to provide the basis for regional redevelopment.

A Comparison of the Geddes and Mawson Reports

Besides Geddes, the Dunfermline Trustees also commissioned the landscape architect T. H. Mawson to draw up a report under the same remit. Mawson and Geddes worked concurrently, and an interesting comparison of their methods and objectives can be made. Mawson's report ran to some forty pages and, in general, lacked the finished presentation characteristic of Geddes's study. Mawson found difficulty in meeting the time deadline and admitted the "the latter part of the text had not been finally corrected". Mawson is far more direct than Geddes and avoids lengthy philosophical discussion. His plan was in the Renaissance monumental style of architecture. It is presented under twenty-six headings, and its main proposals are: a new commercial centre for the town from which radiate boulevards "like spokes of a wheel"; the creation of vistas by clearance of existing properties; a garden suburb to rehouse displaced persons; and an emphasis upon the visual quality of buildings. One of Mawson's new roads was to cut through the centre of the Pittencrieff Park—a proposal also considered by Geddes but utterly rejected in the interest of preserving the Park's organic unity. Only the last sections of Mawson's report were focused upon the problem of layout within the Pittencrieff Park.

Like Geddes, Mawson strayed outside the limits of the Park, but he comes to plan much of Dunfermline anew. The Park and Glen figure as somewhat insignificant items, whereas Geddes makes the Park central to the whole scheme. In another area there was a great difference between the two studies. Mawson left little for the future—his scheme was tight and rigid.

In an advisory plan prepared for Dunfermline in 1946 (pp. 15–17), the consultant, James Shearer, pinpointed major points of difference between the two studies: Mawson's plan is "an example of a plan so drastic that it was never seriously entertained and had it been carried out very little of what is familiar in Dunfermline would have survived". Of Geddes he wrote: "[His] plan is of a different order and although most people now agree that it would have been a major error to impose on the green spaciousness of Pittencrieff Park, the series of large buildings sketched out in the Geddes report, that report as an introduction to Town Planning has had the respectful attention of Town Planning Authorities and students alike all over the world, ever since it was published. In so far as street alteration is concerned, Professor Geddes's proposals were modest. They consisted in linking the public park by two tree lined avenues; he also advocated the extensive planting of trees to relieve the grim monotony of many of our streets and drew attention to the attractive possibilities of a feature which, until then, no-one in Dunfermline had noticed and which happily is still a possibility open to it—the presence of a green belt stretching almost without interruption all the way from Pittencrieff Park to Townhill Loch both as a valuable recreational asset and as an equally valuable amenity." Shearer went on: "my advisory plan incorporates the green belt advocated by Professor Geddes and I without reserve endorse his opinion of the recreative and amenity value of the Townhill Loch as a subject for thorough investigation."

RECEPTION OF THE REPORTS

The reception given by the Trust to the two reports is well documented in the Minutes. The original endowment by Andrew Carnegie was supported by a letter from him to the Gentlemen of the Commission (August 1903). Carnegie suggested that the Park and Glen provided "the needed foundation upon which you can build, beginning your work by making it a recreation park for the people . . . your work is experimental . . . Remember you are pioneers and do not be afraid of making mistakes; those who never make mistakes never make anything." Carnegie also suggested in their pioneering work the Trustees should aim to lead the people upward in a wider social and educative sense. In an address on the work of the Trust delivered in August, the then Chairman of the Trust, Dr Ross, said: "The Park and Glen are ready to our hand . . . , but to extract all the advantages of which they are capable may give us work for years to come"; and, although he also emphasised the need for liberality in the Trust's expenditure, he went on to say: "every shilling will, I hope, be spent with the view to its yielding an adequate return."

In inviting Geddes to prepare a report, the Trustees had taken something of a gamble, for Geddes's views were known to be unorthodox, and, unlike Mawson, he still had to make his name as a consultant. Despite Geddes's plea for a town-wide scale of activity, the powers of the Trustees were limited, and they could act only in those areas which they actually owned. Geddes and Mawson both anticipated difficulties, but both failed to modify their schemes in such ways as to obtain a more receptive reading.

That Geddes foresaw a cool reception is apparent from his correspondence with his wife, to whom he wrote in 1903: "I have, of course, long been prepared for no consideration whatsoever. The previous October, hopes were there. It should thus become a convenient paper reference on those subjects for workers outside Dunfermline as well as, I trust, some interest to the Trustees and their immediate public—however, the problem of short and long term view has always been there." To Mawson, with whom he had frequent discussions during the period of investigation, he recalled a meeting at which differences of attitude were all too apparent—"not only the purification of the stream, but the improvement of the approaches, follow upon a general educative and social policy, and . . . although I am assured that many if not most of my recommendations will be carried out in due time, I do not think it will be in Dr Ross' time at all. Our opposite views about old buildings being only one of the various differences." Geddes does not seem to have learned from several previous experiences, for he complained, in February 1904, that "it seems once more, as in the University for twenty years, I am to have that one encouragement with which every bit of pioneering in thought or action is met, that of the disapproval of my seniors and the indifference and suspicion of one's own contemporaries. That, as I said before, is the real investigator's pay."

Mawson also foresaw that difficulties lay ahead, and that, in part, they were of his own making. In a letter to Geddes written in March 1904 he concluded: "I am afraid that in making my proposals for the improvement of the town I have entered on a very risky subject. One's difficulty is generally in inducing a client or clients to see the work as a whole before details and I imagine that the Carnegie Dunfermline Trust will not prove an exception to the general rule." In letters to his wife Geddes expressed his own opinions of Mawson's plan. The vast differences between their two plans would, he hoped, redound to his advantage by elevating his approach "in the eyes of the Trust". These differences did not impair the friendliness of their relations: "Mawson and I dined together very amicably the other night. His plan is very American and Haussmann so I don't feel crushed. The job is a gigantic one to both of us, not even he with all his experience has realised it, least of all do the Trustees. I am convinced that here, as so often, the less they like it, the more they will be wakened up by it and come to it in time. It doesn't pay, alas, but if we had wanted things to pay we should have kept a public house."

In a letter dated 23 June 1904 Mr Whitehouse, the Trust's Secretary, informed
Geddes that, having received his report, the Trustees had resolved★ "to record
their high appreciation of the fulness of knowledge and the great talent which
he has brought to bear on the subject and . . . to award him their best thanks
for his labours and their acknowledgement that he has furnished suggestions
which may prove to be of much value to the Trustees in their future work":
but that the Trustees also considered that "it would be unwise to adopt any
plan . . . that would greatly alter the present aspect and character of the Park
and Glen"; that "for the present it will be sufficient to continue making such
improvements as from time to time may be found desirable"; that, although
they recognised "the necessity of taking steps to secure the purity of the water
of the Town Burn", and of the "desirability of acquiring from time to time,
if obtainable at market prices, properties which may not only give them control
of the stream, but may also provide additional recreation grounds for public
use", they were bound "to adhere to the principle of limiting themselves in
their expenditure, unless in very exceptional circumstances, to the ordinary
income of the Trust funds", that it would be "inadvisable to embark upon more
schemes than they can personally and efficiently supervise"; and that "the
scheme which at present most urgently calls for their attention is the provision
of further library and reading-room accommodation . . .". Thus although
the Trustees adopted a cautious attitude towards many of Geddes's most
sweeping proposals, they did not categorically reject his report. And, according
to the Minutes★ of a further meeting held on 26 July 1904, at which the Trustees
learnt that the expenses reclaimed by Geddes and Mawson respectively
amounted to "such extraordinary sums" as £798 and £817, "the Committee
regretted that both of the reporters had so largely exceeded their commissions. . . . The greater part of Mr Mawson's report was occupied with
what was practically a reconstruction of the town, and in so far as it dealt
with the Park and Glen, his recommendations were so dependent upon the
acquisition of properties which do not belong to the Trustees and which they
have no power of acquiring that no real benefit could be derived from the
report, even assuming that the recommendations could theoretically be
approved. While the same criticism can to some extent be applied to Professor
Geddes's report, there are portions of it which it would be in the power of the
Trustees to adopt if so advised. After full consideration of all the circumstances,
the Committee agreed to recommend the Trustees to offer to pay Professor
Geddes £750, and Mr Mawson £300, in full of their services and outlays,
including the printing of the reports stated in the accounts rendered, under
reservation of all objections to the accounts if these sums be not accepted."
A definitive examination of the issues thus raised must, of course, await the
publication of the whole of the Trust's fascinating correspondence with
Geddes and Mawson.

★ The relevant Trust Minutes of 23 June and 26 July are appended to this Introduction.

On many future occasions, Geddes was to price himself out of the market by insisting on his own deepest convictions. Often, in later years, his clients were not prepared to embark on costly programmes of development merely on the strength of his assurance that the expenditure would be recouped many times over through the resultant improvement in urban efficiency. Nevertheless, many of his ideas have ultimately been realised in Dunfermline and elsewhere, in response to evolving and changing economic and social needs. By providing him with 100 copies of his report for distribution to his own correspondents, the Trustees helped him to inject an important influence into modern British civic planning in its formative years. Ebenezer Howard summed up a general reaction when he wrote to Geddes that a copy of the report "ought to be in every public library and in the office of every architect of every local authority". Half a century later the Geddesian approach on questions of public participation, conservation of environment, and the derivation of civic priorities has come to underpin our attitudes to town-planning.

The Aftermath of Dunfermline

Dunfermline stretched Geddes. Here had been an opportunity to focus attention on a number of social theories and to give them a concrete application. Geddes was fifty years of age, yet his report shows a liveliness characteristic of a much younger man. It conveys the urgency of Geddes's feeling that social planning must make a great advance to meet the needs of the twentieth century. Geddes showed an understanding of the nature of urbanisation and was, with Ebenezer Howard, exceptional in his commitment to long-term planning. His valid insistence that civic survey must be a preface to town-planning was well taken and was put into practice, but, regrettably, much of his thought relating to the crucial role that planning had in education and social change was lost for a generation.

Geddes was to make this wider field of social planning the battle-ground of his work as a publicist. Dunfermline might have become Geddes's Letch-worth—a living and growing testimony to his philosophy, followed, perhaps, by numerous other consultancies within the British Isles. But this did not happen. A plan for the Edinburgh Zoological Gardens appeared in 1913, but by then Geddes was committed to a career outside his native land. After Dunfermline, Geddes turned his efforts to refining the collection of survey material in the Outlook Tower which he then displayed in national exhibitions throughout Europe and later in the Near East.

It was this work of his as a propagandist of social planning that established his reputation with a wider audience. He came to the attention of educational-ists and politicians who, in turn, provided the overdue opportunities in practical planning. For a decade his main work lay in India and Palestine. He travelled widely and made plans for over sixty towns and cities. Amongst these were plans for Colombo, Calcutta, Madras, Jerusalem, Tel Aviv and Haifa. All these studies show a similar stamp: a deep concern for the conditions of living of the mass of citizenry; an orchestration of systems, economic and social, towards social betterment; a distrust of indiscriminate clearance; a respect for community traditions; an emphasis on the role of planning as a medium for educating citizens to create their own future environment. In all his studies Geddes tried to outline the likely results of following one or another course of action as a basis for decision-taking. He would recommend the "best buy" measured against an ideal, leave a host of detailed work for others to implement, and then move on to fresh fields. As a result much was left undone. Nevertheless, in his travels, Geddes came to influence a whole generation of administrators towards a humane planning philosophy.

At the age of seventy he settled in Southern France and established an international college at Montpellier. His health was often suspect, but for a further eight years he continued to bombard the youthful planning profession with his ideas as to its needed social purpose.

Geddes was out to remake the world, and, needless to say, the task was too big. Had he become a great political figure he might well have pushed a society along his path, but his belief that no one philosophy, creed, or political doctrine held the prerogative of truth prevented this from ever taking place. He tried to influence by means of argument and precept, and, in a period before opportunities through radio and television were available, he came to influence all levels of society in three continents.

Geddes was outspoken in his criticism of existing values and moved into new channels the universal debate relating to the rights of man and the conditions necessary for the attainment of a life more abundant. His goals were basically unsophisticated, yet worthwhile in themselves—the realisation of human happiness and contentment for all. Perhaps the climate of opinion in his day was not conducive to seeing these goals realised with speed, and many of Geddes's methods of attacking a problem head-on did not facilitate the required transformation. Nevertheless, the fact that Geddes was able to bring countless men of power to adopt a less authoritarian and a more humane and discreet attitude to the use of power merits recognition.

Many of the specific aims Geddes sought to achieve (including the conservation of the life-supporting environment, universal education and opportunity, and the right of the citizen to share in decision-taking) have become the collective tasks of groups of men in subsequent generations and have not yet been completed.

Meeting of Trustees, 23 June 1904

404. The Minutes of meeting of the Chairman's Committee, held June 20, 1904, were submitted, and in connection with item No. 397 the action to be taken on the report submitted by Professor Geddes was considered. After a full discussion it was agreed to alter the resolution submitted by the Chairman's Committee to the following:—

The Trustees, having received from Professor Geddes the report entitled: "Park, Gardens and Culture Institutes," resolve to record their high appreciation of the fulness of knowledge and the great talent which he has brought to bear on the subject and the earnest desire he has displayed to render the future action of the Trustees beneficial to the community. They further resolve to award him their best thanks for his labours, and their acknowledgment that he has furnished suggestions which may prove to be of much value to the Trustees in their future work. The report will have their earnest consideration. The Trustees also resolve to place on record the following views:—

1. They are of opinion that it would be unwise to adopt any plan, however attractive in itself, that would greatly alter the present aspect and character of the Park and Glen. They recognise that at present the Park and Glen are characterised by great natural beauty and are singularly adapted to form desirable resorts for public recreation, and they are strongly of opinion that they can best conserve these advantages by limiting themselves to such alterations as may be necessary or desirable in a place of public resort.

2. They realise that much may be done towards intensifying the beauties of the Park and Glen, and, while recognising that it may be necessary in the near future to adopt a general plan of operations, they are of opinion that for the present it will be sufficient to continue making such improvements as from time to time may be found desirable.

3. They place on record their sense of the necessity of taking steps to secure the purity of the water of the Tower Burn, and of resorting to such measures as the law prescribes to prevent its pollution; also, their sense of the desirability of acquiring from time to time, if obtainable at market prices, properties which may not only give them control of the stream, but may also provide additional recreation grounds for public use.

4. In carrying out the work of the Trust they resolve to adhere to the principle of limiting themselves in their expenditure, unless in very exceptional circumstances, to the ordinary income of the Trust funds.

5. They deem it inadvisable to embark upon more schemes than they can personally and efficiently supervise by committees of their number, aided by other public-spirited citizens.

6. They consider that the scheme which at present most urgently calls for their attention is the provision of further library and reading-room accommodation, including the enlargement or the rebuilding of the Library, and the provision of a Reference Library and Reading-room such as will meet the educational requirements of the young people of the town. They also deem it advisable that the proposed Reading and Recreation Room at Townhill should be proceeded with forthwith.

405. The remaining minutes of the Chairman's Committee were approved, but it was agreed to obtain 200 copies of Professor Geddes' report for the use of the Trustees.

Joint Meeting of the Parks and Property and Chairman's Committees

445. The accounts rendered by Professor Geddes and Mr. Mawson for reports on Park and Glen were examined and considered.

The Committee were surprised to find that they amounted to such extraordinary sums as £798 8s. 6d. in the case of Professor Geddes and £817 6s. 7d. in the case of Mr. Mawson.

The written instructions given to these gentlemen were read, from which it appeared that what they were each asked to do was to furnish a report on the laying out of the Park and Glen and the needed structures upon the edge of the Park. No arrangement as to remuneration had been made with Mr. Mawson. In the case of Professor Geddes, the Chairman explained that at an interview he had had with him shortly after the written instructions had been given, the remuneration for his report was fixed at 200 guineas, and it was stipulated that the report should be furnished before the end of December 1903. The Professor was also authorised to purchase some books of reference and to employ a photographer and a surveyor to do a limited amount of work. No authority was given to employ a draughtsman, or architect. The Committee regretted that both of the reporters had so largely exceeded their commissions by dealing with properties outside the Park and Glen, and with topics not submitted to them. The greater part of Mr. Mawson's report was occupied with what was practically a reconstruction of the town, and in so far as it dealt with the Park and Glen, his recommendations were so dependent upon the acquisition of properties which do not belong to the Trustees and which they have no power of acquiring that no real benefit could be derived from the report, even assuming that the recommendations could theoretically be approved. While the same criticism can to some extent be applied to Professor Geddes' report, there are portions of it which it would be in the power of the Trustees to adopt if so advised. After full consideration of all the circumstances the Committee agreed to recommend the Trustees to offer to pay Professor Geddes £750, and Mr. Mawson £300, in full of their services and outlays, including the printing of the reports stated in the accounts rendered, under reservation of all objections to the accounts in these sums be not accepted.

Acknowledgements

Acknowledgements are due to the Carnegie Dunfermline Trustees for their kindness in permitting the author of this introduction to quote so extensively from their Minutes and from their correspondence with Patrick Geddes, and to Mr Fred Mann, their Secretary and Treasurer, for many helpful suggestions which the author has gratefully accepted.

University of Strathclyde, January 1972   P.G.

A STUDY IN
CITY DEVELOPMENT

FRONTISPIECE.—The Abbey Church from North-West side of glen, looking over Queens' House and ivied ruin, traditionally St Catherine's Chapel. The value of the vertical lines of this group as base to West Front and Towers will be noted, as also the value of the old cottage roofs. Observe loss to picture by removing any, especially the lowest of these. (Compare also Fig. 120, p. 183.)

CITY DEVELOPMENT

A STUDY OF

PARKS, GARDENS, AND CULTURE-INSTITUTES

A REPORT

TO THE CARNEGIE DUNFERMLINE TRUST

BY

PATRICK GEDDES

PROFESSOR OF BOTANY, UNIV. COLL., DUNDEE (ST ANDREWS UNIVERSITY)
PRESIDENT OF THE EDINBURGH SCHOOL OF SOCIOLOGY

WITH PLAN, PERSPECTIVE, AND 136 ILLUSTRATIONS

GEDDES AND COMPANY, OUTLOOK TOWER, EDINBURGH
AND 5 OLD QUEEN STREET, WESTMINSTER

THE SAINT GEORGE PRESS, BOURNVILLE, BIRMINGHAM

1904

PREFACE

As title and treatment indicate, this volume is one of practical purpose. Its main contents are a plan and plea for conserving and developing the amenities of a small provincial city, and its constructive proposals are based upon a photographic survey of its present, a re-reading of its past. The work was not only planned, but essentially done, independently of publication, but unexpectedly numerous inquiries from many centres, British and foreign, have shown that the ideas with which it deals are fully stirring, and that the demands it is here sought to supply are widely felt. I have, therefore, to return my thanks to the Carnegie Dunfermline Trust, not only for their appreciative minute of reception of the volume, but for following this up by according permission for its being now made accessible to the public.

Such a monograph—as at once naturalistic, horticultural, architectural, educational, and social, and in all these respects having to utilise past history and present resources, frankly to discuss needs, and boldly to indicate possibilities—cannot be prepared without wide inquiry and general reflection ; in fact, its local questions inevitably raise the general ones of city life and development, and these from well-nigh every point of view. The preservation of natural beauty, the ordered gardening of art and of science, the intelligent conservation of the surviving relics of the past, can only be attempted in proportion as we realise the significance of each of these in the larger world ; indeed, in the general development of civilisation. Still less without such wide survey can future developments be outlined, for the needs and problems of health, leisure, and recreation, of education and social betterment, are becoming much the same for all cities. The purpose of the great gift, towards utilising which this Report has been called into being, has been from the first explained by its donor to his trustees as not only a local but an experimental and general one : " the very problem you have to solve is, ' What can be done in towns for the benefit of the masses by money in the hands of the most public-spirited citizens ' ? " Again, in the words of a recent announcement of the University of London of its inauguration of sociological and civic teaching : " With the consideration of life in any one of our towns of to-day is essentially connected the question of what this life may become if intelligently directed by men who are clearly conscious of the ideal to be desired." To offer answers to these great questions, at once ideal and practical, for any one city, a comparative study of others is necessary, and the volume begun and planned in this old Fifeshire capital has thus not unfitly been in great part written in the vastest of modern cities, and in the midst of university and other teaching and study of " Civics as applied Sociology." *

---

* As this more general treatment of civics has been lately laid before the Sociological Society (Meeting of 18th July 1904, Rt. Hon. Charles Booth, F.R.S., in Chair) I may here cite a few weighty passages from the comments of *The Times* on account of their clear recognition of

The world is now rapidly entering upon a new era of civic development, one in which " progress " is no longer described as in mere quantity of wealth and increase of population, but is seen to depend upon the quality of these. The last generation has had to carry out great works of prime necessity, as of water supply, sanitation, and the like ; elementary education, too, has been begun ; so that to some, even pioneers in their day, our city development may seem well-nigh complete. But a new phase of civic development has become urgent—that of ensuring healthier conditions, of providing happier and nobler ones.

In this movement great Continental capitals have indicated the way : German cities are now leading ; American cities are actively astir. Where one small Scottish burgh may take up an active initiative the larger (and despite our great local gift still the wealthier) industrial and university cities cannot lag ; nor will the great English municipalities, least of all London itself, long be content to follow. In fact, social and municipal activities, hitherto mainly on utilitarian or remedial lines, are now increasingly progressing towards cultural betterment also.

Alike in interpreting things actual, and in designing things possible, I have not hesitated to be definite, even at the risk of criticism. Holding as a naturalist a brief for " regional survey " as uniting all its component special sciences ; as garden-maker urging the employ-

civic betterment as now henceforth upon the plane of practical politics, as well as of their substantial endorsement of the views here enounced.

" In the paper by Professor Geddes—an abstract of which we print—are contained ideas of practical value to be recommended to the study of ambitious municipalities. This is the age of cities, and all the world is city building. . . In a dim sort of way many persons understand that the time has come when art and skill and foresight should control what so far has been left to chance to work out ; that there should be a more orderly conception of civic action ; that there is a real art of city making, and that it behoves this generation to master and practise it. Professor Geddes truly said the land is already full of preparation as to this matter ; the beginnings of a concrete art of city making are visible at various points. But our city rulers are often among the blindest to these considerations ; and nowhere probably is to be seen a municipality fully and consistently alive to its duties in this respect. London may be left out of the question. . . It will be some time before it can be dealt with as an organic whole. But the rulers of such communities as Manchester and Newcastle and York ought long ago to have realised, much more than has been done, that they are not so much brick and mortar, so much rateable area, so many thousands of people fortuitously brought together. They have all a regional environment of their own which determined their origin and growth. They have all a rich past, the monuments of which, generally to be found in abundance by careful, reverent

inquirers, ought to be preserved ; a past which ought to be known more or less to all the dwellers therein, and the knowledge of which will make the present more interesting. . .

Such pride . . . such 'growth of civic consciousness and conscience, the awakening of citizenship towards civic renascence,' will be the best security for a worthy city of the future. . . At present those who are most zealous are too often indifferent either to the past or to the true interests of the future. They snatch at passing, popular schemes, neglecting what would permanently beautify their city. . .

Professor Geddes glanced at the opening civic future, ' the remoter and higher issues which a city's indefinitely long life and correspondingly needed foresight and statesmanship involve,' the possibilities which may be early realised if only there be true civic pride, foresight, and unflagging pursuit of a reasonable ideal. . . It yet remains to be seen what our cities will become when for some generations the same spirit of pride and reverence shown by old families as to their possessions has presided over all civic changes and developments. . . Something more than open spaces, music in the parks, municipal trams and steamboats, and a generous employment of the rates is needed to build and develop cities as they ought and might be. Ruskin somewhere points out the mediæval love of cities. . . Affection might with more reason attach to the modern city if its people knew what it had been and steadily strove to make it better, if there were in every large community patriotism and a polity."— *Times, 20th July* 1904.

ment both of formal and naturalistic styles, each in its due place ; as antiquary and builder in Old Edinburgh and elsewhere, pleading here for the retention and repair, yet the social and educational use, of that open-air museum of the centuries, which is the best asset of Dunfermline, if not yet always the best appreciated one ; I cannot but differ from some of my readers. Not only as an ambitious museum-planner, but as long occupied in educational pioneering, I feel it essential to insist upon the present transformation in education, the closing of its memorising and bookish stage, and to press forward to the education of nature and of activity. Hence my proposals for the actual recapitulation by our young folk of early culture-phases, through primitive life and early industrial evolution, to later historic development, and thence up to the world's masterpieces ; hence I plan out the presentment of these in museum and palace, and suggest it in pageant and drama ; hence, too, I press for the generous establishment of the noblest resources and functions of civic life.

For such reasons, in this volume, local problems and general solutions are constantly discussed together, in a way I can well imagine not at first pleasing to the general reader, to whom guide-book or plans on one hand, general discussions on social and educational questions on the other, usually stand apart.

Amid constructive proposals so many-sided, naturalist and gardener, archæologist and antiquary, historian and art-critic, architect and decorator, musician and dramatist, educationist and museum-maker will all find points for criticism; and I submit these necessarily rapidly-produced designs under correction, and with due openness to their amendment. Yet as the wandering student of old, though seeking ever to learn as well as teach, was wont boldly to nail up his theses against all comers, so do I here. First of all I press the conception of the literature of cities as constituting a vast " Encyclopædia Civica," having for each city its Book of the Past, its interpretative guide-book, geographical and historical ; its Book of the Present, a social survey; and its Book of the Future, the city's book of hope, in which it should be attempted to discern, to plan out, and to suggest its incipient or potential development. Civics as an art, a policy, has thus to do, not with U-topia, but with Eu-topia ; not with imagining an impossible no-place where all is well, but with making the most and best of each and every place, and especially of the city in which we live. Here, then, is such a Eutopia for Dunfermline, with its presentment of the needed Culture-Institutes of this bettered city of the opening future—Naturalistic, Historic, Civic, and each with its local colour and popular use, so offering to every soul full and living contacts with Nature and with Humanity, and relating individual tasks to the social whole.

Furthermore, I submit that the time has come to be fully setting about the same thing in other cities—by the thought and effort of its historic and its progressive spirits, by their co-operation also ; through existing machinery, municipal and other, or through such new forms of civic union as may prove needful ; and this whether private generosity or public wealth be at first available or no.

CONTENTS

5

6   CONTENTS

CHAPTER VII
THE LAIRD'S GARDEN

CHAPTER VIII
THE PALACE GARDEN

CHAPTER IX
WILD GARDEN AND BOTANIC GARDEN

CHAPTER X
SOUTHERN PARK AND "ZOO"

C. STREAM AND GLEN

CHAPTER XI
STREAM PURIFICATION AND ITS RESULTS

CHAPTER XII
PARKS AND BUILDINGS IN THEIR BEARING ON CITY IMPROVEMENTS   .   .   97

CHAPTER XIII
THE GLEN

D. NATURE MUSEUMS

CHAPTER XIV
NATURE PALACE IN PRINCIPLE AND IN POPULAR USE

CHAPTER XV
NATURE PALACE IN EXECUTION

CHAPTER XVI
NATURE MUSEUMS IN WORKING

BOOK II

MUSEUMS AND INSTITUTES: THEIR CULTURE USES

E. LABOUR MUSEUMS

G. LIFE AND CITIZENSHIP

CHAPTER XXVI

SOME EDUCATIONAL BEARINGS OF THE SCHEME

CHAPTER XXVII

THE QUEENS' GARDEN—THE ARENA

CHAPTER XXVIII

MUSIC HALL

CHAPTER XXIX

THE GRAND ENTRANCE

CHAPTER XXX

MANSION-HOUSE AND QUEENS' HOUSE

CHAPTER XXXI

THE GENERAL VIEW: ITS ASPECTS AND INTERPRETATIONS

CHAPTER XXXII

CITIES AND CIVIC PROBLEMS

CHAPTER XXXIII

DUNFERMLINE AS TOWN AND AS CITY

CHAPTER XXXIV

THE CIVIC UNION

PARK, GARDENS, AND CULTURE-INSTITUTES

INTRODUCTION

THE problem of adapting a private park to public uses is one arising normally in the growth of towns, and is yearly acquiring increasing importance. Here, however, the problem has peculiar additional elements of interest. First, this is no ordinary level expanse of grass and trees but of peculiarly varied contour, and of very unequal amenity of laying out. At some points it is already almost all that can be desired, but at others much improvement is needed. Its principal feature is the Glen proper, a ravine perhaps only rivalled as regards scenery among public parks by that of Jesmond Dene at Newcastle; while in wealth and variety of architectural views and remains and of historic interest and associations it is surpassed by no park anywhere.

Though the passing visitor may stroll but cursorily over the rolling park landscape, or dip here and there into the shady dell, the park improver must join with the geographer in laying down first of all a thorough survey of the whole contour, and with the geologist in studying the rocks underlying and exposed, and not only the peculiar incident of denudation to which we owe the Tower Hill but the stream itself which has done the work. To find this entering the park laden with every form of pollution, mechanical, chemical, and organic, is no doubt a partial explanation of the ugly canalising which it has suffered throughout the greater part of its course; but the geologist points out also that it has been a not unpractical, albeit inartistic, method of arresting that rapid denudation of the soft shales which must otherwise ere now have endangered both Palace and mansion.

To urge the thorough purification of this stream for all reasons, not only hygienic, naturalistic, and artistic, but even for social and moral ones, has been from my first visit to the Park, my first proposal, and still is so.

To lay out any park, and particularly this one, without setting on foot all needful measures for purifying the stream would be but landscape-gardening what is at present a drain, and is, I hope, as impossible to all seriously concerned as would be the façading of a slum, or the spreading of Dunfermline damask to conceal decay. Hence for the park a thorough study of the stream and its tributaries above has been necessary

As regards the laying out of the park, the ordinary conditions and requirements of existing municipal parks do not afford sufficient precedent. These requirements as for games, etc., all exist, and can be partly met upon a generous scale, partly postponed until more level ground can be acquired. The problem is further complicated by my instructions to report as to the possible buildings connected with the immediate and future work of the Trust.

To think out a clear initial plan of buildings, all reasonably related, yet all separately capable of extension with the ever-developing requirements of the future, is obviously no easy task. For its preparation it requires at once the fullest local study, the most general inquiry, the most

---

The present volume is in response to the invitation with which I have been honoured by the Carnegie Dunfermline Trust, to report as to the laying out of the Park, and as to the Buildings in or around it needed or desirable for carrying on the work of the Trust. Further than this I have been left completely free in both respects; that is, not only as regards scale and style, principle and detail of treatment; but also free to think out what in my judgment, and keeping in view the needs and practical possibilities of the City and the renewing advance of educational and social progress, these buildings and their setting should be. While I have fully availed myself of this generous liberty I trust I have not abused it: moreover, I must at the very outset make it as clear to the reader as it is to myself that the many suggestions and practical proposals of my various chapters in no way and at no point commit the Trust. They do not even give any indication as to what their policy may be, such as might be gathered had my different chapters with their particular garden, building, or improvement plans been in response to a definite commission of the ordinary kind.

careful reflection. Each building must have its immediate usefulness, yet with moderation of beginnings must provide amply for future growth, and ensure that this, instead of destroying the monumental or picturesque character of the design, should further enhance it. Buildings and sites cannot be even considered until their objects are defined, their uses clearly foreseen. Hence the need of forecasting as far as possible, not simply the general tendencies of the culture activities of the Trust but even the development of the definite branches of these, and of each as housed in its particular dwelling, with its own requirements and possibilities.

In ordinary circumstances the gardener or architect is not called in until his clients have made up their mind as to the accommodation they require and the approximate amount they see their way to spend; but here, from the newness of the whole problem, no such instructions have been possible. I do not, of course, complain of this; it has greatly increased the interest as well as the responsibility and difficulty of this task. Instead of the comparatively simple problem usually set by the Park Committee of a city to the landscape gardener they consult, this has unavoidably developed into that of thinking out, and concretely expressing in plan and perspective as well as description, the essential possibilities of culture resources, their working, therefore, also —that is to say, the problem compels its own restatement, as that of the culture policy of a small but fairly typical city, so far as park and associated buildings are concerned.

A. Photographic Survey

The preparation of this report has thus involved not a few distinct lines of activity. First and foremost a thorough survey of the whole area, one largely photographic. Each main division has been analysed into its essential units, as shown in following plan, and these, again, have been studied from every point of view—in late summer verdure and in autumn colouring, in winter nakedness and in early spring—and as far as possible all these both in sunshine and dull weather.

The results of this survey are partially embodied in large series of photographs, of which a selection only are reproduced here. Of these only very few have been found in commerce, and the great majority have had to be taken.*

A set of these photographs may, with advantage, be preserved by the Parks Committee of the Trust, not only on account of such quality as they may possess, or their frequent interest and use for reference, but as a desirable record of the aspects of the park and its environs before any operations

---

* I have, in this matter, to warmly acknowledge the skilled and artistic co-operation of Mr Norval.

of the Trust. The expense of this survey has been compensated by the disclosure of many points of view hitherto commonly little observed. These, again, are of all distinct orders of importance, from the simplest picturesque detail, say a point of view from which the Abbey spire may be found rising above the trees, a glimpse of park or waterfall, a sunny or shady nook in which a sequestered seat may be planted. But this survey rises also to the largest questions of civic æsthetics—as, for instance, in the illustration chosen as a frontispiece, which appears to me not only one of the most beautiful spots in Dunfermline but one of those noble combinations of architecture and scenery which are rare anywhere. A greater abbey, more picturesque town buildings, a deeper ravine, and nobler trees might all easily be found separately, but seldom do we see a natural composition of these many elements into so satisfying an artistic unity.

B. Contouring and Relief Model

To our photographic survey may be added, as already indicated, a geographic study in detail. The survey, which is a necessary preliminary of every park improvement, has been here carried out by Mr M. Hardy, the active continuator of the late Mr Robert Smith's Botanical Survey of Scotland, and the contour lines drawn at every 5 feet, thus admitting of the construction of a relief model of the Park on true scale. The immediate advantage of this, towards preserving, utilising, or accenting natural features, as especially in the Glen, or in facilitating operations in the Park, will be obvious. I recommend, then, the construction of such a relief; and, further, the application upon its actual surface of pasteboard models to scale of all buildings recommended, either now or at any future time, within the Park or upon the sides of the Glen. These could then be photographed in a well-arranged light, and thus give an almost perfect anticipation of the effect of any proposed constructions. The existence of such a model for Edinburgh Castle has once and again protected it from injudicious improvers. Had Edinburgh such a model, the recent destruction of its main views by the excessive height of the two new railway hotels of Princes Street could never have been authorised; while the case for true improvements would be greatly strengthened, the popular interest in them also. The approaching wreckage of the natural watering-place of Dunfermline— the beautiful coast from Torrie by Culross to Kincardine — by a recklessly-designed railway line might thus have been averted; or the present plea for a Garden City might be indefinitely strengthened. Here, then, is an easy bit of practical pioneering at the very first—the construction of relief models not only of the park but of the region. The educational value of these, too, need hardly at this time of day be lengthily insisted upon.

C. Treatment of Ancient Buildings

A principle, first learned from long experience in repairing and building in Old Edinburgh, but again fully verified here, I may be permitted to emphasise in this introduction. Instead of that merely antiquarian respect of the scanty survivals of the past, which is too often confined to the particular century or period which happens to seem romantic to us, I would respect and preserve examples of the honest and characteristic work of each and every period, whether from our present point of view (also a passing one) it seems to us beautiful or no. This statement must not, of course, be misunderstood. As will be seen hereafter, I do not advocate the retention of things useless when we have a definite use for their space and materials. I plead merely for fair trial before condemnation, for the thrifty and the open-minded—that is, many-sided—consideration of each survival of the past and of its value whether as an actual asset or as a possible one. For, even if not available in its present form for immediate use, I have once and again found buildings too hastily despaired of by others to be capable of cleansing and repair, or of alteration and incorporation with such new buildings as may be required —in short, of renewed usefulness and even beauty.

Any measure of success which may have attended my personal improvement work of the last seventeen or eighteen years in some three dozen closes of Old Edinburgh has been essentially due to the application of this simple principle Old buildings, first admired in picturesque dilapidation by the tourist or antiquary, then ruthlessly condemned as out of date by the utilitarian, or unwholesome by the town councillor, were often found capable of handling from a point which harmonised the partial truth of all these standpoints. Starting with the hygienist, uncleanness has first to be got rid of. Yet this not necessarily by destruction. Decaying matter and smells, the germs which produce these, are not in the stones of the building, but are in the organic dirt superficial to these. Cleanse and disinfect in this way, and the old building may then be wholesomer than the average nineteenth-century one, with its imperfect drainage and other defects. Old mason-work is not discredited by weathered surface; even cracks often indicate a long past settlement, not an increasing weakness, and in any case are more easily repaired than people generally suppose. After cleansing and mending, the antique building is frankly adapted to its modern uses, with sanitation, electric light, and

all; and though in this process a shock is sometimes given to the merely romantic spirit, an ultimately better and truer artistic result is reached, especially when, with use and weathering, the new elements have harmonised into the old. As examples of this, I might cite Lady Stair's House, the last baronial mansion of Old Edinburgh, which was literally discovered, as well as restored, by my friend and collaborator, Mr Aitken; or Riddle's Court, the best surviving burgher one, in which the clearing out of tons of dirt disclosed some of the most beautiful rooms in Edinburgh, Old or New, since then made as wholesome as any.

I must urge these points here, since it is everywhere the first and not unnatural idea of the public-spirited improver, too often even of the busy and hasty architect, to sweep away whatever seems to him an inconvenient, an unwholesome, or an unsightly survival of the past without further examination. But hence it is that the awakening attention to architecture of the past which has been going on throughout the nineteenth century, and which has fully reached Dunfermline, has been too commonly to destroy what it might and should have preserved. Not only have old quarters been everywhere demolished in the name of progress and hygiene, but even the permanent buildings which it was intended to disclose have been largely destroyed by their restorers.

Striking examples of both these changes are familiar to every visitor to the great Continental cities. Following upon the wholesale, even if somewhat too sweeping, transformation of the old forts and bulwarks of Paris into boulevards under Louis XIV., and the creation of new magnificent distances by Napoleon I., came the demolition and reconstruction of the irregular labyrinth of the ancient city under Napoleon III. by Haussmann, whose long perspectives and lofty blocks have essentially set the fashion of the past half century to every municipality in Europe, and, therefore, cannot be neglected here. Viewed from the street, the apparent advantage in directness of communication, in access of light and air, seems obvious and unquestionable; but a more intimate acquaintance with the city and its people from within reveals the fact that, despite the modern rise of wealth, the average Parisian household has actually less living room in the new tenements than before in the old, and this at far greater cost for rent and taxes. The decline both in number and in quality of population, which has at length so deeply impressed the mind of France and of the world, is now seen to have been in no small measure accelerated by these costly improvements. Moreover, with fuller knowledge of the city and its health statistics one sees that the broader streets, the superficial spaciousness, are dearly purchased by the loss of the ample courts, the old gardens, which lay unseen within. For to have to play in the dusty air of the street is one main factor in the weakness of town children.

The moral of all this is the very simple one, yet not fully adopted into the policy of any improving city, that to lessen dirt, overcrowding, and the rest we should not merely relieve our feelings and improve appearances by demolitions, even followed by imposing rebuilding, but, as far as may be, improve the old and build new quarters beyond, so slackening the pressure of population upon habitation, not increasing it.

Coming next to the great surviving monuments, we see how Notre Dame has been restored, cleared of the crowded old buildings which clustered about its feet, and now stands detached upon a vast open place. The same process has been followed, if possible more thoroughly, in Vienna; most of all for the cathedral of Cologne, of which

D. Threatened Demolitions in Dunfermline

I elaborate this point, because during the last six months I have not only constantly heard, but again and again received, suggestions, both by word and letter, as to the desirability of demolishing this and that past element of old Dunfermline. These have included not only the most characteristic and beautiful features of the old town, such as the Abbot's House itself, but each and every building upon the Trust property, without any single exception! Not only is the dilapidated old smithy included in this condemnation, or the old mill buildings opposite, or the cottages of St Catherine's Wynd; to some Queen Anne's House, adjoining these, more immediately below the Abbey, is specially objectionable. Entering the park, to some

FIG. 2.—The Tower Hill as historic and prehistoric nucleus of City and Park. Note loop of stream entering on right and running West (Tower Dene), and thence South under Bridge out of sight, and again East on left (House Dene). The low front walls are modern, but must broadly suggest the inner limit of the original Dun-ferm-linn—the fort on the crooked water. The higher wall in distance is all that survives of the early mediæval tower.

the completion has been the crowning monument of German unity. And all with what result? Too much that of the outside of St Giles' in Edinburgh, with its ancient exterior destroyed and rebuilt; and this practically modern building robbed even of its ancient loftiness by the removal of the clustering buildings which, though seeming to obstruct it, really gave it dignity and height. Turn now to fig. 1 (frontispiece), or the panorama of Chapter XXVI., and judge of the disaster of removing the old cottages and houses below the Abbey towers and spire. Consider, too, the disaster to Dunfermline and Scotland, from the fact that the accompanying figure of our Tower Hill has nothing more of its ancient buildings to show!

the old wall on the right is an eyesore, and to others its continuation in the newer wall bounding the Tower Hill. More than one letter to the newspapers has urged the removal of the double bridge, or its replacement by some more modern piece of engineering. To some the plain and lofty back of the old mansion-house unduly deepens the permanent shadow of the glen at this point; while the dulness of the west aspect of the old stables, the grey simplicity of its southern front, furnish conclusive arguments to others for their removal as a blot upon the beautiful park landscape around.

Other correspondents, it is fair to note, find their special abhorrence not in the work of the fifteenth, sixteenth, seventeenth, and eighteenth centuries, above referred to, but in the nineteenth. Thus if we descend the stream past the old glebe dovecot, apparently wantonly demolished, the lack of harmony between the substantial modern manse and the picturesqueness of the Abbey buildings above is strongly commented on; while if we return and go out by the modern gate and lodge at Pittencrieff Street even these new improvements are not without their severe critics.

I have thus received every possible destructive suggestion, but practically, as yet, no constructive ones. Without, at this stage, expressing opinion on any one of these foregoing points I merely bring them together to show that if such improvement suggestions were adopted by the Trust and City, no present building, save the Abbey and Palace ruins, which are out of Dunfermline's power, would long remain.

The method here adopted is to examine each point upon its own merits and on the principles previously indicated—that of adaptation to our modern requirements, educational, recreative, and so on—with due retention or incorporation of whatever has economic value or artistic fitness.

The reader is, therefore, entreated to approach this question with an open mind, as the writer has tried to do, taking into account all points of view. Many an apparent difficulty will thus be found to be an opportunity; and even when a building is not capable or worthy of retention as it stands, it may serve at any rate as an element in our reconstruction, which will be found at once conservative yet thorough. At the very worst, its materials may be utilised constructively.

E 1. Relation of Buildings and Gardens

It is not long since, after an architect had erected a building in one particular style, the client called in a house-painter, who thereupon decorated it in another; while a nurseryman or jobbing gardener was brought in to put in such and such plants as he or his client pleased, without reference to either of his predecessors. Now, however, matters are improving. The architect starts in far more truly utilitarian fashion, and works out the specific practical requirements of his clients upon plan. From this the elevation naturally arises. The effect of this elevation depends primarily upon its masses; the proportion and the light and shade arise also from this, as does the colour scheme from the appropriate material; while the traditional "ornaments" of this or that "style" to be found in books, and followed as a "precedent," a term which has too long enslaved the architect, may often safely be dropped altogether.

Ornament is at any rate far more temperately used, and, when used, is of a better kind. It expresses material and gives additional interest to surface; it also expresses the purpose and ideal of the building, and the individuality of the artist.

Around the building thus designed there now, and only now, arises the work of the gardener, whose problem is neither to do something wholly distinct, nor merely to arrange a frame or setting for the architecture, but rather to complete it, adding a final base of simplicity, a glowing wealth of enrichment also. After this the buildings and their garden must stand or be changed together, as the permanently related parts of a larger artistic unity.

The great saying of Bacon: "Men build stately before they garden finely, as if gardening were the greater perfection" is thus literally true. And this not only in the history of his own time, with its stately palaces and yet more glorious gardens; it is coming true again in our present century, our own generation: it applies in the present case, and in each individual experience.

Of this principle, thus clearly emphasised at the outset, the applications will appear in the following pages in detail. Only as the uses of each building and its practicable dimensions have become defined, its appropriate gardening— naturalistic or formal, simple or elaborate, grave or gay—has naturally followed. Each group of buildings and gardens will thus, it is hoped, be found in harmony with its practical use, its particular site, and its position in an orderly scheme, in which the various aspects and needs of culture and of social life find their respective yet organised expression, or at least their starting-points of fuller growth. Yet the whole scheme is one of enhancement, not of injury, to the peaceful setting of the mansion-house, amid its park and trees, and to the wilder beauty of the winding dell.

E 2. Styles in Landscape Gardening

A word must be said regarding the styles of landscape gardening, which have always varied with those of architecture, and have consequently been peculiarly variable during the past century. Examples are happily not far to seek: witness formal gardens like those of Drummond Castle or Balcarres, to name only those within reasonable distance; while modern naturalistic work, like Lord Armstrong's in Jesmond Dene, Newcastle, is, of course, also readily accessible.

The landscape gardening of the earlier part of the nineteenth century is here specially important, such as the best surviving portions of the Edinburgh or Kew Botanic Gardens; so, of course, is the better neighbouring park scenery, such as that of Broomhall, Blairadam, etc.*

The conflict of styles is sharply indicated by the many volumes of Mr Robinson, a great naturalistic gardener who will have little or nothing of the formal; and by those of Mr Blomfield, who, while an eminent formal garden-architect, seems to have too little interest in nature or even in plants. But later naturalistic writers, such as Miss Jekyll, have assimilated much from the advocates of formal gardens; while recent architects, like Mr Sedding, are not unmindful of nature.

Some have felt the originality and subtlety of the Japanese to be highly suggestive. Though a first sight of pictures of Japanese gardens may give an impression of quaintness and remoteness, it soon becomes plain that the Japanese is really emphasising the characteristic features of his own environment, alike in natural landscape and domesticated vegetation. He may thus in some ways be claimed for the naturalistic school, yet in the elaborate adaptation of his architectural conditions and domestic needs he is also among the formal gardeners. His formalism and convention are so different from our own that we cannot reproduce it without his actual aid, nor should we wish to do so save, at most, at some one definite point of deliberately exotic interest.

What, then, is the conclusion of this matter? While appreciating all styles, we must here follow no single one, but use each in its appropriate place, here emphasising natural beauty, there creating such ordered and formal beauty as we may; yet finally harmonising all into a larger unity, a Protean one—for only thus can we appeal to each level of age and culture, and meet the many requirements of recreative and educative use, of individual taste and social culture. We thus independently reach for our gardening the principle above reached for buildings—neither too radically destroying the past in the supposed interest of the present, nor too conservatively allowing the past to limit this, but incorporating the best results of the past, with the best we can do in the present, towards the bettering of the opening future.

The proposals and plans hereinafter submitted will thus, it is hoped, be found to give scope and satisfaction to the lovers of naturalistic freedom and exuberance, breadth, variety, and detail; yet also in their due place they utilise the many and stately resources of architectural and formal gardens. This ancient rivalry is no longer mutually destructive; an age of toleration has

* The possibility of reference in Dunfermline to the main books on gardens and garden design is much to be desired, as also access to the leading garden papers, and to kindred publications, such as *Country Life.*

arrived for architecture and for gardening alike; and both great styles, the classic and the romantic, are seen not only to deserve continuance but to admit of mutual enhancement, even to lend themselves to new developments. In a word, then, each style has its own place.

F. Constructive and Critical Point of View

Since, after seven months' preparation, the following plans and proposals have now to face the criticism of many, and the test of years, I may be permitted to offer a word of explanation—the more so since this is not by way of mitigating or evading criticism, but of assuring that it be just and keen. I assume then, that since the problem had been set from the first, not only upon the best usual level—that of utilising and adapting the best that has been thought and done in the world— but beyond this where it is practicable upon the most ambitious height—that of " pioneers always ahead "—there is one question, one implied criticism which must be excluded from the outset as outside the rules of the present game, and this the commonest: " Very pretty, no doubt; but can you show me where this has been tried before? Where has it succeeded? "

Such criticism, if sometimes less clearly expressed, is generally what each and every concrete attempt at carrying out into the needful applications any general counsel of pioneering usually gets; as I know in the present case, even from most of the friends upon whom I have occasionally tried this or that proposal. I understand, and so far sympathise with, this attitude. I love the old songs best, and have seldom cared for any new ones at first hearing; still, knowing my own bias against new compositions, I do not criticise them. A new picture, however, or a new flower is quite a different matter, since here I am more accustomed to the pictorial or horticultural standpoint, and the novelty of the new object or point of view becomes to its advantage.

In short then, I plead that the unconventional nature of some of the following proposals must in fairness be set to their credit, at anyrate not used as an argument against them.

After warding off this one criticism I would now aid all others, by disclosing the point of view needed to share the standpoint of such designs and to overlook them. It is one easily acquired, in some measure, by anybody who will take the pains, or rather the pleasure, for it is a child's one.

Anyone who is not wholly unobservant knows that he is often partially so. The difficulty of drawing or describing any familiar object, say the church steeple, from memory, or the like, is a simple proof of this. Here, too, the camera, still more the view-finder, is an aid: with this the

FIG. 3.—Row of modern villas, Dundee, as united for college use.

FIG. 4.—The same blocks with gap filled, and effect altered by gardening ; with beds of botanic garden (heath and primrose families) ; greenhouse ; and ivies, etc., on walls. A simple example of "gardenesque" treatment, applicable to irregular buildings on level. (Photos kindly lent by Messrs Valentine & Sons Ltd.)

most unobservant may soon cultivate the art of seeing.

For the ordinary purposes of life we need generally go no further. We have no call to bring imagination to our aid; and we have grounds, by no means wholly irrational, for distrusting any who do this. Yet a more careful view discloses that in almost every occupation the higher efficiency is connected with the exercise in some form of the imaginative powers.

The physician we choose or consult is he to whom the frame is most transparent, the lurking death-shadow most plain. The successful merchant foresees the coming market; the skilled officer is he who "sees through the hills"; and so on. Similarly, then, for the gardener, the architect. One appreciates or improves upon his particular plans as one acquires his general point of view—that of not only first seeing the thing as it is, but also as it may be. Medical sight and insight are acquired by nurses, and military insight by soldiers and volunteers, and this often in a high

have no suggestions to offer—one, the pessimist, who can see only the dreary street picture; the other, who likes the pretty one, but "does not see how it can be done."

So much for buildings chosen as of the everyday street style, and of their immediate possibilities with a minimum of outlay. In illustration of the converse problem—that of more ambitious and romantic design—I may cite my long-continued, though still far from completed, attempts to preserve and carry on the essential artistic motive of Old Edinburgh, its picturesquely piled-up masses and roofs, chimneys and pinnacles, and to express this spirit in new groupings.

Of the recovery of picturesque slums, or the improvement of ugly ones (fig. 5), I might give many instances. Keeping, however, to garden problems, let me give, in conclusion, a single illustration of a simple case of the formal terrace gardening I propose below (Chap. VIII.) upon a greater scale in its appropriate place, and as a further illustration of

FIG. 5.—Slum in Old Edinburgh; (a) recent; (b) as proposed and partly realised; (c) alternative design adopted by proprietors but displaced by (b).

degree, one which justifies their habit of criticism even of specialist and veteran. So it is with the intelligent amateur in every subject; and it is hence no small use of plans such as these to serve as exercises for the more general cultivation of this spirit.

Take a concrete and simple illustration of this mode of imagining improvements and of judging them. I find that some at first glance hardly recognise in the two illustrations (figs. 3 and 4) that the houses and ground are the same; indeed, almost, though not exactly, the photographic viewpoint also. Look, then, at the bare blocks not clothed and consider how these bare blocks should be treated here, with the limited purpose of a college lawn and the severe restrictions of a botanic garden.

The skilled eye, professional or amateur, will now detect the weak points in my second picture, that taken after improvement and planting, much as does my own; it will know also which of these points must be left to improve by further growth, and which should be altered; thus its criticism is a mutually interesting and a constructive one. Two, however, of our friends are silent, at any rate

the habit of mind required both for a design and its criticism—two states of a garden entrance in Old Edinburgh before and after operations,* the whole change being the lowering and balustrading of the retaining wall, the disclosure of an existing staircase, and the provision of railing and shrubbery in their due places (figs. 6 and 7).

Further illustrations of the same principle—that of clear observation of the thing as it is, and design of it as it may be, are given throughout this volume (figs 17, 63, and 69).† In many other cases also my illustration exposes an evil without any companion to express its accompanying

* Here, of course, I owe the skilled expression of my rough design to my friend and architect Professor Capper.

† I find that this method is substantially a revival of that employed by Repton, in whose imposing descriptive volumes lithographic plates, illustrative of views of places as they stood, are frequently supplied with a movable slide showing the effect of his proposed improvements. This method can now be carried out with far greater accuracy in these days of photography, and its wider application would be of service alike in the preparation of designs and in the appraisement of them. They afford a means of testing the more familiar perspectives, such as I also supply e.g. (figs. 36a, 49, etc.) in almost every particular.

remedy. To do this consistently far more time would have been needed ; but my reader will now, I trust, exercise himself upon supplying this, as, of course, also in improving the suggestions actually offered. Some, I well see, are only too capable of this, while others are still but indifferent. Of these illustrations I shall here venture to maintain only one as being, so far as I can yet see, in principle and on the whole, the best that can be done under the circumstances (Fig. 95), though for this also I invite emendation.

The reader will, of course, allow for the difficulties of this adaptation of the retouching process, and the imperfection or over-finish in the figures which have alternately resulted.

ment, interest will be continually renewed, and public taste improved. Nay, more, the whole younger generation may thus be deeply and truly influenced towards beauty and knowledge, with the no small reaction upon life and home.

To appreciate the result of a too decisive completion let us return once more to Jesmond Dene. While we admire the completed effects produced by its master hand, we soon also discover some want of adequate appreciation in the community to which this great park has been handed over. Close beside the lovely mill cottage, the picturesque lake, fall, and bridge (Chap. XVIII.) with which Lord Armstrong's whole construction culminates, the present park authorities are building a shelter, doubtless in itself needed, but architec-

FIG. 6.—Detail of reconstruction in Old Edinburgh. Garden entrance before improvement.

FIG. 7.—The same entrance, showing effect of lowering and balustrading wall, and exposing staircase with shrubbery above. A simple example of detail of formal gardening applicable to varying levels.

G. Mode of Execution

While we would not leave things untidy because unfinished, still less without a general design to be steadily carried out, the commoner converse error must also be guarded against—that of leaving nothing to future development. For park and buildings are not in themselves the end but the means towards an ever healthier, happier, and more cultivated community, and towards this end the citizens and their environment must ever be progressing together. The following plans have thus been drawn up with the idea not of finishing the place once for all as a nine days' wonder, but as indicating a comprehensive policy of improvement, which would not only occupy the constructive labour of years, but could ever be further and further developed. A rock garden, for instance, may be made and extended gradually, while its collections are never completed. Yet, to avoid confusion, we need a plan upon which extensions are provided for. On this principle of comprehensive, yet continually progressive improve-

turally as poor as poor can be. Down-stream adjacent parks and their buildings disclose an unexpected deficiency of civic æsthetics ; while, outside the park limit altogether, the magnificently widening valley passes through increasing neglect and pollution and desolation into the utmost squalor and slum. One almost wonders whether this great gift may not in some ways be harmful, since it not only fails to serve as an incentive and start-point to the continued improvement of the valley, but seems too much reduced to a spot of refuge from the neighbouring neglect or continued destruction.

My proposal involves the precise reverse of this. It is, that while adopting a comprehensive design (I trust the present one), and having this still further elaborated with all needful completeness, the Trustees should utilise its gradual execution for the corresponding education of its community. Thus, the place of needed trees once fixed upon plan, their planting might largely be made a matter of social and educational interest, utilising, for instance, "Arbor Day," that admirable

American school holiday, in which the practical and moral, the æsthetic and naturalistic education of the younger generation, and the needed afforestation of the country are being helped on together.

Similarly for the development of gardens, and that of all kinds—scholastic and general, botanic, naturalistic, and formal, of course in varying measure. The same principle of widening participation may be applied also in various collections, both living in gardens, preserved in museums, libraries, etc. Towards such developments the respective working staff may actively co-operate.*

In this report I suggest such co-operation here and there; and its possibilities should be everywhere kept in view, the Dunfermline public thus increasingly coming to feel towards the Trust and its group of culture resources and institutions as do the members of a great college—not only jealously careful of their common wealth but active towards increasing it.

At the same time, I must expressly guard against the idea that a garden can be developed like a cairn, from the sum of independent contributions. This would be like having rival painters on the same canvas, rival decorators or musicians in the same room, or a council of war conducting a battle—despite all ability and good intentions only discord and material disaster can result.

H. Correspondents

At this stage I have to express my cordial thanks to over two hundred correspondents in many quarters of the old and new world, whose suggestions I invited at the outset of this report, seven months ago, and from whom I have received a very large number of replies, always interesting or encouraging, and sometimes highly suggestive. Were I authorised by the writers to print these, they would make up a volume of no mean interest. Many of these suggestions, of course, touch matters beyond my scope; especially do many of the large groups dealing with educational problems and tasks and with social betterment extend beyond the limits of the present volume. But all have been transmitted to the Secretary of the Trust for its respective committees, so that no suggestions will thus fail to receive the serious consideration they merit. I trust that many correspondents who may not find their particular view expressly represented may still feel that its spirit is not wholly lacking.

* Thus, in at present laying out a botanic garden for London teachers in connection with a park, museum, and educational scheme now being organised by the L.C.C., and much akin to that required by Dunfermline, I am asked by the parks superintendent to select and nominate to him among the many working gardeners one who can efficiently tend the plants and who can also best aid the teacher and pupil.

I must frankly confess that after reading, summarising, and re-reading this wealth of suggestions, and, I trust, digesting and profiting by it, I have laid all aside with the strengthened conviction that the problem before us is not one which can be dealt with piecemeal by the simple plan, in other cases so useful, often even so necessary, of simply meeting demands as they happen to arise, or adopting good ideas as they happen to come in so long as funds may last. The problem is one of design, the designing of a unified group of institutions capable of assuring a real and substantial culture development to the city. This assured, all suggestions may anew be considered, and will be found largely to fall into their natural places.

In the following pages, then, these courteous correspondents will find the general view of the problem I have to offer, and I invite their criticism if I have not yet done justice to their view, or at any rate left place for its subsequent consideration when the time of detailed execution approaches.

I. Summary of Method and Point of View

In summary, then, the preparation of this report has thus involved not only the planning of the improvement of a park, and the laying out of gardens upon a scale worthy of the city and of the occasion, but that of an extensive series of buildings of very various uses. In view of the extreme irregularity of the sites, and their peculiarly complex relation both to park and city, these have had to be planned out with especial care, indeed with practical completeness, since to indicate such sites without positive certainty that the proposed buildings could be fitted into them would have been worse than no suggestion at all. In this connection, too, I have had to acquaint myself with the history of Dunfermline, and, indeed, largely to reinvestigate its significance, which appears to me to exceed that claimed even by its many loving annalists.† To this problem I had already, fortunately, given some attention, as also for many years past to the vast modern question of museums. But here, again, fresh planning and replanning has been necessary, since precedents have availed little. The requirements of twentieth-century science have had to be frankly reconsidered, and this from that more comprehensive and unified standpoint, synthetic yet evolutionary, which especially distinguishes the opening period from the recent one, which has been, in the main, so content with its multiplicity of unrelated specialisms. Again, beyond the difficulty of due presentment and worthy housing of science and arts in evolution is that of the vast educational problems which these raise, and this on every

† Erskine Beveridge, LL.D., "Bibliography of Dunfermline." Dunfermline, 1903.

level, primary and secondary, higher and adult. In all these fields, again, it is no easy matter to be all things to all men. For this involves at once devising the means of arousing and leading on popular interest, yet also of meeting the complex requirements and ready criticism of experts in many fields.

At every point, therefore, from park, playground, and garden to museums and palaces, these larger human and social uses must dominate our constructive tasks; theirs the demand which must determine the supply. Once more, therefore, the planner's standpoint changes. No longer has he simply here to garden or there to build, even reconciling as best he can in detail past and present with future, so far as his foresight can go. He must now strive to place himself at a more comprehensive standpoint, the hardest of all to reach—that of the city as a whole—and this not only the particular and concrete city, the local growth, with its advantages and limitations—he must think out for himself anew the civic problem in its many aspects, comparing city with city over the world; and beyond this again he must not shrink from formulating the ideal of the city. This now is no mere Utopia, but is to be stated in terms of modern science, which begins to turn from deciphering the past of evolution to seeking the practical secret of its future guidance. Here, then, is the last and higher plane of social and scientific research—that which recovers the best ideals of the past and reinstates them in the fresh light of evolution as cardinal points which must henceforth increasingly guide our social development on our personal life journey. This is no merely intellectual step, nor even practical one; it involves the whole life, the whole being, and that of the community even more fully than that of the individual. Beyond the evolutionary synthesis of the thinker, or the renewed university of the teacher, there thus arises a conception, already nascent, not only in books but in cities, that of park and gardens and culture institutes as becoming the Cathedral of the People and of the opening time. We now see the modern town evolving anew towards the culture city—city of realising ideals—and thus again becoming sacred in a new sense, yet one which may have within it much of what is best in the old.

With this evolutionary point of view—the sociological, the ethical—our whole perspective changes. It is our social and educational hope and purpose, our conception of civic progress, which must determine our selection amid the many possibilities of life; and if not consciously and for higher ends, then unconsciously and for lower ones. These ideals now stated, their housing may be profitably considered—that is, their buildings fitly constructed and planned; and, this concluded, their garden setting, within the whole city, park, and landscape, becomes practicable.

For these long studies, then, each with its ramifications, its many drafts and sketches, much longer time has been needed than was calculated for, and this despite well-nigh continuous labour. I trust, however, that this may not prove to have been unfruitful. Indeed, when the great number and variety of the questions and the points considered and of the solutions offered is taken into account, it will, I trust, be seen that this fuller elaboration, which has been found necessary to do them justice, will not be found to have been a loss of time in the long run.

J. The Present Volume

Despite much thought and pains, the variety and intricacy of subject, and the sometimes needful abstractness of thought, make this volume less readable than I had hoped. I would plead, however, that the task laid upon me has been comprehensive beyond precedent. In concluding it I venture to predict, however, that over and above the ordinary literature of topography, history, and contemporary life and activity in which cities are already so rich, each and every city will soon come to have at least three new volumes to itself. The first of these will offer the geographic and historic facts of a good guide-book, well illustrated by help of a photographic survey, even fuller than that which I have undertaken for this park and its environs; while all this would be accompanied, as far as possible, by an interpretation of the city considered as a concrete product of social evolution. After this General Survey, which describes material environment and historic development, comes next its complementary volume—the Social Survey proper. This sets out from the standpoint of the present condition of the people, their occupation and real wages, their family budget, therefore, and culture level. The first of these books is partly represented by our current guide-books—Black's or Murray's, Bædeker's or Baddeley's, still better by Grant Allen's, since these are more evolutionary in their treatment; and the second by Booth's Survey of London, or Rowntree's of York.

The present volume has necessarily something of the first of these, though not of the second. Its real place, however, is as suggesting the third desideratum—that which, taking full note of places and things as they stand, of people as they are, of work, family, and institutions, of ideas and ideals, yet patiently plans out, then boldly suggests, new and practicable developments; and these not only for the immediate future but for the remoter and higher issues which a city's long life and its correspondingly needed foresight involves. In short, a Report such as the present—indeed, far more complete and more extensive than the present—should arise as the natural sequel to the two previous volumes—those of Guide and Social Survey.

Here, then, is a broad result of that pioneering injunction for other cities as well as our own, which is the initial keynote struck for the Trust and those privileged to serve it by its founder. Here we reach the due coadjustment of thought and action, as Social Survey and Social Service ; and even the conception of an *Encyclopædia Civica*, to which city after city should contribute the trilogy of its past, present, and future. Better far, as life transcends books, we may see, yet more foresee, the growth of civic consciousness and conscience, of awakening and renascence. This the production of such volumes would at once imply

and inspire—life ever producing its appropriate expression in literature, and literature reacting upon life.

Apart altogether from what may be the qualities and defects of particular volumes such as the present, we see how the very conception of such a threefold series may become of service, since combining the view and the resources of the educationalist with his treasure-houses of culture, of the man of action with his mastery of immediate affairs, of the thinker with his vision of the opening future, and all into the material of the artist. Even his unifying design, its worthy realisation, is thus preparatory to the real problem of the Trust, that of moral and social leadership, at once inspiring and orchestrating all.

NOTE TO GENERAL PLAN.—In order to keep down the number of blocks, for clearness inevitably so considerable, I have crowded the essential detail of each garden and section of the Park upon the General Plan, instead of giving each a separate block in its appropriate chapter, and indicating its mere outline upon this plan, which would thus have retained its simplicity of effect. I see this economy to be a misleading one, so that the plan, which is, if possible, even more conservative of all the existing features, views, and even details of the Park and Glen, as of its surrounding buildings, gives an impression of exaggerated importance of added details, which, especially in the south park, may seem to destroy the real simplicity of general effect.

If these details still appear too numerous and too elaborate, the reader will remember that in such planning it is far better to foresee the possibilities of elaborate treatment, and thence to simplify, than to make a too simple design, which the enrichments which are so commonly desired would be apt to destroy. This principle holds good in every detail ; for instance, that of the suggested drives. These may, of course, be narrowed into promenades or paths if desired, and the neighbouring footpaths reduced accordingly ; whereas, were not all the main possible drives here foreseen, the whole design might have been at any point upset.

I regret not to have been able to prepare garden perspectives corresponding to those of the buildings (figs. 131, 132, 133), and indicating the effects aimed at, especially since these are to many not easily visualised either from the plan or from the text. The beauty and persuasiveness thus lacking might also have been supplied by the help of reproductions of photographs of fine features of existing gardens. But after a little study of such volumes as those of Miss Jekyll or Mr Robinson, of *Country Life*, or of its quintessence in "Gardens Old and New," a fresh study of the accompanying plan will show that very many of the best effects of such notable gardens have been provided for here, and rearranged so as to enhance each other's effect, within a fresh and independent whole.

Estimates for the execution of the different features of the designs are also withheld for the present, the more since only gradual execution is suggested. But both gardens and buildings will be found to require less considerable outlay and upkeep than may on a first impression appear.

BOOK I

A. APPROACHES AND ADJACENT IMPROVEMENTS

CHAPTER I

PARK APPROACHES AND ENTRANCES

A. Choice of Approach

BEFORE us is the plan of the whole park. I ask that the consideration of the following proposals be rendered real and practical by means of a peregrination, one actual to the resident and at least followed on the map by the more distant reader. Where shall we begin ? For many the High Street seems the natural starting-point, for many the Abbey, with its park entrance, or the Tower Hill, around which the whole city has historically arisen. With the recent inaugural procession we might enter by the Pittencrieff gate, with the visitor to Dunfermline from the Lower Station, or, again, from the naval base by the road from Inverkeithing, or from Rosyth, which are both destined to such increased importance in the near future. From the station we would naturally approach by Priory Lane and Monastery Street, while by the last we obtain our first view from the Nethertown. There is much to be said for each of these points of view, and the plan of the present report has been thought over from each in turn.

From the standpoint alike of geography and common-sense we must approach a hill-city from its bottom, not from its top. Were we here at the standpoint of the tourist we should naturally make at once for its landmarks—the Abbey and Palace, thence pass to the Glen, and thence to the finest parts of the park and garden, coming to minor elements only later if time allowed. In this report, however, it is expedient almost to reverse this process, and begin with less salient aspects first. About these there is less danger of difference of opinion, so that not only can principles be more simply discussed but plans of action more easily settled.

For further concreteness, let us imagine ourselves meeting at the Lower Station someone not unacquainted with gardening and architecture, and bringing with him that fresh eye which may help the everyday familiarity of the citizen. Entering from the station, our visitor, though favourably impressed by the old public park and the short boulevard of Comely Park Place, can hardly fail to notice the great defects of the first

and the imperfect adjustment of the two. The latter, he may point out, is easily remediable, mainly by a slight rectification of road, railing, and park wall, with a little planting, by which the street, the old park, and the railway station would all be united, and thus each improved not a little. Coming on through the narrow Priory Lane to the new Technical School and High School, he can hardly fail to note with regret the recently lost opportunity of extending the station boulevard and parkway he has just traversed to meet the school square; and though welcoming the recent widening of the street at the expense of the garden edge of the bowling green, he may regret the bareness of its wall

FIG. 8.—Photograph looking East from middle of Priory Place, opposite Technical School—*i.e.* from middle of the proposed " Parkway"; looking back along the short Station Boulevard (Comely Park Place) to old Public Park. Trees here introduced.

treatment. By planting trees, at any rate where adjacent land is unbuilt on, some effect of this lost boulevard can still be recovered (fig. 9); these trees in perspective leading to those of the park, whose tree-tops are so plainly seen over the manse gate and wall. The possibility of obtaining a new entrance here comes naturally to be discussed, and turning round and looking back towards the station from this (fig. 8) we fully realise how great would be the gain to the amenity and dignity of the city were the two parks, old and new, to become connected by a continuous boulevard, a " Parkway." Hence he cannot but urge that this be put upon the city's plan, even though it can only at once be realised by these few trees, and perhaps not fully for a generation. For tree planting involves patience as no other calling does.

The disastrous loss to the improvement of a city through looking at each of its public parks as a well-defined " property " enclosed within its own boundaries is here at once realised. In any and every city (even in those comparatively well laid out or richest in parks, like Edinburgh) we may readily see how its present beauty might have been doubled had the approaches and interconnections of its parks been adequately studied, instead of independently conducted, on one side by a Parks Committee, on the other by a Streets and Buildings Committee, and so, practically, by

FIG. 9.—Photograph from same spot, but looking West towards Manse, with new (Pittencrieff) Park beyond. Proposed new entrance at end of street. Trees again introduced.

unlucky chance. Here at the very outset the landscape gardener may at once define his habitual viewpoint—that of combining into picture, coordinating in literal perspective, the standpoints of these two civic committees, and of helping, so far as he can, towards coadjusting the immediate field of the park superintendent with those of the city architect and of the burgh engineer. To be efficient in his task he must take note of all that comes into his park pictures, which necessarily include park approaches and environs, no more avoiding this point or that feature, because of proprietary or other differences, than does the hygienist in his way, but equally free with him to say what in his judgment is wrong, and suggest what may still be done, or, at any rate kept in view, to remedy it.

B. Approach Selected

Since this Manse entrance is not yet acquired, and since, moreover, we agreed at the outset to begin at the lowest level and to dispose of simpler

matters before entering upon difficulties, we leave this, and also the present East entrance, the old " Portgate " by the Abbey, for later consideration (Chaps. XIV. and XXIII. respectively), and descend by Moodie Street towards Nethertown, noting for preservation Mr Carnegie's early home, and below this, for improvement if possible, the featureless gable of the adjacent house and the present unoccupied field—an excellent site, it may be noted in passing, for a possible future School Garden. Of this the needed gardener-superintendent's cottage would cover the gable above referred to, and improve the street. (See Fig. 10.)

Reaching Nethertown Street, we have fortunately here such breadth as offers the possibility of planting it as a boulevard like Comely Park Place (indeed why not with the improvement of grass verges as at Helensburgh ?). (Fig. 11.)

Here, in fact, would be a first-rate immediately realisable Parkway, which would be practically in line with a new entrance to the park at the foot of the Glebe, of which the acquirement is obviously of great importance. Pausing at this point, we note the various elements of the landscape, the fine tree-clad west bank of the stream, the pleasantly rising but naked manse hill with the valley narrowing upwards, the irregular grouping of the old mills, the tower of the Abbey Church. (Figs. 12 and 13.)

Again and again along the slopes to Forth or Tay we find such a " den " or dell, a more or less deep-cut, tree-filled ravine widening out into an enlarged valley of more fertile aspect—in short, passing from dell into orchard and field. This being the general and natural character of a landscape of this kind, our business as gardeners—taming Nature, yet developing her natural resources of beauty—is to plant upwards, thus continuing trees from the boulevard and from our proposed Nethertown entrance to the top of the manse hill. Large and lofty trees at the highest points along this ascending east side of the Glebe, soon to be the edge of the park, are obviously desirable to frame the valley in trees on both sides, the present high and unsightly wall (figs. 14 and 16) being, of course, removed. Common maple (Scots " plane ") would here do well ; and immediately west of these should be planted flowering trees—first the wild gean, white in spring blossom and orange-scarlet in autumn foliage ; within these again a variety of crabs and other apples, so interesting in fruit as well as in flower, and acquiring with age a gnarled picturesqueness of form and beauty of bark all their own. Rowan, service tree, and hawthorns of sorts would also be added, the common

FIG. 10.—View up Moodie Street, which would frame the Church Tower. Widening practicable. Field to right suitable for School Gardens: blank gable to right could thus be covered by gardener's cottage.

FIG. 11.—View of Nethertown Street from near Hospital (East of Station), looking West towards new Park. Trees introduced, showing immediate effect, here so easily practicable, of Boulevard Approach to Park.

hawthorn occupying shade thrown by the larger trees.

With the shelter thus provided fine varieties as of double cherry, and even of almond, with its early pink blossom, may be planted ; while even where the Glen narrows into shadow thorns will still blossom, furnishing a " Hawthornden " transition from the orchard effect below to the deeper ferny shade above. On the future gate-lodge climbing shrubs like the blue-bush (*Ceanothus*) the orange thorn (*C. pyracantha*), the dark-foliaged and scarlet-berried cotoneasters, would all find place. The main effect obtained by the acquisition and improvement of the Glebe would thus be that of a well-sunned orchard slope, sheltered by trees from east and west with grassy bank running down to the dovecote and the stream.

Should the adjacent field to the east be acquired,

The general principle of the needed rearrangement will be understood from a glance at figs. 14 and 15, for, as inspection of the ground will show, it is needful and easy to widen and straighten the present connection between the Nethertown Boulevard and the avenue of Lovers' Loan. To do this we must, of course, push the stream northward, and here rises the possibility, as the contours show, of altering the present artificial course of the stream, chiefly by excavating to northward of its present course, along the roadside, so as to furnish a not inconsiderable estuary-like lake or pond, of which this south side would still be straight, but the outlines to east and west would be quite natural ones. Any excavated material would be partly used to fill up the deeper portions of the present course, and so leave no spot which might be too deep for children wading ;

FIG. 12.—View from West end of Nethertown, looking up the valley field (Glebe) and past Manse on right (east) to Monastery ruin and Abbey Church. Park trees on West bank of stream. View shows expediency of adding glebe to Park.

the proposed planting may be readily adjusted to this ; or if buildings are erected in it by other proprietors of such a character as to enhance the amenity of the park, peeps of mutual advantage can be arranged.

The design for this south - east (Nethertown) entrance lodge must naturally be determined by the architecture of the buildings to be erected above, and so cannot be discussed at this stage. In any case it should be simple and unobtrusive upon the larger view. Imposing gates and lodges are only needed where the landscape otherwise lacks interest ; with great architecture as here within sight, they must be kept as simple as possible.

C. East Lake

The question of roads from this entrance next falls to be considered, and some conjoint understanding between the public authorities, adjacent proprietors, and the Trust is here plainly desirable.

and, further, to construct a small bird island, where nests would be secure from molestation. But some material would be needed for raising the road and improving the slope also from Elgin Street. A small skating-pond, though one not very rapidly freezing, owing to the trees sheltering it on the western side, is thus provided. This will be of beauty during the whole year, and afford a natural home for swans and for a considerable number of aquatic birds, of which an interesting selection may easily be maintained at very moderate expense.

The ruined dovecot should, of course, also be rebuilt (fig. 17), and would furnish a picturesque foreground object, composing with the picturesque masses of the old buildings above on the hill. This dovecot peninsula might also afford lodging for a seal, or even sea-lion, on its southward side, a duly protected bear-cage or bear-pit and pole to the northward. The position of the different animal houses of the proposed small " Zoo " has been carefully considered, with the kind help of one of our most eminently successful authorities, Professor Cunningham, F.R.S , late Director of the Dublin Zoological Gardens ; but this subject will be returned to later. (Chap. X.)

It will be noted that this slight raising and extension of the stream would sacrifice a certain number of trees along the west edge of the present stream. These would be more than compensated for by judicious planting along the edge, and also by planting new ones upon the other side of this belt of trees—i.e. upon the east side of the main park beyond.

The effect of the proposed changes may be realised from figs. 17, 18, and 19.

D, Previous Need of Stream Purification

The polluted state of the stream, however, renders this whole proposed improvement —i.e. the very first park improvement we come to, and one of obvious beauty—quite impracticable for the present. We theretore leave the glen and its stream till we have discussed its thorough purification in a later chapter (XI.), and in the meantime address ourselves to such park improvements as are practicable independently of this, though not thereby recommending these, however in themselves desirable, as worthy of precedence. This is indeed the fundamental condition both of the naturalistic and the artistic improvements which lie before us ; a condition closely connected, not only as symbol but as practical help or hindrance, to the whole task and problem of material and moral betterment upon which Dunfermline is entering.

E, Lovers' Loan, etc,

Proceeding along the widened road shown in fig. 15, we now reach the avenue of Lovers' Loan. Fig. 20 shows not only its beauty but

its defect. The existing footpath on the south side is too narrow, while on the north side there is none, and the park wall, unfortunately, hides the stems and roots of the trees. The following

FIG. 13.—Detail ot preceding view ; from S.W. corner of Manse Garden wall, point near middle in preceding. Mill chimney to be removed. Drive from Manse Entrance to proposed new East Bridge (Chap. XIII. and plan) would run along line of wall indicated about 2¼ inches above lower margin of block.

illustration shows the improvement of removing the park wall to the south and carrying a light fence behind (fig. 21). As shown on plan, the main drives proposed around this southern portion of the park should have an entrance and issue here, and a new lodge at this point would admit scope for a somewhat more ornate architectural treatment than that at Nethertown.

May not an amicable arrangement between the road authorities and the adjacent proprietors

FIG. 14.—View from same spot as in fig. 12 (West Nethertown Street, near proposed South-East entrance), but now looking West towards old avenue to South of Park ("Lovers' Loan").

FIG. 15.—The same view, showing proposed emendation, by widening roadway and damming stream so as to give artificial pond or East Lake. (The over-polished transformation of the writer's rough sketch in course of the retouching process must here be allowed for.)

FIG. 16.—Panorama looking South from Manse Hill. Stream and Park on right. Town to left (back of Moodie Street) and South.

FIG. 17.—The preceding view, but now showing effect of East Lake (Fig. 15), and of planting East side of Glebe if added to Park.

FIG. 18.—Further detail of this East Lake, showing nearer effect of west lake margin seen from boat or east side.

FIG. 19.—Further detail of west margin, from its own side. (This and the preceding view are taken by Mr Norval from Otterston Loch in vicinity, and are thus quite realisable here.)

FIG. 20.—View along Lovers' Loan, looking West. Note narrow footpath on South, and high Park wall concealing tree stems to North.

FIG. 21.—The same view retouched, showing this North wall removed, also advantage of new pathways outside trees on each side (the trees to North are really on a higher level).

be possible here ? Might not a strip of ground be conceded by each proprietor, north and south of the present road, so as to give a boulevard proper, with a footpath on either side of the main avenue ? Upon the outer edge of each footpath a new row of trees might also be planted; while the gaps in the main avenue would of course be supplied.

Turning northwards up the Coal Road (fig. 22), is not a similar arrangement possible, thus continuing our initial Parkway along the south side of the town and park up the west side also ? Why

may furnish an argument of enlightened self-interest, and present the planting of trees as a shrewder " investment in futures " than many more common ones.

F. North Entrance and its Neighbourhood

After pausing at this important crossing, and noting the monotonous street perspectives up and down, we pass eastwards, and soon reach the North entrance, with its new gates and lodge

FIG. 22.—View of Coal Road, looking North uphill. A similar treatment upon each side is naturally indicated (cf. General Plan), thus giving a West Park Avenue.

not continue the avenue still farther, so improving the new suburb arising to north-west of the park ? For this some trees already exist (on the way to Grieve Street and Golfdrum), and serve to indicate how great would be this improvement.

It is the clear and increasing policy of all park improvements really worth the name, by due development of such approaches to send out at any rate the beginning of boulevards radiating into the actual city or the future suburbs in every direction possible. That difficulties exist is obvious, but this class of improvement is so obviously needed for the approaching future that it cannot be neglected; while the substantial economic gain to proprietors, as well as to the city,

buildings opposite. These are admired by some, severely criticised by others, but at any rate are so new, efficient, and substantial as to make no alteration justifiable, save by the planting of ivies, roses, jessamine, and the like upon both lodge and railing. As representing the style of our own times, they also take as obvious a place in our open-air museum of architectural styles as any of their predecessors.

Pausing again for a moment at this crossing we note the desirability of again improving a park approach by planting a northward avenue up Maitland Street and of putting in trees along the edges of the adjacent school playground. In all such matters of planting, even in comparatively narrow streets we cannot do better than follow the example of Aberdeen, which, despite a more inclement climate, has taken the lead among Scottish cities, and can show many miles of results already admirable, indeed conclusive, to all who value the evidence of experience.

G. School Gardening

The question of a School Garden in this neighbourhood naturally arises ; but, as on entering the park we see that no plot of ground can be given up for this without far too serious damage to park amenity, I strongly recommend that any ground provided for a garden to this school should be in its own immediate neighbourhood, especially as this adjacent ground seems still available, of course with greater convenience to the school itself. The supply of extended recreative and garden grounds to other schools, especially those still upon the growing edge of the city, while obviously most desirable, does not come within the limits of the present report. I submit plan, however (Chap. VII.), for one such School Garden, designed to indicate the possibility of combining both recreative and gardening uses, and it would be easy to work out very varied designs adapted to respective sites. These would enable each school to develop characteristic elements of interest and corresponding branches of gardening, so that each might be best in some way. All schools and children will find their interests considered, so far as limits allow, in the treatment proposed later for the Park and Gardens.

FIG. 23.—Highest ground of Park in North-East corner. Old Dovecote Tower to East. Roofs of Pittencrieff Street cottages seen through Boundary Plantation and behind wall. Backs of high new Tenements to West. Proposed site of sunk Playgrounds with Shrubberies, Flower beds, etc.

CHAPTER II

NEIGHBOURING PROPERTY AND HOUSING IMPROVEMENTS

A. Neighbouring Housing Improvements

WITHOUT entering upon the general Housing Question or the housing policy of the Trust in relation to it, the present problem, that of the park, its approaches, and adjacent buildings involves some brief discussion of the subject within these limits.

Returning to the North entrance, possible sites at once suggest themselves, not only as well adapted for improving the approaches by open spaces, housing improvements, or both, but also on account of the serious risks of permanent injury to the amenity of this important entrance, as of others, should they be built upon in the ordinary tenement fashion, of which examples are not far to seek. It is manifest that such sites can be used not only more picturesquely but more economically by the Trust than by a private speculator, for the former can more fully utilise them.

From the northern part of the Park, east of this main entrance, the uninteresting backs of new and comparatively lofty tenements form a regrettable interruption of the picturesque lines and pleasing colour of the red-roofed cottages which elsewhere predominate, especially westwards. These bald brick walls and low-pitched, slated roofs, so well seen during the long months while the trees are bare, give an ominous indication of the possible future aspects of the Park boundaries. The ugly and monotonous high boundary wall of the Park is also far too much in evidence. See fig. 23 above.

There is nothing necessarily undesirable in having houses looking into the park. On the contrary, the more windows with this pleasant outlook the better. Nor is there any objection to tenements in themselves: some such lofty buildings, at due intervals, the writer (himself responsible at Edinburgh for the lofty tenements of University Hall, with their outlook upon West Princes Street Gardens) would naturally rather welcome than oppose, provided due architectural care be taken in their grouping and design.

FIG. 22a.—North Entrance.

Here, then, is a suggestion: that the Trust let it be openly understood to all surrounding proprietors that where they are willing to make their present back a pleasing frontage, in any way, however simple, whether by building, harling, or verduring, and where tenants keep their garden so as to make this presentable and pleasing from

31

the park, that here, at this point, the Trustees should lower their wall to a height of 2 or 3 feet, and surmount this by a railing, so as to exchange the mutual view.

The trees, mostly limes, which fringe the northern plantation might also in not a few cases be lowered, in fact be pollarded, with gain of sunshine to the dwellings and their gardens, and without loss of general effect to the plantation—limes lending themselves admirably even to the severest treatment. Per contra, where the backs of buildings are objectionable, the Trust should leave its existing trees and wall, and still further shut out the view of any building they object to as of the irregularities of their own wall by further plantation, especially of tall-growing varieties of yew and holly, so as increasingly to conceal them in winter.

I see no reason why the more improving neighbour proprietors should not be further encouraged by a privilege which would give increased value to their property—namely, the grant of a private entrance from their garden direct into the park; of course, controlled at night-time by an over-key by the park-keepers. This arrangement has been in operation for many years in Edinburgh between West Princes Street Gardens and the adjacent houses.

B. Hygienic and Domestic Improvements

I assume that a certain number of these houses —two especially—of Pittencrieff Street and Chalmers Street adjacent to the park will gradually pass into the possession of the Trust. Is it not possible judiciously to use them so as to influence, no doubt gently and gradually, the general housing of the town apart from larger building schemes to which my present instructions do not extend? Beyond the ordinary repairs, sanitation, and simple, tasteful decoration which may be all taken for granted, what else can be done? I submit that there are at least two sides—the Hygienic and the Domestic—on which these Trust properties should exhibit a definite and conspicuous advance. First as regards hygiene, I would urge that the Trust attempt an initiative, which would no doubt like every novelty be ridiculed or opposed, but would soon be justified by health statistics—namely, the adaptation to the ordinary house of facilities for that open-air life which the open-air treatment for consumption is tending to naturalise among us. This treatment is itself so comparatively new that few realise that it is now passing beyond the task of curative medicine altogether into that of preventive hygiene—that is, of housing and building generally.

The old dread of open windows, particularly at night, is now known to be a survival of earlier times, when ague and malaria were rife even in Scotland; but it has now no such common-sense justification. Hence not only the ground-floor verandah summer-house, but next the open-air sleeping-box of every consumption sanatorium has, as soon as hygienic education allows, to be incorporated as part of the ordinary and reasonable sanitary standard of the intelligent home; the better educated house-mother having henceforth to expend the same conscientious solicitude in seeing to her children's and her own open windows that she has formerly expended upon closing them; indeed, by-and-by feeling the same sting of shame at noticing a closed window that she already does over a dirty one. And since it is naturally the more domestic and sedentary sex that suffers, especially from consumption, the provision of that upstairs balcony which is a main hygienic resource of woman's life in other countries, and next even of the out-hung sleeping-cage, has to be henceforth more and more largely considered. The actual immediate gain to our deficient housing accommodation from this easy supply of actual "outdoor apartments" will only be derided by that section of the public whom the open-air treatment has not yet converted.

I submit, then, that it is for a pioneering body like the Trust to insist upon its architects keeping in view this consideration throughout its whole body of housing schemes, and not merely to be content with enforcing that far greater attention which may be expected from them as to due placing of buildings to sun and air than is shown in ordinary feuing schemes.

The domestic point of housing improvement which I press for all properties acquired by the Trust is that of improving kitchen and scullery accommodation. This may seem a small matter, but, if so, this can only be from masculine limitations or from feminine modesty. After spending more time in America than many more prolific writers I may unhesitatingly set down my adherence to the view that those American superiorities which begin to surprise and disconcert old Europe, very largely turn, indirectly as well as directly, upon the superior culture and status of women. This is no doubt commonly known; but it is not sufficiently realised that the leisure for this culture and this improved status is to an enormous extent derived from that diminution in domestic drudgery which distinguishes the American from the European home. When this begins to be realised masculine chivalry will take the form of improving the kitchen and its appurtenances, alike for Cinderella's sake and for her mistress's. It is this lessening of drudgery, lessening of fatigue and worry, that leaves the women of the household—mistresses, daughters, and maids alike—time, and consequently strength and inclination, for the culture activities of the Women's Club, with its wide and widening interests, and for the further improvement of the home. It sets free from domestic work also a larger proportion of women for business, thus notably increasing the American commercial forces, and still more recruiting that profession in which, above all others, America at present both in numbers and in average culture excels—that of the woman teacher. I have as I write the opportunity of regularly meeting both primary and secondary teachers in each of the great quarters of London—north, south, east, and west—and while these, of course, present many individuals who would be distinguished even in America, there is no doubt that such leaders are less numerous, the average less high, and the total number and proportion of teachers to population seriously deficient, as, indeed, the London School Board has lately been recognising.

To adopt every improvement, then, that housewife and architect can devise is thus a matter of increasing importance in domestic comfort, wellbeing, and leisure, in civic prosperity and culture, in national and racial struggle. The more familiar aspects of the case, from economy of fuel to bettered decoration, and diminution of dust, dusting, and disease, as from better cooking to diminished intemperance, need not here be insisted on. But in summary I submit that in the various exhibitions, competitions, or commissions with which the policy of the Trust may be concerned, attention should be paid not only to the beauty of front aspects but even more strictly to the convenience and wholesomeness of back ones. It is highly encouraging to note in the work of various recent architects increased attention to these matters of domestic and sanitary detail. Such improvements have artistic value also.

The complaint that such improvements raise rents is not a serious criticism. They will soon tend to lower rents also for the houses which remain behind the age. The essential problem of prosperity, individual, civic, and national alike, is to improve real wages ; as this is done by more and more truly productive industry the money wages must, and do, follow.

Other matters of housing I may safely leave untouched, as I am not here to enlarge upon this attractive question of general city improvement, which would require a separate report altogether. Enough if I recommend the holding of occasional exhibitions bearing on the various aspects of this.

C. Housing Improvement Generally

Instead of pressing for any large improvement of this or that point, involving extensive purchases of property, I advocate rather the purchase of properties at many points along the margins of the park, where, in the natural order of things, properties are changing hands every year. Thus,

without hastening to make any one extensive improvement which would too rapidly raise the value of unpurchased property in its neighbourhood, the Trust would soon possess a fair number of properties, with neighbouring and intermediate ones constantly falling in. Pending the development of contiguous properties some would be let as usual ; some used, as we shall see below, for various detailed objects of the Trust. Of large architectural proposals there will be no lack later ; existing buildings and their utilisation, as far as may be, are the first care.

When several contiguous properties, especially upon the streets bordering the park, have been acquired, we have thus sites available either for housing improvements or for such large permanent buildings as the future may require. These would be well shown from the park also by a judicious local thinning of the plantation belt on that point. Such possibilities will make the Trust increasingly independent of pressure from particular proprietors.

Many possibilities of street improvements have suggested themselves, but I hold back sketch plans and detailed suggestions, which might at present only defeat their own realisation, since tending to raise the price of properties concerned.

The progress of Dunfermline improvements under the Trust, while, of course, in many ways of obvious advantage to the whole community, carries at the same time a special advantage to property owners in a rise of capital values. But this must inevitably and soon become expressed in a tendency towards a rise of rentals more commensurate with this increased value. Thus it has come about before now that an Improvement Trust, undertaken primarily in the interest of the working people, has also tended, so far, to their disadvantage as compared with the property-owning classes. Hence the working man points out, with some natural disappointment, how improvements can raise his rent but cannot raise his wages. Per contra, the property owner loudly complains wherever an Improvement Trust tends to cheapen dwellings by increasing the number of better ones or by entering into building competition with him. But the reply is fairly made that, since it is already helping his capital account by making its improvements, and so by-and-by his rentals (it may be these also in some measure by reducing the number of dwellings by substituting public buildings for private ones), it must do something on the other side for his tenants also. Thus, to keep the balance even, the Trust must put its massive weight partly into each scale.

Below these economic reasons for purchasing and improving properties adjacent to the park I now come to the deeper social one. If there is any one point characteristic and clear in the advance of social thought throughout the past quarter century it has been the return from the purely

Individual and the State points of view, emphasised by the economists, to the older conceptions of the Family as the elemental community, and with this of the City, as for many purposes, if not most practical ones, the true State, and not a mere voting unit. We have passed the time when civic progress could be sneered at as " parish politics," or as " a matter of gas and sewage."

With this point of view, in fact central to it, there is thus rising upon the first plane of social importance the Home. Its improvement, its culture, is beginning to transcend in importance those too purely institutional developments of the preceding hundred years which have been so long favoured by all political and economic schools. This newer movement of thought towards home and city happily agrees in emphasising the position of woman, and this no longer as a mere political " individual," a mere " economic man," but again as home-maker, civiliser, on all sides, therefore, as citizen.

Hence before proceeding to discuss the museums or picture-galleries, which, as student of science and art, I rejoice to design, or even these gardens of pleasure and of science for which I personally care most of all, I press this question of home improvement, since in the long run the whole culture policy of the Trust will be measured in terms of the comfort, culture, and character of the Dunfermline home.

But how is a Trust to meddle with homes ? Gardens may, of course, be directly helped, criticised, or even set in competition, but no organisation can or should intrude upon the inviolable privacy, the absolute independence, of the individual home, which must ever ultimately be what its denizens unconsciously and consciously make it.

Yet within its limits the Trust may do much— first, as that most needed sort of model landlord and good house factor who, accepting the ordinary existing rules of the business game, yet sees to it that his share of the duties and responsibilities is fulfilled to the utmost. But it is not the problem of a model landlord to supply more houses merely of the average quality, still less to increase a minimum accommodation for minimum rents, though there are many philanthropists who think so. This is merely extending that low standard of civilisation at the one or two-room level, which has already sufficiently degraded Scotland among the peoples, and which tends to lower wages as well. The task now before us is a quite different one—first, that of giving the tenant better accommodation for the same money in actual floor and cube space, in sanitation and decoration, in garden and outlook, or, if possible, in all, and thence leading him on to a new and better house altogether. This must necessarily be a dearer one, but the increase of wage-earning power which better conditions develop should meet this

Such a model landlord finds his return not in a higher percentage but in choice and permanence of the best tenants, with consequent regularity of letting and maintenance of property. It is, therefore, with the simple everyday business methods of Miss Octavia Hill, which have been practically adopted with no less success by the Edinburgh Social Union and by kindred Glasgow and Dundee organisations, that housing improvements may reasonably begin.

This sound business, at first more of factoring than of building, once begun, with such park boundary properties of the Trust as may be required for amenity's sake also, larger building schemes will doubtless follow. But these have not to be considered within the present limits.

There are immediate uses to which such adjacent dwellings may be applied. Thus, though the existing and prospective lodges will house some of the working staff of the Trust, more houses may be required. Though the bothy, customarily supplied for unmarried gardeners, would be, naturally, near the winter garden or greenhouses of the Trust, at least one such cottage might still be usefully found in this neighbourhood.

Though young men are always free to find lodgings in the ordinary way there is something to be said for their living together ; and experience of houses of residence for students (who are much like non-students) shows that common living is of advantage to a majority. Experience also proves that though the provision of residence for women workers is less developed, because more difficult of solution, it is yet perhaps more needful and this not only on economic grounds but on psychological and social grounds also. These are not homes, yet, beside their immediate usefulness, they help to fix standards of comfort and refinement, so important to home life later.

D. Social Survey

At this stage, also, we must fully keep in view not only the immediate sites but the use which can be made of them towards social betterment.

The current change in economic thinking, from academic theory and working-class struggle for money wages, to the observation and improvement of real wages, centres essentially upon this housing question. The " Family Budget " is again being seen to be as essential to the theory as to the practice of economics, and this very word begins again to express its ancient meaning, the order of the home.

The " Family Budget," to investigate which is the last great advance in economics, means the actual quantity and quality of home space, of clothing and feeding, of warming and lighting, of education and reading, of civilising or debasing pleasure, week by week and year by year ; and it finds its definite resultant in the characteristic types of populations. The usually more or less depressed, when not positively demoralised or diseased, populations of towns are thus being studied everywhere, occupation by occupation. These are now seen to be the essential facts of modern town life. They are not to be forgotten in Dunfermline, and least of all by any agency like the present, expressly created for raising the standard of the population by converging every available resource of civilisation.

I press for such a Survey of Dunfermline as that of London by Charles Booth, or by Rowntree in York, and I submit it as one of the most immediately practical and important suggestions of this report that the Trust either undertake or aid such an inquiry, or in some way see that it is carried on, up to the fullest level of foreign as well as British economic and social survey. For efficient social service, social survey is no less needed than are charts for navigation or maps for war.

One part of such an inquiry, that regarding the health condition of school children, has been begun in Edinburgh and Aberdeen with all the resources of contemporary medical science, and a social survey should be even more comprehensive.

These suggestions, then, dispense me, within these limits, from further reference to the housing question, or to the material condition of the people, which each offer ample scope for separate reports altogether.

While thus limiting myself within the letter of my instructions to park and environs, it seems necessary to guard against any appearance of lack of sympathy with larger housing schemes. Far from this, I assume that these will be fully and separately considered ; though, as having been long personally concerned with the gradual improvement and piecemeal repair of many of the closes and slums of Old Edinburgh, I may be permitted to hope that this more modest, yet not ineffective, line of action may be also taken with their not infrequent analogues here. Into the bibliography of this vast subject I shall not enter, save to refer to two small books just published (May 1904).

T. R. MARR. "Housing Conditions in Manchester and
        Salford." Manchester University Press. 1s.
T. C. HORSFALL.   "The Example of Germany." *Ibid.*

CHAPTER III

SOCIAL INSTITUTES AND CENTRAL INSTITUTE

A. Social Institutes

THE possession of some of these dwelling-houses near the park would also give the Trust an opportunity of testing upon a moderate and experimental scale one or two of the Social Institutes which have of late been so strongly recommended by the Rev. Dr Paton, Mr Arthur Sherwell, and others—first, as successful substitutes for the public-house ; and second, as reacting usefully upon homes in their districts. To give this principle fair trial it must be tested, for young women and for young men, for older people also, and on the whole separately. If two or three such clubs can be grouped in the same tenement or in adjacent cottages this will admit of greater economy of management—e.g. in heating, refreshment supply, etc. A single large room for entertainments and other special occasions would thus suffice for the whole group, and other economies would be compatible with all due individuality of separate organisations. Apart from capital investment, the expenses of a moderate start, for rent, repairs, and taxes, of heating, lighting, cleaning, and caretaker, of interest on furnishing and depreciation, need not exceed £100 annually, while a substantial portion of this might be recovered by subscriptions and by small charges on games and entertainments, leaving only the balance therefore to be met by the Trust. It is not unreasonable to hope that such clubs would in time become self-supporting, if not even yield a margin of profit, which might be employed to reduce the initial deficit upon starting new ones.

I am aware that many prefer to begin upon a larger scale, with a People's Palace, or the like ; but I submit that both types are needed, and the smaller first. This small type of institute, where one may meet one's own friends and neighbours, but not the whole town, is a needed element of temperance reform, of civic progress, and, last but not least, of that education in social life, in responsibility and administrative experience which would in turn react usefully upon the larger citizenship.

Here again everything must ultimately depend not upon the Trust directly but upon the vital personal initiative they can find for management, and this must be of that rarest kind, which can at once collect and inspire a social group and yet provide for its own replacement from within its ranks.

Dr Paton's and kindred Social Institutes are said to be successful in this respect. My own long experience in the organisation of student's houses in Edinburgh has been that such a group once started soon becomes, and on the whole thoroughly remains, worthy of the utmost confidence which can be placed in it ; indeed, it often exercises stricter regulation from within than could possibly be imposed from without. Moreover, the educative value of giving such responsibility far outweighs the occurrence of occasional undesirable incidents, while even these are found invariably to provoke a healthy reaction, which is the best safeguard against their recurrence in the future.

To the Decoration and Furnishing of these Social Institutes I would attach much importance, pleading for the adoption of a standard in advance upon our average domestic one, yet this in the direction of simplicity no less than of improved adornment. Simply stained and waxed floors, with only the fewest and simplest of rugs and mattings ; simply but pleasantly distempered walls decorated with those good and cheap reproductions of masterpieces which may now be no less within the reach even of the poor than are the cheap papers. Simple tables and cane chairs, and some of those cheap but restful deck-chairs, which can be used either indoors or in the garden, complete the essentials at an expense substantially below that of the ordinary furnishing of the corresponding home. This combination of economy and beauty in furnishing, actually known as the " University Settlement Style " in Whitechapel, in New York, and Chicago alike, is becoming adopted in the homes—especially, of course, of the newly married—and it serves as an excellent base upon which the further adornment, so instinctive to the home-making sex, may be carried on. The reaction of all this upon home life and family ideals has still to be sufficiently realised.

This economy in furnishing will help towards a more liberal outlay upon an essential to each of these institutes and clubs—a Piano of the strong make, yet good quality, supplied to the better schools. Furthermore ; I am urged by musicians to suggest the addition of a Pianola, since this admits of the reasonably adequate rendering of music of far higher quality than comes within the range of the amateur. I am aware that the expense of such instruments is at present considerable, but they claim to be durable and capable of repair. Moreover, I have been asked : Is this not practically a necessary complement to that wise and generous encouragement to music upon which the Trust has entered ? To provide first-class concerts is excellent, but most of us would appreciate them and profit by them far more if we could first prepare for them, and also recall them by hearing their main pieces at will by help of this instrument. In providing several Pianolas at different centres of the town the Trust might also economise by having only a single library of scores, which could easily be circulated. At a central institute, at least, the experiment might easily be made of having one good instrument of this kind to start with.

The provision both of indoor and outdoor Games is next worth considering. Thus along the whole length of one side of a garden or back-yard wall should run such an open-air shelter as can easily and cheaply be erected by carpenter and slater, and of which the posts can be wreathed with roses for summer and jessamine for winter. This shelter, well bottomed with ashes, would serve as an outdoor apartment, and would thus help in that education towards open-air life which it is a main use of this whole report to instigate. The seats and light tables being easily cleared away the long space becomes available as skittle or bowling alley, an admirable resource for either sex and all ages, in wet weather especially.

With all this should go the supply of one or two elements of the open-air gymnasium. The old impression that gymnastics are only for young men has been dispelled by girls' schools, and as this better-educated generation has been growing up some have continued its gymnastics, so that we are beginning to have gymnasts of all ages, just as we have cyclists, pedestrians, and riders up to old age. In the public gymnasia of advanced cities like Boston there are large regular classes for elderly men ; and the gentle, yet active, and open-air hygiene so essential to vigorous old age is also in active progress. Such institutes will not interfere with the great public gymnasia, etc., any more than do private baths with public ones : they will in the main help each other.

I hold very strongly that these initial typical units of the social institutes of the opening future are, and should be, of a modest and domestic character ; in advance certainly of the average home,

yet rather repeating themselves in a fresh street than attaining any great single development. Their relation to the temperance movement also indicates this.

Here again, as with students' houses, experience proves numbers to yield advantage, to give variety and interest, only up to a certain very moderate extent ; after this unity is apt to suffer. Where numbers increase, the establishment of a new house is found to be the better policy. In short, for busy people a friendly and homely atmosphere is wanted—not a large club, with its too passing acquaintance.

B. Residences

A certain natural growth, however, is legitimate and desirable. Residence, primarily for the unmarried, but sometimes it may be also the married, may naturally arise in conjunction with this or that social institute ; and, since standards of comfort necessarily vary with average income, like groups tend to be formed, here of working girls, there of teachers, clerks, nurses, etc., and similarly for men of different incomes and occupations.

In conjunction with each of these houses the various forms of social activity, as of amusement and entertainment, would arise just as they do in larger cities. There the small university settlements and the like are steadily growing up into great and active institutions, the true analogue of the religious and social sisterhoods and brotherhoods of the past. With this growth new buildings become needed, and these naturally take appropriate forms of architectural beauty. Adjacent to parks or to other open spaces, the value of such institutes is naturally greatly enhanced, and their success correspondingly promoted. Boys' and youths' clubs, for instance, can thus especially be promoted.

One mass of buildings, fortunately already the property of the Trust, presents itself as both in situation and architecture peculiarly appropriate to the purposes of such an initial social group—assuming, of course, that active and capable leadership, at once moral, practical, and intellectual, which is required. Starting with one of the dwellings of Queen Anne's House (figs. 24 and 25), this could include others as required, and gradually incorporate the old cottages northward, with due repair, or rather, in this case, rebuilding. Of the beauty and fitness of these old buildings I have already spoken ; and though these, as I constantly find, are far from being sufficiently appreciated in Dunfermline, I can only say that I know of no Oxford or other college, much less of any university settlement, which would not be proud of possessing a range of such historic and archi-

Fig. 24.—Queen Anne's House, East front, and St Catherine's Wynd, looking up to City Buildings and High Street. View looking North from steps of Abbey—West entrance.

Fig. 25.—West side of same range, looking North to City Buildings, over Queens' Garden in Glen. View taken from Park drive, fifty yards west of former point.

tectural representativeness and interest, from St Catherine's Chapel to the Portgate, with its buildings from each of the great ages of education —mediæval and subsequent—grouped under the abbey spire (fig. 26). Here, better than in any other buildings obtainable, can be naturally fostered at once that spirit of sympathetic appreciation and conservation of the past, of practical utility in the present, and of adequate outlook towards the future, which is essential not only to a liberal culture but to a fully sympathetic and useful life. Such a group of houses would readily adapt itself to residence for both sexes, the method which works so admirably in some of the best American settlements—as notably Hull House, Chicago. If a separate centre under exclusively feminine management is desired excellent sites are obtainable even in this neighbourhood. In this connection I would strongly press that the whole policy of social institutes must be largely influenced by women. First of all, therefore, the relevant committee will have to find the right woman.

To many who are accustomed to think in terms of large political changes rather than of small social leavening ones, these proposals must necessarily seem " petty " or " indefinite." Yet one cannot as yet simply map out a town into districts like municipal wards, or school-board areas, and there plant down a social institute and expect it to work. At any rate, I am not aware of such methods having succeeded anywhere ; whereas that sporadic, irregular, and unsystematic growth from many individual centres, and of as many kinds, is steadily transforming the slums of Whitechapel and of Old Edinburgh, of New York and Chicago. Thus Toynbee Hall and its associated group have quietly gone on and prospered, and in less than twenty years have spread into activities, influences, and results which would need this whole report to do them justice ; while the famous People's Palace, started from the first upon a far greater scale, and with apparently everything in its favour, has gradually settled down into little more than a local technical school. There, as so often, the most generous of philanthropic foundations from without is but little compared to that which struggles up from an ideal within. But here in Dunfermline may we not have the combination of both advantages ? May we not hope to see living personal groups, generously, yet wisely—that is, gradually—encouraged to enlarging growth and usefulness ? My conception, then, is of the rise of one after another of these gradually growing centres, each naturally selecting its own membership and lines of activity, and its individuals giving some portion of their time to the work of the institute, and thence taking part, it may be, in wider social service. It is in this way that in the course of a few years the settlements

come to furnish effective members to all kinds of public bodies, and are hence so notably aiding that movement of higher citizenship now so obvious in London and in American cities.

The detailed working of such social institutes, their adaptation to and contracts with people of all ages, their entertainments and activities, need not be described here. Enough that the elements

Fig. 26.—Ivied ruin, traditionally of the Chapel of the Convent of St Catherine ; with Queen Anne's House on right, and Abbey spire above.

are already present in Dunfermline, like other towns, indeed abundantly, both in connection with churches and with lay organisations, general and special ; while acquaintance with the work of university settlements and kindred bodies can be obtained in all the larger cities. It is obvious that although the universities have had considerable share in their establishment there is no necessary relation between the two ; capable workers and leaders constantly appear independently of educational institutions altogether. Yet the peculiarly central position of Dunfermline among the five university towns of Scotland will make it easy to utilise this connection in many ways. No greater combination of advantages can be desired for social and educational workers.

So far, then, our minor Social Institutes and Residences, their possibilities of growth. These,

however, next require, at least will be greatly
benefited by, the establishment and corresponding
progress and development of a Central Institute.
Let me now attempt to sketch this.

C. Central Institute (Halls, Library, etc.)

Each growing group of social activities will
work more efficiently in proportion not only to its
healthy rivalry with others but to its living touch
and interchange of ideas, as far as possible even
its actual co-operation with these. The simpler
kinds of intercourse, from individual acquaintance
and mutual hospitalities, from entertainments
and matches of all kinds, will naturally arise, but
beyond this we need a Meeting-place of persons,
and a Clearing-house for ideas, an Information
Bureau of many kinds. This in turn requires
efficient Reference Libraries of various definite
kinds, so giving us a literal Athenæum, a home
of social and intellectual life, a radiant centre of
educational, civic, and moral activities.

This, then, next requires a conveniently situated
—that is, as nearly as possible central—group of
buildings, and now upon a large and public scale.
What are its elements ? In the first place, both
small and large Halls for meetings, entertainments, lectures, of all kinds ; and, on the other hand,
an adequate Library.

Obviously the elements of both of these already
exist in St Margaret's Halls and in the Public
Library, happily adjacent, and it would be in my
judgment sheer waste to build new ones to replace
these, even were a more convenient site obtainable,
which I fail to see.

While Dunfermline has the honourable distinction of possessing the first of the great series
of Carnegie Libraries it is also undeniable that
—doubtless in great part for that very reason—
this is less adequately developed than are many of
its successors. Now surely is the time to bring
it up to date, which in this case means not only
abreast of the modern average, but again serving
as an example and initiative. For this purpose
it requires in the first place substantial structural
extension, and this is practicable on the present
site by moderate alteration and addition. The
present librarian's house should be thrown into
the library. No dwelling should be placed here,
so that the whole available space up to St Margaret's Halls and the Bank garden might then
safely be built over, thus making one continuous
block of buildings from Maygate to St Margaret's
Halls inclusive.*

I have not thought it necessary or desirable to

* I am aware that this would require the special sanction
of the magistrates, but if the dwelling were removed the
usual reservation of open ground from building space might
safely be relaxed just as it has been with the site entirely
covered by St Margaret's Halls.

submit any detailed plan for this, since the two
existing buildings have doubtless their own
architects. The simplest inspection of the two
buildings and the vacant ground will make it
obvious that they can be easily and economically
connected, the present ground plan of St Margaret's Halls, with their existing passages on east
and west side alike, making such connections easy
without any serious structural alterations upon
this portion of the proposed unified block. Might
not the Trust Offices here also conveniently find
accommodation, so giving a yet more effective
combination ?

The present unattractive reading-room might be
easily improved and adapted to a children's library,
and a new and larger reading-room provided for
adults upon the open site.

I can well imagine that the time is ripening for
the establishment of branch libraries, at any rate
in 'he remoter suburbs, such as Townhill and
Baldridge Burn, but these lie beyond my limits.
Nor need I here enter into the obvious need
of improving the existing general library, or
rendering it accessible through a larger portion of the day and week than at present, as of
improving and increasing the scanty supply
of current literature accessible in the reading-
room. But I must be permitted to urge the
desirability—in fact, it appears to me the urgent
necessity — of adequate departmental Reference Collections in those departments of activity
which the existence of this Trust involves. I do
not propose that Dunfermline should attempt
to rival the great general libraries of Edinburgh
or Glasgow, much less the University Libraries in
their special subjects, but I do press that it is not
merely desirable but indispensable, if the Trust
is to carry out any policy of pioneering, that it
should know the best that is being thought and done
in the world in its various departments. That is
to say, it needs an Education Library, it needs a
Social Science and Social Betterment Library,
it needs a Horticultural Library ; and each must be
first-rate of its kind—that is, it must include not
only the essential books and serial publications of
Great Britain and America but also those of the
great Continental countries, since to pioneer in
education or in social betterment without knowing
what is being done in Germany or France, what is
being thought in Italy and in smaller countries,
is inevitably to fall and to keep behind the times,
as on the whole has been the position of affairs in
Scotland during the past generation, if not before.
Much lost ground has now to be made up. In
short, these three libraries at least are no less
necessary for the work and future of the Trust
than is a medical library for an active medical
institution, a law library for a legal one, a theo-
logical library for a clerical one.

I am aware that these proposals involve large

capital expenditure for the space and books, and large annual expenditure also, yet I feel bound to submit that these should be faced early, as practically among the first charges upon the present and future of the Trust, though doubtless with the growth of the city and the possible increase of its rate of taxation for this purpose, as in Dundee, the Trust may by-and-by be somewhat relieved.

While I plead that these three departmental libraries be developed to an extent which would make them effective for the Trust and the city and central in Scotland, if not beyond, I have also to plead for other reference collections upon a more moderate scale. These are required to deal with Art and Industry, with Natural Science, with History (particularly Scottish but also general), and with Music ; in fact, it may be a question whether this last should not be developed upon the scale of the three great collections aforesaid, but this is naturally for more expert counsel than mine.

These secondary collections, however, will naturally arise with their corresponding institutions ; thus the Natural Science Library may be left for consideration with the Nature Buildings hereafter to be discussed. Similarly the Art Library with the Art Buildings, the Music Library with the Music Buildings, although I do not necessarily thereby argue that the whole of these collections should be kept apart from the main one—that would settle itself in practice. The essential thing is that not only the Trust but any citizen should be able rapidly and efficiently to work up any of the great social, educational, or other questions which are now so fully before them.

To handle the question of Housing, for instance, requires not only the literature in English, including such publications as those of the recent American Tenement House Exhibition, but the vast amount of information which is to be got on the Continent—notably, for instance, from the Exposition of 1900, or from the Paris Exposition of Cheap Housing last year, of which particulars seem not even obtainable in London. The housing progress of German cities is, again, far too little known in this country, and so on. I plead that this knowledge be made possible in Dunfermline. So with countless other subjects. Kindergarten or manual training involves obviously German literature no less than American ; while the literature of Art education is naturally very largely in French. And so on ; it is needless to multiply instances.

The necessity of such a group of reference collections, not only to the Trust and its working staff, but to the teacher, the social worker, the horticulturist, and so on, is surely obvious ; while not only the credit but the stimulus to Dunfermline, from also bringing to consult its books kindred workers from Scotland, and in vacation time from England and the Continent, with visitors from America, would be considerable. That all this involves skilled library assistance is, of course, true. Here I submit that one of the very first pieces of pioneering with which Dunfermline may and should be identified is in the improvement of the whole library system by raising the standard of Bibliography. For lack of bibliographical equipment in Great Britain the usefulness of our existing library system is but a fraction of what it might and should be, and the advantage not only of German learning but even of the American popular library lies very largely in the fact that the learned German and the intelligent everyday American can lay his hand upon the literature of his subject in a way still almost unknown in this country.

I have already traced one great element of American superiority to the improvement of the back kitchen. I next press that another great American superiority lies in the possession of an adequate card catalogue, for this, as an apparatus of learning, study, and research, stands to our common library catalogues almost as repeating rifle to flint musket. To accustom not only the student and special worker in every department of human knowledge but the common-sense person of every kind who wants information about anything to know and use an adequate library and card catalogue is one of the most urgent and necessary of all the small and easy, yet momentous, requirements of our present education.

I estimate this as comparable to the adoption of the metric system itself, and I entreat the Trust, whatever it does or leaves undone, to seriously consider the claims of Bibliography. A small sub-committee of business-like men who would acquaint themselves with the work of American libraries in this department, who would take the trouble to realise the immense usefulness of the International Institute of Bibliography, who would seriously investigate proposals like those of Dr Emil Reich and other prominent bibliographers in this country, and issue a short report upon the whole movement, would render an immense service to culture in this country upon every level. The present occasion is a thoroughly auspicious one, and would but recover for Dunfermline its historic initiative. I therefore forward with this report the documentary material I have received from the bibliographers above named, as also from Mr Victor Branford, the indefatigable secretary of the Sociological Society.

B. PARK AND GARDENS

CHAPTER IV

THE PARK—NORTHERN PORTION

A. North-East Section—The Children's Park

FROM the north entrance a new drive runs eastwards uphill. Along the north and west margins of the park it passes 20 to 40 feet within the line of the present sunk wall or " ha-ha," which should be here balustraded, with footpath behind, and with occasional steps connecting it with the drive. This path would be provided with seats at intervals, from which the commanding view would be enjoyed.

We thus soon reach the dovecot tower (fig. 23), which I propose to treat as shown in fig. 27, thus

be kept in order by park keepers, spontaneity and pleasure are apt to be spoiled. Hence the device indicated on plan (yet not pictorially to be judged on this)—that of a connected succession of small circular and oval Playgrounds, laid down in ash or fine gravel, and connected by short paths with slopes or steps, ascending or descending according to the levels of the ground. Wherever the levels allow, and where important tree roots would not be interfered with, these playgrounds would be sunk, say from $1\frac{1}{2}$ to $2\frac{1}{2}$ feet—so not only giving increased shelter to the children but keeping these playgrounds comparatively out of sight in per-

FIG. 27.—Dovecote Pavilion—Shelters, Lavatories, etc.

picturesquely and inexpensively giving the desirable shelter and retiring spaces, while preserving an old effect and increasing its architectural interest. The doves should, of course, be reinstated ; indeed, at various other points of the park dovecotes would yield points at once of scenic interest and living charm. One variety had best be kept to each—say, fantails here, homers at another point, and so on.

This portion of the park, the most accessible and convenient, should, therefore, be especially laid out for the young children and for old folks, who do not care to ramble far : this contrast of ages is also one of the happiest combinations of human life—the old finding their keenest pleasures in watching the activities of the young. But with children comes in the difficulty that their playing is destructive to the grass, at any rate ruinous to the verges ; while, if they are to

spective, so that the verdant park view would not be appreciably interfered with. Still more is this the case when we note the low masses of shrubs and flowers on the plan which practically complete the concealment of these playgrounds without excluding sun. The flower arrangement is discussed later (Chap. IX.).

By putting circular seats around the large trees here, with lightly-gravelled spaces also connected by paths, not only with each other but with the main drive and by steps with the higher balustrade walk, we have thus a network of paths and spaces upon which the children would race and chase without injury to the lawns, or otherwise wearing out the turf. These, too, can be used in all weathers, and without wet feet ; while, of course, in sunshine the grass is still as accessible as need be.

In one of these playgrounds, that nearest the

42

Dovecote Pavilion, where mothers and nurses would naturally sit, I should place a good-sized mound of building sand and in the other a ton or so of miniature bricks, so providing those architectural and engineering facilities so enjoyable and so unconsciously educative. In each of the two smaller circles I propose a flying-stride ; in another are indicated rows of swings, parallel bars, trapeze, ladder, see-saw, and the like—in fact, the apparatus of an open-air Gymnasium ; while the westmost circle remains completely vacant for round games and the like.

This arrangement is also favourable to use by separate parties and groups of children, so that a variety of different games can be going on at once without clashing. The question of a games superintendent, and the whole educational use of games, their philosophy, psychology, and morals, are not to be neglected. I doubt not our educationists are becoming alive to all this ; yet these subjects have of late mainly been worked at in other countries and languages. Here, surely, in Dunfermline, should be the ideal conditions for a fresh experimental reinvestigation of the whole subject, surely not the least important to a pioneering trust for promoting the greatest happiness of the greatest number. For it is the children who offer the numbers, and their happiness is far more easily assured. Spontaneous though play be to the young, nowhere may a true educationist have a greater influence than as play leader, and that such experts are still so scarce is testimony to the rare qualifications needed—physical, mental, and moral, temperamental most of all. It is no insignificant evidence of the growing leadership of America that play teachers are there becoming recognised : in Dunfermline may we not hope not only first to find one but next to train others ? Like many other apparently idealist progresses it would soon literally pay the community ; for one play teacher, with her or his hygiene of healthful activity, would soon far more than save costs in reformatory and prison, in depressed labour and apathy most of all. We have lately learned that the consumptive is generally only so for lack of the services of that preventive hygienist who is now rapidly approaching power. The Hooligan still seems a hopeless problem to the passing educational order, since so largely a product of it. But the educational hygienist is already beginning to cope with him, the play leader perhaps especially moving on the policeman from his present prominence.

The renewal of the little dell west of these playgrounds, with its vanished water-course, as a Children's Dell, is discussed in connection with the Glen : Chap. XIII. *D*.

The remaining features of this section of the park will be discussed in a later chapter, that dealing with the possible Bridge Street Entrance (*cf*. fig. 28 and Chap. XXIX.).

B. North-West Section of the Park—Basin

Placing ourselves once more at the old North Entrance where it opens on each side into the

FIG. 28.—Adjacent East Plantation border, with boundary wall behind, looking towards city. City Buildings' Spire through trees indicates line of High Street and possible future Grand Entrance.

park we may note the excellent park view, with the old circular basin in the hollow (fig. 29). This I propose to treat with balustrade and fountain as shown in fig. 30, and with shrubberies and seats surrounding this as indicated in plan. We may first clear and slightly widen the winding path through the plantation belt, and next carry a 16-feet drive round in front of the old ha-ha, as shown in plan. The ha-ha is preserved and balustraded up to and somewhat beyond a broad stairway opposite the basin, connecting the path and drive. Beyond this the ha-ha disappears, being filled up and sloped away as contours require, thus restoring on the west the impression of continuous park and plantation up to the present Coal Road, while this effect of enlargement is next carried further by lowering this whole Coal Road wall from Pittencrieff Street to Lovers' Loan and by carrying along its upper edge the new footpath shown on plan. For simplicity's sake this is drawn as a straight line, but it would of course spare any trees of value. The advantage of this may be judged from photograph of Coal Road at present (fig. 22).

This lowering of the wall will be found to be a notable gain to the park landscape, while there is no serious loss of shelter, this being increasingly given by the dense plantation belt on the opposite side of the road.

C. Men's Gymnasium, etc.

Return once more to the Pittencrieff Street entrance. Having provided in the north-east section for young children and old folks we may here consider the requirements of the young men.

furnishing of the open-air gymnasium on this scale ; but an indication is given, as also of seats for performers and spectators.

This north range thus offers a considerable range of interest to the young men and boys.

D. Shrubberies, etc., Women's Pavilion

Coming out upon the ha-ha its more sunny portions can be picturesquely treated by plants like the magnificent sea-holly, etc. Besides these in front the beautiful flowering currant family can be displayed, with mock-orange and other flowering shrubs for spring, and also hydrangeas and other beauties of autumn. The main body of the ha-ha would be cushioned with stone-crops, sempervivums, and saxifrages, thus continuing that combination of wild garden and shrubbery, wall garden and botanic garden begun in the last

FIG. 29.—Old Circular Basin in low-lying ground near North-West angle of Park. View of Park to Northward.

As elsewhere pointed out, there is in this park no suitable level ground for the greater games, but a Bowling Alley and Fives Court are provided along the north wall, without any loss of park space or undue thinning of trees. These buildings might also be very plain and inexpensive, being easily screened by ivy trellis, dogwoods, and huge umbellifers, which would all thrive perfectly well in this shady region.

Passing the basin we now reach the corner feature so plainly indicated on plan, intended not merely for exceptional use as a spacious turn or waiting-place for carriages but as a youths' Open-Air Gymnasium. For simplicity's sake the trees are left out on plan, but the better ones can perfectly well be spared, without inconvenience. The ha-ha being here effaced the surface can be gently sloped down to meet the level of the main drive. Around this space seats are shown. It is unnecessary to show the detailed

portion. Around and west of the Basin the same general principle continues, so providing an interesting seasonal succession of flowers and shrubs along the whole north of this section.

Coming now to the west side, it will be seen on plan that besides retaining the good trees of the plantation as usual I show new bits projecting from 20 to 40 feet beyond the present ha-ha. Of these I would plant the more northerly with leguminous trees and large shrubs (pseudacacia, laburnum, etc.) : and the southerly one with rosaceous trees, thus again combining picturesqueness and variety of effect with botanic unity of interest.

Continuing southwards from the gymnasium our new drive sweeps southward between these new patches of trees on the west and a corresponding mass of shrubberies on the east, on which crabs, the larger cotoneasters, flowering cherries, thorns, etc., would be planted so as to repeat that magnificence of flower which was suggested at the very outset of these park studies at the Glebe, seen on entering from Nethertown, as the most conspicuous and characteristic feature of our whole seasonal design. These rosaceous trees in all their variety and beauty I propose to carry southwards to the Coal Road Entrance of the main east and west avenue, working out as far as space allows the varied resources of this most beautiful order of plants, as regards shrubs as well as trees. Here is, in fact, the possibility at once of creating one of the most beautiful and constantly improving features of the whole park, and of a not inadequate arboretum selection suggestive to horticulturists and students alike, no less also to designers, whose interests have constantly been remembered throughout the park by the selection of the more decorative species of all kinds, herbs included.

Our path now rises gently to the highest point of this section, nearly 100 yards south of the basin. This height I propose to crown by a

which we come farther south ; while, of course, the same water-supply suffices without extra expense. The ample use of water along this whole east side and foot of the park is, in fact, relieved of all extravagance by this consideration, and we now see on the general plan that this system of lakes and small intervening watercourses not only gives the whole west and south sides an interest in which they are at present deficient, but also furnishes the right contrast to the deep den on the east side of the park. This thus lies between two watercourses, great and small, and so doubly invites the visitor, first to a more prolonged walk, and then to a fuller enjoyment of the characteristic beauties of each. Could the custom of a frequent ramble of this kind, from a mile and a half to two miles in circuit, be induced, the usefulness of the park would soon be deeply felt in many ways. To form this habit among an increasing number the ordinary attractions of the average city park have

FIG. 30.—The same, with balustrade added, and central fountain. Shrubberies (shown on General Plan) are next needed, to relieve the otherwise monotonous effect of this.

square Pavilion, with four pediments and central dome, the arrangement which works out as most convenient from the standpoint alike of accesses, of views from without, and from within. The effect must be imagined in the accompanying figures 29 and 30, and by help of the general plan. This might be reserved for women, and furnished somewhat more daintily accordingly, especially with ample reclining seats, as befits a rest-house.

E. Small Lake and Open-Air Theatre

In the little Lake, which is shown in plan in the natural depression at this point, we have here a feature not only of interest and beauty as an unexpected feature in what is otherwise a comparatively insignificant spot—it also performs the artistic service of giving scale to the larger lake to

to be increased in such ways as this, especially since for one who appreciates the larger aspects of landscape, here of course present and not to be interfered with, there are many who are attracted by the variety and interest of details. Hence the justification of the present design, that of varied enrichment of the margins of the park, while leaving all its present fine general aspects undestroyed, indeed developed also by improved foregrounds and the like.

Return to the Women's Pavilion and its southeastern portico steps : a path runs up the little height to a square space with seats, from which pleasing views are obtained. Almost due south of this the peculiar disposition of shrubberies shown in plan indicates a proposed small open-air theatre of the simple yet effective kind suggested by the theatre of the Villa Gori at Siena (*Century Magazine*, 1903). The various amateur dramatic companies, both adults and of school age, should thus each be able to carry out its own performance on summer evenings or afternoons with its own audience, undisturbed by the general body of visitors to the park.

We come now to the main east and west drive (the old Culross Road), which is shown straightened along the line of its ancient avenue, alike for landscape and for historic reasons. Crossing this we see the large lake.

F. Central Avenue from North Entrance

Entering once more from the north, some improvements will be seen to be desirable upon the Entrance Drive. Thus, I should at once replace the present high iron fences by a single low bar, 9 inches or so above the ground, and, next, lower to 2 feet 6 inches or thereby the present high park walls, at present so conspicuous at the north-east entrant angle, surmounting these with as little railing as may be judged necessary, just as has been already done on the west. The advantage of these trifling changes to the first impression of the park, necessarily a most important matter, will readily be appreciated.

The present open Central Drive may be widened at least a foot on each side with advantage, and its margins improved, since at first it runs upon an obvious ridge above the adjacent park level on each side, and then through a no less obvious cutting. By lowering the slope of this cutting, and using the earth to fill up the deficiencies to northward, both defects are easily removed.

After careful consideration of pros and cons, I recommend planting the almost treeless extent of this drive as a tolerably close lime-tree avenue. This is the only place in the park where such a straight avenue effect can be arranged; and the result obtained would far outweigh such partial interruption of transverse views as it involves. The general view from the heights of the north-east section will not be seriously interfered with, while many of the minor views will be improved; the interest of the lower level portion to east of the avenue especially, the more when we note also the desirability of planting up the rising ground and renewing the little water-course as a children's dell, as becomes so evidently desirable from the study of the main glen to which we come later (Chap. XIII.).

G. West and East Avenue—from Coal Road Entrance

From near the central crossing of the preceding avenue with this older one, where past convenience has, therefore, located the old stables, considered in the next chapter, fig. 31 has been taken, its trees on right indicating the line of the ancient road, from the Tower Hill and City westwards. In the following illustration (fig. 32), as in plan also, I show this road reopened, with a rough suggestion of position (not style!) of lodge and gates. Outside these gates we are upon the old Coal Road, of which I have forecast the widening as a West Park Avenue in Chap. I., and also above (§ B). It seems also natural to foresee the reopening of this old road farther westwards, along the boundary of the fields from the lodge on to join the existing Culross Road at Urquhart Bridge. Thus, in addition to the Park being bordered to south by avenues, we should in the next place have a fine Westward Boulevard, agreeably continuing the Park from the City point of view, and furnishing an easy and beautiful approach to it from the country, instead of the present steep and unattractive one. This improvement would obviously react very favourably upon the western development of the city, and is, in fact, an excellent illustration of how park approaches may be developed, alike for the benefit of the city and of proprietors. This matter seems, therefore, one naturally adjustable as an ordinary matter of street or rather suburb-planning, and not one which directly involves the Trust.

Returning now from this entrance westwards, we come to the temporary refreshment pavilion, which must postpone, during its years of service, the full reopening of the ancient road to and from the Tower Hill, although, on the other hand, a path on this line becomes indispensable, so restoring the historic route, with no small gain to the imagination.

For the continuation of this reopened bit of road, eastwards to the main existing portion north of stables, I submit, but need not here reproduce, alternative plans in full detail, showing the crossing of the main north and south avenue, both by a bridge and on the level, and may leave these to speak for themselves, the former being in my view the more picturesque, and the latter certainly the more easy.

Descending eastwards towards the glen, the road now passes under the bridge of the old drive, skirting the Glen northward; and we may here note the desirability, both of artistic and suggestive picturesqueness, of recalling in some way the old fortification and outlook which must for many centuries have stood here as the needed outwork and defence of the Tower Hill (its " Petit Chatelet," in fact).* This I should do by erecting a bridge-turret, which may well have existed here of old, since the road it carries is no mere pleasure-walk, as it seems to-day, but is on the line of obvious military importance, alike for defence and for attack. Here, too, upon this bridge-turret, might

* A modern expression of this picturesque feature of ancient bridge work may be seen in the grounds of Torrie, near the mansion-house.

FIG. 32.—The same showing proposed reopening of Old Drive—the old Culross Road—the former direct line from Abbey and Tower Hill towards Culross and West generally, with rough sketch to suggest need of new gates and entrance lodge (though not design of these, as limitation of retouching process here evident).

FIG. 31.—View along Old Avenue to West (Coal Road) entrance.

well be placed (as my friend Mr Duncan suggests) the statues of mediæval guardians of the Tower— one, its military sentinel, and, St Michael the other. Continuing eastwards, we now descend towards the double bridge which, though severely restored in the late eighteenth and early nineteenth centuries, strikingly suggests that evolution from low to high levels so characteristic of modern times. Its main aspect, after very full consideration, I should leave wholly untouched, but its weak and unseemly wire balustrading should be replaced by a substantial parapet. This should be of the simplest, wholly without ornament, but lightened by openings, as in fig. 33. This parapet wall I should continue, with buttresses at intervals upon the present retaining wall of the Tower Hill, which also requires a gateway entrance at each end. These, as in the illustration, recall the fortalice by their general character without elaboration, which would be unsuitable to the modest size of the old Tower and the rugged simplicity of the style of its period. These gateways and the whole range of pierced parapet of bridge and Tower Hill may, with advantage, be ivied, so that for this reason also elaboration would be wasted upon them.

Continuing still farther west, the Abbey comes in sight. Here the drive needs widening, and this I should do not upon the south side but upon the north, building out for that purpose a simple bold series of round arches, rising from the old garden below. The effect of this simple, massive, curved arcade, sweeping round as a base for the Abbey, would be to give this at once the effect of a cloister, of approach, and of a stately base also, so greatly enhancing the view from this point. From the garden itself also, of which the importance will be realised later, as also from other points of view, such as that of the frontispiece, this arcade would be a most important improvement.

As the present roadway continues eastwards, it unfortunately sweeps to the left, and thus loses its ancient and appropriate alignment to the west door of the Abbey. This I propose to restore, as shown in plan. The increase of steepness, which this will be seen to involve, can, of course, be done away with by beginning the ascent farther back, and this would be easily arranged with the widening just referred to.

The further improvement of this entrance and approaches will be discussed later (Chapter XX.).

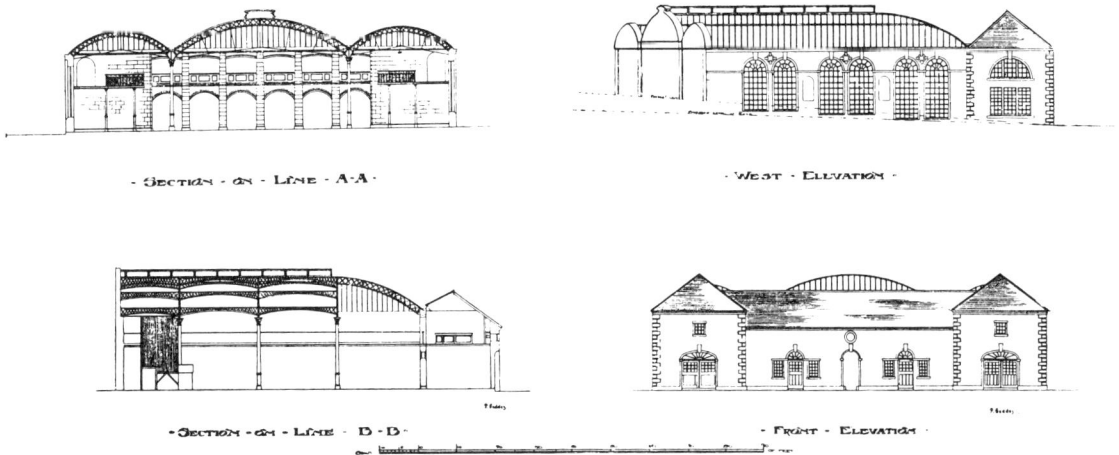

· SECTION · ON · LINE · A·A ·

· WEST · ELEVATION ·

· SECTION · ON · LINE · D·D ·

· FRONT · ELEVATION ·

FIG. 35a.--Elevations and Sections of Stables, partly reconstructed as Shelter and Orangery.

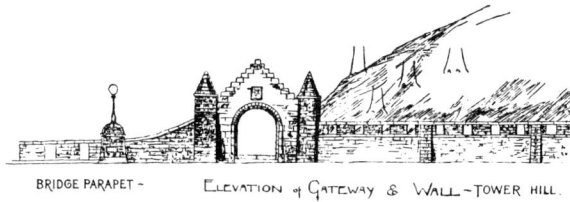

BRIDGE PARAPET ~   ELEVATION of GATEWAY & WALL ~ TOWER HILL.

FIG. 33.—Detail of Parapet of Double Bridge, Tower Gateway,
and Parapet on Retaining Wall.

CHAPTER V

ORANGERY AND MANSION-HOUSE

A. Old Stables as Shelter and Orangery

THE open-air theatre above mentioned of course raises the common grumble about the difficulty and uncertainty of our weather, a complaint grievously exaggerated, since everyone who seriously follows any really outdoor pursuit, sport or athletics, gardening or botany, knows how very few times, after all, in the year his pursuits are really interfered with. Still, a shelter is required, alike for occasional gatherings of the citizens and for ordinary protection from showers, with cloakrooms, lavatories, and so on ; and here I am fully convinced that there is no spot so central and so convenient in the whole park as that afforded by the present old stables (fig. 34). Hence the accompanying plans (fig. 35 a, b), show the old front building retained and the north wall also, while the east and west sides are rebuilt, the building thus forming a spacious glass-roofed hall, with a platform at the north end, which will also serve as a bandstand. Internal accommodation and architectural effect are at once greatly increased by the spacious gallery running round the whole building and affording exits and entrances from the Tower Road—that is, from three sides ; indeed, when we look at plan, from all four sides if need be. Such accommodation and approaches are practically impossible elsewhere, and such speedy and easy access and exit are of real importance in providing for crowds and for excursionists.

The needful cloakrooms and refreshment rooms are provided for in the old front portion of the building, the latter also in the upper storey continuous with the gallery promenade. The needful lavatories are shown in two well-separated blocks, both to the eastward, and thoroughly concealed on either hand.

While the practicability of these proposals will hardly be disputed I imagine objections on grounds of amenity. Grim, dull, miserable, dirty-looking, dilapidated, even squalid, are the usual adjectives, and the first instinct of the park reformer is thus to sweep the whole thing away. But, let me ask in return, does the critic appreciate such advantages as the building has ? Does he see, for instance, in this stern and simple building the style,

probably indeed the master hand, not only of the most eminent architect which Fife has ever produced, but, in fact, one of the greatest architects of the eighteenth century—Adam himself ? Does he recognise in this simple front the character not only of the stables and of the mansion of Valleyfield but the stately lines of the University of Edinburgh, the Register House, and of Charlotte Square ? If so, he will not readily destroy this notable feature of our open-air museum, this one memorial of our one great local architect, and of the eighteenth-century style. Or, if he has not noticed this, must he not look again ? For it is with architecture as with pictures ; we would rather possess a great work by the master, but we need not carelessly destroy such small study by him as we possess ; we are fortunate in having even so much.

The perspective (fig. 36) shows the main south front unaltered, while the western aspect is, I trust, greatly improved by continuing it with the large orangery windows Adam so often employed. I submit, however, an additional sketch, showing the possible improvement of this frontage, based upon more ornate examples of Adam's work, and thus faithfully continuing his tradition. The front is thus enriched, without losing its simplicity and horizontality, which contrast so well with the lofty perpendicular lines of the mansion, and were obviously designed so as to enhance each other, as they undoubtedly do in the approaching perspective, which combines to the observer's eye the effect of figs. 36 and 37 in a way I cannot represent here.

I would plead with those who are not accustomed to analyse their likes and dislikes in buildings to give this point a fresh fair trial on a few of their walks through the park. They will jaso come to see that their objection to this building, as to Pittencrieff House as well, is largely on account of its colour. The extreme severity and simplicity of this front to our modern eye, accustomed to that extreme over-enrichment of detail which is a main vice of the street architecture of our times may, and do to most, seem mere bareness ; but this impression will, it is hoped, be partly diminished by the help of the accompanying photographs and drawings.

FIG. 34.—Interior of old Stables at present, showing extensive area and possibility of further increase as shelter and orangery by taking in area of cottages to left and sheds to right.

CARNEGIE-DUNFERMLINE-TRUST.
PROPOSED CENTRAL SHELTER
· ON · SITE · OF · PRESENT · PITTENCRIEF · STABLES ·

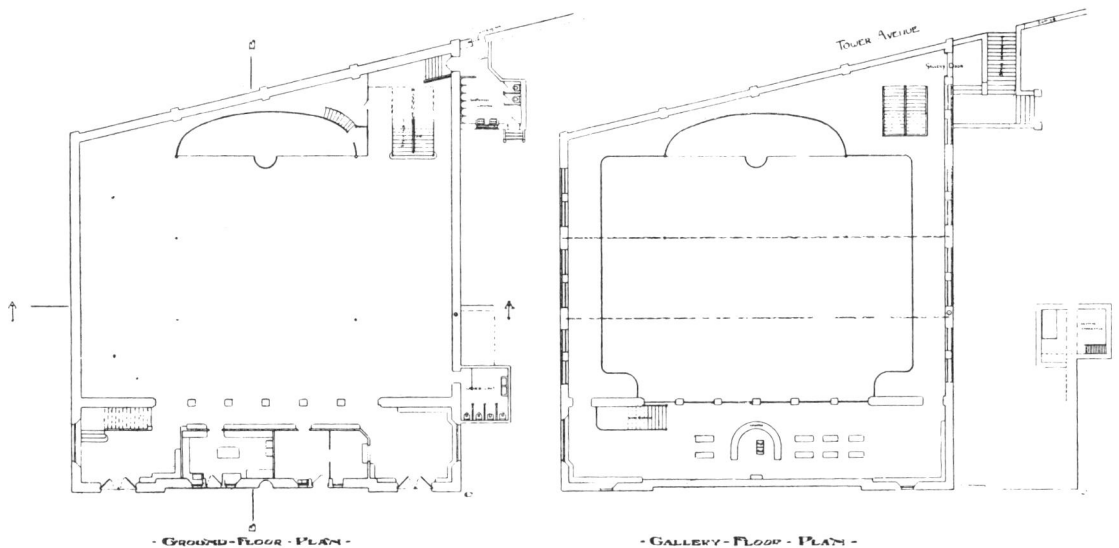

· GROUND-FLOOR · PLAN ·   · GALLERY-FLOOR · PLAN ·

FIG. 35.—Plans of proposed Orangery, waiting-rooms, etc.   (a) Ground floor ; (b) Gallery floor.

FIG. 36.—South-West aspect of old Stables. View taken North-East across lake basin, but retouched, showing effect of proposed **lake and bridge**; also, in perspective, the West side of proposed Orangery. Window opened in Adam's South-West block, the remaining cottage rebuilt.

FIG. 36a.—Architectural perspective of the same, without Orangery, but with pediments and balustrade added.

Let it be clearly understood, then, that my plea is on no merely historic ground ; this old block is a real and useful element of the composition, a genuine beauty to the lake scene I propose to create ; and I appeal from its hasty critic to the architect and artist of every school. Here is a clear case of the unison of historic and artistic considerations with economical and practical ones. The survival of a few buildings which depend for their effect upon proportion and simplicity, not

FIG. 37.—Old Mansion-House, Eastward approach from Stables.

name really expressive both of its essential proportions and its architectural style as now re-planned—the Orangery—and invite the reader to compare this with the orangeries of Adam at various great mansion-houses, or even in its present state with the museums of Kew. Surely what is valued as good architecture there cannot be so despicable here. As for the dark and shadowed frontage, this may be partly relieved at the west angle, but not as a whole, since it is too useful a shadow for the lake picture to which we are now coming. For the greater portion of the interior, as will be clearly seen, is perfectly well sunned, while the shady portion of the interior, that of its south wall, will facilitate a contrast with ferns and other shade-loving growths.

The main beauty of this spacious park-hall would be as an example of the possibilities of a Cool Greenhouse, which need not be heated at all save during the extreme frosts of winter. Leaving aside any detailed enumeration of the too seldom utilised resources of this type of gardening, I may point out its possibilities as a Camellia House, not only beautiful with ever-green foliage all the year round, but glorious beyond description in the early spring, just when flowers are most enjoyed. Through the summer and autumn the galleries would be festooned inexpensively from end to end, as a pillared avenue

upon ornament, is something to be thankful for and to be guarded. In such a case it is the duty of the gardener and architect to resist popular sentiment, with the clear conviction that it may be the passages of his report which give little satisfaction at the moment which may be afterwards seen to be of most value ; especially when, as in the present case, they may help to prevent the irreparable destruction of features and elements of beauty which may be all the more needed because they have for the time fallen out of general appreciation.

Let me propose, then, for this Central Shelter a

of flowers, with creepers of every kind trained upon them, festooned and swinging from the roof.

We set free also within this great enclosure a few well-plumaged birds. We arrange for a small aviary of song birds in the gallery, and our dingy old stables have become a tropic paradise. Similarly the change from exterior dulness is emphasised by placing a statue in the central niche and by using the little piazza within the new external balustrade as a convenient and natural place for tea tables and seats. From this balustrade the guests of the refreshment rooms would feed the peacocks, and also readily attract the picturesque bird life of the adjacent lake.

B. Mansion-House

While thus dealing with old buildings it is natural to pass on to the old Mansion House, of which the fate has so long hung in the balance. No one will dispute the picturesqueness of its approach (fig. 37) ; and it may be safely assumed that the many protests during the past winter, not only of antiquaries but of artists and architects, have awakened the Dunfermline public to a greater sense of its real merits. External improvements are easy, without serious change. Pending repairs, and the presumable clearing out of bedrooms and garrets as a long gallery, the possible improvement also of the elevations from the outside, I would suggest that the building be washed anew a pleasant cream colour instead of the present orange, here too garish, there too dirty. It is to this and its contrast with the dull purple grey of the window facings that the frequent dislike of this old building very largely depends ; and the effect of this small and inexpensive change would, therefore, be generally appreciated. Hence the sooner this slight improvement can be carried out the better.

It now remains to consider the treatment of the shrubberies on either side of the old lawn ; that on the east, already with many rhododendrons, should be developed further and fringed with a heath collection, which would give flower through eight or nine months of the year. Two small decorative bedding-out masses, conveniently again round the small fountains, occupy the angles of the lawn on either side of the gravel sweep in front of the house.

At the southward apex of this gravel sweep is also shown on plan a sun-dial ; this might best be of the type at Newbattle, perhaps the noblest in Scotland, indeed one of the finest anywhere.

The contrast of these enrichments with the plain old tower of the mansion will be found greatly to enhance the effect of both.

This sternness I propose to relieve further by a due planting of climbers, from the early clematis to the winter cotoneaster, and to train high upon the wall the fig and vine, with tall climbing roses. Upon the east and west ends ivies and yellow jessamine may be mixed. For the recent poor garden seat have already been substituted two better ones. Finally, if, as seems not unlikely before long, the present roof has to be renewed, the old-fashioned attic windows of the original design might be advantageously replaced, the grimness of

the building to many eyes being largely due to the eighteenth-century abolition of these (fig 38).

As to the use of the house, I first suggest it as primarily part of that historic museum in which this park should excel all others. Within it might be lodged the historical collections, pending the creation of that large historic museum to which I come later—perhaps the natural history collections to begin with also. When special museums, as later suggested, are constructed other use will readily be found (Chap. XXX.).

To give this building its exact historic character and interest, that of the Puritan and Cavalier period, we have happily a fitting and obvious resource in the splendid statues of " The Puritan " and " The Cavalier," by Macmonnies, which were so prominent at the Paris Exposition of 1900, and of which I doubt not adequate replicas could be

Fig. 38.—Old Mansion-House, from outside ha-ha fence of lawn to South.

obtained. Or, failing these, minor statues of kindred type would give back to this building a historical character in all eyes hardly less distinct than that of the mediæval buildings themselves. The statues of Scott's characters upon the Waverley monument in Princes Street show that Scottish sculptors only await the opportunity to give us work of individuality and interest. The statues of the National Portrait Gallery may also be referred to. These statues would readily find their places to east and west of the house.

C. Pinetum and Cedar Group

Leaving now the mansion we may enter the little wood upon its right or western side. Here a path leads to an old well, probably that of the old mansion, which should, therefore, be cleared out, the well head simply built, and the spot adorned with seat and shade. This whole place, despite several fine trees, is somewhat forlorn-looking, but might readily be reorganised, preferably as a small Pinetum : it is one of the few points at which coniferous trees can be used with advantage in this park.

The next is of more importance, since serving to complete each and all of our whole series of gardens. Noting once more on plan—pinetum and lake, the rock garden, and formal garden—what final element is needed which will dominate and compose each and all ? The answer is that this can best be done by a group of Cedars of Lebanon, which will be equally valuable from and for every one of these points of view, and will steadily increase in beauty for centuries to come. The comparative exposure to the south-west wind here is quite favourable. It is far severer exposure than this that has made the great cedar of Culross Abbey one of the most notably picturesque trees, not only of the neighbourhood or the country but outside of Japan.

The roadway border of the pinetum, from the lawn to the lake and stables, should be bordered with shrubs, preferably early spring and autumnal ones, such as witch-hazel and mezereon for the earliest spring, hydrangea (H. paniculata, etc.), and the like for autumn. And as the east shrubbery border of the lawn is edged with rhododendrons and heaths, so the opposite border may be fringed with a lily garden, linked to its shrubbery by yuccas and the like, and its beds kept bright, not only with lilies proper but with their kindred, the season round, from snowdrops and crocus to gladiolus and torch-lily. This type of " monocotyledon garden " has not only a considerable botanical interest but an artistic quality and character of its own, a popular interest even, as I know by experience at Dundee, where I have carried out this style of bedding for decorative purposes throughout the seasons, from the snowdrops and crocuses, through the hyacinths and tulips of later spring, and the day-lilies and fuchsias of summer, to the torch-lilies of autumn.

CHAPTER VI

LAKE AND ROCK GARDEN

A. Lake

WE now enter upon a new quarter of the park, the western, which is here shown occupied by a shallow Lake, measuring 150 by 70 yards, and thus admitting of a moderate number of boats, and of many skaters at the appropriate seasons. The situation is a beautiful one, the lake mirroring the requirements would obviously be of great beauty. That the lake possesses sufficient variety will be seen from plans, process blocks, and, best of all of course, on the ground itself, the various added elements being there most clearly imagined, the western willow-green fringing the existing belt of trees, and a cedar group occupying the higher ground to south-east. To this cedar group I

FIG. 39.—View in West section of Park South of preceding—showing depression of proposed West Lake and the trees of West plantation border along its wooded margin.

fine trees to east, west (fig. 38), and north, while a good architectural effect is given by the necessary bridge, fig. 36, Chap. V. This will be seen also to compose well with the old stables, and I trust fully convince their severest critic of the need for retaining them. The loss to this picture which would result from the removal of the stables will be obvious from a study of the illustration.

Here, then, is a main element of our architectural composition, but this, again, finds its completion and contrast in the Boat-house, conveniently usable above water level as a tea house and rest house. This, again, is a building of which the attach great importance, as will be seen fully later. It is to the whole surrounding design—of lake, rock garden, mansion-house lawn, pinetum, and formal garden—what the keystone is to the arch. (See Chap. VIII.)

The general form of this lake is in accordance with the contour lines; and where excavation has been necessary beyond these, especially at the north-west, the consequently steeper shore adapts itself to a picturesque rock treatment.

About the middle of the north shore stands a boat-house, with refreshment room above. The addition to its northward shady side of a possible rain awning would greatly increase shelter in showers.

The promontory is left simply grassy, with a mere stony edge, so as to allow the eye to travel across the path up to the trees, some distance behind. On the east side the present road passes over an embankment, which at this point is replaced by a bridge, as shown in plan and perspective (fig. 36, Chap. V.).

The bridge thus divides the lake into a large, bright, and sunny west portion, and a small, dark, shady east one. The arches stand between 6 and 7 feet above water level, thus making it possible not only for boats to pass but for skaters to run through in full career. But though the whole lake would be kept shallow, nowhere exceeding 3 feet, the usual precautions will naturally fall to be taken by the park-keeper of closing these arches until the frost is thoroughly assured.

Here the illustration (fig. 36) indicates the effect producible by the construction of the lake and bridge. At each end of the bridge are disposed great clumps of picturesque water plants, such as bulrushes and reeds, their narrow foliage contrasted by the gigantic leafage of Gunneras and other decorative plants. One or two of the finer willows might also with advantage be planted here.

Proceeding now southward along the corresponding path we come to a small island with nesting clump, arranged again with a footbridge, this time simply wooden, and high enough not to obstruct the skater.

Eastwards are built a series of " pockets," broadly corresponding to those of the small pond at the Edinburgh Botanic Garden, for the culture of water plants, intermediate in size between the rankest forms at the bridge and the finer ones around the pools of the rock garden to be considered later.

Behind these, south of the dry path along the edge, runs a bog garden and bog shrubbery, with beautiful plants too numerous for mention.

Towards the south end of the lake is the outlet, with its necessary dam concealed by the planting of a thicket of willows. This is continued along the west side northwards to the rocky shore, this willow plantation thus shading into the existing plantation belt (fig. 39), so that sufficient thickness is assured and the desired effect realised. The ha-ha would here be effaced.

B. Japanese Tea-House *

Returning to the outlet, where the dam is crossed by a bridge there would naturally be a fall of

* This passage was written before the opening of the present war.

about 8 or 10 feet, which, by economy at night, could be run with sufficient quantity for picturesqueness. A pool is shown below. This brings us almost down to the row of noble old plane-trees shown in photograph No. 40. The old grazing park shanty shown in front of these I propose to replace by a Japanese Tea-House.

This can no doubt be designed in a kind of way by European hands, but I submit that it would be more satisfactory to have, not indeed

FIG. 40.—Site of proposed Rock Garden, separated from Lake to North by high trees. The ha-ha fence in deep shadow under West boundary plantation to be effaced, and the existing natural depression deepened as watercourse and main valley of Rock Garden. Japanese tea-house suggested on site of present sheds.

the framework of this building but its essential detail and adornment, executed in Japan, the experience of Mr Mempes and others having already proved that this is both practicable and economical.

I have later suggested many things for the technical school and for the local artist, but this is not one of them. We can no more produce Japanese ornament than Greek statuary, and in this case it is not even desirable that we should try, the imitation of Japanese art in Europe being mere clumsy forgery.

Why, then, do I suggest a Japanese building at all ? Primarily because the park is intended to give a recreative and complete change from our daily environment, and change of scene and association is one of the most real sources of such recreation. Very few of those who are to use the park will ever see Japan, and I therefore ask for one little genuine bit of it here. There are other reasons. Of all nations the Japanese have succeeded most completely in combining physical health and strength, necessarily therefore the essentials of hygiene and comfort, with the utmost simplicity and economy ; yet all these again with many of the very highest elements of personal refinement, and with that marvellous art which is at once the noblest of luxuries and the most enduring of economies.

To our old intercourse with China we already owe the beverage, the porcelain, and the flowers of our tea table, even the silk of our hostess, and there are many reasons for thinking that the civilising influences of Japan may soon be felt as no less important and profound.

This tea house, then, with its large open-air verandah, its simple yet subtle decoration or exquisite vase and carefully arranged branch of flower, would be full of artistic lessons, none the less real for being unobtrusive. It is, of course, very largely the influx of Japanese art feeling which has substituted for the ascendency of the traditional Royal Academy picture that of the masterpieces of our own Glasgow School; and it is now time that the same gentle but saturating influence be more fully popularised, till even for the humblest kitchen its too crudely decorative almanac may develop into a kakemono. The independence and individuality of modern painters, despite all this influence of Japan, has been well illustrated by the character and work of Mr Whistler, so that we have nothing to fear from such contact. It is a fertilising, not a deadening one.

Such a Japanese tea house would also serve as a Japanese Museum, and would exhibit now and then treasures lent by our Scottish collectors; thus again the park would constantly be tempting the many art lovers of Dunfermline to a healthful excursion to its farther extremity. Here, also, is one of the many ways in which in these park designs has been kept in view the enrichment of the staple industry.

Behind the tea house, around the trees, as also on its west side, so as to give an alternative of shade and sun, it will be noted that a large space is cleared of turf, slightly levelled, covered with ashes, and provided with seats and tables. Here, in fact, is another of those temptations to that open-air life for which, despite indoor habits, and popular prejudice, our year's average climate affords a very considerable range of days and hours.

C. Rock Garden

Leaving this tea house a new landscape opens southward. The slope of the ground shown in the photograph (fig. 40) indicates that cultivation has nearly effaced a tiny natural dell, but with a little excavation and raising of banks this may be easily recovered into a little watercourse, the water being provided from the outlet of the lake. At this point, then, naturally arises the question of a possible Japanese Garden. But while we can bring over Japanese carpentry and bronze we cannot bring a garden, and the mechanical imitation of the Japanese style would here be even more impracticable than ever.

The whole Japanese style of laying out the ground and disposing its rocks differs from ours. It expresses at once their difference of artistic style and of nature outlook—that is to say, not only a different technique but a different poetry, a different symbolism. The symbolic stones in which they delight mean nothing to most of us; their conventional model of the great volcanic cone of Fuji could say little to us of what it means to them, and so on in detail.

By all means, if a Japanese landscape gardener should present himself in this country, let him be invited to lay out a Japanese garden. This would be most interesting; but, pending his appearance, I submit that we can best share and express the Japanese spirit in developing our own naturalistic style, thus utilising its suggestiveness as our best painters do, but wholly avoiding any attempt at copying.

Happily, there is at least one exception to this self-denial; some small example of the Japanese Iris Garden is thoroughly practicable in these conditions; hence I propose to plant the sides of the little pond in front of this tea house with a wealth of Japanese irises, so completing its architectural suggestiveness, and having, alike in building and gardening, a little bit of genuine and typical Japan.

Below and eastwards of this Japanese iris pond we pass naturally enough into the Scottish Rock Garden. Here the southward slope of the ground, amounting to about 30 feet—say 1 in 9—gives excellent opportunity of bold and picturesque treatment. I take considerable space for this, so as to make a really good rock garden, one in which both plants and visitors should have ample room. Children will always run up and down the rocks of a rock garden, and it should, therefore, be constructed from the first with paths and steps sufficiently broad to admit of their doing this without injury to the plants or themselves. Hence my roomy and winding rock paths, nearly one-third of a mile, with occasional pools and masses of shrubbery, are arranged so as to give continual variety and fresh points of view and interest.

It is unnecessary here to give the design in large scale detail, as photographs of good rock gardens are sufficient to give an idea of the general effect. I attach great importance here, as with the wild garden or the lake vegetation, and even the irises which we have just passed, to growing first of all the more common and vigorous species with the utmost possible abundance—this not only to gladden the spectator but to enable the superintendent to give away liberally of his abundance to schools, and even to grant all reasonable individual requests, from designers and students especially.

While this rock garden affords the conditions for growing a wealth of beauty practically undreamed of by most of us the actual capital outlay of construction is not very great, and the upkeep is quite within the powers of a single man, assuming that the costly care of tender rarities and weaklings be left to the great botanical collections as at present.

Finally, our rock garden is screened from north and west and its general effect harmonised into the rest of the park by the belts of flowering shrubs shown on plan. Here, then, so far as outdoor gardening is concerned, we leave for a time the botanist.

This long irregular range of paths, with its innumerable nooks, sheltered often by flowering shrubs, is further designed, as the plan can only partially indicate, with blind alleys and nooks in which the child or student, the ordinary visitor and the convalescent, may sit at once in shelter and in sun. That education towards open-air treatment, which is a main hygienic aspect of the park, thus finds here one of its most attractive and effective points.

D. Rock Garden further developed— Evolutionary and Geological

So far we have sketched a good ordinary rock garden like others. But beyond such individuality as laying out might give, may we not introduce here as well as elsewhere some fresh departure, some element of that pioneering which is an initial injunction for all these designs. Two such possibilities there are, of botanical and geological interest respectively.

While it is the first merit of a rock garden to grow and show its individual flowers to the utmost perfection, its general effect may also be excellent, and for this our valley formation gives every advantage. The wealth and variety of species is nowhere better displayed, and I should arrange these in a certain harmony with the natural orders disposed later around the park (Chap. IX.), and also with that genealogical tree stretching from lowest to highest plants up the slope of the "shade garden" of the Tower Dene (Chap. XII.).

The interest, not merely to the technical student of evolution but to the everyday observer, of seeing such an evolutionary arrangement before his eyes, might be made a new and fascinating popularisation of science, one of educational value beyond its immediate botanical one. For, while everyone is nowadays familiar with the idea of the perpetual branching of the genealogical tree as a symbol of evolution, no such comprehensive attempt to realise this has been made as I here propose. I am well aware that, with the advance of our knowledge, rearrangement would be necessary; but do not our plants require just such periodic lifting and dividing ?

Without entering upon the details of this, I may say that practical experience both of laying out and of teaching from other gardens justifies what has been proposed.

More generally interesting and impressive would be the Geological novelty in rock gardening here practicable. Too often the rocks of such a garden are irregular, even chaotic; sometimes, as with the Japanese, picturesque arrangement is attempted; but our better builders aim at reproducing the effects of natural outcrops of rock. Here, then, are the advantages these different builders aim at—variety, pictorial effect, and reproduction of nature : can we not carry all three further here ? Science with her plans must underlie art with her colour perspectives ; so let us ask the geologist the fundamental question: What is the ideal of geology — its fullest ambition ? To survey and explore the structure of the world, to bare and bore its crust until the succession of strata from the earliest times up to our own can be displayed; and, again, to look back from the simple everyday processes of change to the world-making which is their sum.

All this the geologist strives to condense into his survey, to set forth in his museum with its succession of cases, and to teach in description and diagram ; all at best, however, mere suggestions or symbols of the magnificent reality. Can he not come nearer expressing this ? The geographer has long ago got beyond his flat map to his model in relief, and this step is beginning to transform and vitalise our whole geographical thought and teaching. Why not now something similar for the geologist ? If the geographer has a world-model, surely he may have a World-Section ? Let us go to work, then, and prepare under his direction such a section, or rather three-fold series of sections— the central one for our own islands, comparatively so well-known; within this another for our immediate neighbourhood, for the rocks directly below and around us ; and outside all such an outline of the world formations as present knowledge can offer.

Adjust now to this design the large scale plan of our rock garden. This may be considered not so much now as broadly rectangular, but rather as the quadrant of a circle whose centre is at the south-western corner. Around the widest sweep of this large arc we arrange for the world formations ; along the middle the British ones ; while near the centre of the curve —i.e. at the garden's eastern foot—comes the presentment of our immediate strata.

Here, then, is a fascinating problem for our Naturalists' Society, one for which they will need all the help that geological surveyor and teacher can give them, but which with this is not impracticable. We have to allot so many yards or feet for this and that formation, so many feet or inches within this for each important subformation, and then actually to build this, as far as possible with genuine and representative rock samples, gradually collected here and there for the purpose. As we gradually build our visible model of this and that formation the ripple marks of its ancient beaches thus appear upon our pathway, even its characteristic fossils may be seen in their due place and succession, not chipped out from these into a glass case. The intrusive basalt or other igneous rock is easily supplied, the glaciated surface also. Even classical sections and characteristic exposures may sometimes be suggested, if not reproduced in miniature. In fact, the more one brings to bear on this problem the experience of the geographical model in relief the more one sees its splendid possibilities.

It may be justly said that such a model is not easily made, yet that is surely another reason why it should here be attempted. The rock garden, of all gardens, best admits of gradual growth, and even, where need be, of detailed change; and it is surely advantage to find a section of the garden and park which lends itself so perfectly to elaboration and improvement, which are so desirable for continued interest.

The collection of the needful constructive material—rocks and stones, minerals and fossils—may at first sight appear difficult; yet this is the business of museums, and that upon a far more elaborate scale. These aim at comparative completeness; while here we should be satisfied with good types. The expense of carriage is nothing serious; a good deal of the required material comes to our ports in ballast; while the practical transportation even of large stones is an everyday matter of builders' experience.

Returning to our plants, we have here an excellent mode of exhibiting that characteristic relation to appropriate soils which is a condition of perfect culture. The geographical distribution of our different plant types might thus be largely related to the limestones, sandstones, and clays of our geologic model.

We need not even wholly leave out the paleontologist; for though the inexactitude of premature popularising has long made him shy of reconstructing the creatures of the past in all their strangeness, this we see of late years again begun, as notably by the eminent scientific authorities of the American Museum of Natural History. Durable casts of some of their striking reproductions are easily obtained, and might here be placed upon their most appropriate pedestals, the real rocks of their own time. Escaping, then, that backwash of discouragement and ridicule provoked by the too crude dragon restorations of fifty years ago, we may safely utilise the labours of the more exact and not less artistic fossil restorers of to-day, and even come to share them.

While the historical interests of the geologist and paleontologist are thus recognised, what of the actual physical geologist of to-day? How can the simple visitor, the beginner in geology, be helped to see the great processes of world-making? May not even this be in some measure contrived in miniature by the help of our little stream? Can we not set it to cut a cañon here, or fill up a lakelet there? I do not propose attempting to construct a model glacier, for instance, but I will not take upon me to deny the possibility even of this; certainly I should desire to set up, in a summer-house in the adjacent plantation, one or two forms, such as Prof. Lebour's or Mr Cadell's, of the machine for actually imitating the stupendous operations of nature in the compression of strata—such making of foldings and dislocations closely illustrating the making of mountains and valleys themselves.

Here we reach the natural conclusion of such pioneering proposals—that he who would see the world may literally do worse than come to Dunfermline.

FIG. 41.—The Laird's Garden at present—taken from near South-East corner. Present greenhouses along North-East wall to be removed. , New conservatory to occupy North wall, behind low, dark yew hedge—height not to exceed wall. This wall should carry path along its length (see fig. 4).

CHAPTER VII

THE LAIRD'S GARDEN

A. The Laird's Garden

As yet the horticulturist is not satisfied, much less the architect, the artist. After all, the ordinary idea of a garden is one of vegetables, flowers, and fruit, and from this indispensable, indeed main point of view wild garden, rockery, and the rest are minor affairs.

It is time, then, to betake ourselves to the old mansion garden, which an additional act of generosity has now thrown also into the common wealth. The general aspect of the garden has both its good and its bad points, but the latter (fig. 41) may be gently transformed without losing the former. The principle already applied to buildings holds good also for gardens : that good work should be respected and incorporated, not destroyed.

The decorative feature of the garden, its long central grass walk, with herbaceous border on either hand, hedged by espalier-trees, I propose practically to leave alone, merely improving the at present unsatisfactory oblique ends, as shown on plan. I should also lengthen this main walk by setting back the entrance gate 40 feet westwards. The small circular basins shown at each end of the walk will greatly improve each extremity. I assume the future rebuilding of the greenhouses, but for new ones the more natural and advantageous situation is, of course, at the north wall, not the north-east as at present. At present also these, from too many points of view, gravely interfere with tho magnificent view of the Abbey and Palace (fig. 44).

But before entering upon details let us ask : What in common-sense is the best public use that can now be made of this old private garden ? I submit that this should not be laid out as a pleasure garden simply, for which its outline and present character do not very well adapt it, though these difficulties could, of course, be got over. But, as we shall see, we can make a far better pleasure garden elsewhere ; and, in my view, this old one should still practically remain, and even be called the " Laird's Garden." It should be permanently used to show what any good ordinary garden, in our conditions, may reasonably be expected to produce. Its future, in fact, like its past, should be entirely determined from the homely point of view—using " homely," of course, in its full significance. And since the first concern of a homely garden is to produce vegetables, let us have kale, leeks, and all the rest, each in its best varieties as well as its best culture. Thus the well-to-do villa resident who keeps a skilled gardener will see what he may fairly expect to grow, while even the simplest and poorest citizen who has a plot of ground at all, and who has to use it to make both ends meet, will see here the best varieties of vegetables and flowers, take note of their labels, and lay in his packets of seed, or buy his young plants from the nurseryman.

Most important and most instructive to advance horticulture among us is the due rotation of crops in the garden, and so at convenient points should hang the cropping plan of the different plots of the garden for three or four years, so that the visitor may again in this respect go home instructed, and avoid his common mistakes of growing the same crop season after season in the same ground, or of making haphazard or unsuitable successions.

Another important lesson should also be put up monthly or fortnightly—the diary of garden operations for Dunfermline—so that we should be shown,

set I have pleaded for the retention of the fine old grass walk, with its old-fashioned flower borders and espaliers. By all means let us improve the selection of these, both as regards fruit and flowers, but let us keep them in the main ; even the small rock garden also, which is now thoroughly established, and needs little care, and may easily be kept by the garden pupil and imitated at home by the intelligent amateur.

There is not room here for a great fruit collection ; hence all the more care should be given to the selection of a small typical orchard of the finer sorts alone, the coarser trees being already planted freely as decorative trees, especially at the glebe and north-west side of the park.

FIG. 41a.—Present garden, looking West ; old central grass walk and herbaceous borders to be preserved.

not only what to grow and how to grow it, but reminded when to sow, transplant, prune, and so on—a no less important matter.

Here, then, our gardener would become a teaching horticulturist ; under arrangements easily framed he would become a natural leader in the regional horticultural societies and the like, and, of course, be in ever-increasing touch with the schools. It might readily become an honour and a pleasure to the best pupils in the schools to be allowed to assist him in particular operations, or even be granted the responsibility of some particular garden plot for the season. A selection of more advanced pupils would be admitted into the inmost and secret penetralia of the gardener—his propagating houses at the back—and there, behind the scenes, would be initiated into the final secrets of preparation and stage management of the floral drama. The same principle, of course, holds good for flowers and fruit. Hence at the very out-

At present it is right to say fruit trees are usually discouraged in public parks and gardens, and curators are more prone to tear them up than to plant them ; and yet in face of this I plead for the reverse policy. Here, in fact, is one of those opportunities for Dunfermline pioneering, which is needed if we are to become the fruit-growing country we might and should be ; the simple remedy against boyish depredations being to interpret these intelligently, as showing the need for more and more fruit planting still, until not only the towns and villages but the roadsides of Scotland are as fruitful as those of Germany.

Again, of course, the unfortunate prejudice against our own climate disguises the fact that the good Scottish gardener is everywhere producing results of which his countrymen rarely dream. All the more since the dimensions of the park are not sufficient to admit of any substantial departure in the matter of forestry, I press that here, in orchardry, our initiative possibilities be exerted to the full.

Some of the ground will be needed for reserves for the rock garden and for propagating plants for the formal garden of which I have still to speak.

Besides preserving the old-fashioned herbaceous borders there is room for a bit of the gorgeous bedding-out lately so popular, and also for a rose and rose arch here and there. Without these our garden would not be truly typical.

At this point, too, a word may be said of the greenhouses. The small existing scattered houses should be removed as early as may be, and the semicircular ground at the back, north the of present drive, should be carefully laid out for frames, propagating houses, chrysanthemum stand, etc.

B. Altered Drive

The present traffic of the public through this drive should be closed off by gates, and an entirely New Drive made close to the edge of the ravine. This is practicable, with much less under-building than may at first sight appear. The present cherry-laurel hedge would be transplanted about three yards inwards to make room for this road, and working space thereby so much curtailed. This would be practically compensated by the present broad roadway becoming more available for working purposes and also by a better arrange-ment of space, which I do not plan here, since this will fall naturally to the general superintendent of the gardens. The gain to the drive by the sub-stitution of the magnificent view of the ravine it at present loses would alone more than compen-sate for this change ; hence, on double grounds, I strongly recommend it.

C. Conservatories

I now come to the question of the conserva-tories and greenhouses. While the existing range might no doubt serve some time longer for limited use it is not suitable for the public. I therefore supply plans indicating my view of the general type of conservatory required.

First of all, I give up the idea of a great lofty hall, suitable to palms and multitudes, and content myself with something more modest, yet more varied and interesting. Entering at the north-west corner, that next the mansion-house, we pass into a long fern corridor, lit only from the roof, its ferns growing not only on the ground level but irregularly grouped upon the walls, hanging, too, in baskets from the roof, with here and there in centre and at sides tree ferns in large pots sunk into the ground, so as to keep the whole building low. From a roof-walk above this, which could easily be carried along the top of the wall, would

be obtained that finer view of the palace and abbey group (fig. 44, Chap. VIII.) which I offer in place of the more familiar one, and also similarly improved views in other directions.

On this corridor to the north, if a room can be spared from the working range and the bothies behind, I would convert it into a filmy fern house, always delightful and interesting. From this quiet corridor we pass southward into the large conservatory, descending a flight of steps, upon a level excavated for the purpose, so as to keep this roof also low—a point to which I attach the very greatest importance, alike for the sake of growth within and of the landscape with-out.

Southward, in front of this again, but now separated only by glass, not by a brick wall as in the former case, runs a long corridor, thus parallel to the fernery, but in contrast to it, and chiefly filled with the finer climbers of all sorts. This triple range of houses—fernery, conservatory, and cor-ridor—thus collectively provides the advantages of a winter garden, being excellently suitable for a promenade, even for afternoon receptions, or with electric light for evening entertainments From this corridor to the southward open three houses ; say a miscellaneous house in the middle with a succulent house and orchid house on either hand. If funds allow, a " Victoria regia House " would be a most interesting and beautiful addition, and small collections of useful plants, insectivorous plants, etc., would be easily provided. These three may again be connected by transverse passages. These are not shown on elevation, as on the whole I think the very sheltered space enclosed by these three projecting houses may be better used for the growing of delicate plants, otherwise difficult to cultivate out of doors. Examples of the success of this method may be seen in the corresponding situation at the Edinburgh Botanic Garden or in the scarcely more favourable climate of that of Cambridge. In sum, then, our range of houses combines the essential advantages—of course, upon a small scale—of the winter garden of a great city park with the greater beauty and variety of botanic garden houses.

I need not speak further of the plant arrange-ment of this conservatory, a matter of more detail than need be entered into here ; but neither good examples nor fresh ideas are lacking.*

Leave now this conservatory and look at it from without. Its elevation (fig. 42) is in con-ventional style, and while I stand by its interior

---

* Thus Mr Backhouse of York suggests an idea more daring than anything I have ventured to imagine—the re-production under glass of a typical subtropical landscape, in its geographical as well as horticultural aspects. The large, low greenhouse of the Jardin d'Acclimatation, laid out as a promenade, will also be remembered by visitors to Paris.

arrangement as interesting, even beautiful, I frankly confess to its architectural plainness—inherent, as yet, in all our architecture of glass, at best here mitigated by keeping down height as far as possible. Next to the old mansion, in view of the Abbey and Palace, and in winter especially, its hard outlines and cold glitter cannot but strike a jarring note. These unprepossessing features can be abated by giving up the custom of outside painting in white, and, further, by giving the whole house a somewhat more architectural character, for which there are some artistic precedents,

D. South Promenade on High Terrace

Before leaving the Laird's Garden a final word should be said of its walls. I recommend lowering the south portion of the east wall by at least 6 feet; the rest may also be lowered when the present greenhouses come to be removed. On the south I show a promenade on top of the wall, obtained by setting back the present holly hedge an average of 15 to 20 feet from the curved frontage, and surmounting the wall by a balustrade, with a garden house at either end. The trimmed hedge should

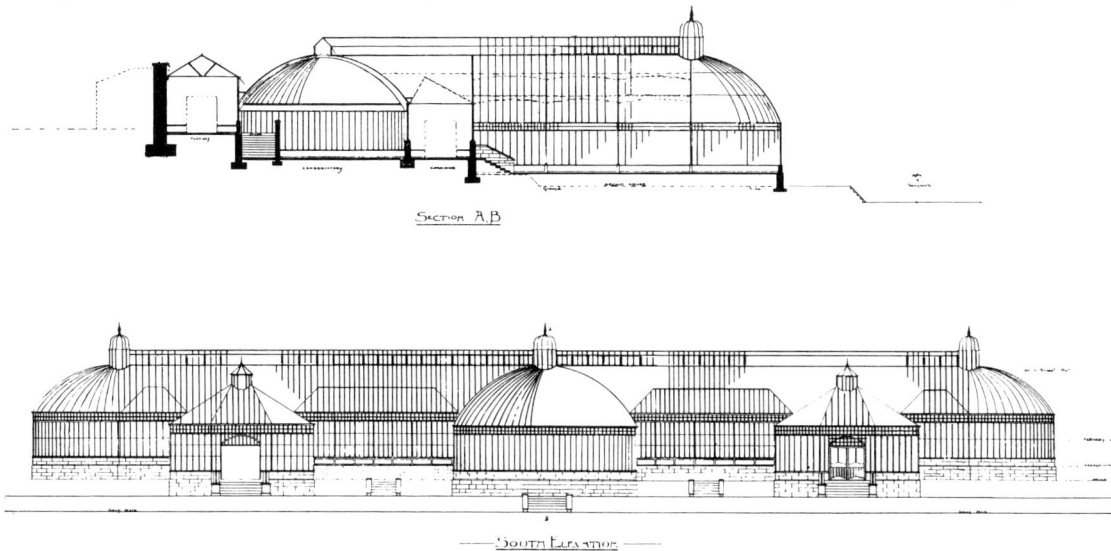

FIG. 42.—Elevation and Section of Conservatory, etc., as developed in usual style upon scheme indicated in chapter and general plan, showing desirability in view of this situation between Mansion and Abbey (despite height to be further moderated)—(a) of architectural improvement beyond usual Conservatory style; (b) of screen of higher growing trees at sufficient distance; or (c) of exclusion from this Park altogether. (Drawing by Mr W. Ramage.)

though none completely successful. But for the present I leave this building in the ordinary horticultural style in order to point out two alternatives. One is that it may still be screened; say, by a row of pear-trees in front—not so near, of course, as to shade the house, yet so as to conceal its roofs in perspective. The other point I put rather as an inquiry than as a positive suggestion: What of erecting this glass palace in the other park altogether? There it can easily be placed, and also screened; there are no great historic buildings around with which it would clash, and it would also give greater attractiveness to this park, which is a substantial city asset, well worth improving in its turn. In any case there should still be a small greenhouse here, or, say, even the fernery, sunny corridor, and greenhouses, without the large conservatory; this would be the essential feature of a centre building elsewhere.

be treated with square bays, in the old fashion as shown in plan. We have thus sheltered places for flowers, occasionally interrupted by spaces for seats, these seats and promenade alike commanding an excellent view; and one still more interesting when the Formal or Palace Garden below, with its tennis courts and bowling greens, to which we come in the next chapter, is considered. (See Chap. VIII.)

Behind this hedge runs the upper garden walk, thus in shade, and widening out into a central square, in which I indicate a simple circular basin. This is a beautiful feature of many old gardens, and one of usefulness also, both for watering the garden from this high point and for carrying a hose down to the formal garden, described in the next chapter, below this wall altogether. The possibility of circulating on this front terrace between sun and shade will also be noted.

Below this promenade and upon the wall below I should grow vine, fig, and myrtle, and other plants of special interest, a series connecting well with the formal garden also. This would be a little Mediterranean terrace garden, for with a little protection in winter one can do wonders upon such a well-sunned and well-sheltered wall.

So far, then, the Laird's Garden, a developed yet simply domestic type for general example and for horticulture.

E. School Gardens

The relation of this garden to the schools will naturally largely depend on the horticulturist in charge of this department, and I would submit that this requirement should be taken fully into account in adjusting the staff. Few gardeners can

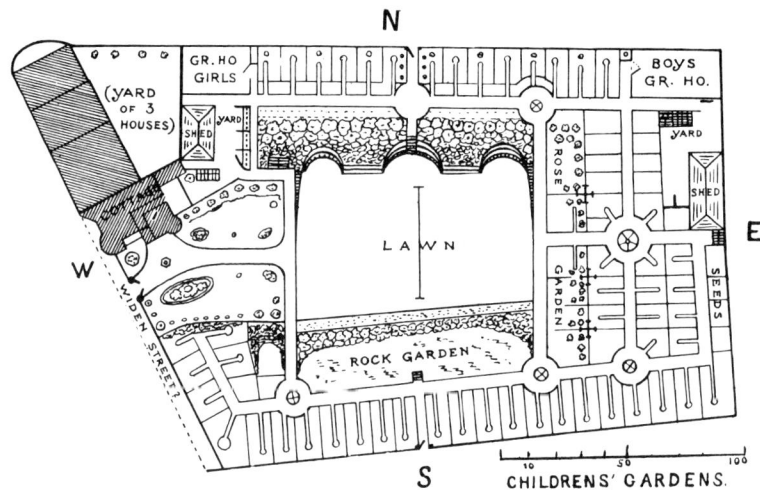

FIG. 43.—Plan of Trial Garden, including 75 small gardens for individual children, and with two small greenhouses and appropriate working-sheds and yards. These may be reserved for boys and girls respectively, or employed for different uses as preferred. Note also Superintendent's cottage (improving Moodie Street, which should also here be slightly widened), lawn, etc. (See fig. 10.)

teach and few teachers can garden : the problem here is to find a man or woman who can do both.

With this garden should be, of course, related the school gardens, now in the near future, and of which I submit one of countless alternatives plans (fig. 43) as a type attractive to beginners.

In our own country the school garden movement is still in its infancy. Of the total number of school gardens in the British Islands I have no statistics, but I fancy I am sanguine in hoping that there may be by this time as many tens as in France there are thousands. The whole matter is as yet in a phase of sporadic initiative : thus for many years I have occasionally found a school-governing body or a pioneering teacher willing to accept a plan and plants ; but even then the garden has usually been considered a very small and secondary affair, in no wise taken up with the thoroughness we have seen on the Continent. Especially through the exertions of the late

lamented Mr Rooper, H.M.I. in England, now I trust being continued by the many cultivators of the Nature Study movement, as notably by Mr J. C. Medd and others, educational opinion has been to some extent awakened, but for practical purposes we may see the movement even now largely begun.

I have lately been privileged to prepare for the School Board of Aberdeen a design for a botanic garden on a larger scale than customary. This is for the use of the High School, where botanical and horticultural teaching has long been ably carried on by my friend Mr Bentley Philip. In progress also I may mention a larger garden for the London County Council ; this is situated at the Horniman Museum, and is specially intended for the use of teachers and the visits of their classes —other examples might be given.

In this matter of School Gardens the initiative of Dunfermline is an old story ; witness the old and charming flower border of the Hospital Hill School, the botanic garden of the Technical School, and the small garden laid out in connection with several of the newer schools. In this respect, however, there is still much to be done, and at the present period of educational transition a further active initiative would be of peculiar value. Especially is it not realised how much more has been done in foreign countries than at home.

Here I cannot do better than cite from a recent American pamphlet.*

The Austrian public school law reads : " In every school a gymnastic ground, a garden for the teacher according to the circumstances of the community, and a place for the purposes of agricultural experiment are to be created. School inspectors must see to it that in country schools school gardens shall be provided for corresponding agricultural instruction in all that relates to the soil, and that the teacher shall make himself skilful in such instruction. Instruction in natural history is indispensable to suitably established school gardens. The teachers, then, must be in a condition to conduct them."

" Ten years ago Austria had eight thousand school gardens. France has now more than thirty thousand of these schools. Nearly all of them belong to the primary and elementary grades. Indeed, in France a man who lacks a necessary knowledge of horticulture and the ability to teach

* J. M. Good, "The How of Improvement Work." *Home Florist*, Springfield, January 1901.

it cannot receive an appointment as master of an elementary school under any consideration. Sweden grafted the school garden upon her public school system more than thirty years ago, and each of her public schools has been allotted from one to twenty acres of ground for gardening purposes. Russia has taken up the school garden work with energy. In 1895 the two hundred and twenty-seven garden schools of one province contained one hundred and eleven thousand fruit trees, and nearly two hundred and fifty thousand forest trees. The school garden idea originated in Germany—the nation to which the world is indebted for this and many other advanced educational ideas. In the city schools the gardens are confined to botanical and decorative flowers. In the country schools and gardens rival the agricultural colleges in the scope of their work. In large cities, where land is very valuable, it is usual to have a large central school garden outside the city, which supplements the small garden about each schoolhouse. This garden supplies the school with all the flowers needed for study. A recitation hall is built in this garden, to which the teachers and their pupils come each week. The work is confined to the high school grades. During study hours silence and order are maintained as in other classwork. Pupils are required to take notes, write essays, etc., and receive diplomas at the conclusion of their course."

From a very concrete statement of the case for school gardens—accompanied also by an excellent bibliography of recent American literature of this subject—which I have just received from a valued correspondent, Mr Warren H. Manning, Secretary of the American Park and Outdoor Art Association, I cannot refrain from citing a few passages :

"The school garden movement will lead, as it has in Germany, to a much more practical education than that now in vogue. It is the kind of education that has more to do with the everyday life of a majority of the students than that of a more academic character previously in vogue. It is the kind of education supplemented, as it is being and will be, by industrial training along other lines that will make students producers almost immediately on their graduation from the public school, instead of compelling them to drift about in great indecision for a number of years, until they finally find an opening, or of leading them into clerical positions or professions for which they are not fitted, and from which they can have little opportunity to become really progressive or valuable citizens.

"This work has developed into a type of school gardens having two distinct purposes in view. One is that of making the grounds more attractive by the use of hardy vines, shrubs, and trees grouped about the base of buildings and against fences in positions where they would shut out unattractive views and screen undesirable structures.

"More recently the industrial phase of the school garden has entered the field, largely as an outgrowth of the movement to have vacant lots utilised by poor people for the cultivation of vegetables and flowers. In such gardens ordinary garden crops are cultivated, methods of propagation are taught, some attention is given to insect enemies, fungus diseases, value of birds, and the like. The most interesting recent development in this connection is the growing appreciation of those who are responsible for the care of our public parks and public reservations, and of those who are responsible for the educational systems of communities, of the importance of a closer co-operation between these two interests. Already in Pittsburg extensive greenhouses have been erected in connection with Schenley Park, in which children of the public school are given an opportunity to study the growth and development of plants under glass. Furthermore, they are encouraged to take advantage of the park as a place for nature study."

These citations might easily be multiplied and enriched by reference, for instance, to Arbor Day, to fruit-culture, to window-gardening, bee-keeping, and so on, as also to popular instruction in landscape gardening. They might be supplemented also by evidence of the moral and social results of gardens upon their cultivators ; and this, again, by concrete evidence such as that of their reforming effect upon the active hooliganism, and the even more deadly loafing habits, of town life, against which our current school education can do so little, for which, indeed, it so largely disposes, if not actually prepares.

Of my own plan herewith (fig. 43) only a word need be said, that it is intended not at all as a typical school garden but as a Trial Garden, in which children might have tiny individual gardens allotted to them for culture, as well as some general training in dealing with larger beds, and in which a playing green, available for croquet, lawn tennis, etc., is also supplied. From this trial garden it would be a distinction to be drafted off to the School Gardens proper, or, best of all, for the highest instruction and responsibility at the Laird's Garden and other gardens of the Park. For a large development of gardening then, this Trial Garden would be not only the best argument, but the means of at once preparing the children and their parents, the public and the authorities, for a vigorous adoption of Continental and American example in this matter. Nor does the influence of such gardens end with school life. It will be the child who has passed a due proportion of happy and busy hours in its tiny garden here who will want a house in a Garden City later, or who at any rate will be ready for that provision of allotment gardens in the suburbs, which might here so easily be provided for those whose homes may still be in town. In every way, therefore, the proposed plan is largely one for sowings.

FIG. 44.—View of Palace, with Abbey Church and Fratry Hall above, showing general group, visible from many points, but specially good from view-point chosen, the top of present North garden wall, thus showing advantage of belvedere turret, or, still better, of narrow promenade walk on top of wall—giving, on the whole, the finest series of views in whole Park.

CHAPTER VIII

THE PALACE GARDEN

A. Formal Gardens

WE have now developed most of the different types of garden upon a substantial but not unusual, much less immoderate scale. There remains, however, one great type of gardening, indeed in not a few ways the greatest of all—the Formal Garden—that designed and presided over by the architectural, not the naturalistic spirit, by urban art instead of by nature, utility, or science. While personally maintaining the preponderance of the naturalistic and the practical points of view I must recognise that the claims of the stately and architectural garden require also to be reasonably considered, even frankly accepted, and this upon an adequate scale, although also within very definite limits, so as not to effect the general character of the whole park scheme, but rather to enhance it more fully by its contrast.

And here in this park, with its neighbouring historic palace of the Renaissance, as well as its later mansion, both dating from the best days of formal gardening, the creation of such a garden is but a natural and legitimate revival of the stateliest elements of one of the greatest periods of art. That this has once and again flourished in Scotland magnificent examples like those of Drummond Castle survive to show ; while the " King's Knot " under Stirling Castle is an interesting example of the creation of a spacious formal garden, probably by the very king to whom the present façade of the palace is due. Such a garden as I now proceed to describe may thus already have existed here, or not far away ; and its creation anew is thus in every way appropriate to the surroundings. As due indication of the dignity and beauty of these, and consequently of the type of garden required, I here insert (fig. 44) that view of Palace and Abbey referred to in the preceding chapter.

What are the elements of such a Palace Garden ? These, of course, have varied like architectural styles with the times and their makers. But, broadly speaking, we recognise in them all the magnificence of perspectives, length of promenades, and breadth of levelled lawns, well-trimmed and monumental evergreens and standards ; we find the large restful spaces of lawn contrasted with complexly-designed pattern gardens, their well-set box-edging separating their mazy walks from rich masses of coloured foliage or gorgeous blossom.

Where the slope of the ground admits, as fortunately here, terrace rises above terrace, each varied in its proportions, its panelling, and its balustrading, its formal yews or splendid flower-beds, while all the terraces are interconnected by spacious stairways of every combination of floral adornment upon architectural design.

The architectural use of water in such gardens is constantly of the greatest value. Beside the formal basin, with its peaceful level contrasted by statuary or enlivened by the play of fountains, the separate fountain also finds its place in the centre of minor panels of lawn and flower beds. The use, too, of the picturesque old sun-dials, so prominent in the gardening of this period, is nowhere better illustrated than in our old Scottish gardens. Beautiful effects are also obtained by the judicious use of vases, of leaden statues, and, best of all, despite all that may be said against our climate, of marble statuary against the dark background of evergreens. These stately and monumental effects are next to be lightened by full and free use of roses, lilies, and all the other glorious resources of the garden colourist ; and the whole results in a new and magnificent presentment of the seasonal pageant, now displayed from the side of architecture and art, as formerly from that of nature and science.

B. Tennis Courts and Bowling Green

One's first idea is to transform the Laird's Garden, but, apart from its unsuitable outline, I submit that a far better and more natural use has been found for this ; while the best place for the proposed formal garden is upon the spacious area in front of the Laird's Garden and the mansion-house lawn (figs. 45 and 46). Yet here again the first idea is rather to reserve this for games—but what games ? There is length, but scarcely adequate breadth, for a single good cricket pitch ; and this is not the right place for cricket. I have sufficiently pleaded for the acquisition of more suitable ground to south and north of the park. Moreover, it is time to protest against the too common fashion of

67

laying out parks for boys' and men's games alone. Hence, just as I have proposed reserving the northeast corner of the park for children and old folks, I submit this level space should primarily be understood as the Playground of the older girls and young women of the town and reserved for such games as they can fully take part in. These games, then, are primarily tennis and croquet, to which we may add bowls ; and the laying-out of this large space with tennis courts and bowling greens is thus, it seems to me, the most practical and useful purpose to which it can be applied. But tennis courts are not in themselves sufficiently beautiful to satisfy the eye, and to plot down such courts in the ordinary way would be to spoil

Moreover here, as at so many other points, we may thus reconcile the claims of wealth and art, of tradition and culture, with those of simple popular pleasure, and even play. Our Palace Garden is thus fully a People's Garden also.

C. Design in Detail (*see General Plan*)

Hence, then, the present plan is a combination of both requirements and principles just mentioned. Referring to the plan, it will be seen that this shows one full-sized grass bowling green and two fair-sized tennis courts, which had better be ash-bottomed for all weathers ; four small grass

FIGS. 45 and 46.—General view of site taken as panorama from near middle of its Southern border, looking Northward up its gentle slope. Beginning with 46, the East border of the future garden is the wooded Western edge of glen— the North boundary is made up first by the high and somewhat sinuous retaining wall of the Laird's Garden, on top of which is shown in plan a High Terrace Walk. West of this comes a line of Trees and Shrubbery separating the Laird's Garden from the Mansion-House lawn. In 45 is shown the Mansion-House with its lawn and ha-ha fence, and farther West its South-West shelter plantation (behind which is Pinetum and shaded end of proposed lake). To left should appear the main entrance drive, united from those of all three entrances to North, East, and West. (See General Plan for design of proposed Formal Garden.)

the most conspicuous point of the whole park, a real waste of the beauty of this splendid public property.

Shall we, then, give this up, and return to the ordinary formal garden of promenades alone, as at Drummond Castle, giving up games altogether ? Not so ; the difficulty is an opportunity ; we may exclude neither, but combine them both. Let us have our tennis courts and bowling greens, but arrange their necessarily straight paths with flower borders and the like. Thus we have our formal garden also, and that of the best type, in which that too great dispersion of interest, the too elaborate detail which is the defect at Drummond Castle is permanently avoided by the existence of these useful open spaces.

lawns for tennis or croquet, and three small ovals, one larger and two smaller, all large enough for children, making ten play spaces in all.

To all these the formal garden gives a centre with its basin and fountains, a frame for them also with its hedges and lawn borders, its terraces and standard yews, its four small fountained and box-edged panel gardens. Of these, the two larger are to westward, the two smaller to eastward, of the basin ; while a long flower border completes its southern foot.

Along the whole southern front runs a long walk, with central circular pool and fountain or statue, while minor fountains, or possibly small garden houses with view platforms on top, some what in the model of a city cross, occupy the centre of the square bastions at each end. From each bastion projects a rounded balcony seat. East and west runs a walk towards the semicircular ends of the garden at east and west. On the longer eastward half of this path project two other semicircles, again with seats, one with a central dial, the other with a lofty rose pillar. A columned rose pergola here offers beauty and shade.

The preliminary contour survey shows a large of about 20 feet on this whole width of garden, hence two 5-feet terraces are shown upon the north side next the ha-ha and garden wall, thus leaving other 10 feet, of which 6 would be accounted for by the southward terrace wall, leaving 4 for a terrace farther down on the other side of the long

giving this garden at once a more complete and varied beauty, and an added historical interest, indeed, making it an open-air museum in its way.

The plans of the ends next need some interpretation. We may begin with the simpler, because less favourably sunned, western one. Here the path running round the square and oval lawns looks westward into three grassy bays in a dense mass of evergreen shrubbery and trees—laurel and laurustinus in front, hollies and yews and cypresses behind. The plan of the two smaller bays shows a pedestal for a bust or small leaden statue. In the large central bay a larger statue and pedestal is flanked by a flower bed on either side, and has a small flower bed in front also.

elliptical drive, which now encircles the whole. This will be useful also as easily furnishing a half-mile running track—while on either side of this drive also races up to 200 yards can be watched by a fair number of spectators, though of course athletic " events " would not be admissible here.

Different methods of treating the long borders are indicated in different parts of the plan, either with regular yews, rows of flower beds, or the like, or largely left vacant in grass. Short and gentle stairways lead down into the lawns, since these are slightly sunken, a method both beautiful in itself and sheltering to the players, for to this depression we must add the height of the hedges above.

In the detailed treatment of these borders, and of the other different units, an attempt would be made to express the characteristic merits and effects of the different styles of formal gardening from the Roman, so plainly indicated in Pompeii, as well as clearly described by classic authors, through their various renaissance developments— Italian, French, Dutch, English, and Scottish—

Passing now to the east end a similar principle is carried out, but on a larger scale, with five semicircular bays overlooking a sunk oval lawn, with small triangular flower beds at its extremities. Of the five bays three have here statues, now of marble, with an arrangement of flowers beside and in front of the pedestals, as at the other end ; while the two minor bays may have busts or vases. From the deep evergreen mass, at this end some 40 feet at its thickest, should rise large irregular groups of cypresses, so in a few years beginning to produce one of the great effects of Italian gardens, and leading back the eye gradually to the high trees of the deep glen immediately behind. It will be noted that the main drives on both sides of this garden unite here in the wood, and thence run up towards the back of Pittencrieff House or down to the bottom of the park. This again affords an agreeable yet not violent contrast between the naturalistic and the formal styles ; the two are so arranged that they cannot come simultaneously into view at any point. In the same way at the west side the

FIG. 47.—View taken from outside the middle of wall fence of Mansion lawn looking North-East through its East shrubbery over Laird's Garden to Abbey and Palace. Old South wall of Laird's Garden seen in distance.

FIG. 48.—Preceding view retouched, showing effect of proposed balustrading upon these walls and of terracing below, with combination of formal and natural growth. (This large stairway is that shown on general plan as leading down to Fountain Basin to South.) Fig. 49 (further detail) withheld.

main drive and running track pass down between the tennis gardens to the east and the rock
garden to the west, without at this point looking
into either, but simply passing through a sufficiently interesting border of flowering shrubs
on either hand. As an alternative to this I
strongly recommend a lofty hedge of trimmed
evergreen yew or holly. I indicate such an effect
as at once simple, quaint, and effective. The use
of such quiet spaces and their value as resting the
eye for fresh views is seldom sufficiently appreciated by modern designers or their critics.

Again, in full relief and contrast to our elaborate
yet fundamentally simple formal garden, we have
the simple mansion-house lawn and laird's garden above and the quiet spaces of the park
sloping away below. At the west end is the rock
garden, and at the east end, between the towering
cypresses and the woodland avenue, runs a shady
path through a wild garden of primroses under
hazels, a natural extension of the wooded dell.

The slope of the ground is not sufficient here
to give us the lofty terrace effects of Drummond Castle ; yet when the ha-ha of the mansion
lawn and the high wall of the garden promenade
are surmounted by a balustrade and the formal
garden has its double terracing, as shown in plan,
a considerable picturesqueness is obtained. This
is enhanced by the building of the necessary
stairway in the line leading from the central basin
to the lawn above (figs. 47 and 48) ; as also by the
erection of a garden-house at each end of the high
wall promenade of the Laird's Garden, the western
one with staircase also (figs. 47 and 48). This
garden-house and terracing would compose at every
point with the noble mass of Palace and Abbey,
the latter furnishing a long and stately base, the
former the needed foreground echo of the spire.

A fuller idea of the whole scheme will be obtained from looking at this whole garden upon
the general plan, and from each of its main
approaches and points of view. Time has not
permitted the preparation of full bird's-eye perspectives, still less of the model to scale, which
would be desirable for the complete elaboration of
the whole design in detail before execution; enough
for the present if the general conception has been
made clear.

CHAPTER IX

WILD GARDEN AND BOTANIC GARDEN

For a wild garden no park could be better adapted. The glen and the plantation borders await us, and afford the opportunity of working out this feature upon no ordinary scale of perfection, at any rate so far as the more shade-loving species are concerned.

But what of the sun-loving forms ? Of these the finer floral sorts are provided for in the flower gardens at different points, notably the tulips and hyacinths of spring, the roses, lilies, and carnations of summer, and the chrysanthemums of autumn. Water-loving species have ample home in the extensive line of lake, pool, and brook along the western side, and Alpine species are accommodated not only in the large rock garden but will find admirable homes in those large sunward spaces of the ha-ha which I specially preserve for this purpose and propose to adorn in this way. (Here the reader may be assumed to have access to Miss Jekyll's beautiful volume of " Wall and Water Gardens," which dispenses me from a more detailed exposition of the possibilities of this subject.)

Instead, therefore, of either preserving or destroying the existing ha-ha as a whole, I have made each point of its circumference the subject of careful study, and its preservation at some points, its removal at others, will thus become intelligible. But it is not enough to work out with the gardeners the appropriate styles, the sites of shade and sun, nor even to work out with Miss Jekyll or the painters the appropriate seasonal effects. For as yet, in all this garden, the botanist has been in the background. Yet the problems of laying out a botanic garden have been, as natural to the writer, perhaps more anxiously considered than any other portion of the scheme. For the requirements of the botanist are not satisfied by the mere labelling of species, nor even by disposing them in some measure in their geographical and geological relations, such as suggested for the rock garden, or, again, in characteristic groups such as the Mediterranean plants proposed upon the high south terrace wall under the Laird's Garden. He must have his plants arranged in their natural orders. To many this at once suggests laying out monotonous formal lines of beds such as meet the visitor to the great botanic gardens, if not a mere cat's graveyard effect of epitaph labels.

But such botanic gardens, despite the high authorities who arrange and maintain them, are really survivals of tradition rather than the last word of science. For they are pre-evolutionary catalogues, not evolutionary ones. They are avowedly made from books, notably " Bentham and Hooker," not the books from them. That their so-called natural system is pre-evolutionary is evidenced by their geometrical arrangement, so that this freer one would be far more truly scientific.

In this way I do not hesitate to say that the small botanic garden arranged by my lamented friend and assistant Mr Robert Smith, in front of the Technical School, is superior to most of the recently arranged botanic gardens in its attempted presentment of the affinities of the natural orders. And since this garden is found sufficient for the requirements of elementary teaching, and since, moreover, the Edinburgh and Glasgow collections are so accessible to advanced students, there is something to be said for going no further, especially as no portion of the park remains which could be adapted to the purpose of a separate botanic garden without injury to what—botanist though I am—I am bound to admit are most general needs.

As at so many other points, the difficulty here becomes an opportunity, and after much thought I venture to think that I have solved the problem. For, instead of a specific botanic garden at one spot, the whole place is a botanic garden ; and this not merely of that simpler, freer growing type which preceded the hard and linear arrangement at present predominant, but also in its very freedom more evolutionary both in general arrangement and detail than any botanic garden has been before.

It is an old and still too common experience that in seeking knowledge we may lose beauty ; yet it is not impossible also to use our knowledge in service to beauty, varying it and enhancing it.

To the ordinary visitor the succession of plants will still appear naturalistic ; indeed, if artistically designed they may appear almost accidental. Yet not only the beginner in botany will soon find the natural orders in their most easily grasped succession but the professed evolutionist, I trust, will also find interest and suggestiveness in the mode of treatment adopted.

A. Botanical Arrangement

Leaving technical details to a possible paper to the Naturalists' Society I may simply point out here that the natural orders of higher flowering plants should begin, on the righ thand from what may probably become the entrance from Bridge Street, with the simple ranunculus family and their allies, peonies, magnolias, and barberries, poppies, crucifers and fumitories, hypericums, resedas, and violets, geraniums, with the pink family and their picturesquely vegetative allies, the rhubarbs, and spinach. Of this whole series the sun-loving varieties occupy wall pockets in the ha-ha, small beds in advance of this, or occasionally on top of the wall ; while the more shade-loving species run back into the plantation belt.

This method of gradation from sunny plants in rich and moist soil to the sheltering dry and sunny wall, and thence again behind to the shadiest shrubberies, affords an almost ideal variety of conditions, no less to the botanic gardener than to the ordinary flower lover. Their interests and methods are thus here reconciled.

By a careful selection of species it is quite possible to keep up a continued interest along this whole region for the greater part of the year, from the winter aconites of February to the Christmas rose, and the like in considerable measure also for many of the other orders

While this section of the park, then, illustrates and includes the large group of natural orders best known to most naturalists as " thalamiflorals," of which the buttercup is the initial type, the next section of the park, the north-west, has similarly its wild garden and wall garden, its plants and shrubs around the basin and elsewhere, drawn from the next great group of orders, the " calyciflorals,"* of which the rose family is most familiar. Hence beautiful cushions of saxifrages may drape and adorn the ha-ha wall, with the allied houseleeks and stone-crops ; while the shrubbery saxifrages, like flowering currants,and mock-orange,will afford a wealth of beauty in spring and early summer and even in autumn with plants like *Hydrangea paniculata*.

In shrubberies around the basin the beautiful and water-loving spireas and their allies would predominate ; but beds are also shown of fuchsias and evening primroses, etc. ; while the more shade-loving umbelliferous plants occupy the plantation belt behind the saxifrages, yet with the splendid sea-hollies coming forward into the sun.

* While using this grouping, so convenient to the beginner, the teacher will, of course, point out that this also is traditional and partly artificial, and that the order of nature is not so simply discovered.

Now running down the west side the rose order in its shrubbery and tree forms would be amply represented, the arrangement utilising all its varied adaptability, from sun to shade and from water to wall.

Beside the roses, their allies the leguminous plants are also similarly illustrated with another wealth of blossom, from the early spring and summer laburnum to the latest flowering sweet-peas at the pavilion on the height.

West of the lake our willow plantation would similarly be of no small botanical interest, and this without interfering with its effect, in fact, enhancing it, and so on with the water plants.

In the rock garden, as in the others, the claims of botany are again perfectly reconcilable with those of beauty ; and even in the formal garden itself a scientific knowledge would greatly enhance the interest of its displays of spring bulbs, of summer and autumn flowers. Tulips or chrysanthemums are not less beautiful to those who know them as supremely instructive yet perplexing to the student of variation, nor are lilies less interesting to those who are wont seriously to consider how they grow.

Along the drive, to southward of the rock garden, would come the main display of rhododendrons and azaleas, far exceeding in their splendour those of fig. 4, and running off into these the whole heath family, of marked interest alike to gardener and botanist, should be illustrated here.

For the primrose family both shady glade and sunny plot are provided, and similarly for minor allied orders like the sea-pinks, sea-lavenders, etc.

Descending now towards the Lovers' Loan, a great feature is made along the east side of the drive and the fringe of the den plantation of the campanula family and their developed allies the composites. Here, in fact, is perhaps the culminating example of this possible combination of seasonal beauty in favoured environment with scientific interest. For ample succession of flowers is most easily kept up from the spring doronicums, which would here fill the shady plantation from April till July, onwards through a wealth of blossom in summer too numerous for mention, to the asters and chrysanthemums with which the floral pageant ends.

The connection of the trees of the plantation with the herbage of the foreground is provided by a plantation of composite shrubs like olearia, etc., behind the kindred herbaceous plants. This brings us down to the Lovers' Loan Lodge, on the opposite side of which is shown a small group of allied orders—madders, valerians, scabious, and teasels, the latter, of course, recalling the composites, and almost exceeding them in picturesqueness.

In front of the lodge entrance are grouped the labiates, in masses of lavender, rosemary, thyme, and other fragrant shrubs and herbs, such as mints and balms. Beside are the allied orders, all easily cultivated and decorative, such as phloxes ; borages, from the tallest comfreys and alkanets to the modest forget-me-not ; the figwort family, from the Veronica shrubbery to the snapdragon and mimulus ; the purple and white foxgloves, and so on—all uniting to make a magnificently varied yet scientifically allied entrance group.

Travelling westwards, and again passing the madders, we come along the bottom and lower western side of the park to what should be a most interesting and beautiful selection of the caprifoil order—elders in their wealth of blossom and fruit, weigelia and honeysuckle, laurustinus, snowball and snowberry—here again at once both in scientific collection and seasonal flower varieties.

Above this comes the beautiful ash order, from the privet and lilac to the flowering ash and thickest forest tree.

In such ways, then, the front region of the park is mainly characterised by the "corollifloral" orders. Next, after the willows already mentioned, come the other "incomplete" and catkin-bearing trees ; hazels, elms, oaks, beeches being also introduced at convenient points in course of the gradual improvement of the plantation border to the south-west and south, but also on the east plantation belt leading to the den. So far, then, a broadly simple yet adequately scientific arrangement of flowering plants has been provided.

The pinetum and cedar group do some justice to the coniferous alliance, as also the proposed new clump of Scots firs in the south-west section, though this, for the sake of contrast, should be mixed with birches.

It remains only to consider the Cryptogamic plants ; and for the majority of these the glen affords the most exceptional advantages of culture, even with considerable variety of conditions.

In the development of the glen, then, I propose to make a special feature of a Fernery—this great fernery beginning upon the spacious bank northwest of the tower bridge, thence gradually extending with the years through, upon, and down the dell, and offering every facility of conditions for the fern gardener—until, before long, the den might become, with the enhancement of its present charms, and without serious expense, one of the most remarkable fern gardens to be seen anywhere. Science and beauty are here again fully co-operating, not competing (Chap. XIII.).

With the general term of fernery I include facilities for growing mosses, liverworts, and the like ; while with the increase of our knowledge it would not be impossible to do something to encourage the growth of some of the more interesting of lichens, and even of fungi for the cryptogamist of autumn.

Nor are the possibilities of the den exhausted

here, other special features of beauty being its adaptability to shade-loving plants throughout the seasons, from snowdrops, celandine, and narcissus onwards. This, however, will be more fully discussed when we come to the chapter on the Glen (Chap. XIII.), which again must be postponed till after the purification of its stream (Chap. XI.).

B. Further Aspects of Botanic Gardens

In revising this chapter I feel that I have here, perhaps more than anywhere, come short of expressing, either to the general reader or to brother botanist, that many-sided presentment of plant life, alike in its protean beauty and its manifold intellectual interest, in which once more this varied park should become a microcosm of the larger world—the world of Nature, the world of Science. In such brief space it is impossible adequately even to outline these. Enough if this practical possibility has been suggested here of utilising the best traditions of the great schools of botany, yet of proceeding beyond these toward a yet fuller and more characteristic presentment of the plant world. That is of the order of its evolution—in historic time and in geographic space—in adaptation of soils and climates—in adaptation, too, to other forms of life, and to man himself, and also in some indication of that natural order of descent and kinship which is now partly deciphered, partly awaiting more complete discovery.

By such laying out as I have proposed for the gardens, of this park much might be done, not only for local education and for regional naturalists, but even for the larger world of science. The great metropolitan gardens are necessarily hampered by their laying out in the past, which it would be unpractical, even sacrilegious, now to destroy, since science rises upon its own past like coral reef or wall, and thus grows upward into the future. The present opportunity is thus one of real importance to natural science everywhere. Where before has there been such a chance of converging the resources of science, at once systematic and evolutionary, with those of horticulture, from utilitarian to magnificent ? Let no one fear the loss of beauty from such a comprehensive proposal of scientific laying out, of viewing the whole park as a great botanic garden. Recall how, with our very first view of the ground (Chap. I.), there appeared the proposal for the appropriate planting of the sunward-sloping glebe as an orchard neuk, narrowing into a hawthorn den, and for echoing these with a kindred arrangement upon the northwest side of the park also, each, then, with an effect at once Japanesque and homely. But this spring paradise of blossom trees above the lake, this blaze of autumn glory below the ancient towers, will only be all the richer for having technical qualities of design, for being an evolutionist's type-selection of characteristic variations of the Rosaceæ.

The child prying among the humblest liverworts and mosses by the stream, the designer revelling amid the verdure mazes of the dell, will again but be the richer when the naturalist-gardener has gone before them, like Ariel with his fern seed invisible; till not only each successive dene, but each different point of exposure and moisture, of rock and soil, within these has its distinctive point or mass of beauty, yet all seeming more natural than before. The narcissus glades, the iris patches

variety of form and colour to the display of the tulips of Holland, the roses of England and of France.

Nor need the economist fear extravagance, since the rule has been laid down from the outset of leaving the costlier rarities and the weaklings to the existing great collections, and here of specialising on commoner things, and at most upon what, with due care and reasonable skill, even the amateur cultivator may grow.

Beyond even all this there is yet a larger conception, an ideal again—that is to say, a point which, though no doubt somewhat distant, is sufficiently definite, steady, and lumin-

FIG. 50.—Narcissus, Iris, Podophyllum, etc. (From Photograph lent by Mr Barr of Covent Garden.)

by the stream, will look none the less natural because their arrangement has been by a selection from the treasures of the specialist in this matter: it is to the courtesy of the very foremost of these that I owe the accompanying figure (fig. 50).

Passing to that contrast and complement of Nature at her greenest and wildest in the shady dell to the stately terraces, the floral magnificence of the palace garden, which should give this park such rare pre-eminence over the vaster pleasances of greater cities, our sunward parterres will be all the richer that their annual pageant has been restudied from the monographs and collections of snowdrops and crocus species, round to those of the chrysanthemum and Christmas rose. Such fresh presentment can but give new wealth and

ous—to show us the right direction to be moving in. This time the ideal is of utility, and at first even the homeliest. The newspapers have of late been popularising the fact that one of the simplest products of the industry of our island— the common field or garden potato—may be ennobled by skilful culture till it actually sells at £30 or so for a single "seed" tuber, three or four times its weight in golden coin. Here is but a vivid popular example of that practically limit-less development of our natural and our cultivated species which is one of the greatest arts corresponding to the biologic sciences. Here, in fact, is a development of industry, later than those of chemical or physical science, of mechanics or metallurgy, yet destined to no less predominance, no less transformation of civilisation in its approaching turn. It is surely none the less utilitarian because, instead of destroying Nature, as with too many recent progresses, it develops her. In our Glen (Chap. XI., figs. 57 and 60) we see more than enough of ashes where, till our own day, there was beauty;

it is time here fully to show the renewal of beauty from ashes, to utilise and to subordinate the powers of industry to furthering the progress of life. Nor does such gardening end with flowers or fruit, such breeding with doves or lambs, but begins anew to have human and social applications, to claim hearing from the philanthropist, the educationist, the reformer. These have too long been alternately traditional or utopian, formal or iconoclastic ; while, as all these are seen to fail, discouragement and reaction have naturally followed. But it is time again to be renewing the best of all these efforts upon their true foundation, their literally natural one—that of a better conditioning of the development of life. The social effort of the opening future will base its practice upon organic knowledge—indeed, of this our bacteriology and hygiene are the beginning—and more and more its social theory will be seen to rest upon vital experience. Hence the great historic teachers have ever sought to turn men again to nature, and have chosen more than their parables from the flowers ; while our modern systematisers of science, however contrasted in other respects, like Comte and Spencer themselves, are yet unanimously agreed in founding the social sciences upon the biological ones.

Putting this more definitely still, the opening generation, for whose sake it is that we are here planning and preparing, has now to correlate the respective arts associated with these sciences, and to apply them more and more boldly to all forms of life, to our own species as well, and this not only in field and forest, in park and garden, but in the renascence of cities, the advance of nations, the policy of races. This advance is being seen no longer merely in terms of the struggle for existence, but yet more in terms of the degree in which we may raise this struggle into the culture of existence. Despite the apparent predominance of a crude Darwinism the evolutionist thinker has now passed beyond this ; he begins to foresee the replacement of our current social policies and politics, with their crude naturalistic theory of mere intersocial and individual war, by a more complete, a more human view, in which hunger becomes increasingly curbed by love, competition transformed by mutual aid. To this theory a corresponding practice, a line of social action capable of no less definite statement, albeit a still too unfamiliar one—that of eugenics, of experimental evolution, organic and human, and this not only in environment but in breed and race. Towards these great social ends, then, of evolution, not only in nature but in human life, the garden is the school and even the laboratory.

Educationists are accustomed to think of physical science as practical, the biological sciences as mostly recreative. Be it so ; our park will be more recreative than ever, as our gardens become re-creative indeed.

CHAPTER X

SOUTHERN PARK AND "ZOO"

WE may now claim to have satisfied the demands of the wild garden with unusual fulness, so that it should not only be possible but increasingly attractive to walk up or down the glen, and still more to go round the park almost every day of the year, and not only welcome old friends but see something new. The claims of the simplest lover of nature, of the teacher, and of the trained naturalist, of the landscape lover and gardener, I trust have all been reasonably, even liberally, met.

The landscape aspect of the park to southward has now to be completed.

Entering once more from the North Gate, passing the orangery, lake, and cedar mount, we descend between formal garden and rock garden. Our main drive descends in a sweeping curve between the rock garden and formal garden, each best closed from the other by a yew hedge, which I should recommend to be grown up to the vastest scale and trimmed in the quaint fashion of our forefathers, although in some new combination of their traditional devices, such as that indicated in plan (fig. 137)—the simple sweep of curvature of the convex side being here contrasted with the strong light and shade of the concave side. This broad and simple treatment, besides its own impressiveness, is designed here to give the necessary repose and contrast with the rich detail of the rock garden and of the ample landscape into which it presently opens southward. Here we are, in fact, upon the present open space of the park, a very uninteresting one, comparing unfavourably with the much more picturesquely planted northern half.

To appreciate the treatment necessary here we may best follow the western drive downhill, now nearly upon the lines of the ancient roadway, to the new lodge and gateway shown to occupy the present break in the avenue of Lovers' Loan.

Looking upwards, the lack of interest is now more manifest, our photographs (figs. 52 and 53) showing that the problem of planting has never been grappled with at all, and that here much remains to be done. The utter monotony of this expanse is as yet little interfered with, even when the formal garden and rock garden occupy the more level space above, for they only come as far as the two lime-trees standing near the centre of the park.

A. "Campus."

Some large open space is here necessary, and this may best come on the eastern side of the park.

The necessity, too, of some such large open space is well brought out by the admirable function with which the park was opened last November. Though the tennis courts and formal garden now occupy the spot on which this took place the access to this south field on various sides is easier than ever, and the space suffices for a great concourse. This also explains the disposition of the large circular platform which the formal garden projects into this field, so that an open air meeting on a great scale, so far from being done away with, can be better held than ever.

Here, in fact, is the civic "campus," suitable for larger fêtes, ceremonies, or gatherings than can be accommodated in the Arena, to which I come later (Chap. XXVI.).

It is possible that some alteration of levelling may be desired on this field, but this would easily be managed, especially in view of the shrubberies at its foot, and thus would present no serious difficulties, practical or artistic.

We now come to the south-west portion of the park ; but first a consideration of the needed "Zoo."

B. Zoological Possibilities

Geologist and botanist will, I trust, admit that their requirements have been carefully considered, but they must not forget that a similar responsibility exists to the zoologist. With all this variety of wild and tame gardening cannot something similar be done for the even more fascinating interest of animal life, both wild and tame ? Since we have gardens of all kinds, practically even a Botanic Garden, why not also a yet more attractive "Zoo" ?

77

Let us begin with animal as with the vegetable life, taking nature as we find it, or rather as it should be, and may easily be.

Fish

First of all, then, even before the bird life of the glen and plantation, comes the fish life of the stream. Assuming the necessary purification, a great deal may be done to restock the stream, especially since its enlargement into more spacious pools—and the creation of the proposed lake—would secure this. It is no idea of mine, but

Aquarium, both fresh and salt, and to establish this on a moderate scale there is no serious difficulty. From great and costly undertakings like the Brighton Aquarium or the defunct one of Westminster we are apt to think of these as of great expense and difficulty. But the methods of aeration of tanks are now so simple and so perfect that there is not the slightest difficulty in keeping moderate-sized aquaria flourishing without change of water even for years. In a London museum with which I am well acquainted, with great and well-displayed zoological and anthropological collections, it is still the small aquaria which are obviously far most attractive to visitors old and young. Yet this aquarium has cost fewer hun-

FIGS. 52 and 53.—Panoramic view of Southward slope of Park below preceding sites of Rock Garden and Palace Garden. The standpoint is near present Lovers' Loan entrance, looking North-West to West Plantation, and thus showing from an important future entrance, as indicated on general plan, the vacancy and monotony which render this large and well-sunned portion of the Park so comparatively unattractive. The need and effect of the clumps shown on general plan in association with zoological paddocks will be realised from this panorama.

a practical and independent suggestion I owe to two of our leading Scottish fishery experts, that a small installation of hatching troughs might be set up, conveniently towards the head of the little valley or orchard neuk below the Manse ; and, even though it be long before the stream can be quite suitable for its natural trout, there are less exacting species. We may thus look forward to anglers, old and young.

Aquarium

Following upon the preceding there naturally arises for consideration the provision of an

dreds than the rest of the museum scores of thousands.

With this can easily be associated, if not a pond, at least small vivaria, with tortoises and harmless snakes, frogs, and their kindred ; also an insectarium, in which the marvellous transformations of insects can be easily shown and followed. The provision for schools of small aquaria, and the revival of the old fashion of keeping silkworms, caterpillars, and the like will again accompany the spreading love and educative use of natural history among the younger generation. This aquarium may also conveniently be associated with the Nature Palace, and is suggested in the plan and large perspective upon its eastern side.

Bird Life, Aviaries, Poultry-yard

The ornithologist may be safely left to work out detailed possibilities : it is enough to point out here that these are larger than is often realised. The existing rookery is a valuable asset to begin with ; while the stream and its expansions, besides the large and small lakes, would furnish the right habitats for an interesting collection of water birds, over and above the indispensable magnificence of swans. Islands, as shown in plans, being provided, the nesting and breeding of many of these species would be assured ; while even their feeding is in no small measure attended to by the visitors. Might it not also be possible to establish a small heronry, of which there is at least one magnificent example in the county, and doubtless more ? Returning to domesticated life, the quaintness of the stork, the grace of the crane, would not be forgotten. This brings us to the question of aviaries, again a delightful and inexpensive resource. Such ample space can be given as practically to take away all that impression of painful captivity which is given by many older collections, with their small aviaries, of too close confinement.

Song, plumage, habits of interest, would all guide the formation of such a small representative collection, which need not regret omitting the too melancholy captive eagle or the disgusting vulture ; the birds of prey may be for practical purposes sufficiently represented by owls, to whom partial captivity seems less oppressive.

Just as the Laird's Garden should be preserved as a centre of horticulture, so our Aviaries, indeed our whole animal collections as far as possible, would have a similarly practical and human interest—that is, they should primarily have regard to the creatures we call domesticated, but which have had so vast a share in civilising and domesticating man. Just as I press for a model kailyard, so I ask for a model poultry-yard, where any visitor could see and be advised as to the best sort of fowls for his or her purpose, just as for the best varieties of kail and peas at the garden. This need not be on any great scale ; in fact, it can be most useful upon a moderate one.

Keepers

Instead of the ordinary male keeper of a zoological garden, our whole aviary, wild and tame (and, indeed, why not the main zoological management ?), might well be in the hands of an intelligent and sympathetic woman naturalist and poultry expert. Such women have always existed in the past, and they are again educating themselves to technical and business efficiency. Examples and initiatives such as that of Lady Warwick need only be mentioned here, but should be fully inquired into, since full of suggestiveness to our present problems. In all schemes like the present a large place should be assigned to women, not only in connection with poultry rearing and with gardening, but with museum curating also, and, doubtless, with other activities as they arise. I have spoken already of Miss Jane Addams' Labour Museum at Chicago, and may also say that no London or other Natural Science Museum known to me has, in proportion at any rate to its size and resources, a more notable educational usefulness and influence than that of Whitechapel, directed by Miss Hall. Other analogous instances might be given.

Larger Domesticated Animals

In one main remaining aspect of the zoological collections, the place of women may be still more prominent. Theirs has always been a large share in the care of the minor domesticated animals ; and, best of all, theirs has been the great educational, moral, and social task of developing those childish instincts of sympathy with animal nature which it is one of the great defects of our present education so largely to stunt and starve. Speaking alike as a paterfamilias and as an educationist, I must strongly plead that to ensure for our children a loving intimacy during childhood, not only with dove and chick, with kitten, puppy, and rabbit, but with lamb and calf and all other accessible gentle young life, is to my mind quite one of the very deepest possibilities and duties of parental and of educational usefulness. Here is one of the truest ways in which we may protect ourselves from withering into that too common masculine world of mere administration and information instead of education proper. After a too long administrative and informational age we are beginning again to learn that true education starts with the culture of the feelings, and proceeds towards that of intellect ; not *vice versa*, as our current codes, primary, secondary or higher, have been too long supposing.

With such womanly influences at work the naturalist need no longer fear violence to either the natural or exotic life he would fain protect or naturalise. Just as the single typical school garden which I ask the Trust to begin with (Chap. VII. *E.*) will in time be found to arise at almost every school, of course in its due local form, so by-and-by live pets will claim their corner of the usually too desolate playgrounds. In all this twofold movement, that of natural history and home life together, our woman curator would be invaluable.

In summary then, I do not propose any extensive competition with the travelling menagerie, but rather to complement this, by encouraging—first, the wild life of our own region ; second, the associated forms most easily naturalised within it ;

and thirdly, above all, those domestic animals, not only on account of their material usefulness, but still more on account of their sympathetic and moralising value which is so urgent a present-day desideratum of our education. The Hooligan has been too long treated by punishment and repression : we begin to understand him as largely the product of our educational machine, the starveling of its stony bread. It is time, then, to give woman-gardener and naturalist a chance of fair competition with school-code maker and policeman.

Besides, then, that literal annual provision of lamb and calf for our children to which I look forward in the nearing future of education by experience and reality, why not also more permanent pets ? Why not only a dog or two, a whole family of Persian cats, but even a troop of donkeys, another of Shetland ponies ? Children would pay their half-pence for rides no less readily than for sweets ; so here, again, one of the greatest educational resources of humanity might be simply and inexpensively democratised, and the literally chivalrous thus begin again to replace the merely horsey. Since such children's steeds pay the private speculator at every summer watering-place, there is surely no risk of their not reasonably earning their living in this place of resort, open and active all the year round.

South-West Paddocks

The plan clearly shows the mode proposed for breaking up the vast western portion, upon which the impression of blankness principally depends. Here the plan must be its own explanation, since time has not permitted the preparation of perspectives.

It will be seen that this western space of about five acres is broken up into large and small paddocks, varying from 2 acres to 100 sq. yds. Here, then, are many spaces, applicable to one of the most desirable interests of this park—its " Zoo "—and with due accommodation suitable to different species, from the small deer park to the mere cage run sufficient for the smallest quadrupeds. A detailed study of the plan will show that this careful attention to the requirements of a Zoo has not prevented the composition of the tree clumps into large and unified masses, nor their disposition so as to give vistas, but has rather facilitated this. I submit, in short, that here, as elsewhere, the real requirements of useful work and general picturesqueness are not separate.

Following the contour lines, the outlet of the lake above gives us the opportunity of continuing it, not only down through the rock garden, but thence down along the edges of a number of the animal paddocks, where it can widen out into pools, sometimes cemented, so as to prevent

trampling and soiling of the edge while running in and out from the general courses of the little stream. This again gives opportunity of picturesque gardening with water-loving plants, and also of showing the animals in their fullest beauty of reflections and at convenient nearness to the spectator, so that this southmost walk would become a favourite haunt of that truest sportsman who has exchanged his gun for the camera.

The partial separation of this portion of the Zoo from the rest would not occasion any serious inconvenience in work, since, after all, the distance is so slight. Yet the picturesque connection can be kept up by occasionally turning sheep, or even cattle, into the main Campus, which I leave, for the present at least, untouched, save for beds of shrubs and flowers opposite the entrance, which are easily defended by a light, inconspicuous fence along the north side. Though a very few specimen trees, or even small clumps, would probably be desirable, these should be left till the main improvements are finished, and then put in as finishing touches with the most careful design.

For donkeys and shelties a moderate paddock space is provided in this south-west corner of the park. In others of these paddocks should be displayed some of the supremely beautiful members of the deer and antelope tribe. A picturesque rocky prominence would be constructed in one or two of the smaller paddocks, one for the display of antelope or deer and the other for a family of goats, which are thus seen to incomparably greater advantage than imprisoned upon the level. Even of the common sheep such a climbing rock gives an altogether new idea ; while to see the play of lambs in such conditions is one of the greatest seasonal delights possible to a healthily simple human life. Yet how few have ever seen a really first-rate tournament of lambs, much less provided them with the needful hillock for their game of " King of the Castle."

Exotic Animals

To these various types of sheep, goat, and oxen, deer and antelope, might well be added some strange intermediate forms, like the yak, or other species adapted to our climate. And beside the pony paddock, why not a zebra ? If these thrive and pair at Penicuik they might also flourish here.

We are thus coming to admit some of the animals of the menagerie and permanent " Zoo," and among these, no doubt, those quaintest of creatures, the kangaroos, would claim one of our paddocks. The great carnivora, the monkeys, and other thoroughly exotic types, I should personally prefer to leave to the menagerie ; but I recognise that many feel in these the very keenest interest, and that some moderate representation of such types may fairly be considered. In this connection I may especially refer to the example and advice of Professor Cunningham, now of Edinburgh, whose long experience and extraordinary success with the Dublin Zoological Garden has proved beyond question that the supposed delicacy in our climate of the monkey, lion, and the like has been due to the unwholesome heat and closeness of their customary housing in older establishments, and that thorough open-air treatment succeeds with them exactly as it does with ourselves. Of the great wild beasts, I should most recommend, as among the most attractive, a couple of brown bears, for whom pit and pool and bath can also be so easily provided, and for whom captivity becomes thus practically but a form of domestication. At once peculiarly quaint and human is the seal, still better the sea-lion, for whom a tank might easily be constructed, though it is fair to say his fishmonger's weekly bill might alarm the treasurer of the Trust. A Lion House with open-air cage with glass roof, combined with a refreshment-room building (an arrangement which the experience of Dublin and other gardens is found to justify) is shown upon the large perspective and main plan.

We have not yet made sufficient zoological use of our beautiful dell. Why not naturalise here a beaver family, and let them build a dam, with ample provision of tree-thinnings, with which the park improvements would supply them ? The success of the Marquis of Bute in Scotland, and of Sir Edward Loder and others in the South, shows that there is no insuperable difficulty ; while in the stream below the manse, a little above the proposed lake, their dam would be most conveniently situated. In *Country Life*, for 29th December 1900, will be found an excellent plan and process-engraving of the beaver dam of Leonardslee.

An otter would be dangerous to our struggling fish population, yet he might easily be confined by a low, yet unclimbable, wire fence to a small portion of the stream. A fox and a badger might each have his lair at some point of the long bank of the stream ; these animals would not be seen often, yet the early photographer would catch them. Even a wild boar and sow might rear a family in similar comparative freedom ; and here again a pair of goats might have their scrambling place. Overhead too among the trees should range a family of squirrels, their alleged harmfulness to specimen trees here mattering little among our irregular ones, and in any case being readily abated by more generous food.

C. Further possibilities of "Zoo"

So far, then, our general project. It is capable of further elaboration and of much detailed improvement, but I trust is defensible in the main.

Vital to its character is the departure, more thorough than is possible in the collections of great cities, from the idea of a menagerie of strange creatures, a wild beast show of prisoners in cages. In our Zoological Gardens we are apt to miss that sympathetic contact with life, both natural and domesticated, which the botanist and the gardener respectively express, and the problem of pioneering initiative in this matter, of real progress in Zoological Gardens, is thus to increase, not the quantity of captive species, but the quality of our appreciative relations to the wild, and of our companionship with the tame ones. Criticism will no doubt suggest improvements upon my proposals for the development of wild life in the glen, and the utilisation of the lake and the park paddocks ; we should thus reach the most perfect attainable expression of the variety of animal life in beautiful natural environment both of glen and meadow. Thus our "Zoo" affords an opportunity of great enhancement of our naturalistic gardening.

Nor is the other aspect less important in its opportunities—starting anew with the grass paddocks and such space as may be available at the glebe, our complementary presentment of animal life, not simply as wild from the hunter's point of view, but as tame from the shepherd's and peasant's, is surely no less important, though the social and scientific point of view is a changed one. From the restoration of wild nature at home, or the presentment of it abroad, we pass to the association of animals with man in the history of civilisation, with its gentler but surely not less needed appeal to the collaboration of woman and educationalist. Here again there is room, and even more than before, for constructive criticism, the more since, while many precedents exist for keeping animals in comparatively natural conditions, I know of no attempt such as I have pleaded for, that of selecting, arranging, and evolving the everyday farmyard into a recapitulation of the relation of man to his domesticated animals throughout the rise of civilisation, and of complementing this by arranging as far as may be its corresponding recapitulation in the individual experience of our children, not only by awakening their curiosity, even their admiration, of wild nature, but their sympathies, their love.

The great recreative value of a zoological garden is due to its reawakening the primitive interests in us all, and so of bringing us back to the child level, free for the time of our maturer thoughts and cares.

But can we, or at least our children, do this in some yet more thorough way ? That surely would be the ideal Zoo, in which not only should the animals be happily free or happily tame, but in which we ourselves should be again in nature, free in greenwood or forest belt or grassy glade, like Adam watching and naming the creatures, or, at any rate, like Mowgli in his jungle. Again, and more than this, we should again be taming and civilising them, feeling their gentle influences in return. And though in town and chamber we may forget all this, in summer holiday at least we remember, and not only delight our children and educate them beyond the world of books but renew for ourselves the past year's outworn activities for the next by participation at some point with their primitive life, now in sport or in the woods, on the pastoral hillside, or again at the farm. To supply something of these elements is thus the highest problem of our Zoo ; and its adequate solution would be a real piece of pioneering alike in park development, in recreation, and in education. Here at least are beginnings ; on the more civilised side with our woman-keeper with her chickens, her calf and lamb, her ponies and the rest. But for the more primitive side, the elemental return to nature, something more is required, and for this we must find the means of return to nature more fully—that is, recalling and recapitulating our own past—in plainer phrase, of putting man into our menagerie. This, too, we see sometimes done in great exhibitions and the like, but too much in its inferior aspect, of strange captives to be gazed at behind their bars. But the child is wiser ; he does not want to *see* the savage merely, but to be the savage ; he does not

play with Crusoe, he is Robinson himself upon his isle. So the final achievement in Zoo planning would be to devise the ways and means of this return for our children, and in spirit at least, with them, for ourselves. Bringing this idea now to practice, we need the primitive cave, the lair, the log-hut, the tree-house, and all the rest, so reconstructing not only Robinson's home and look-out, or Mowgli's lurking-place, but the primitive types of human dwelling-place throughout the ages. Where is such a primitive village possible ? There is the very place for it on the west bank of the proposed East Lake, the rising wooded margin of figs. 16 or 17.

Here one has not only the glen above with its wild life, the lake with its birds and fish, but the Zoological Gardens, east and west, on either hand. In such an environment who would not be more of a naturalist, more of a Thoreau, more of a primitive, more of a child ? And would not this be recreation indeed, this going back to nature, this re-creating of the elemental past, this re-creation also of the essential phases of civilisation anew ?

Here, then, we pass fully from zoology into archæology and anthropology, and from naturalistic into social education. While the discussion of zoological possibilities thus closes, the other needs for its treatment a fresh chapter (XVII.).

FIG. 54.—Panoramic view of West side of St Margaret's Glen above Park—the North-West corner of latter to South (left hand) in distance. The backs of the houses of Chalmers Street run along the top of the high west bank. On right—to North—is lower portion of grounds of Wooers' Alley.

C. STREAM AND GLEN

CHAPTER XI

STREAM PURIFICATION AND ITS RESULTS

It will be remembered that the initial park improvement of our approach was of the widened stream (Chap. I., figs. 14 to 19); but that this was seen to be impracticable—indeed, all Glen improvement impossible—without the purification of its central essential element, now so deplorably contaminated, the once pure and beautiful hill stream. To treat this, then, we must overleap our park walls and follow it, if need be, to its source. This clear, we can then, and only then, speak of improving the Glen at all. But as we have already seen that at least half the value of a park lies in its approaches, here is, of course, the main, the natural approach; more than ever we must keep our eyes about us for such collateral and convergent improvement as its banks may afford, now in pleasant nook or in spot of noble associations; or again, in larger open spaces of rest or play, the more since these are necessarily connected with our main park by the finest of natural parkways, the varied course of the stream itself, with its incessantly changing landscapes. Thus, then, we are not leaving our Park, but naturally continuing it along with us upstream, redressing its present sadly depreciated value, and enhancing this with each practicable extension. We are not expending our wealth, therefore, but investing it in real estate. and this in the truest increase of beauty and use, of accessibility and variety, of recreation and health to the generations of the future. Here it is again possible, and surely, if anywhere, it is desirable, to be pioneering ahead of the wants of those to whom the present modest limits of our existing Park walls may seem sufficient, or who may be satisfied with this present improvement of its own quarter of the city without similar concern for the larger quarters to northward.

A. Parks and Playing Fields

On our first impression Dunfermline may well seem amply supplied with public parks, and this even as regards considerable future extension of population. Yet if we look again from the standpoint of playing-fields, available especially for the games of boys and young men—a matter obviously not only of recreative interest but of the most definite hygienic importance, of economical significance also to the working power of the population, indispensable too as a safety-valve for energies which otherwise find less desirable channels—we see that Dunfermline as yet has practically hardly any park at all. For neither the public park to the east nor this new park to the west possesses any adequate level area available for games. To level such spaces would, moreover, cost a great deal, and would seriously deteriorate the new park for other purposes.

The ambiguous term of park may, indeed, for the moment be usefully abandoned. We have pleasure grounds of the rarest extent and beauty, but these are really leisure grounds, not playing-fields, and they should be as far as possible preserved for their natural uses. Their appeal is to childhood, to maturity, to age; and such level ground as they possess should be preserved for the gentle games and recreative activities of the girls and the large working-woman population of the city, and practically not offered to the young

83

men at all, so far as football or cricket are concerned.

Even from the point of view of the present city, much more from that of an expanding one, this larger park problem must be speedily faced.

Before doing this let us notice the actual resources, not of the greatest towns but of the

At Perth the two Inches, both quite level, make up an area of fully 175 acres, and at Stirling the park area is just under 200. In this way it will be seen that Dunfermline, despite its peculiar advantages, is still far from being abreast of other towns as regards parks, much less ahead, as its ideal and its public responsibilities henceforth demand.

FIG. 55.—View of West side of Valley below (South of) St Margaret's Cave. Suggested improvement of back terrace of Chalmers Street U.F. Church as new access from Park quarter to Cave. Here a fresh notation is employed which may need explanation. Instead of having my sketch worked into process block by process engraver, with corrections, retouchings, and inevitable consequent imperfections, despite apparent finish, I have here simply sketched upon the photograph direct, as with chalk upon a blackboard, without any retouching at all ; so that while photographic verisimilitude is here abandoned, the comparison with plan is clearer than before, and criticism of the suggested effects more easy.

actual neighbouring burghs, distinguishing in these the level ground from the braes when these are present. Thus in Kirkcaldy the Beveridge Park measures 95 acres, of which the greater amount is level enough for games. A view of this park on a Saturday afternoon or summer evening is most instructive, for while the braes have only an occasional solitary pedestrian or couple the level fields are alive with players many hundreds strong. In short, level ground is for athletic purposes alone of real use, greatly though undulating and glen scenery have the advantage as regards beauty.

Passing to St Andrews we find the links amounting to nearly 300 acres, with sea-shore walks in both directions practically without end.

Do I then, in view of this great public acquisition so recently made, venture to propose yet further extension, with corresponding responsibilities, financial and other, to the Trust ? Frankly, Yes. I see no escape from this. I cannot hesitate to urge this in two directions, both north and south of the present new park. Let us begin northward, with the general view of St Margaret's Glen (fig. 54). In the first place, I strongly urge the acquisition of a path, as far as possible double, on each side of the stream above Bridge Street—indeed, this as far as possible along its tributaries ; also so supplying gradually improving accesses to the district of Baldridge Burn, as well as Broomhead and beyond. I plead for the acquisition also, as opportunity may offer, of ground on either side of this proposed path. This would furnish, here it may be only space for a seat surrounded by a few trees, or there for a drinking fountain or the like. Again, a bank may be planted, or a level site reserved from building for a bowling green for men, or a tennis court or croquet lawn for girls. At some other point a small field may be reserved for school or occasional music, and so on, to form the habit of coming out of doors a little more largely for or with her little ones, and could bring her needle-work or knitting in her hand, yet with the cer-tainty of easily returning without fatigue to prepare the midday or evening meal, the gain of bodily health and mental serenity would be great

FIG. 56. (Rough Pen-and-Ink Sketch.)—This may be taken together with preceding, as continuous to Eastward (the Church Terrace sloping due East in fig. 55 being seen in Northward perspective on the left side of fig. 56). To the right of the stream and in the distance lies the Saint's Cave, environed by weedy and overgrown trees, mostly poplars. The proposed bridge is indicated.

for allotment gardens, while a larger field should now and then be obtained for recreative purposes for the games requiring ampler ground. These are not parks, however, of any great acreage. The multiplication of a large series of open spaces, how-ever small, will be increasingly found to be of greater hygienic value to populations than is the modern system of large parks at comparatively great distances. These the bulk of the population practically reaches only on summer evenings or on Saturday afternoons ; whereas, to raise the general standard of health, we need many more open spaces easily accessible to children and within easy hail of home. Such spaces, too, would be of immense value in tempting out the working mother and elder sisters with the smaller children, and the provision on such spaces of roofed yet open-air shelters, with comfortable seats, would be found of immense value in such ways. If the housewife could be induced by judicious example,

and the home happiness notably increased ; the proportion of illness diminished also, even the actual life expectation appreciably improved. Not even all medical men adequately realise, much less the general public, or the (too exclusively mascu-line) municipal and governing bodies, how very large a proportion of the defective elements in our city life, particularly in Scotland, is due to the too great confinement of mother and bairns within the narrow limits of what is actually or practically a one-roomed home, with its deteriorated air and its deficient sunlight and beauty, even where cleanliness and order are maintained, and much more when these, through overcrowding or the like, become deficient.

B. St Margaret's Cave

I submit next that besides the double path in St Margaret's Glen above Bridge Street the public property around Queen Margaret's Cave should be improved as one of these open spaces. In view of the great expense involved I do not recommend, in our time at least, the acquisition and demolition of any buildings on the north side of Bridge Street or even of Chalmers Street or Bruce Street. If, as I hope, the long-dreamed-of new bridge be some day thrown across the valley, continuing Pittencrieff Street to Carnegie Street, and so opening up that whole quarter of the town to new development, accesses at each end for descent to the glen would naturally be provided. One of these would be very much upon the lines of the existing right-of-way, the brae on which the children are climbing in my photograph (fig. 58). It is, of course, unfortunate that a new tenement should have been erected facing Pittencrieff Street, right in the way of this needed bridge, but upon so great a public improvement the additional expense of removing this would not be too serious.

For the present, then, it would be sufficient to obtain such improved accesses to St Margaret's Cave and Glen as follows :—That the Trust should acquire from the Chalmers Street United Free Church an access, as shown (fig. 55), to their back green, sloping down to the stream below ; that this should be terraced much as is the existing garden immediately to the south ; and that thus by sloping paths and steps one should descend to the stream, which should be crossed by a bridge, either communicating with the ground of St Margaret's Cave already in possession of the city, or better as follows.

I further urge that a similar application be made by the Trust to the Free Church opposite, and that a path be made downward from Bruce Street through their back ground to the stream, and that this new bridge at the bottom be made between these two church gardens (fig. 56), with path to Cave.

The result of this simple and comparatively inexpensive improvement would be that the public would have a new and attractive access from both sides to one of the most interesting and historic spots within the city, one at present practically useless, since its present approach is not only obscure, but squalid and repellent.

In this way, too, we should have literally united churches brought together with that spot of early traditions in which all the various denominations feel a common interest. On the one side of the small new bridge required I would, therefore, place a carved panel, bearing on one side the emblem of the Free Church, on the other that of the United Presbyterian, and in the middle their present conjoint symbol. On the north side, towards St Margaret's Cave, might be placed her own symbol, or say marguerite and crown, with some device commemorative of the Celtic Church on the one side and of the later Abbey on the other.

May I further venture to suggest that the congregations concerned might give (as other riparian proprietors have already expressed their willingness to do) this access to the public through the Trust without charge ? They would themselves be sufficiently gainers by the improvement of their ground and accesses and by the pleasing and restful transformation of what is at present useless or unsightly. The incentive to public spirit would also be of general value beyond the congregations concerned, and might lead to other improvements in connection with Church Buildings ground throughout the town, such as will readily suggest themselves, though beyond my limits here.

The four illustrations (figs. 57 to 60 on same page), all taken within a few paces of each other on the west bank opposite the cave, will here interest the reader. That supply of dust to children's lungs, by which our present urban enfeeblement would alone be thoroughly ensured, will be noted on the left above ; while of the stream treatment the two stages of development photographed in successive weeks, in the lower figures, surely need no comment.

C. St Margaret's Garden

Passing now northward of the cave we note how the tall trees of this ground have completely spoiled the garden adjacent, which now lies waste. This might surely be easily acquired, and should be planted with elders and other shade-loving shrubs, thus deepening yet further the quietness and coolness of the region round the cave. This brings us to the square-walled ruin, that of an old weaving factory, now long disused and roofless, with a narrow lane to the south and some tumble-down outbuildings to the east. Surely this might be acquired for little or nothing. What should be done with it ?

I urge the retention of this ruin practically as it stands and its treatment as follows :—The walls to be pointed with cement, the tops especially cemented so as to prevent further dilapidation. Ivy then should be planted on the outsides of this. The narrow approach might easily be widened, of course by demolishing the wall on its south. Upon entering now by the existing doorway a spectacle of desolation presents itself, yet here are elements of great picturesqueness and suitability when transformed as indicated in plan. The walls upon the interior show the recesses of windows now walled up, and these might easily be adapted to lodge wall plants—a method of great beauty occasionally employed by old-world gardeners no less than by modern ones, witness Edzell Castle near Brechin.

The interior space might easily be brought into cultivation as a flower garden, and this I propose to treat in special commemoration of our local saint, whose ascetic cave of retirement and medita-

FIG. 57.—Example of everyday disposal of ashes upon bank of stream opposite St Margaret's Cave.

FIG. 58.—Immediately adjacent public path to Cave—an old right-of-way in daily use by children, as their only access to stream.   Till lately this was practically the only open access to glen, and, in fact, all the public park or lung of this quarter of the town.   Seat at top.

FIG. 59.—Example of a sewer descending from street above, opposite Cave; nominally leading to sewer along course of stream, but really leaking into it.

FIG. 60.—Same drain photographed within a fortnight later.

tion will have its effect and interest greatly enhanced by thus providing it with a natural complement, a little cloister-like garden paradise.
Upon the inside of the southern wall ivies might
again be grown, with a border of shade-enduring
herbaceous plants like white spiræas, etc. Continuing this bed all round next the wall, let us lay
down within this a path of gravel, or, perhaps still
better, pavement, of say 4 ft. 6 in. broad, and within
this lay down a square lawn. Cut out four large
corner beds in this, and in the middle place such
a very simple sun-dial as might have been in use
in her time, or, still better, a small fountain. Better
still, a statue of the saint herself ; for here beside
her cave, rather than in any more conspicuous
place, should be the monument of this woman
whose spiritual forces were here so constantly
recruited, and who has left so deep a mark upon
our city and country. The treatment of the
garden might readily be such as to carry out the
sentiment appropriate to the place and purpose.
White flowers should here largely predominate,
from snowdrops round the year to lilies, and thence
to Christmas roses, with special predominance of
the white marguerites which especially commemorate her, and of which a selection can easily
be made flowering through the summer into
autumn. Upon the south side of the north wall,
which gets ample sunshine and yet perfect shelter,
a wealth of white damask roses might be grown,
not the last florist's varieties, but such old-fashioned
roses as she might have grown herself.

Violets, dames' violets, and other flowers of
modesty and fragrance, fragrant herbs too, like
rosemary, lavender, and thyme, would naturally
complete this little garden and give it some notes
of variety ; and thus the sentiment of the place,
already developed by its union with the terraced
gardens of the two churches, would find its natural
completion and climax.

Thus at peculiarly little expense for this whole
improvement a spot of interest equal to any
element of the park, and in its way unique, would
be easily secured.

This whole garden should now be further
sheltered and concealed by planting elder-trees to
east and north ; and thus a new wealth of flower
would appear above its walls, with complete
isolation from being overlooked by the rest
of the glen. The seats of this garden would
furnish places of rest and meditation to which
many a busy person might steal away for a few
minutes from any part of the surrounding town.

If the old garden to eastward were acquired, its
ancient wall facing southward would again make
an excellent support for roses, which should here
be of the brightest and richest variety, and with
a border in front of herbaceous flowers of every
colour, so as to give the most vivid possible
contrast to the quieter beauty of the saint's garden
within and to its own deeply-shaded southern side.

D. The Toom

Leaving now this whole St Margaret's shrine behind us we come out to one of the everyday realities
of the modern industrial town, in the vast double
" toom " (fig. 61) of miscellaneous abomination
and rubbish which is at present, perhaps, the most
distressing and discreditable feature of the whole
treatment of this unhappy valley, of which till our
own day the beauty remained undestroyed. This
is, of course, only an extreme type of the deplor-
able treatment of the stream and valley by its inhabitants, and this from practically the first houses
upon its course to the last, with too few exceptions.
It is hence most urgent that, if our stream improvements are to have any reality at all, this entire
spot should be acquired and dealt with. I am
aware that this toom meets a real need as a place
for the disposal of earth from foundations, etc.,
and that its removal will impose upon all future
building operations in this neighbourhood a certain
appreciable expense for carting rubbish elsewhere.
But there is no spot in the whole city, so far as I
can see, in which this mischief could have been more
disastrous, or of which the improvement would
even now yield a greater return of beauty. For
the mischief though great has not gone so far as to
be irreparable. These spoiled banks can still be
planted, and with only a little modification can be
made to return to the wooded aspect natural to the
dell ; a literal " Hawthornden " thus replacing
the present hideous sore upon the amenity of the
city. Upon the level top of this toom, which
commands a wide and beautiful view (see photographic panorama, fig. 54), seats should be placed,
and surrounding these a group of tall-growing
trees, conveniently the common maple (Scots
" plane "), might be planted. Here, in fact, is one
of those spaces opening off the neighbouring streets
for which I have previously been pleading.

There is also here the distinct vestige of a
little lateral stream, and this might still in some
measure be rescued and improved, at least towards
its fall into the main burn, where it would be
crossed by a simple rustic bridge.

E. Improvements Up Stream

Continuing up stream our prospective path
leads us along the foot of different gardens to the
property of Wooers' Alley. This, I understand,
can be acquired on reasonable terms, and I unhesitatingly urge this acquisition. Its beautiful
terraces and paths might easily be improved still
further, and to this trifling acreage the artistic
value of quite an additional little park be thus
given. At the highest point also one or two
cottages might be erected, or still better, I should
say a tenement block of dwellings, with open
galleries, or at least ample oriels and fairly high-

pitched roofs, so as to give a picturesque finish to this otherwise at present rather confused corner. Around such a higher mass the existing buildings would then group quite naturally and picturesquely.

Upon the opposite side I have ventured to converse with two neighbouring proprietors. The one assures me that, while he has other interests to consult, the Trust may depend upon his cordial good offices with his fellow-proprietors. The

something of a boulevard effect. Under the arches might be arranged an open-air gymnasium (indeed, why not several of these, each allotted to its appropriate age and strength?). Swings for children, a flying-stride even, with parallel bars, horizontal bar, and the like, cost but little, and are unfailing sources of pleasure and healthful recreation; while a few seats at the margin would be welcome, not only to the tired gymnasts but to the lookers-on. The existing viaduct is shown in fig. 62, and the

FIG. 61.—"Toom" constituting main modern feature of East side of Valley immediately North of St Margaret's Cave. Its interest as an open space to adjacent quarter of town is indicated by preceding view (fig. 54) taken from it. After due grading, careful planting would readily conceal rubbish.

next proprietor at once authorises me to inform the Trust of his cordial willingness to give off such a path as is desirable along the whole bottom of his property, simply upon the natural condition of the Trust constructing its path with such retaining wall as may be needed to keep his garden above from sliding off into the stream, and to protect him from uninvited visitors.

Leaving Wooers' Alley we cross the street at Buffie's Brae, and note opposite the fine railway viaduct, with the underlying ground happily already the property of the city. This ground I urge should be partly employed for widening the street, with trees planted so as to give at least

improvement here so easily possible indicated in the following fig. 63.

This brings us next to the Harrie Brae Dyeworks and their outlying ground, a region of many picturesque elements even as it stands, and of great possibilities. I must again strongly urge the acquisition of this property, alike as a great element of this reformed valley region, as a lung to this whole neighbourhood, and, of course, also as a means of removing the abominable pollution which constantly surprises the visitor to Pittencrieff Park below—the stream suddenly coming down changed from its usual leaden hue to every objectionable shade of blue, red, or green. Be it clearly noted that I in no wise suggest this as a mere unremunerative outlay to the Trust. My treatment (Chap. XVIII.) of the mills below the abbey and palace will sufficiently show that, so far from having any objection to industrial buildings, I accept and even welcome their presence, and only press their employment in ways consistent with the ordinary claims of hygiene and public beauty. With the buildings (fig. 64) I have practically no fault to find, though if any funds be available for their improvement I should readily undertake

This now leads us to the ground of and street of Low Beveridgewell (fig. 66). While the tributary stream of Baldridge Burn runs in from eastward, laden, alas! with every pollution, bottomed with broken crockery and ashes, and interrupted by tin pails, old linoleum, and every other evidence of lapsed civilisation, here the main stream is covered in altogether and runs through a culvert. It is hard to say which is more to be pitied, the frank open-air pollution by the private citizens, or the covered-

Fig. 62.—Existing Railway Viaduct, etc.

Fig. 63.—The same view, improved by planting and laying out this ground.

to increase their picturesqueness, as I trust my designs do for the mills of Monastery Street; nor need the various spots of building ground which this property might yield a speculative proprietor be neglected by the Trust. I would recommend their building on them much as he would do, yet get increased picturesqueness with it all.

See photograph (fig. 65) of the three cottages to the east of these dye-works. There is no domestic group more picturesque in Dunfermline, yet there is nothing to which any architectural expense or ornament has been added.

in sewer treatment which we owe to municipal art. Little matter if, as is obviously of elementary necessity, we correct both. Up Baldridge Burn our suggested path can still go on, on one side at least—that of the iron works—and farther up perhaps on both again. The cleansing of the stream here as elsewhere is of no great difficulty or expense, since the removed rubbish need not even be carted away, but can be decently buried in deep holes dug temporarily for the purpose along the bank. While the stream is so utterly dirty nobody need have the smallest compunction about adding more dirt ; but, per contra, let the Trust cleanse the stream, in due co-operation, no doubt, with urban and local authorities, and thereafter the better citizens at least would think twice before they would again do anything to pollute it. Upon the occasional offender the continual passers along the proposed path would have a certain moral effect, while even the hardened offender might be readily dealt with without legal or police interference by the simple yet pungent expedient of photographing her or him in the act (see my preceding fig. 58). The polite communication of a copy of such a photograph by the secretary of the Trust to its subject would generally be sufficient ; if not, more publicity might be readily given.

Coming now to the main stream in the culvert, I advise that this be reopened and the stream conducted no longer in the natural course, which is filled up for good, but along a regular and formal basin. The street is here broad enough to give a sufficient boulevard, and with this should be undertaken the improvement of the long-neglected-looking bank, which, I understand, has been actually offered by the proprietor to the city on condition of some such general improvement. I understand that the expense at the time deterred the city from undertaking this, but the Burgh Engineer's plans exist, and might be readily revived—it may be adjusted to the larger scheme I am now advocating. The Trust need not, of course, relieve the city of the whole expense. I am far from suggesting any violation of its fundamental instruction in the owner's letter ; but only that in view of the resultant public space at top as well as bottom the Trust might fairly undertake that difference of outlay over and above that of ordinary street improvement, which deterred the city on a former occasion. The opportunity here presents itself of a fine piece of formal boulevard, a sheltered yet sunny promenade also. On top of the bank a small open-air gymnasium, a band stand, or both, might also be erected with great advantage to the neighbourhood. For the present, however, I leave my photograph (fig. 66) of the existing desolation to

speak for itself, and withhold its natural companion—that of the scene transformed.

This now brings us to the estate of Broomhead, of which we may especially note its 12 acres to south of the stream, its acre or so occupied by stream and banks. The 4 acres of gardens and grounds around the mansion-house, and the large field behind, up to the coal-pit, may for the time

FIG. 64.—Old Dye-work and Mills on stream.

be left out of consideration, though any building scheme in which the Trust may engage would naturally look at these among other sites. Of these 12 comparatively level acres of Broomhead, with at least one side of the stream, if possible both, I strongly urge, however, if not the immediate acquisition, at any rate the obtaining of an option upon these, so as to prevent their passing into the hands of the speculative builder and becoming irrevocably lost to the Trust. For here, nearer the centre of working population than the

FIG. 65.—Old cottages East of Dye-works.

FIG. 66.—Existing state of Low Beveridgewell, showing possibility of releasing stream from culvert, laying out boulevard, planting the earthen bank, and placing bandstand seats or open Gymnasium above. Broomhead Park is seen in distance.

FIG. 67.—View up Mill Lade near its origin.

FIG. 68.—Bank with Scots pines opposite Golf-course. Here the stream is shown widened out. The margin would next be made less tame by a little planting, etc.

Pittencrieff Park or the Public Park, is one of those open spaces and playing-fields of which we have seen the necessity if Dunfermline is to even approach the standard of its smaller and neighbouring cities. To mitigate the expense of this ground a certain number of villas might be feued off the Wellwood Road to eastward, and also one or two more, or even a block or two of tenements erected on the level ground at the south-west. though I must admit the economy of such curtailment is open to question.

Leaving Broomhead, crossing the Wellwood Road, and continuing up stream, we note by the roadside a tiny wooded glade, with small tributary streamlet, which might be made a picturesque feature upon our double path. On the north side we come to the golf links, along the foot of which our path should surely easily be secured ; while on the south we have the bleaching-works of Messrs Marshall. These gentlemen allow me to report that they will be happy to grant the Trust the needed ground for the proposed path along their feu from just above their water tank to their upper limit, a distance of say 150 yards. Here, then, we emerge once more upon the farm of Headwell, with its fine avenue leading eastwards to the Townhill Road, an avenue which it is earnestly to be hoped may be long preserved and maintained. The care of all such spots would naturally become one of those public interests which might conveniently be undertaken by that citizens' union towards which I offer suggestions (Chap. XXXIII.).

Keeping, however, to the stream, or rather striking up to the lade which runs through the town, and rejoins the main stream in the glen below the Abbey Mills, we find a charming picture upon its banks (fig. 67). Soon, alas! we come to the high barbed fences and notices commonly suggesting an ancient but disputed right-of-way, the natural path from the city up to the Town Loch. Here, too, are signs of an ancient mill-dam, which may be at any future time restored into a lakelet. From this runs to Townhill a fine avenue, and beyond this the picturesque and rocky bank, with its Scots pines, the first example of this invaluable landscape element we have yet come to (fig. 68). This little portion of the valley in itself contains more elements of beauty, not to speak of possibility, than many a city park in a large town, and I suggest the desirability of acquiring this whole access. To be able to rest or picnic among these Scots firs would be a privilege many would appreciate.

Continuing our regional survey beyond this point, we soon come to a union of streams. Choosing first the smaller, that towards the village of Wellwood, we see the water running in apparently pure. We ascend the stream through pleasant banks, which again with a little planting of hawthorns and roses would beautifully continue our

path, now, of course, a single one, without any diminution of land to the fields above. We are soon struck by an unmistakable presence of sewage fungus in the water, which thickens and thickens as we approach the village, until at length it fills the stream. This obvious abomination is naturally not to be tolerated even under the existing low state of public opinion, and the construction of a sewage tank for this village is clearly a matter for its local authority. The borough of Dunfermline is certainly justified in asking, and I am assured possesses all the legal power for enforcing, some such effective measure of purification from the county. I trust that the County will compensate itself and relieve any natural feelings towards such an attack, and further aid the Trust, by active reprisals upon the City, at the other and lower end of the town, where it receives the burn a thousandfold worse polluted than here, where it is the unmistakable offender.

Returning now once more to the main stream we may follow this up to the Town Loch itself. That this should be, on amicable arrangement with the proprietor, improved by planting, and that paths and seats be set round it, surely should not be impossible. For here, despite a considerable length of country walk from the main body of Dunfermline, we again re-enter its municipal limits at Townhill, which though somewhat outlying, is surely entitled to receive some attention and improvement on the part of the Trust. In conjunction with the neglected wood to eastward, also a city property, the banks of this loch should, in fact, afford the public Park of this quarter, and the citizens of Townhill should be able to walk up and down to town along this path or by either of the two lateral avenues which we have seen communicating with it. At various points also along the direct road from Townhill to the city—that is, practically to the old Public Park itself—improvement by tree planting wherever possible might go on, and we should, therefore, have almost belted the city. In fact, when we remember how easy it would be still to restore something of the old avenues of Brucefield south of the Public Park, and with comparatively little alteration to connect these with the proposed Nethertown Boulevard and Pittencrieff Park, we have thus a scarcely broken park girdle around the city. I press this class of improvement above and beyond all the dainty devices which suggest themselves for the interior of the park itself. These can be done at any time ; whereas this proposed improvement must be grappled with speedily before it is too late. If there is to be any reality in our return to nature, in our endeavour to brighten the lives and improve the health of our working citizens, it is emphatically to be done, not first by perfecting the great public parks, which are after all mainly accessible to the leisured classes during the greater portion of the working week, but by dotting the whole of the city in a way I have only ventured to suggest along this fringe with such small open spaces, yet also connecting these, as far as may be by roads and paths which may be constantly taken by the pedestrian on his way to or from work, or for the few minutes' breathing space available at meal hours, and by women and children at any time. The American city, hitherto even more oblivious than our own of the beauty of nature and the worker's access to it, has now with American thoroughness begun to look at this question in this comprehensive way and to see that " Parkways " are almost more important than parks themselves. And if we are really determined, at any point whatever, to faithfully and boldly carry

wards also. While the northward extension is amply justified by the fact that the existing factories and their working population are in this quarter, and will naturally continue to develop along the existing railway lines, so involving the utilisation of the healthy and thoroughly suitable southward slopes of Townhill, etc., the great body of increase to population is still expected southwards. Railway communication also will develop here, and from Pittencrieff Park one readily foresees a natural line of development of industrial buildings along the line of the Charlestown railway also, of which the siding is already plain in view from the Park. Let us now photograph this view—*i.e* from the gas-works on the east to the siding on the west—and proceed to fill up the picture (fig. 69) with the natural and

FIG. 69.—View looking South-East from near foot of proposed Yew Drive—*i.e.* near top of lower portion of Pittencrieff Park, showing existing Gas-works and chimney to left, and beyond these to the right the probable industrial development along the line of the Charleston-Kincardine Railway, to be expected with the expansion of the city.

out the instructions of our donor's letter and to attempt a policy of municipal pioneering in the interests of the people I submit that this chapter of my report is the fundamental one, since it is the one yielding the most definite returns to the health and happiness of the citizen and the most useful and urgently needed example to the towns and cities of the kingdom. For it is not enough to build new garden cities ; we must face the far more difficult task of making garden cities of our existing old ones.

Yet at Townhill the opportunities are almost unique in Britain, since the city is already its own landlord, albeit hitherto very far from a model one. Why not a model one henceforward ?

F. Park Extension Southwards

Will even this proposed fairly comprehensive belt of open spaces northwards suffice ? Certainly not without some corresponding extension south-

normal developments which must be expected, say on a moderate allowance a dozen good large industrial buildings of various kinds, with not less, therefore, than eight or ten average chimney stalks all belching away. Even the most ardent enthusiast of Dunfermline progress will surely feel some regret at the march of this right up to the Lovers' Loan at the foot of the park ; while the permanent and enduring criticism of the present Trust by the future generations, for whom the park will thus have been practically and increasingly destroyed, may be imagined without attempt at further argument here. Towards warding off this real and imminent danger—this creation of an industrial quarter where none should be, the filling up of the present beautiful valley with a vast huddle of factories and tenements corresponding to, at best, the district of Dalry now running west along the corresponding valley from Edinburgh—what is to be done ?

I see nothing for it here but to face the acquisition, on terms as moderate as may be, of as much as possible of this level area at the foot of the park. Here are the playing-fields required by the vigorous youth of the town. Their acquisition would render the Lovers' Loan practically an avenue within the park, and would guarantee its permanent amenity from destruction. I recommend, indeed, the acquisition of the park south of the railway as well as this one north of it. There are already cricket fields in this direction ; while the racecourse to the west also shows the need and use of open level ground in this quarter. Here, too, among these fields is the natural site (indeed the drained one) of a lake, larger than those possible within park limits, and of the utmost beauty to the landscape, the utmost recreative value also, not only for winter skating, but in summer for boats and for bathing. Here is one of the best of open-air recreations not elsewhere practicable in Dunfermline, and for which the Carnegie Baths would be the school. To combine the whole of this large acreage into one noble park is really the policy which I submit future generations would increasingly appreciate and profit by ; whereas to omit this great improvement for the sake of subsidising more ·generously for a few years this or that smaller undertaking, albeit apparently of more immediate usefulness, would be a really shortsighted policy, a forgetting of that pioneering and forethought which is the very object of the Trust.

G. Further Advantages

Is any further and more concrete and local argument needed towards this plea for the development of the beauty of the whole valley, from loch to plain ? The so-called Glasgow School might almost be called the Kirkcudbright School, many of the noblest landscapes which it has produced having come from the comparatively large colony of painters who make the little town their main or summer home of inspiration and work, though exhibiting in the great city. The aggregation of these painters at this spot has arisen in response to its richness and variety of surrounding beauty, and the wealth of its seasonal effects, from the earliest snowdrops to fullest autumn glory. These wonderful effects, these noble woodlands, so magnificent that one of their fairy glades has had the common name of " Paradise " before the painters discovered it at all —all these look " natural "—that is, undesigned— even, doubtless, to many of the painters. Yet they are really well known to be the creation of the second Earl of Home, or rather of Patrick Nasmyth the painter, whom he employed as his landscape gardener, and by whom these seemingly accidental effects were designed—vast pictures sketched and laid in upon the level with saplings, instead of upon the upright with charcoal.

Are we told that we shall not see the trees we plant ? Even were that necessarily true the moral argument for doing so would be all the stronger.

With parks and parkways, paths and woodlands stretching from the present racecourse and playing-fields up to the Town Loch, to Townhill and back again, Dunfermline will also become a town not only attractive to painters but productive of them. For designers, too, upon whom the prosperity of the town so much depends, and ever increasingly must depend, the best artistic society and example is constantly desirable. These two branches of the profession would increasingly become unified with gain to both, and through them to the community also. Thus larger aspects of technical education would soon react upon everyday practice and schools. In our efforts at social betterment we have long enough been familiar with the vicious circles. It is surely needful to consider the possibility of the vital spirals of ascending progress.

CHAPTER XII

PARKS AND BUILDINGS IN THEIR BEARING ON CITY IMPROVEMENTS

IT now remains to consider the relation of our improved park and its associated new or renewed

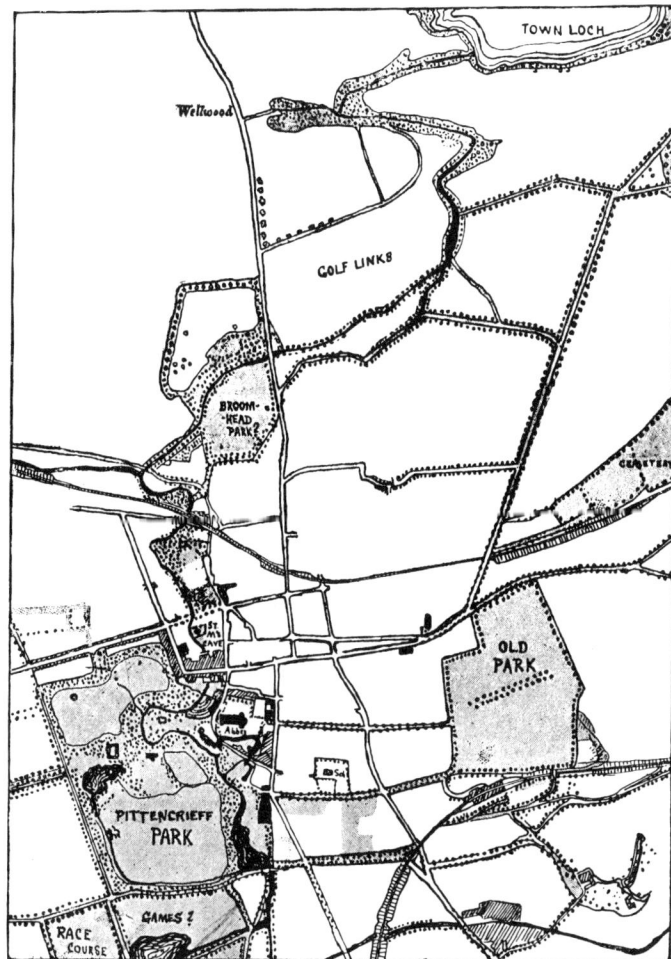

FIG. 70.—Sketch outline map to illustrate improvements advocated in this and preceding chapter—viz. (1) the connecting of the two city parks by park-ways; (2) the improvement of St Margaret's Glen and development up to Town Loch and Townhill Wood; (3) the extension of the existing beginnings of an avenue system along the main roads and future streets; (4) the extension of the Park Southwards towards play-fields and present race-course.

buildings to the general improvement of the city. City improvers, like the gardeners from whom

they develop, fall into two broadly contrasted schools, which are really, just as in gardening itself, the formal and the naturalistic. Each has its place and use. The formal school appeals to and follows the example of new Paris or Washington, the latter finds its ideals in Bruges and Nuremberg, its suggestions in Old Stirling or Old Edinburgh. And as we have found place for both schools of gardening in the park why not for both schools of city improvement, each in its due place, here in Dunfermline? If ever a city had a chance of arranging its future for the best it is now larger Dunfermline, which to the opportunities of Park and Trust adds the coming naval base, the natural expansion of its main industry — a singularly steady and permanent one. With all this it may expect also the development of its cultural and residential aspect and the growth of new industries, such as printing; indeed, innumerable subsidiary industries both utilitarian and artistic. The fact, too, that instead of a city debt it has a " common good " of exceptional magnitude is also greatly in its favour.

I am not suggesting any fanciful or exaggerated culture comparison, but simply using a plain geographical comparison, when I remind the reader that Dunfermline, with Inverkeithing (and now Rosyth or St Margaret's), is becoming a city of the complex type of Edinburgh and Leith: that is, the type of Athens and Piræus; and this combination of hill-city and port-city has always been, and may reasonably be expected to continue, peculiarly favourable to the attainment and maintenance of relatively high culture, both civic and personal. It is in this connection that the solution of the rival claims of the formal and the naturalistic city improver settle themselves accordingly. For the very maintenance of modern city life, the arrest of its present degeneration, broad

97

and airy streets, well-spread cottages and spacious gardens are urgently necessary ; while good and rapid communications, not only for horse, vehicle, and tramway, but broadened out for autocar and cycle, have to be kept in view from the very first, so that communication between Old Dunfermline and its new maritime suburb be not only easy and rapid but attractive. In a word, I press for combined action on the part of the City authorities and County Council with the Trust and with the Government, so far as they are concerned (and this is further than is always seen), for the planning of a really adequate modern city and modern road system, neither of which, it must be remembered, as yet exists in the civilised world. I have not acquaintance with the plans either of the Admiralty or with those of the Garden City Association, if any yet exist ; but I plead that the occasion is of transcendent importance not only to local but to general progress. To allow this supreme occasion to be lost, and the future city to arise in the ordinary way, as a muddle of a new port with a huddled industrial and residential town, and of all these with the usual confusion of railway communications and inadequacy of road and street ones, would be a disaster to the world and a disgrace to all concerned, not to speak of the deep and dangerous strategic blunder and waste this implies and educates for. No one can live for any time in London, or even attempt to do a day's business there, without realising the enormous calamity, the permanent and increasing waste of life and energy of all kinds, which has been entailed upon seven generations past, and perhaps as many future ones, by the non-acceptance of the simple and admirable plan of Sir Christopher Wren for the rebuilding of London after the Great Fire of 1666. That the greatest and busiest city in the world should still be centred in a mediæval labyrinth, and thence spread out through practically mere unwidened village roads, and even unstraightened cowpaths, in ever-increasing confusion, and then cut up and blocked in every direction by railway "systems," tramway and 'bus lines, without a suggestion of systematic or linear order, involves a daily loss of money which would have paid the difference on Wren's plans. Kingsway and Aldwych are examples of the costly apologies now being paid, piecemeal, to the memory of Sir Christopher ; while the disadvantage to London in the ever-sharpening struggle for existence of its now largely incurable crookedness goes far to cancel its great natural advantages. I do not here submit any proposal for the planning of the extended city, though this will yet range up to the park, and should at once be considered from it, since my present instructions do not admit of this. Let me at least point to the progress in this direction which is being made both by American and by German cities.

Returning now to the present Dunfermline, the "Old Town" of future parlance, I hold that here is the place for the conservative treatment, the naturalistic, in the sense of making the best of things as we find them, just as below and around it for the more formal. This does not prevent the formation of open space wherever possible ; in fact, it encourages it, and makes street widenings at this or that point as may be convenient or as occasion may arise, but it does not enter upon any regular plan of improvement comparable to that which should be designed for the new city which is to come. I rejoice that in the chairman's inaugural address to the Trust, already referred to, the American criticism of Dunfermline as a "dirty and ill-built town" should be so frankly considered ; yet to make it well-built, and even beautiful, requires, I believe, merely a generation of that comparatively gentle and gradual transformation which has been in progress for the last half generation in the Old

Town of Edinburgh. This, I maintain, is yielding a far better result for a town of this type than could the greater schemes of clearing and widening which have been from time to time proposed for it.

This is not to say we should not have a general policy of improvement of Old Dunfermline ; in fact, its main lines are fairly obvious and may be easily indicated. To relieve the mean, ill-built, and over-crowded aspects, which so strongly impress every visitor to the present city, a first great yet easy improvement would be to unite the two parks by adequate "parkways" or boulevards—(1) by extending the boulevard of Comely Park Place to the manse entrance of the park ; and (2) that from Lovers' Loan, the Nethertown entrance, and the proposed Nethertown Street boulevard both by Woodmill Street and Brucefield Avenue to the Old Park ; again (3) the continuation of Abbey Park Place into Park Avenue (a change which needs interference with but little property) would form an admirable and attractive street from the Public Park to the Abbey, thus again practically connecting the two parks ; (4) coming to the High Street line, the improvement to Bridge Street by a new park entrance would also be a very admirable one, as also the new "Carnegie Place" I have suggested on the roof of the new music hall, like that on the Edinburgh Waverley Market. In the middle portion property is no doubt too valuable to be interfered with, but much may be done for its continuation in Viewfield Place, and still more from St Margaret's Church onwards. From behind Hawthorn Bank and in front of the old park the street and road should be planted as a boulevard, or, since prejudice against large trees in the street too largely survives in Dunfermline, let us say a laburnum avenue, which grows to no great height yet to great beauty, not only of blossom but of picturesque gnarled growth.

In this way we see the possibility of no less than four broadly parallel parkways, each with its own features and interests, and all this at a very unusually small outlay for the results ; in fact, an expense which might be fairly faced by any small city, even without external aid.

So much, then, for the southern half of the town ; what of the less attractive northern portion ? (5) James Street should share at its west end in the improvement last suggested, and without any great expense both this street and its continuation in Queen Anne Street admit of great improvement here and there, without any expensive scheme of widening, but by simply forming here or there some little open space such as can be obtained by removing single buildings of small value. Nor are architectural features wholly deficient. The historic Erskine Church needs only a few trees, especially a row upon the east side of its ground, to show it at its best and greatly to improve its quarter ; while the position of the Post Office and the needed bettering of the approach to the ever-increasing important Upper Station makes the improvement of this line of street a matter of practical certainty in the future.

Proceeding northward, the next line (6) is that of Reform Street and Carnegie Street, at present certainly unattractive enough. But the proximity of the new baths and the recent adjacent improvements arranged by the Trust render the improvement of this quarter a matter substantially begun. Carnegie Street is certainly at present not very worthy of its name, but the needed rebuilding of much of Chapel Street affords the opportunity of laying out here a little place or square towards Bruce Street. Hitherto we have dealt exclusively with the east and west streets, and left the north and south ones unconsidered, but (7) the widening of Damside Street is surely specially obvious. (8) The erection of the new bridge, so often desired, that across the valley to

Pittencrieff Street, should again be kept to the front in any plan of improvement, and a tramway or motor-omnibus line running along this route to the Upper Station and beyond would naturally arise to connect what are at present inconveniently (*i.e.* wastefully) remote districts. This line would, moreover, promote building westwards. It is in no small measure the dreary monotony of Pittencrieff Street and James Place which at present largely checks improvement in this direction, but such housing improvements as those which have been above considered in connection with the park (Chap. II.), with the associated street improvements which are also so obvious, would doubtless lead towards renewing the natural western extension of the town to the great advantage of all concerned. The laying out of the irregular ground west of James Place would especially lend itself to the creation of a delightful suburb—a " garden city " in miniature or germ—still better, a garden village.

When we look again at the map in this larger way we see (9) Harrie Brae and Mill Street no longer as mere backways of Dunfermline. These are boulevards, which, with the stream improvements already pleaded for in Chapter XI., should be continued (10) to Rumbling Well and Baldridge Burn ; in fact, continued beyond these ; and with a tramway line or suburban station in this direction a new suburb might readily arise. The old quarries, still in the open country, in this quarter are favourable to transformation in the future as the nuclei of new open spaces and public gardens ; while even the abundant presence of old mine workings would, I trust, also be of service in helping to discourage too crowded building. The connection of this district with Pittencrieff Park by converting the present narrow road into a boulevard continuous with Coal Road (which might now be correctly renamed as West Park Avenue) would also be a great advantage both to the working-class quarter of the main thoroughfare of Rumbling Well and the villa quarter centring in Grieve Street.

Let us return once more to the Upper Station and then again enter the manufacturing quarter of the city. (11) We have already seen the advantage to the workers of the proposed improvement of St Margaret's Glen and the use of green spots like Wooers' Alley as city lungs and workers' breathing spaces, especially at breakfast and dinner hours, when the two large parks are equally inaccessible. The improvement, already outlined in Chapter XI., of Low Beveridge Well and the addition there argued for Castle Blair Park would also thoroughly develop this quarter.

Among the vacant fields south of Headwell Bleach-Works expansion is also going on, but again without sufficient plan. Here (12) a good east and west boulevard should be kept in view from Broomhead Park to Townhill Road. In fact (13), the whole of this quarter, up to and including Townhill,

should be the subject of a timely and thorough design. With a tramway up and down the Townhill Road, say rather Townhill Avenue or Boulevard, this important suburb would be greatly improved ; still more when we bear in mind the alternative (fully indicated in Chapter XI.) of what would practically be a country walk from Townhill or Kingseat Hill by the existing Chamberfield Avenue to St Margaret's Well, and thence down the burnside or ladeside to the tramway line of Pilmuir Street or through the Castle Blair Park to Mill Street.

The preceding dozen suggestions are but intended to open the subject ; thus, for simplicity's sake, the question of the north and south roads and avenues has scarcely been more than touched at one or two points, and the obviously needed improvement of the old Public Park has not been entered upon at all. Enough if these pages indicate the approaching time when a city will no more be destitute of a comprehensive yet ever extending and improving collection of maps and plans for its future improvement and development than a ship of the charts of its voyage. To the confused and sordid labyrinth of modern towns no small proportion even of their apparently non-material evils are due, and I therefore make no apology for this brief excursion beyond the strict and necessary limits of my immediate problem of the park and its associated improvements. In fact, these are associated improvements.

Again, imagine such a scheme of improvement gradually being worked out ; imagine the result, even in half a generation, of such a policy, and consider whether the crooked little Old Town would not thus become no less beautiful in its way than the more formal New Town upon the lower levels towards the sea. That would have its stately avenues, its long perspectives, its charming garden city also, with its blossom-covered cottage houses, but this would have the still greater antique charm of variety, picturesqueness, unexpectedness, which can never fully be designed. With its high views, its sunward slope, it should even be the more healthful and attractive of the two.

In conclusion, then, we look at our map as a whole ; we see the little, old hill city preserved in all essential characters, even renewed ; its group of culture buildings around the Abbey Church and Monastery, its stately Palace and venerable Tower ; we see its two Parks brought together by their verdant parkways and this splendid central group spreading out its radiating avenues to suburbs, country, and coast towns, ancient and modern. Here, then, we should have a complete city, Old and New, which would be in its way the first in Scotland ; in fact, an example and encouragement to city progress throughout the United Kingdom, and even beyond—a little northern Athens and Piræus indeed.

FIG. 71.—Waterfall of Jesmond Dene, Newcastle, to indicate possibilities of an artificial fall of about the same height as that proposed, even without planting. (Photo kindly lent by Messrs Valentine & Sons.)

CHAPTER XIII

THE GLEN

A. Improvement of Stream—*concluded*

WE now start again from the Town Loch and return down stream. Some day this loch, as already suggested, will be the central lake of the Townhill Park, the cynosure of a little Garden City. Enough, however, for the present if this water be pure and its effluent be kept so ; with recovered respect for this, the essential condition at once material and symbolic, all else that either hygienist and landscapist can desire will assuredly follow.

A very practical question is the utilising of this loch more fully for its practical purpose as a reservoir for the stream, and of economising its flow as far as may be, so as to avoid ugly and unwholesome drying up of the stream in summer. Three possibilities here suggest themselves—the first, the bringing in of additional brooks, is from the contour of the country most difficult, and may, I fear, for the time be practically disregarded. But is it not possible to help the course of the stream from water pumped or run from the different mines ? I believe I am correct in stating that substantial increase might be thus given to the stream at more than one point above the

park without any great expense. Especially may this be the case if any large pumping scheme be set agoing for the town's property in conjunction with adjacent proprietors. A third method, and one also reconciling amenity and utility, is the construction not of any new large reservoir but of as many small dams as possible along the course of the stream. This method would yield charming successions of lakelet and waterfall, and would give an aggregate accumulation of water of considerable value towards our present purpose. In this country people are too apt to think of a stream as something visible in its course, but anyone who thinks in terms of geology, or who has had experience of Eastern irrigation, is accustomed to realise that the great body of the stream is " the underflow " out of sight below the visible bed altogether. By increasing this such ponds are of much more value than their storage capacity would indicate.

The advantages of settling impurities and giving a pellucid stream through the park, of supplying fish-pools also along the whole course, will be obvious. If any doubt the picturesqueness of such artificial dams, with their pools and falls, I need only point to the many examples afforded by landscape and park gardening. Great civic improvements are now beginning, for American cities especially, by utilising the vast reservoirs required for water supply, by treating them at the same time as lakes, thus gaining park and water landscape with inappreciable extra expense. Here, in fact, is one of the coming improvements of all our cities ; so that instead of the landscape lover, as hitherto, having to protest against or mourn over the operations of the water engineer, he will welcome and co-operate with him.

I do not, of course, take upon myself here to indicate the precise position of these ponds without the assistance of an engineering survey ; enough if we note the existence of at least one now drained at the bottom of the valley lying between the Golf Course and the opposite slopes of Venture-fair ; in fact, lying between the scenes shown in photographs (figs. 67 and 68, Chap. XI.). For the same reason I do not enter upon the question of whether or not another of these lakelet reservoirs be possible above or below Wooers' Alley, although even small pools would be of great additional beauty.

In the case of storm and spate the presence of such ponds would naturally help to mitigate any local risks of inundation, though, of course, they could not be sufficient to completely remove these. That would be a matter for the engineer south of the town, into which we need not yet enter beyond pointing out how admirably the existing contours of the ground near the Charleston railway and siding south of the park are adapted for a fair-sized lake. Thus, then, our park would again clasp together new expanses of beauty on either hand. At length we come to the end of this long insistence upon the stream improvement external to the park. This has been necessary and justifiable, since the stream is still the vital centre, as well as the historic cause, of the whole park and city alike.

B. The Glen Proper

Entering now the park itself, we have here as its central and historical portion, that extraordinary loop upon the stream (fig. 2) to which the Tower Hill owes its existence—the Dun and Tower therefore, and the City itself. Here, again, the creation of new pools or lakelets is possible and legitimate. Though from the fitful flooding of the stream and the friable nature of the shales through which it cuts no material evidence of surviving constructions can be expected, I think it not impossible that in early times the stream around Town Hill may have been artificially raised so as to furnish an adequate moat, greatly strengthening the defences of the Tower. Be this as it may, the present ditchlike walling of the stream is intolerably ugly, and must be dealt with. But

here Mr J. G. Goodchild of H.M. Geological Survey, who has been kind enough to go over the ground carefully with me, points out that the rate of denudation of the soft rocky banks is so rapid that the removal of this wall would soon have disastrous consequences ; but there is, however, no objection to altering or disguising it with rock-work or with verdure, or to such raising of the surface of the stream as I am suggesting. He also lays stress upon the conservative value of the ivy, which here and there sheets the banks ; so that here as everywhere the demands of utility and beauty, of conservatism and betterment come to practical agreement.

While speaking of the geology of the valley, let me here recall that amid the many historical events and associations in which it is so rich, the greatest of all is apt to be forgotten—the fact that it was probably here, along the banks of this stream, that the world-transforming industry of the collier took its modern origin. Historians dispute this priority between the monks of Dunfermline and those of Newcastle ; and it is clear that what was known to one branch of the order would not long be a secret to the other. Can our geologists rediscover this ancient working ? If so, it deserves the most careful preservation, and it is well worthy of artistic commemoration also. Here is a theme for the painter ; still better, an ideal subject for that great Belgian sculptor who has so often found his inspiration in the coal-mine—Constantin Meunier.

C. The Glen—unit by unit

For convenience sake, let us divide the course of the stream into its geographical units. First the Queen's Garden, which in a subsequent chapter (XXVI.) we develop as the Arena. Even independently of the construction of this, the existence of a lakelet as a reflection mirror would be a great gain to beauty, while its fall below gives us the needed centre and focus of a new picture looking eastwards towards the Abbey (Chap. XXVI.). This is, in fact, our second unit, the beginning of the best part of our winding glen or dell, den or dene (not to be misspelt *dean* as at Edinburgh).

Not only for clearness in the present outline, but for the convenience of those using the park, may I be permitted to suggest a definite set of names for the remaining units of the Glen, respectively overlooked by Tower, Mansion, Palace, Mills, and Manse, as, therefore, the Tower Dene, House Dene, Palace Dene, Mill Dene, and Manse Dene respectively ? Each is a natural unit with features of its own which have now to be further developed.

Starting, then, at the top of the Tower Dene

(which may here for the time being be roughly suggested by that of Jesmond Dene, fig. 71) with our new waterfall from the Arena lake, we have half way down the half-natural, half-artificial makings of another waterfall (fig. 72), and this a little more art will easily render much more natural-looking. On the right is seen the nearest approach to a rocky cave which the stream affords; in a dangerous and nearly collapsing state, it is true, yet capable of being easily preserved by a little judicious underbuilding, which should be supplied without delay for fear of an accident, which might easily be fatal to anyone sheltering within it. At several other rocky points along the stream such skilled underbuilding is needed, notably under the Tower approach opposite; and there is no reason why this should be unsightly. Ivied strength cannot offend any eye.

Here the stream begins to turn southwards towards the bridge, and here, again, another lakelet is possible, with small fall below.

D. Tower Dene, Children's Dell, etc.

Though the serpentine sweep of the Glen gives it an ever-new and individual interest we still miss one feature which would be of great value—the coming in of some smaller tributary stream of which the minor valley would give a new scale and dignity to the ravine, a greater effect of breadth and depth. Here above us is the one point where nature (though apparently not unaided by the debris of the miner's art) has of old supplied these, though on no great scale—the tiny dell in the north-east section of the park, though waterless and completely dammed off from the Glen below (fig. 73).

To give this, however, something of its possible beauty and continuity with the main valley, and again, if possible, bring down a little stream with its opportunities of picturesque fall, is here most desirable, and fortunately easily practicable also. The hollowing out of this as a watercourse, the slight heightening of its banks, their planting

—these are all obvious, and though a drive whose course we cannot now alter appears to interfere, this difficulty again becomes an opportunity of new effect by simply carrying the streamlet in a short tunnel below the path—this, in fact, giving us the always picturesque effect of a single-arched bridge. From below this the stream would descend in a succession of small falls and pools to the main stream, so giving a fresh interest to the whole Tower Dene. The water would come

FIG. 72.—View of Tower Dene, looking East towards Abbey Church, faintly seen in distance. Note walled-in stream, small fall, etc., also small cave in dangerous state below tree.

naturally from the large fountain of the main entrance (Chap. XXVIII. and General Plan). The association of this as a Children's Dell with their playground in the Park above (Chap. IV.) will also be noted.

For this whole water supply a 2-in pipe would suffice, easily supplied from the city mains, or more economically worked from a ram concealed at the new Abbey Fall below, or possibly also near St Margaret's Cave. In such ways the water supply of the large and small west lakes, its continuation through the Rock Garden and along the west and south of the park, would all be easily managed without any serious withdrawal from the existing stream. For dry weather, however, it would be desirable to have the town supply to fall back upon, and unless the main stream can be substantially reinforced this auxiliary had better be provided from the first. Even assuming the purification of the stream a special

FIG. 73.—View of South side of Double Bridge, and small fall in House Dene. Note that there are at present practically two separate pictures, but that they may be unified by the needed improvement, that of raising fall on left side, though less formally than present retouching indicates.

filter should also be supplied in connection with the lifting ram, thus guaranteeing the greatest possible purity to this ornamental water.

Shade Garden, Spring Garden, Fernery, etc.

The spacious southward slopes above this upon the north side of this Tower Dene admit of simple yet beautiful treatment. After re-

moving a few worthless trees, mere weedy poles, this shady glade should be planted with the richest wealth of daffodils, sheeted in drifts of blossom, not merely dotted, each main variety amply represented so as to give not only greater interest but larger succession of bloom. The higher wooded banks should be more fully planted with ferns, of which the growth is here peculiarly perfect, and also sown broadcast with primroses and foxgloves and other shade-loving wild flowers.

This wild wealth of spring and summer beauty should next gradually pass westwards into the shady banks and shrubberies traversed by the existing paths, and also be well seen from the double bridge and its drive. From these, northwards, I would carry out and develop a suggestion which I owe to the Rev. Mr George, and which, though long a puzzling difficulty, I now see to be realisable at this point, that of a Fernery and Shade Garden, which should at the same time express something of the development and classification of vegetable life from the simplest cryptogamic plants upwards to the flowering ones. Towards working this out I have again lately studied the collections of Kew, and more especially the famous Spring Garden at Belvoir Castle. While profiting by these examples, I would combine at once an order of planting expressive of the present standpoint of the systematic and of the evolutionary botanist, so that we should literally ascend the tree of vegetable life. Starting from the stream level, with its humblest water weeds, we should cultivate upon the rock-work of its banks the liverworts and other simplest cryptogamic land plants ; then the mosses, the ferns, and their congeners ; and thence pass to a similar outline representation of the seed-bearing and flowering plants. By introducing here and there amid the needful rock-work the example or reproduction of the appropriate fossil form, and by putting out in summer-time some of the more delicate plants such as cycads, which are needed to complete our outline of the vegetable kingdom, a very fair general idea of plant life can be obtained. A literal bird's-eye view of the vegetable kingdom would thus set forth, with perhaps unprecedented simplicity and clearness— this Tree of Evolution, fitly completing and indexing that general presentment of the main orders of the vegetable kingdom which is disposed throughout the park, especially along its borders.

This will also complement that display of the essential succession of geological formations which I have proposed above (Chap. VI.) as the essential substructure of the Rock Garden. Here, then, once more we reach the proposition that whoever would see the world most clearly and most simply (I do not, of course, say most richly)—this

FIG. 74.—View a little farther down House Dene, showing back of old Mansion-house to left (South), and on opposite bank a little nearer than the large tree, Wallace's Well, fallen in. Old paths effaced.

FIG. 75.—The same view, with Wallace's Well simply rebuilt, and roughly-suggested rustic footbridge, uniting old paths now renewed. The Mansion-house shows also one of proposed new turrets suggested in Chapter XXIX.

time the world both of geology and botany—may well come to Dunfermline.

E. House Dene

Passing now south of the double bridge to the House Dene, what can be done for its main features ? The bridge is shown in fig. 74, and this from one of its best points of view, that of the existing small fall. This should, again, be somewhat heightened and improved, the resultant pool above this fall then mirroring the bridge, and so doubling its present beauty.

Upon the improvement of the mansion I enter elsewhere (Chaps. V. and XXIX.). As regards the stream, the banks need little more than ivy and enlargement of its masses of bays, yews, and elders. I propose to renew the path along the bottom, and connect it by a light wooden bridge with the renewed footpath leading to " Wallace's Well " upon the north side (figs. 75 and 76). Whatever be the connection with Wallace, if any, this Well may probably have been connected with the water supply of the Tower, but its tradition of medicinal value must also be kept in view. If after cleansing it turns out to be drinkable, we have here an interesting little feature, an additional attraction.

F. Palace Dene

This brings us practically to our next unit — the Palace Dene. To raise and to widen out the stream is here of all places most important to afford the reflection mirror needed to perfect the picture of the Palace ruins, and more fully justify that comparison to Warwick Castle which is often made (fig. 77). This is easily done by raising the level of the existing Linn, which,

in any case, needs improvement from its present too obviously artificial character (fig. 78). After attending to the trees and their slight further thinning, due to the widening of the stream, and extending the ivy sheeting and planting of the banks, there is here little to be done on either side.

Looking down stream, we again note the im-

FIG. 76.—View looking down Palace Dene ; block retouched to show stream raised and widened (in fact, somewhat too much so), and with stiff edge, easily modified in execution. Note advantage of small Mill buildings beyond palace in grouping with them and continuing their extent, again notable from almost every point of view.

portance of the old mill buildings as extending the magnitude of the Palace ruins, and the group it forms with the Abbey above. Of this whole mass it now behoves us to find the best view points. Better than the familiar ones from the west side of the Dene will be found the view offered above, owing to its better display of the Monastery ruin and Abbey spire above the Palace. This (fig. 42, Chap. VII.) may compete with the frontispiece in the claim of being the best view in Dunfermline. It is taken from the top of the north garden wall, and hence surely justifies the construction of a light stair case, leading to a railed walk, replacing the present cope, or at least to a belvedere turret—why not both ?

By thinning out the worthless trees, and by a little judicious pruning of the remaining ones,

blemish is obviously the iron railing which at present protects the path (figs. 42 and 76).

Here, therefore, without forgetting that this is Crown property, not the Trust's, I venture to suggest, in the interests of common amenity (indeed, in some measure of safety also), that for this unsuitable railing be substituted a low stone parapet, as introduced on the left of my fig. 78, in place of the present railing in fig. 76. An inspection of this will show how the buttressing and underbuilding of this carried downwards, as it must needs be here and there to the rock below, will further aid the picturesqueness of the whole composition, and also prevent any danger of landslip within an appreciable time.

FIG. 77.—Mill Dene and Linn, showing present too formal treatment, and easy improvement, especially in view of slight heightening of stream of Palace Dene proposed above.

this whole picture may be considerably improved, since parts of the building would then be visible through openings in verdure, and not merely, as at present, through the winter branches alone. The slight thinning of trees at bottom, involved by the widening of the stream, will also be an advantage. In extending the ivy sheeting and planting of the bank there is also a little further improvement to be done.

Studying this Palace view more closely, we note how largely its noble effect depends upon its massive buttressing, while the corresponding

While speaking of the Crown property I may also venture to say that the present rough earthen steps are not in keeping, and that simple and substantial stone steps, with low parapet or balustrade on one side, would be a substantial improvement to the whole architectural composition. The expense would not be considerable, and the present constant repairs would be put an end to.

I recommend, therefore, that these two matters, along with the elsewhere suggested widening of the Palace Yard and Monastery Place, with its consequently desirable setting back of the wall and railings in the former place, and lowering it in the other, be submitted for consideration by the Trust to the Crown authorities. The opening of the late proprietor's accesses to the Palace, which has presumably devolved upon the Trust, should also be arranged for.

G. Mill Dene

Of the Mills I shall speak at length in Chapter XVIII.; while of the picturesque interest of the Mill Dene, with its two falls both improved, its present bridge rebuilt, and a new one thrown across from the foot of the Mill Garden westwards, nothing more need be said than that this section of the glen would obviously be one of the most interesting and varied of all. The mill stream I also leave for consideration in Chaps. XVIII. and XIX.

New and interesting views both of Mill Dene and Manse Dene would be obtained from the proposed new bridge (see fig. 79), of which the usefulness as connecting the two sides of the glen for driving purposes will readily be appreciated. At other points this would be impossible without much greater expense, and, indeed, serious alteration of the landscape, but here the levels readily admit of its presence as an improvement not a transformation. We drive from the future Manse Entrance to the foot of the Mill Garden, then across the stream and down a wide old path, easily renewed as a drive, to meet the east drive of the main park, and thence turn uphill or go round. A little study of the plan will show how greatly this bridge will increase the extent and the variety of the possible Park Drives. This bridge I have sketched in but the slightest way, but its comparatively long span indicates steel as here the suitable material. Apart altogether from any peculiar fitness here on personal grounds, this would obviously be the most characteristic constructive addition we can make in our day and generation to the open-air architectural museum of the Park. Why not make its construction an occasion and a stimulus for the engineer as artist? In our still comparatively early steel age, he has hitherto been mainly occupied with the more elementary problems: let him now express the finest capabilities of this most marvellous of materials.

H. Manse Dene

Of the Manse Dene widening into its lake figs. 80, and 14 to 19 collectively, showing the possible improvements, are sufficient. The whole study of this proposed improvement, in relation especially to the Nethertown Boulevard

FIG. 78.—View of Abbey ruins, with suggestion of buttressed stone parapet to replace present iron railing. The parapet is here too prominent, and the cope especially needs improvement; the difficulties of retouching must here be allowed for.

and its improvement to Lovers' Loan, is thus possible. It will be seen that the transverse dam afforded by the raised road is not a wholly desirable ending for our lake (fig. 17). I have preferred to give this an arched and therefore bridgelike treatment, and to suggest the planting of trees on the south side of the road, both for reflections and for concealing the poor buildings behind, rather than the other alternative of giving this dam an earthen bank with trees upon its slope down to the water, though I fully admit there is also much to be said for this naturalistic treatment.

Here at length we have returned to the improvement with which these park studies began, in summer-house of oak boughs and heather thatch, which might reproduce in its interior the "mirror grotto," formerly so popular, and I believe still surviving, at the Hermitage at Dunkeld and elsewhere. I am well aware that this is not offering a high form of landscape art, but it seems to be so real a resource of delight to children and other simple observers that it seems reasonable to supply it.

FIG. 79.—Suggested Steel Bridge between Mill Dene and Manse Dene, thus admitting of great extension of Park Drive system. The footpath to the right might easily avoid any need of steps up to bridge and drive by a slight increase of gradient.

Chapter I.—that widening of the stream into a lake at the foot of the Glebe which gave us the whole series of figs. 14 to 19, but which we were then obliged to abandon as impracticable, pending the purification of the stream. This now exhaustively treated, this proposed scheme can be realised; indeed, some day, I trust, continued southward, as already advocated in Chap. XI *F*.

I. Possible Hermitage Grotto

At some convenient point—either here in the Manse Dene above the primitive village by the lake or at a spot just below the proposed new Arena Fall—I would erect a rustic

I trust, however, that this may not be the beginning of any subaqueous grottos or other costly conceits, for in such ways the arts have too often wandered away into mazy elaborations of unreality. These fascinate and delight for a season, but a reaction soon appears. The waste of labour, of wealth, needed elsewhere, becomes suddenly manifest, and a utilitarian age thus follows. To others the unreality is most painful, and scientific Philistinism results; while to others, again, such elaboration of lower interests in preference to higher ones awakes the protests alike of Puritan and iconoclast. On all grounds, then, it is safer to do as I have tried in these pages; and, while fearlessly elaborating great constructive designs, to keep these always in touch with the reality of labour, with science also, and, above all, with those high realities, those cardinal points of direction, which we call ideals.

D. NATURE MUSEUMS

CHAPTER XIV

NATURE PALACE IN PRINCIPLE AND IN POPULAR USE

A. Site

COMING along Priory Lane we see the venerable fragment of an ancient gateway which connects with a portion of the city wall behind. Though any suggestion to displace this ancient landmark must be resisted, the question may arise of trying to adapt to this, or harmonise with it, the gate pillars of the new entrance here proposed. But this does not yield any satisfactory result : I therefore recommend frankly leaving this as it stands, without any attempt at incorporation, still less restoration. An ivy plant may be placed on the west side, which will soon climb up and give it a bushy top, without unduly concealing this interesting bit of old masonry. Of course, the top should be cemented and any weak joints well pointed, but after this treatment ivy can do no harm ; its only mischief to old buildings arising when it is allowed to conceal actual dilapidation and to thrust its shoots between the joints of stones, which its growth then, of course, bursts asunder and may even bring down

It is here at the manse that, after full consideration, I have finally fixed upon as the best site for the Natural History and Art Buildings (see figs. 9 and 12). This choice has been determined not only by the gradual exclusion of the one or two other possible ones for various reasons but by the peculiar advantages here, first of all of general accessibility, and this, of course, not simply from the railway station or the Technical School but as the most convenient centre between the present Old Town and its future expansion, which must now necessarily be mainly southward. Though the proposed tramway route goes by the Inverkeithing Road this will still be very convenient, and there is every probability that before many years a new line may be laid, passing this entrance.

The large tolerably level site desirable for a spacious Nature Building is to be found here by utilising the manse garden, of which the slope is a gentle one. I, therefore, recommend the acquisition of manse and garden as well as glebe, equivalent accommodation being readily found for the present manse elsewhere.

To replace this an existing, possibly historic house, say the Abbot's, might, perhaps, be purchased, or one of the existing villas, say in Comely Park or its neighbourhood, may be acquired ; or, again, a new site might be formed west of Pittencrieff Park, say upon the Coal Road, and a new building erected which might be the beginning of a better style of domestic architecture than the too conventional villas to the east or north of the town.

While the outhouses should be at once demolished for the new entrance the manse itself should be allowed to stand for a time until the museums are largely completed. In its various rooms, some of which are of good dimensions, I should propose at first to house the incipient library and museum of the Naturalists' Society, as also the beginnings of other collections, artistic, technical, anthropological, etc., which cannot too soon be set agoing. Let us devote one large room to the beginnings, say of geological and mineralogical collections, others to zoology, botany, etc., each with its honorary curator, an official who should be readily found amid the large and capable membership of the Naturalists' Society. Similarly tor antiquarian or art purposes : open the room and find the curator, and the collections and specimens will soon be coming in.

This principle of assigning small rooms to minor collections—one to entomology, another to ornithology, a third to minerals or fossils, and so on— gives the all-important beginning of small independent collections of value, which would go on increasing, pending the erection of the permanent museum building.

B. Nature Palace in Popular Use

We now come to one of the most important and necessary buildings which can be erected by the Trust. While a naturalists' museum, or even a music hall or art gallery, can only appeal to, or even contain, a comparatively moderate number of citizens, there is urgently needed in our cities some spacious and attractive place of recreation and meeting.

Suggestive indications towards such a building are afforded by the magnificent winter gardens of several of the Glasgow public parks, and also by the People's Palace on Glasgow Green, which, in addition to a covered promenade, serves as a centre for exhibitions and entertainments of various kinds.

The Museum of Science and Art in Edinburgh use as a promenade and popular assembly-room and as a centre for bazaars, periodic industrial exhibitions, flower shows, etc.

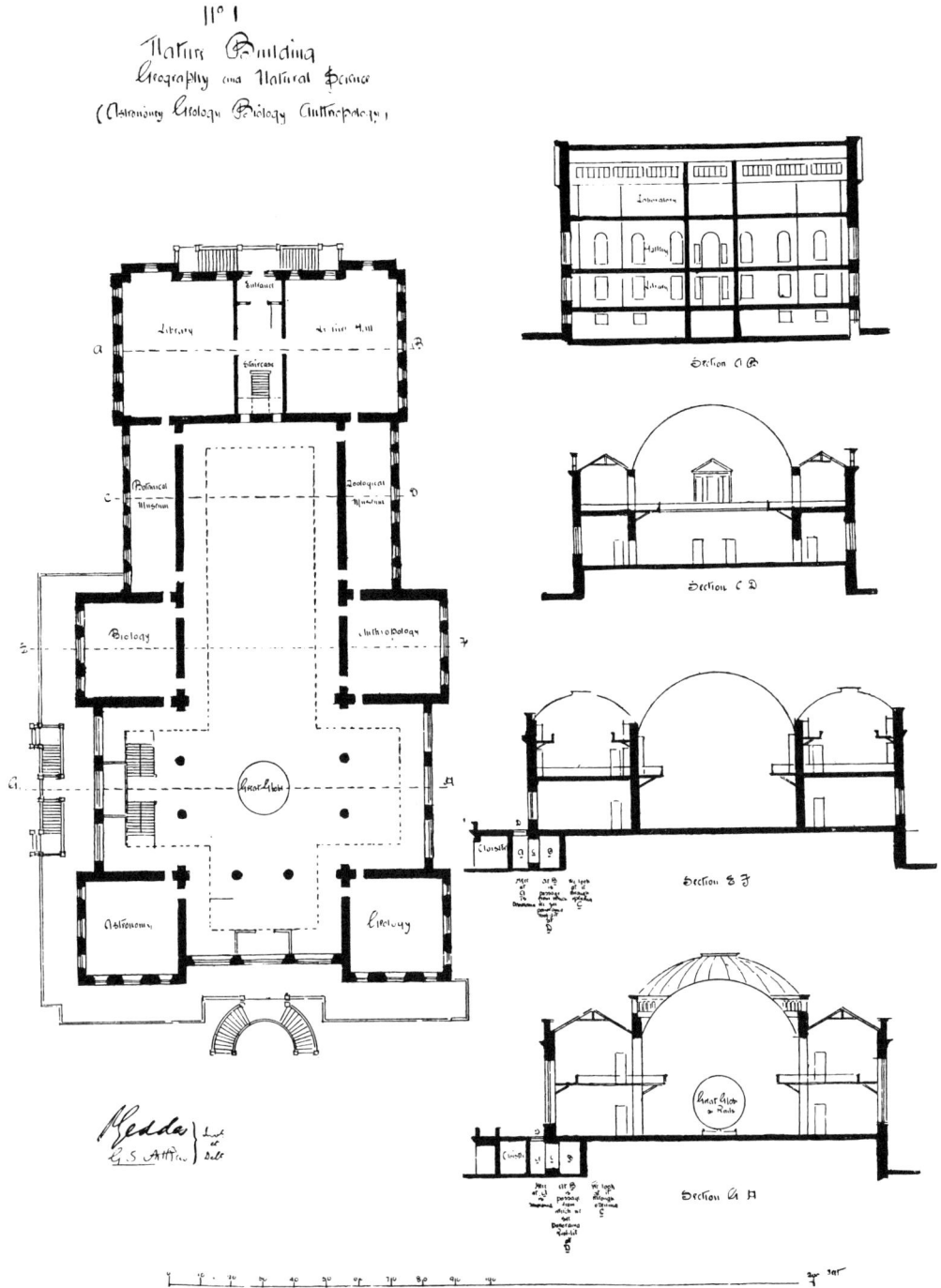

FIG. 80.—Plan and sections of proposed Nature Palace. Details as described in text, save that the four fountains at extremities of great hall (XVI. C.) are not inserted.

may also be kept in view—a museum well adapted also to receptions and conversaziones. The Waverley Market of Edinburgh is constantly of

While the creation of an example of each and all of these types of institution is obviously beyond our needs, the question at once arises : May we not design something to combine the essential advantages of all these institutions, and be Museums and Winter Garden, People's Palace and Waverley Market all in one ? Could this be realised, such a place would be of continual and varying interest throughout the year, and become increasingly attractive and useful both as a popular resort for Dunfermline and a means of additional attraction to visitors.

The standard example of such an institution for half-a-century has been, in fact, the Crystal Palace, though it is, of course, not necessary to imitate its vastness. Its cross-shaped plan, however, is equally adapted to the present moderate scale, with the important difference that I propose filling up the four square spaces left at the intersection of the cross by blocks of museum building and of continuing these to join the entrance block chiefly occupied by the Naturalists' Museum, etc., which would replace the manse (see plan and sections, fig. 80).

The economy of construction effected by this combination, and the possibility of architectural effect, especially in the north, west, and south, and also from a distance through the groupings of the four small domes around the large central one, will be seen from the accompanying plans, elevations, and perspective. It will be seen that the lighting from the glass roof of the main building is supplemented by the great windows of its east, south, and west fronts. The treatment of this in stone like a vast orangery, or like the Edinburgh palm-house, will be seen to be architecturally more satisfactory than could be any construction in glass and iron alone. The possibility of roof-lighting of the upper storey of each of the four angle-blocks completing the square around the cross allows of utilising their whole wall space and of omitting external windows. This admits, again, of much more monumental treatment (figs. 81 and 82).

While in buildings of historical character we may naturally employ the older architectural styles, as will be seen later, a frankly modern treatment is here necessary—a mediæval museum, even at its best, as at Oxford, being too incongruous with the modern science or arts it has to house. After consideration of the various styles adapted for modern museum buildings, not only of Edinburgh and Glasgow but of London and American cities, I think we cannot do better, especially here in Fife, than adopt what we are apt to forget is a local tradition, that of our greatest native artist, perhaps the most important architect

that Britain has produced since Sir Christopher Wren, and one surpassing many more famous masters of the Renaissance—I mean Robert Adam, whose home at Blairadam, in our own countryside, perhaps makes us forget his rare and acknowledged eminence.

The massive and austere dignity yet subtlety of his proportions, the temperate reserve of ornament, the use of the low and natural dome in preference to the lofty false domes of former and subsequent fashion, have rendered his work less popular throughout the nineteenth century, and it must be admitted that even important works like the Register House and the University of Edinburgh are somewhat severe, even cold, and lacking in popular interest. More ornate examples of his work, such as the great south front

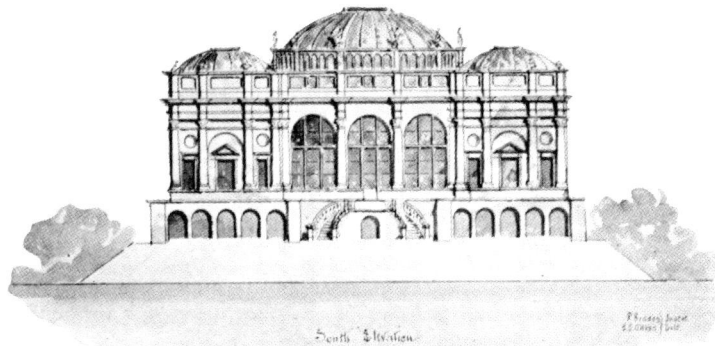

FIG. 81.—South Elevation of proposed Nature Palace—on top of Manse Hill (cf. fig. 14).

of Kedleston, have, therefore, been of more suggestiveness.

Leaving, however, the external architectural treatment to speak for itself, and returning to the essential matter of usefulness, this may be imagined in detail by help of the accompanying plans and sections, from which the external aspect, although here first described, has really arisen.

The floor of the main building measures 160 × 50 ft. = 8000 sq. ft. Adding to this the area of the two transepts, each 25 × 50 ft., we have 750 sq. ft. To this must be added the extensive promenade or exhibition gallery, which runs round the entire circuit of the cross for a length of 520 ft. Giving this a breadth of 7 ft. of clear floor space, independent of allowance for wallcases, this adds another 3640 ft. of promenade, making a total accommodation of, say, 12,400 sq. ft., 1377 sq. yds. Allowing one square yard for easy standing room per individual, we have thus accommodation for a convenient, but not a maximum gathering of 1200 people.

A musicians' gallery might project beyond the promenade gallery at the north end of the nave, and a platform or bandstand might also be placed at any convenient spot upon the main floor, or arranged more prominently, say, at the south-west angle of the cross.

For a flower show or the like long temporary trestle tables might run down the middle and arms of the cross, conveniently with a central passage. The same arrangement might be adopted for annual industrial exhibitions, like those which are proving so successful in Edinburgh and Glasgow.

Of the long gallery promenade any required portion might be utilised for wallcases; more beautiful, however, at any rate for the transepts and south end of the building, would be the method of running flat showcases along the inner parapet edge, leaving the outer wall free for plants—particularly flowering climbers, etc., which give great beauty and variety to the columns and roof. Difficult though it may at first sight seem

tions of all the ordinary kinds—geological, botanical, zoological, and anthropological? Frankly, no—not beyond a well-chosen small collection of types, such as of the Perth Museum, at the very largest. Though personally strongly interested in such museums I cannot recommend the reduplication of a set of these in Dunfermline. Without preposterous outlay these could never become of value to the specialist; the local student would do much better to make excursions to one of the larger neighbouring cities, while the Trust will find it far cheaper to send even whole schools to Edinburgh than to create such museums here. Even were valuable specialist collections offered gratuitously

FIG. 82.—West Elevation of Nature Palace.

to ensure dryness, it is not impossible to keep vertical cases of sufficient height upon the walls and yet have the plants above them on the wall-head under the spring of the roof, the narrow gangway easily provided above the wallcases admitting of tending these.

The great orangery windows to the south would house a group of sun-loving palms and acacias, while to the east and west more shade-loving plants could be arranged, thus giving three very distinct types of beauty and vegetation, and meeting the criticism, not unnatural on such a plan at first sight, that we are in danger of over-shading our plants. The greater portion of the hall would be amply reached by direct sunlight.

So far, then, the aspects of this proposed building as Winter Garden, People's Palace, and Waverley Market—i.e. as place of promenade and music, of exhibitions, flower shows, etc. The needed cloakrooms, refreshment-room, and even assembly-rooms, will be found on plan.

What now of giving it the additional and educational interest of a great Museum?

C. Nature Museums in Principle

Let us return to the Naturalists' Museum, with its primarily regional character. Shall we aim at having, as in larger cities, a set of general collec-

I should doubt the wisdom of accepting them, unless for exchange with other centres.

While I, therefore, strongly press the abandonment of any ambition to possess the sixth best collection of skeletons in Scotland or the like, do I therefore propose shutting up our knowledge of the world to our own region? By no means. The abandonment of reduplication of the existing museums thus clears the ground for the preparation—and this with less outlay—of a far more interesting, more beautiful, and more instructive type of museum — one not as yet represented either in Scotland or England, nor, indeed, at all adequately elsewhere—a museum of which the motive is no longer the preservation of a variety of special collections, each artificially isolated from the living whole of Nature, but the presentment of Nature herself in her most characteristic aspects and regions—a museum, not primarily of geology, botany, natural history, anthropology, and so on, yet of the whole of these within the living unity of Nature, scene by scene—in short, a Museum of Geography. Here, alas, the geographer will too readily meet prejudice and opposition to his claims. Just as botany still too popularly stands for dog-latin and dried plants, so geography is painfully associated in our minds with the memorising of boundaries or statistics. But this past, at anyrate passing, exaggeration of the letter of science is the very reason for now seeking to realise the artistic expression of its living reality and spirit.

The botanist rightly treasures, and when possible extends, the precious herbarium bequeathed him by his predecessors; yet he increasingly knows that his main work is with the life and flowering of nature, and that he is no longer a mere herbarium clerk, but the awakening spectator and interpreter, for his few short years, of the glorious pageant of Nature through all her regions and seasons. But this is to say he has become a geographer; and so, indeed, has every other man of science—the geologist, the zoologist also, the anthropologist most obviously of all. The geographer's is thus the comprehensive concrete mind, answering to, and supplementing with the needed facts, the philosopher's upon its abstract level. He takes all the various results of the different sciences and reunites them into a series of living and characteristic world-scenes, in which latitude, configuration, and relief, rocks and soils, climate and rainfall, flora and fauna, nature races and civilised races, industries and institutions—nay, with these, even ideas and ideals — are all expressed as the elements of an intelligible and interacting whole — the dramatic unity of the World and man — say, also, of Man in his world. Can we adequately conceive and realise such a museum as this, we shall have reached the unexpected proposition that anyone who wishes to see the world may best come to Dunfermline.

CHAPTER XV

NATURE PALACE IN EXECUTION

How can such a project as that outlined above be practically carried out ? Is it not beyond the resources of what is, after all, to be only a provincial museum—one, moreover, clearly subordinated within a larger general policy, that of aiding the recreation and life-brightening of the workers and children of the community ?

As the various special natural sciences return into that Geography, that general presentment of the world in evolution, of which they are but the analyses or the fragments, however apparently specialised away, everyone must be more or less aware how great an improvement is going on in geographical education. For not only are primary and secondary schools everywhere becoming comparatively well equipped, but even several of our British universities have begun to recognise and make some small provision for the subject. The Nature Study Exhibition of last year, or the Geographical Exhibition of January 1904, now available to borrowers (why not, therefore, in Dunfermline ?), are examples of this progress, as also the rise not only of geographical journals in connection with the London and Edinburgh societies but of others specially addressed to teachers.

Far more important, however, was the magnificent Paris Exposition of 1900, from which, unfortunately, our country has profited too little. As its predecessor of '89 was characterised by the technical marvel of the Eiffel Tower, so this Exposition found its appeal of freshest interest and wonder in its extraordinary and undesignedly simultaneous outburst of geographical illustration from almost all nations and quarters of the globe. This was not only in relief, collection, and picture, but most of all in Panoramas, these embracing every possible development from and beyond the two types more or less familiar in this country— the unrolling picture and the vast single panorama occupying an entire hall. Moving panoramas were developed with remarkable combinations of artistic and mechanical skill—witness the " Stereorama " and " Mareorama " of 1900—and the method of fixed background pictures with foreground relief was developed on every scale of magnitude and perfection, from the colossal panorama of Mont Blanc exhibited by the Alpine

Club, to the tiny peep shows of different minor scenes which accompanied this. The same method was also usefully and successfully applied for the illustration of architecture—witness the Exposition de l'Art Public. One such peep show in Edinburgh, for instance, would do more to protect and advance its beauty, by its appeal at once to the trained architectural critic and to the popular mind, than is possible to the entire lifetime of a too purely critical Cockburn Association.

No visitor to the Exposition, child or adult, who saw the panoramas of the Swedish Pavilion, with its marvellous snowy Lapland night, its Stockholm sunset, will ever forget their admirable fidelity and beauty, their combination of realism and of art ; while in many other national and French departments of the Exposition scarcely less skill was displayed. A climax of union of geographical truth and landscape beauty was reached in the Alpine models, like those of the Swiss Village, especially when skilfully illuminated, as they were through the most glorious changes of sunrise and sunset, of night and day.

Here, in fact, was developed, from long familiar beginnings, practically a new class of exhibition and museum in one, in which the veteran explorer and geographer, the trained artist and the simplest visitor, rustic or child, could and did alike find the most keen and active pleasure, with genuine and enduring instruction to boot.

In all that enormous waste of good work which goes on at the breaking up of an Exposition nothing was more lamentable than the scattering of these panoramas ; yet this was inevitable, since they had been prepared from all sorts of separate points of view, without any approach to unity, or even common scale. Nor does, probably, any existing museum possess adequate facilities for showing panoramas, small or large.

Here, then, is a concrete opportunity in Dunfermline : the knowledge, the skill, and experience which produced these panoramas is largely still available, is practically unemployed. Let us import some of it here ; in fact, let the curator or assistant curator of the proposed museum be one of those geographical artists, and let him go to work upon a series of subjects carefully chosen, with the help of a geographical committee. The scale might conveniently be that which the ex- ample of Sweden, above referred to, has especially shown to combine economy of production with excellence of effect. In the accompanying plan I have allowed, as an average, 8 feet depth, 12 feet breadth, and 8 feet openings, but this can easily be varied and modified (Chap. XIV., fig. 81. See indication of these on left in two lower sections).

The building being provided, the creation of a series of, say, fifty such larger pictures, with, per- haps, as many smaller ones at half or quarter that outlay, would thus give, at a gradual outlay of from five to seven thousand pounds, an idea of the world, such as not even the traveller like Hum- boldt, the descriptive geographer like Reclus, has yet possessed.

The expense of such small panoramas would be moderate, chiefly for " time and lime." I take this broadly at £100 each, and believe I am well within the mark. The completion of each pano- rama would be at once an educational and artistic event in the city ; and the growing collection would not only command the attention of geographers in Scotland and beyond, nor even of the intelligent public, but be at once attractive and educative to the spectacle-loving visitor of every kind and age and level.

Leaving precise definition to a special paper, more suitable to a geographical society than for the present purpose, it is enough here to give a first rough indication of possible and desirable panoramas, selected so as to convey an impression of the most characteristic regions of the world, especially these which may be regarded as of most interest to us on general scientific grounds, or those of national intercourse.

The series should naturally be arranged running from north to south, with due attention also to east and west. The visitor entering at the north, and keeping his left hand to the east, so as to travel with the sun, would thus pass through the characteristic landscapes of the old world. He would begin, say, with Nansen's sea of ancient ice ; pass into Lapland, with its Lapps and reindeer ; descend to the pine forest of Norway, with its sturdy woodman, its boat builder on the fiord ; thence through Denmark or north Germany to the Alpine landscape ; thence again to Italy, to South Italy or Greece, to Asia-Minor or Syria. A series might lead through Mesopotamia, Persia, the Himalayas, and India to Ceylon ; another through Manchuria, Korea, and Japan, through China, Burmah, and the Malay Peninsula ; yet another to and through Australia and New Zealand.

Or, coming down again from the north upon the western hand, he would similarly start with a Greenland or Alaskan glacier, and the Eskimo encampment at its foot, and pass, by a Canadian forest and lake scene, with its half-breed trapper,

to the vast wheat fields and orchards of Manitoba or the apple orchards around Quebec. From a farm scene of New England he would pass to the cotton and tobacco plantations of the Southern States, and thence again to the great dismal Cypress Swamp of Florida or the orange-groves and ranches of California, and once more to the gorgeous cañon architecture of the Yosemite, to the mighty trees, the cactus desert.

A West Indian scene, conveniently from one of the glorious landscapes of Jamaica, would naturally here find place. Crossing to the mainland, say at Vera Cruz, we should see something of the marvellous landscape of the Mexican railway, climbing from its palmy tropical sea coast, through a changing forest, up to the temperate plateau overtopped by eternal snows. Stepping south- ward, the Panama Isthmus, the Pacific and the Canal route, would lie before us, well-nigh as plain as to Cortez or Lesseps themselves. Southward still, the debatable land of Venezuela, the vast plains, the mighty Amazonian forest, the pastures of Argentina, or the nitrate fields of Peru ; the quaint Araucaria forest of Chili, the plains of Patagonia, the shores of Tierra del Fuego, would successively appear, even the mighty cubic ice- bergs so familiar from Antarctic expeditions. It is a characteristic little fact that not only is Scotland holding her own in the present fashion of Antarctic discovery, but through a Scottish explorer she actually initiated them. Our Scot- tish patriotic pride has been too purely con- centrated upon the leading bards and their heroes ; few know that, taking, say, even a foreign history of some department of geographical exploration, there are mentioned as many Scottish travellers of note and productivity as from the greater England or any other of the great nations of the world. To our people, then, such a geographical museum must especially appeal.

Such a range of panoramas may, I repeat, without any undue expense, and within a very moderate terms of years, be constructed along the east and west side of our building ; while along the south might be arranged a similar series of panoramas of Africa, say from Algeria and the Sahara, with a characteristic oasis ; through the Egyptian delta, up the Nile, and by its monu- ments to the great dam ; onwards still to Abyssinia and the Soudan, and through Zambesia, Uganda, over the great veldt to Table Mountain and Cape Town, and thence over to a scene or two in Mada- gascar ; nor could a vivid series from Morocco to West Africa and the Congo be forgotten.

The completion of each panorama would, I say again, be an appreciable geographical event ; and the temporary (indeed partially permanent) exhibition of the geographical and artistic material, photographs, books, etc., employed for its pre- paration would similarly have notable educational value and interest. I do not hesitate to claim that, were such work once fairly in progress, it would exercise a peculiarly stimulating effect upon the schools, and this for more than merely geographical studies. Even those who most believe that learning is advanced by punishment would find a not ineffective lever in exclusion from the " private view " of each new fairyland.

I attach importance also to the broadly correct orientation of such panoramas as have been outlined ; this orderly placing of these world landscapes in relation to the cardinal points enabling, indeed compelling, the spectator to enlarge his whole resultant image of the world, beyond his everyday visible horizon, into a scarcely less real and vivid presentation of the entire world in all its main regions, and in their approximately true places around him. Thus, as the series became comprehensive the visitor would not only know more of the world than any one mortal has ever seen, but realise it also, and see beyond his too narrow limit of daily street the larger world of Nature and Humanity.

A. Special Nature Museums

The various special sciences of the geographer—the geology and botany, the zoology and the anthropology of the world—would thus be prepared for, their large aspects being imprinted upon the spectator's mind in a way which no museums, much less books, have ever yet succeeded in doing. Moreover, it is after such a comprehensive preparation, such a generally intelligent outlook upon the world as a whole, that we can best succeed to form a reasonably separate idea of its geologic or biologic constituents. Thus we come into a position to utilise special museums and to develop them ; and these we may now proceed with advantage to consider, so filling up the four angles of the cross, and each under its respective minor dome.

In the first of these let us place the Astronomic Museum, too commonly neglected altogether, or represented by some poor orrery, commonly out of order. An initiative such as Mr Goodchild's in the Edinburgh Museum, and a reduction of some grandiose endeavour like M. Galeron's " Globe Celeste," would show its possibilities on the ground floor ; then the models of the solar and stellar systems, in which such eminent and original teachers should have their say. Above would be the observatory itself, with telescope and apparatus available to the public under due guidance, as in Edinburgh. Of the supreme educational advantage of astronomy, its high place at every great period of education, and its total eclipse during the blind, sordid age of codes, examinations, and payments by results we are now leaving, there is sufficient evidence. I need not enlarge upon it here, in confidence that

no body such as the present, seriously considering the best provision of the elevating resources of culture, can omit the claims of astronomy.

The value of some new attempt upon adequate scale of an astronomic presentment of the universe, not only of the solar system but as far as may be of the incomparably vaster stellar universe beyond, would again extend far beyond our own citizens, and give a real impulse to the truly Higher because deeper Education of the world.

Geology with its long past, biology with its protean life, even anthropology, with its scarce less protean variety yet unity of human nature, can only in their greatest aspects approach this high intellectual and emotional appeal—this sublimity of a due presentment of the astronomic universe. Every scheme of education throughout the remotest past of mankind, through all its great constructive culture periods, has recognised the need of guiding, directing, and developing men's interest in the stars. It is true, I repeat, that in the conventional primary, secondary, and higher education of the times astronomy has come to occupy a less place than at any previous period of history ; but this I take as no small element in the explanation of the moral and philosophic inferiority of our current medley of imperfect specialisms. In the education and the recreation, in the whole uplifting of the people, astronomy, then, must have its liberal place. I am glad to learn from Mr Peck, the astronomer who of all others best combines with scientific work the widest educational and civic appeal, that the realisation of such a project by establishing a small but efficient observatory upon an adequate scale would make no very alarming demand upon the financial resources of the Trust. From Mr Goodchild, M. Galeron, and others I also find that the establishment of an astronomic museum is, as museums go, a quite minor matter.

In our second dome let us represent the Geological aspect of the world in its widest sense, including oceanography and meteorology, or, in perhaps less familiar yet really more vivid phrase, " the account of lithosphere, hydrosphere, and atmosphere."

The lower and upper storeys of the adjacent dome might be similarly allotted to the Biological world—the presentment of the " biosphere," with its plants and animals, its " phytosphere and zoosphere." Separate museum galleries are also shown upon plan.

The fourth block might conveniently offer in its lower storey the presentment of the simpler Human world—that of prehistoric and of anthropological research ; while its upper storey might be devoted to a new panoramic presentment upon smaller scale (corresponding to the admirable little " maquettes " of the Exposition de l'Art Public of 1900) of characteristic scenes and cities of the civilised world—that " politosphere " which completes and transforms the aspects of Nature.

I am quite aware that these panoramic projects may be received with disapproval by the purely analytic geographer, and with incredulity by the " general reader " whose reading is apt not to be general enough. But, from the first, I may appeal to the higher, the synthetic, geographer, like Reclus with his "Géographie Universelle," Schrader with his World Maps, to Bartholomew with his Physical Atlas, or, may I hope, to the President of our own Naturalists' Society, Sir John Murray, with his rare combination of first-hand world experience with precision of regional survey. While as to the incredulity of the general reader, though it is too late for him to see the actual wealth of the panoramas of 1900 of which I have spoken, it is easy to answer by simply offering, under duly defined business conditions of reasonable time and moderate expenditure, to deliver the goods.

B. The Great Globe

One final element is now needed for our museum, yet the centre and starting-point of the whole—the Great Globe itself. In the very centre of our building, then, under its great dome, let us erect this Globe. This would not, of course, be upon the colossal scale demanded by M. Reclus for his stupendous Temple of the Earth, which will one day be realised, and which will make the city which possesses it the world-capital of geographic science ; it would not even be on the scale of that National Institute of Geography, recently proposed by Mr Bartholomew and myself (*Scot. Geog. Mag.* 1902), but on the moderate and easily practicable scale of the globe of the Paris Exposition of 1878, of 10, or even of 5 metres, say 32 or 16 feet in diameter, the latter the very smallest upon which a true relief of the greater features of the world's surface can be at all adequately shown.

Both the educational uses and the popular interest of such a globe have been so often and so fully demonstrated, and the details of its construction are so well known, that I need not here repeat them. Suffice it merely to say that not only the due rotation, the effective lighting and display, but the detailed inspection of any required portion of its surface may all be easily provided for ; as also that, by simply placing the stand upon rails, the removal of the globe from the middle of the dome to the edge of either transept might be easily and instantly effected whenever, for other purposes, an uninterrupted view of the entire Palace would be required.

I repeat, then, that, pending the creation of a first-class geographical institute, such as those above indicated, in one of the great capitals, there would be no place for seeing the world like Dunfermline. The recreative interest, the educative power of such an institution should soon be appreciated by a city which prides itself upon sending forth its active youth to win for themselves place and fortune in the world ; and yet also—here and there at least—not to rest content with this, but to take up its burden and its progress upon their willing shoulders.

If to any reader, be he man of the world or professed educationist, this Nature Institute may appear excessive, I reply that it is for his sake that I labour this point of view so fully and so far. Were I asked, as, indeed, I here practically am asked, to sum up the result of thirty years' study and travel and reflection upon nature, of many more years' delight, and to plan out the best of this for the pleasure and the development of others, I can but answer as I am doing. Of the long drama of nature we are privileged to be for a few years the awakening spectators, we cannot all do this by help of ever-extending travel ; let us all the more have access to its descriptive and artistic result, so bringing before ourselves the scenes and regions of the world, the glories of them ; and then, leaving our little planet's bounds, let us pass to the solar system with Copernicus and Galileo, and thence extend our eyes throughout the stellar system with the continual advance of astronomy.

Yet in the same quest, and with but a modification of the same optic powers, we may, and must, make an intensive, a literally photographic and microscopic, survey of our immediate region—that one which it is natural to know and to love best, and which, by common consent of geographers of the world, here possesses at once peculiar wealth of beauty and depth of significance. Our regional studies, then, have to extend in their largest landscape and geologic aspects from cloud and mountain top to sea, yet also to microscopic scrutiny of rock and earth, of verdure and life— nay, of every peopled water-drop by the way. Telescopes, microscopes, stereoscopes are all now available for popular use, even for the museum visitor's most inexperienced handling, and should be generously supplied—that is, increasingly as the demand rises for them.

Our Nature Building, then, is once more a perpetually changing and developing panorama for childhood, and in all these studies it is no modest metaphor of Newton's or Darwin's, but the simple fact, that we are children all.

CHAPTER XVI

NATURE MUSEUMS IN WORKING

A. Curator and Naturalists' Society

As to heat our building we need a competent fireman, and he a sturdy and willing aid, so to run this Nature Museum we need a living curator, well seconded by likeminded younger men or women. One of those geographer-naturalist-artists for whom I have so specifically asked might do this. It is no small misfortune for the world that no such building has yet been placed at the disposal of any of the living masters of geography like Reclus or Schrader ; yet if their rare combinations of the scientific and the artistic power cannot often be found in one man, these qualities can frequently be got separately in two.

Upon the keeper of this building devolves a still higher than scientific and artistic responsibility—he has to be also the educational driving force of it, and his office is thus a literal ministry of culture from the naturalist point of view : I may use this term in all its denotations and connotations, all its " sense, meaning, and significance." While he must have due permanent skilled assistance, a larger volunteer staff will of course be available from the Naturalists' Society ; every such society, and this particularly in the east of Scotland, containing not only individuals of considerable experience and even accurate knowledge but of genuine and original aptitude. Permit me, then, a word of this : it touches the highest policy and usefulness of the Trust.

It is not sufficiently realised, either by educationists or the public, that in our British Islands there are characteristic regional aptitudes, almost as distinctly as there are veins of mineral wealth. Yet we know of the songfulness of Wales ; and if we explain this merely by its element of historic survival we are undeceived by an expert like Madame Patti, who tells us she built her castle where she did because she had found a place where the people's voices sing.

We are rising beyond that vulgar idealisation of Quantity of Empire, which is but the expression of geographic imagination in the rough, to the real, the urgent, question of practical politics—that of the Quality of Race—and of which even the struggle is in terms of culture. Soon we shall see a psychological survey of the children of Scotland following upon Mr Tocher's current anthropological survey, Dr Leslie Mackenzie's and his colleagues' hygienic one, just as these have followed upon the geological survey or that upon the ordnance survey and the political map.

I submit, therefore, that so far from going beyond the practical problems of the Trust I am pressing one of the most vital and educational of them in calling their attention to the fact, which every historian will confirm—that is, every student of natural science who knows anything of its development—that the east coast of Scotland has furnished many and marked examples of men of naturalist genius who have broken through all the difficulties of their circumstances to an original grasp of things, so that the names of Robert Don or Hugh Miller, of Thomas Edward or Robert Dick are but the popular examples from a list which might be amplified, probably at least fortyfold.

That from such a strong infusion of local aptitude world-initiatives should arise need not be wondered at. Of these Sir John Dalzell, one of the first marine naturalists, ornithologists like Mac-Gillivray or Wilson, botanical explorers like Fortune or Douglas, are better known abroad than now at home ; though of these men of widely acknowledged eminence some names, like those of Murchison and the brothers Geikie, have become familiar to their countrymen.

With this large proportion, again, of eminent ability it is not to be wondered at that this region should again and again have produced the man of supreme ability and initiative in the whole world at some particular stage and time. Of such names those of Hutton and Playfair among the founders of geology, of Lyell as its greatest organiser, are surely well known ; while with little further study we find Humboldt's *facile princeps botanicorum* in Robert Brown of Montrose.

I am well aware how this to some readers may seem away from the point. I reply this *is* the point, this the objective of the Naturalists' Society of Dunfermline—to improve themselves as naturalists on the simplest level I have cited and to educate their successors as better naturalists, and among these to search out and find and encourage that native nature-genius which exists among us.

All teachers at times are despondent, and even in the richest gold-bearing regions and reefs the arithmetical percentage is extraordinarily small. The real point is that this is appreciable and obtainable ; and as we see science literally recovering the sympathy and the patience of her sex, as in these dazzling days of Madame Curie with her radium, we need not fear but that the more refined psychology of the future, largely through the women teachers who will best apply their science, will discover and rescue that genius, which is as yet the most wasted of all human resources, the most deeply hidden, yet the most widely distributed, of treasures.

No person in this century is sufficiently ignorant frankly to deny the increasing importance of science, yet no educational authority as yet adequately recognises the possible usefulness of a good Naturalists' Society like that of Perth, or the greater possible usefulness of the easily better one of Dunfermline—easily better now, not only because more richly endowed or more numerous, but because of the relaxation of that deadening urban education which peculiarly sterilised for nature studies the whole generation from 1870 to 1900.

Despite such reservations we owe much to the popularisation of the three Rs ; yet we may now get much more from that return to nature of which our very park and its purposed nature-building here are but the beginning.

I have treated this building at special length, partly because I am here within the field of my own fundamental interests, training, and educational duties, but also because it affords a convenient example of that treatment which pervades the entire report.   Just as one does not first make gardens and then erect buildings to spoil them, so one must not set up buildings first and then move in—handsomely furnished lodgings for dead institutions are common enough already. We must begin in this case, and in every other, with the active life and progress of the subject, and consider its place in the general progress as well as in the local weal. To forget this general progress of science and culture, of country and humanity, and build only with the stunted interests of the present Dunfermline in view would be to continue that narrow provincialism which has blighted too many of her endeavours already ; just as her public library reading-room, which is not worth a stranger coming to, is little worth a citizen going to.

Little reflection will show that the one and only building which can be constructed from external measurements and financial estimate alone, independently of living use, is a coffin. To this class no doubt many institutions belong ; hence so many speak, and so many more feel,

even of museum or university, not to mention yet more dignified institutions, as being each in its way but a sarcophagus of culture. Such architecture has its qualities, but surely not those we seek here to realise.

B. Working continued—The Children

In searching out these hid treasures of individua genius, still undistinguished in the crowd, we see that, even were it but for the very sake of these, our essential standpoint, almost the only one we need thoroughly consider, is the juvenile one.

Our curator will have more opportunity than any other person of seeing the children of the town, for he has not only his Nature Palace to attract them, but his " Zoo," an attraction no child can withstand.

To prepare for the children, both directly and through their teachers, small exhibitions, loan collections, picture and book collections, on this and that subject by turns, would be a great part of his own work, by-and-by also the essential work of a skilled assistant, most conveniently a specialised member of the library staff.

He would give not only such indoor demonstrations, with occasional lectures and frequent lantern ones, but still more he would conduct outdoor walks in the Zoo and the park ; he would thence encourage or lead excursions through all the regions accessible on foot or cycle ; and thence, again, direct those longer excursions by train which have been for a good many years one of the educational initiatives of Dunfermline schools.

In this first-hand contact with nature, with its stimulating find of fossil or flower, comes the training of the future paleontologist or botanist, the historian or classifier. Conspicuous examples of young ability to use the ever-enriching resources of their city for themselves might thus rather be in danger of too much encouragement rather than, as commonly hitherto, too little—but such error is soon corrected.

Hitherto we have spoken of this building almost entirely in terms of its " grown-up " uses, or for children in their studious and nature-loving moods. But its largest use will be as a Children's Palace— a shelter from climate and season, not only in the harsher days of winter but at all times of inclement weather—at least an actual place for play, its spacious floor available for march or dance, for roller-skating rink or romp even. Such children's play, which has natural limits of time, need not deteriorate its other usefulness—the Naturalists' Library and Galleries, the lecture-room, the curator's and workers' rooms, being all easily protected by double doors from noise. For many elder adults of the town such play hours would indeed be chosen for visit ; while if any shrink wholly from their babel, interests are provided in the park elsewhere.

C. Children in Art and Nature

All this young active life must bring in dust with it, and so spoil the air. Here, again, beside ample ventilation, those fountains which our climate renders less necessary in the open air may here be introduced, and I suggest, alike for ornament and for hygiene, no less than four of these, one at each extremity of the cross, their spring and spray always cooling, moistening, and cleansing the air.

To design each of these with its own character, and to render the actual fountain form of each variable at will, is an easy task; while, with simple and inexpensive installation, the gorgeous effect of electric fountains—again varying in colour and brightness as in form at will—may readily be supplied. Such a spectacle would itself afford a source of vivid pleasure—an evening attraction " certain to draw."

Shall we design these still further? Good examples are not wanting, the Renaissance designers having, perhaps, especially excelled both in play of fancy and in perfection of form. Yet spouting dolphins and blowing tritons have lost their spell; we need a simpler, directer, fresher motive, and here in the children playing around the fountain (why not wading in its basin?) is the artistic motive we seek—one already used, too, in good examples, Renaissance and modern.

Let us take, then, this simple motive, with its popular, its universal, appeal. Yet, applying this, as architecture must do, with the whole conception of the building before us, what follows? Our four fountains are in the four quarters of the world; so, instead of repeating one type, our own, to conventionality, let us give to each fountain its individual character, none the less interesting for being anthropological and social also.

At the northern fountain, then, the tall Scandinavian and the smaller Celtic type, so amply represented in our own households, naturally predominate, but to its south the Mediterranean child. In the eastern fountain, beside the now essentially Aryan type of Persian and Turk, would come the characteristic individuality of the great Asiatic races—Indian, Japanese, Chinese. In that of the south the contrast would be yet more distinct—say of Arab and Malay, of negro and of Australian; while on the west the half-breed Canadian, the Indian, the Mexican, concluding with the to us so distinct yet so kindred individuality of our own American child-cousin.

For such sculpture, science has of course ample materials; but what artist has taken advantage of it? After all, not so few. An American artist has lately travelled the world, painting its types of racial beauty, from north to south, from east to west. A vivid example of good sculpture of this kind, satisfactory alike to artist and to anthropologist, may be seen any day on Princes Street, Edinburgh, in the two noble lamps which stand before the building of the Life Association of Scotland. The most ambitious example of this ethnological sculpture is that of the large groups symbolic of the continents which occupy the angles of the London Albert Memorial.

Yet the two street lamps aforesaid furnish, perhaps, the best as the most simple and precise example; and here, too, we see the true function of this alliance of art and science in the illumination of the everyday street—the help of the passerby. Here, in this example, is the actual symbol and business sign of one of those corporations of business men which, like that I now address, has for its task merely that of being a little farthersighted than its neighbours; and so has the courage to express its ambition to the everyday world.

For the educational and moral purposes of the Trust, its social and cultural ambitions, such as association of art and science has many possibilities. The symbolic suggestions of such fountains would be as manifold as their aspects; and even those who least care for art and its gentle ministry may most need to be reminded by it, as here, of the variety and interest of humanity as of nature, and helped to see their fellow-man of different land and race and colour, no longer as " half-devil " but as truly child.

BOOK II

E. LABOUR MUSEUMS

CHAPTER XVII

PRIMITIVE VILLAGE: OPEN-AIR MUSEUMS

A. Primitive Village: Site and Outline

THE high bank of the stream opposite the Glebe now claims our attention. Here, above the footpath which would run along the west side of the stream, widened as lake, is a wild bank peculiarly attractive to the activities and instincts of children, and particularly of boys, who might here be allowed larger freedom and latitude than is possible at other places, where damage might be more easily done, and where noise would be more disturbing. Its main road of access would be controlled from the new bridge up-stream (that from the Mill Garden), while its existing thickets of holly, etc., should be extended so as to form a practical but not apparent hedge of shrubbery.

Let it not be supposed that either damage or noise is to be encouraged ; on the contrary, I propose here to organise and utilise some of that constructive energy of boyhood of which boy mischief is mainly but the leakage or the explosion, and to devote it to the construction of what might be made in course of no long time at once a not inconsiderable attraction of the Park, as well as an immediate addition to its educational resources. What I propose for this spot is that our boys gradually construct for us a noteworthy part of the whole open-air museum, by reproducing as far as possible a number of these dwellings of early man in which Scotland, if not so much this particular neighbourhood, is so rich. In the exposed escarpment of cliff we should hew out, under due direction by a mining expert, one or more caves. In the more level portion we should excavate and build one of these underground " Picts' houses " which Mr MacRitchie especially has shown to be the homes of those ancient possessors of the land, who have been transformed by tradition and fancy into brownies and fairies.

A convenient spot exists for the erection of a larger rude stone dwelling above ground, with its surface covered with earth and turf ; practi-

cally, therefore, a tumulus, yet bringing out the idea that the tumulus was a place of habitation before it became a tomb. Near this rude stone huts might be erected ; one with primitive overlapping stones giving the false-arched roof familiar to visitors to the hermitage on Inchcolm, the ruins of Dunimarle, or the Treasury of Atreus at Mykenæ. Next, we should build with sod bricks like the Roman Wall ; and, again, with branches and clay in " wattle and daub," thus illustrating in germ the styles which have developed into such beauty, especially in English village and mansion.

Coming down the lake margin, this affords a convenient situation for the artificial island platform and huts of one of the " crannogs," which once existed in Scottish lochs (*e.g.* Duddingston), if not even for the more developed lake-dwelling proper—that of the Swiss lake in which the platform was erected on piles in deeper water.

Again, with the thinnings of trees from glen and park-belt, our boys should readily construct log-huts of various types and styles, and so on. This whole scheme thus at once furnishes a succession of holiday workshops during the progress of each construction, and a play-house and a picnic-room afterwards, the girls here coming in for their turn to finish and to adorn, and to preside over the hospitalities of this or that primitive home. Still, in the main, the first log-house constructed would serve as a joiner's workshop for the next ; and by-and-by for many kindred activities, such as the construction of bird-houses and beast-hutches which would naturally be carried on here. With the leadership of a sympathetic and inventive workman-teacher there is no limit to the variety of interests which might be provided for.

Every visitor to the favourite surburban resort known as " Robinson," outside Paris, with its many summer-houses, perching largely even in the trees, has seen that such play-houses are full of attraction and charm, even to children of a larger growth ; while if any scepticism remains as to the educative usefulness, or the local applicability of these proposals, it may surely become sceptical of itself upon the reflection that the immortal Robinson (Alexander Selkirk) was a Fifer. Why not, therefore, let his classic home be again reconstructed here ?

The interest of such a return to nature, and in such a spot, in woodland bank and glen, and between lake and park, between the two halves also of one Zoological Garden, can be readily imagined. Such a group on the side of the Seine was a main feature of the Paris Exposition of 1878 ; but here is a far more natural environment.

B. Educational Uses

There are doubtless some so severely grown up, that such proposals may appear to them simply chimerical, but these can surely have never lived the life of the boy-rambler or the field naturalist, much less roughed it with traveller or explorer. Not only from some personal experiences of these kinds, but from everyday later and present life, as paterfamilias, and as teacher sometimes of boys and youths as well as young men and teachers, the writer keeps well within what he has experimentally proved in saying that undertakings such as those suggested are not only practicable but easy with boys such as abound in all schools, with youths such as are at present running to waste at street corners. I am told that boys prefer mischief ; and doubtless so did many of us till we got the chance of doing something better. Only is this true in the too common case where they are left without leadership capable and resolved to lead them to that constructive activity which should be, if it is not, the very impulse and reality of a boy's education. Our present exaggeration of mere classroom notes or drawings, mere workshop exercises, however skilful, leaves this unsatisfied, even where it does not, as too commonly, provoke permanent distaste of work altogether. Putting this still more clearly, let me say this : that while governing bodies, local or central, in Dunfermline or in London, are congratulating themselves upon the good reports, the high marks, and highly finished drawings of their examinations, even the models of their exhibitions, the fact remains, as anyone who gets on terms of friendly confidence with schoolboys or with technical students may soon discover, that much of the most skilled practical teaching is leaving as its main result upon their pupil's lives little save a thorough distaste for its continued exercise. From the Latin or French or arithmetical " exercises " which wasted so large a proportion of our own boyhood, we, of the older generation, could at least escape in adolescence to art or science or

industry, and take up one or other of these with virgin interest and fresh eye. But now that in our would-be progressive educational bodies and official ones we have laid our heads together, and dissected our Art into " Grades," Sciences into " Stages," and handicraft into " Workshop Exercises "—i.e. the whole of these into a mere variant of Latin grammar and exercises once more—the result is that the spring of the young worker, artist, or scientist is being broken. They have had far too much of mere exercises for opportunities which came too late, if at all. What we now need is opportunity. In a word, the modern education of Exercises has again to be replaced by the past and future education of Experiences.

I am not here speculating or suggesting, but emphasising the truth, everywhere being verified by experience, that it is rough activities like those of the boys' camp, and of open-air play construction generally, that are the best preparation for that higher technical education to which we shall come further on. Similarly to utilise that strong destructive impulse which is one of the signs of the coming of vigorous manhood, I would find volunteers to help to demolish, when the time comes, the unsightly wall between glebe and park ; indeed, to move the stones to any point where they may be required. A windlass, for instance, is a marvellous and ever welcomed engine for at once relieving and utilising surplus boy energy, even disciplining and socialising it— collective action having here such a rarely obvious and immediate collective result.

Am I told that boys will injure the bird and animal life of the Park ? Doubtless, if, as at present, too often left uneducated with regard to it. But I may here cite the experience of my friend Prof. Hodge of Worcester, Mass., who in two or three years co-operation with the teachers of the town in the nature studies now prominent in America and incipient here, has so transformed boy conduct and boy influence throughout that large manufacturing city that instead of the numerous complaints of nest destruction and tree injury which were formally made on all hands, public and private, only one complaint was heard of in that connection last year, and that from the parents of a boy who had himself been too soundly trounced by his own comrades for a bird-nesting attempt of the very kind to which the same gang were in previous years devoted. For in the meantime they had learned to make bird-boxes, and take a friendly interest in the nests instead of a destructive one.

With the valued aid of my friend Dr Haddon, F.R.S., President of the Anthropological Institute, and with the advantage also of criticism and suggestion from Dr Munro, whose recent fascinating paper * will, I trust, receive the attention it deserves, I have drafted a scheme of illustration not only of the various types of habitation of the palæolithic age but of the neolithic and the earlier and later bronze ages also, with their respective monuments. This, however, I may keep in reserve until it can be more fully elaborated—the above description, with some suggestion in fig. 83 and in the large perspective (facing p. 228) being sufficient for the present, since the scientific interest and the educational value may be best considered apart from the details. To complement and continue this general presentment

I may, however, content myself by pleading that any to whom this educational scheme seems unpractical may refer to such recent literature of practical education as we owe to Parker and Jackman, Stanley Hall, Dopp, and other writers, or at least note that these emanate from America, and most of all from Chicago—surely not the city likely to be over-reverent of mere archæological survivals, be they in material form or in educational practice. This conception of education by progressive experience, and this of direct action and reaction with the completest attainable environment, is, in fact, the needed comple-

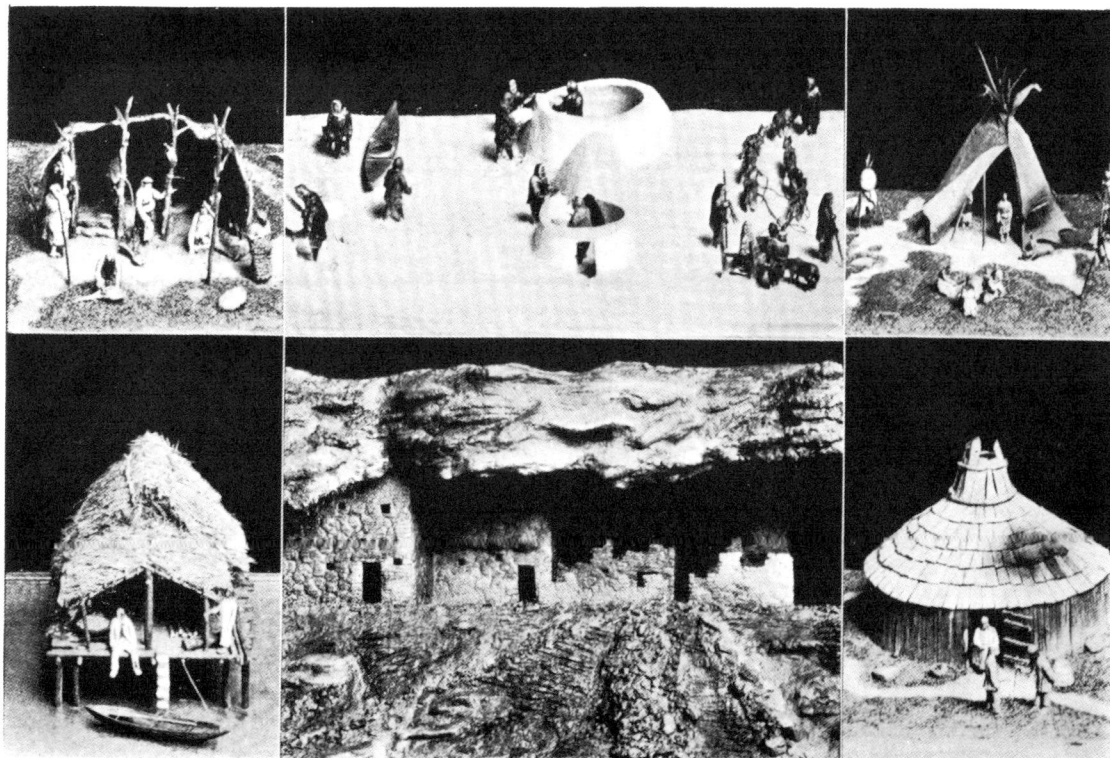

Primitive Indian Shelter.
Lake Dwellings (Venezuelan).

Eskimo Snow Huts, Sledge, and Kayak.
Cliff Dwellings (Arizona).

Sioux Tent.
Round Hut California.

FIG. 83.—Primitive Dwellings (Buffalo Exposition, 1901, from Report U.S. Museum).   Washington, 1903.

of the world from various points of view, astronomic and geographic, geological, botanical, and zoological, which we have already considered in previous chapters, by the correspondingly simple yet vivid and comprehensive exposition of the early relations of man to nature, and of some of the main phases by which he has risen to his present mastery, is surely of value too obvious to need argument.

Its educational value might also be much more fully argued for, if of this any doubt remains.

* "Man as Artist and Sportsman in the Palæolithic Period." Proc. Roy. Soc. Edinburgh 1903; and Grant, Princes Street, Edinburgh.

ment of the too purely subjective educational theories and practice of the past ; and when we observe that the leaders of this return to nature are among the foremost of living psychologists, as well as of pedagogues, any dread of a return to barbarism, or of a mere imitation of Diogenes or Thoreau, may be dismissed.

Again, since rapidly to recapitulate the main phases of the past is nature's way of passing beyond these, even of acquiring the impetus for passing in turn beyond the present phase, it may well also be ours. Or if a concrete proof be needed, that this very inquiry into the remotest past may be associated with a forelook into the future, I may mention this fact, too little known either to archæologists or to modern industrialists and inventors, at their opposite ends of the historic scale, that the man who first interpreted flint implements and excavated caverns—M. Boucher de Perthes, to whom the demonstration of the antiquity of man and the foundation of this modern archæology are historically due—-was also one of the most ardent advocates, if not the initial projector, of international exhibitions nearly a generation before 1851. " Tools and the man I sing "—this was his real standpoint, his practical motto. Would you prepare a young boy to be, some day, an electrical engineer—inventor it may be ? Set him to rediscover the fire-drill of the savage—the secret of Prometheus.

C. Correlation with Zoological Garden

Here then we have reached, from a fresh point of view, the very same practical proposals as those to which we came as the needed final development of the Zoological Garden (Chap. X.). Each plea has, I trust, its own weight and cogency ; and surely when now considered together their appeal must be far stronger. Naturalist and archæologist have of late had commonly too little to say to each other, though the " Natural History of Selborne " is a classical example of the thorough harmony of these points of view ; and now this open-air school and museum of anthropology unites the essential standpoints and results of both ; craftsman and adventurous boy do not usually co-operate, yet here they are at one ; even psychologist and pedagogue are not often so fully agreed, yet here all meet and co-operate. We see, too, that this scheme develops an otherwise unused and unimportant fringe of the park into a new unit, and one in its way as interesting as any, one enhancing the zoological garden by climax, the horticultural gardens by contrast, and furnishing, too, the needed link between the wild glen and cultivated levels, the civilised park and city around. We realise, in short, more and more of its manifold aspects and interests, from those of imagination at play to those of science and morals conveying upon industry. It is to be remembered, too, that the whole scheme, here necessarily unlike most others, is almost a costless one. For it is of the very essence of the scheme that it be realised, be it slowly or quickly, by the voluntary and unpaid labour of boys and youths, with no outlays, therefore, from the Trust beyond tools and supervision. Under all the circumstances, then, I venture to hope that the beginnings of execution may be at least made the subject of a sufficiently organised and patient experiment so soon as the right man or woman to inspire and superintend it can be found.

D. Open-Air Museums

One of the most notable of recent contributions to our knowledge of museums and their possibilities will be found in the admirable article by Mr George Brockner in *The Studio* for 1900, entitled " Open-Air Museums for London : A Suggestion." This is easily accessible, as also Mr Bather's recent invaluable Presidential Address to the Museums' Association Meeting at Aberdeen (Proceedings, Museums' Association, 1903), which is indispensable to every serious consideration of the subject of Museums in general. Hence it suffices here to give a simple idea of the Open-Air Museum from the accompanying figure (83a), which I owe to the courtesy of *The Studio*, and which represents the model of the design now being executed for the Open-air Museum of Christiania. It will be seen that this expresses the types of simple domestic and public architecture of town and country in Norway.; and this as far as possible from surviving examples, and with due garden setting and appropriate interior furnishing, so that the exact material conditions of civilisation in the past can be here precisely realised.

From this illustration, and still more from the whole paper from which it is borrowed, my repeated insistence upon this comparatively unfamiliar idea will be better understood, as also the even greater corresponding value of these surviving relics of Old Dunfermline, upon which I have so repeatedly insisted in this connection. Like my preceding plea for School Gardens, for a Great Globe or the like, however my proposals may seem in advance of public opinion or educational practice in this country, they are but to utilise the experience or the scientific outlook elsewhere attained, and if possible to overtake the successful educational pioneering of other countries. The absurd irritation, or even accusations of " lack of patriotism," of " faddism," or the like, so familiar to every one who has endeavoured during the past decade or two to inform his countrymen of foreign advances in educational theory or practice has at length abated ; but the practical difficulty of having these modern resources and ideas even fairly tested in detail, much less introduced, still remains. For in the present phase of educational transition, as the writer well knows, nearly everyone readily grants one's general appeal but is afraid to give trial to any of its particulars.

Upon such lines, then, there is no small field and opportunity, even of national pioneering, before Dunfermline. And in cases such as the present, where pioneering is but the adaptation and combination of ideas and methods of proved efficiency, the period of preliminary consideration may naturally be shorter than in cases where precedents, home or foreign, cannot be brought forward

E. Correlation with Technical Education and General Culture

As I go to press a valuable letter comes to hand, this time from one of the pioneering educationists of America, Dr Felix Adler of New York, who, as at once the head of a great city school, and as the inspiring leader of the ethical movement in America, naturally approaches the education problem from a very different pole from that of naturalist and gardener, which predominates in these chapters.

"What I have to say now may be inapplicable to the local conditions, or perhaps it is already embraced in your scheme. At any rate this is my thought : A policy of culture for a small yet typical city is what you have in view. It seems to me that culture should centre about people's vocations ; that it should be gained not after one's work but in and through one's work. The labour problem to me is essentially the problem of so reconstituting the conditions of manual labour that the work shall become mentally, æsthetically, and morally stimulating. Hence I should sug-gest not only a good technical and art school in the neighbourhood of your factories but a museum of inventions, illustrating to the eye the progress of inventions from primitive times to the present, and helping to create the historic spirit. A really good labour museum on a sufficiently large scale does not yet, I think, anywhere exist. If you can build one you will be a pioneer.

"I hope that the time will come when a part of the manual labourer's daily work-time will be spent in educational study, and the time so spent will not be deducted from his pay. The school and museum will then be recognised as an integral part of the factory system."

On every side, then, I may take it that these proposals for a primitive village will, in principle, recommend themselves to practical educationists both technical and theoretic ; and our next problem is, therefore, to carry on the line of planning beyond these primitive beginnings, to the simpler manual arts and industries, and thence again to the complex mechanism, the finer arts of later civilisation and modern requirement, so uniting the claims of technical education and of general culture.

Fig. 83a.—Model of Open-Air Museum, Christiania. (From *The Studio*.)

FIG. 84.—Old Mill and miller's cottage at top of Jesmond Dene Park at Newcastle, preserved as focus and climax of park landscape. Blasted rocks of new waterfall, and new bridge in foreground.

CHAPTER XVIII

THE MILLS AND SMITHY

A. Aspect of Existing Buildings, etc.

As already said, there is probably no park in Britain so obviously interesting to the visitor from Dunfermline as Jesmond Dene at Newcastle, since there we have a larger and broadly similar " den " or " dene," with the advantage of greater scale, more water, and finer trees. It is also a remarkable piece of naturalistic gardening, the work of a fresh and original mind accustomed to operate both upon the greatest and the finest scales in various fields of industrial activity— that of Lord Armstrong, who personally designed and superintended the whole work before handing it over to the Corporation of Newcastle.

As we ascend the dene and admire its many beauties these culminate in a concluding scene, or rather group of scenes, which is the pride of Newcastle, and deservedly so, as fig. 71 (Chap. XIII.) and the accompanying fig. 84 indicate. Yet what are the main features of this ? A small lake, from which the stream issues in a fall perhaps 12 or 14 feet high, like the Linn in the glen ; artificial like it, but better done. And secondly, a little ivied cottage group—the old mill and its humble dwelling (fig. 84).

Coming now to our own Glen, I am surprised by the indifference displayed to the beauty—the real and remarkable beauty, the still greater possibility—of the falls along the mill lade, downwards to its joining with the main stream of the Glen. The idea of suppressing this fall in the interest of the main burn, or for any other reason, is too much like those which I have too often heard for destroying each (and therefore every one) of the old buildings of the Trust, and is similarly to be protested against on every ground. I yield to no one in my demand for a purified stream, and, of course, I quite approve turning the lade into the main burn, as is perfectly easy, whenever that may be necessary or convenient ; but that is a very different matter from admitting proposals for doing away with it altogether. A steep mill race, available for forty feet of falls, is too precious an asset to part with easily !

I ask comparison of the accompanying photographs of this fall with those of the Linn of Corrymulzie, a fall familiar to every visitor to Braemar —indeed, famous throughout the Highlands. With little alteration, practically the rearrangement of a few stones and some planting, the essential charm of such a lovely little fall could be reproduced here ; this despised lade thus furnish-

126

FIG. 85.—Existing Mill Lade ; ruins of old mills on left. Large modern mill buildings on right to be removed.

FIG. 86.—The same, with old mills repaired, and uppermost mill wheel restored. The stream slightly cleared of stones above so as to reopen natural slight irregularity of its course. The present bridge is rebuilt, and the wall replaced by a simple parapet. Finally, the lower portion of stream is cut back into a small fall.

ing a principal naturalistic feature and beauty of the entire park, estate, and even city ! This is a strong statement, yet one emphatically within the possibility of realisation (figs. 85 and 86).

One sees what has been made of all this at Newcastle, and then returns to Dunfermline, to find opportunities for better falls than the Linn, even if not so ample as Lord Armstrong's ; still more to see that our local group of mill buildings is far more complex than those which have been so skilfully utilised here, and even now are more pic-turesque from their best points of view than is the completed picture at Newcastle. But to note also how rare is the appreciation of this in Dunfermline is to obtain striking proof of the way in which lifelong habit and familiarity may blind us to the beauties at our very doors ; witness also the com-mon indifference to the merits of other and more imposing buildings. I am only stating what

FIG. 87.—View of existing mill buildings from opposite garden wall, showing picturesque group, with Fratry Hall and church spire above.

every fresh eye sees ; that in these mills, as in the old houses under the abbey, or, again, as in old Pittencrieff House, even in its very stables, there are features which would be the making of a park in many a greater city ; and, further, that it is on the utilisation and improvement of these features that the real success of our park design must depend—all our new adornments being successful as they group around, lead up to, or contrast with these essential features.

I am credibly informed, and my own experi-

ence goes to confirm the idea, that the preserva-tion of all these buildings can only be in the very teeth of the opinion of a majority of the public. But, if so, here is the use of such a report as the present. Its new constructive proposals can wait, but destruction is irreparable : it is necessary, therefore, to modify public opinion in this matter, or it may be too late.

Some help may be got from the conservative pleadings of many who have been concerned with construc-tive improvements in Scottish cities, our foremost living ar-chitects, our artists and art lovers as well as antiquaries. We may cite too the warmth of appreciation, not only of these trained æsthetes, but of the passing tourist with his camera, whose snapshots not only of the Fratry Hall, of the Abbot's House, or some other jewel of Old Dunfermline, but his views of the Mills or Queen Anne's House, of the mansion or stables aforesaid, wring from the citizen at least the admission that these, after all, " look not so bad in the photograph," yet somehow not well in reality. It is, of course, an absurd idea that the camera image or the eye of the trained and critical observer is not a test of reality ; while indiffer-ence (or at any rate non-train-ing) to composition, to light and shade, is so ; or that an off-hand decision that an old building should be destroyed is a fair preparation for discussing its merits. Yet though I have heard this sentence of Jeddart justice for each and every one of these old buildings not once nor a dozen times, I must yet press for trial and reversal now.

Let me begin by conceding that photographs or drawings are so far perplexing to the plain observer, since they express deliberate selection of the best points of view. Yet why should these best points of view be usually unknown to the destructive critic, who has in the majority of cases frankly to admit that he has never seen these points at all; indeed, would often be puzzled to find the spots from which they were taken ? It is a modest and a practical proposal that paths, when necessary, be made or cleared to these spots and that seats be placed at them, so that our critics may in fairness be able to go there and reconsider their former verdict.

What contrast in architecture anywhere, for instance, can be more surprising than that of the two aspects of the palace ruins—the back a gaunt, dilapidated two-storeyed wall seen from the north, while seen from the glen the visitor is startled by a front which may be fitly compared to that of Warwick Castle (figs. 44, 77). No doubt in a smaller way, yet quite truly, the same principle holds both of the old mills and of the old cottages below the abbey, and especially of the former.

Will the Dunfermline reader, who can so easily do this, frankly and open-mindedly make this experiment on the spot? That is, of comparing in succession the views from the level, and then from the hollow, of palace and abbey, of cottages and mills in succession, before refusing to consider the present discussion? For the reader elsewhere figs. 87 and 88 will doubtless suffice, since he comes to them with a fresh eye.

But admitting there is beauty, is there not also ugliness? Certainly yes; granted at once. The north side of the palace wall, and especially the north elevation of Pittencrieff House, are greatly deficient, and though even here the trained eye might urge extenuating circumstances, these might not be sufficient to gain its case. The Monastery Street aspect of the mills is at present poor enough (fig. 91, Chap. XX.); while the photographs of the monastery itself show the humble old white-washed smithy as on the whole a blot upon a great architectural composition (fig. 93, Chap. XX.); and on plan (fig. 115, Chap. XXIV.) it will be seen that I propose wholly removing both of these, with the result of opening up the street into a fine public place, such as the city has not had hitherto (Chap. XX.).

And if this street widening be approved by the modern spirit, as surely it must, I trust that it will also disprove any accusation of mere æstheticism, or mere sentimental adherence to things old for old age's sake, independent of historic value; but will gain me fair hearing while I attempt to show the real reasons of my apparent conservatism.

Leaving now this question of beauty, I am next

asked—Have these old buildings really taken any part in history? But here my difficulty is that my interlocutor usually does not mean history at all but biography—a minor, though important matter. Fortunately for old architecture the many houses in which Queen Mary happens to have slept in her peregrinations seem partly thereby preserved; yet such an incident is not, of course, a serious historical reason at all, albeit this

FIG. 88.—Slightly different view of the preceding, with more picturesque light and shade, and altered composition.

second Helen of Troy was again well-nigh queen on the chessboard of Europe. History is primarily social: it is by their place and part in social changes that places, buildings, individuals have historical importance at all. Thus, as regards a great church, it gains greatly, of course, in interest from its illustrious foundation and its historic sepulchres, but surely all will agree that its main significance comes from its place in larger history—that of thought and feeling, faith and cult, and their expression in architecture.

Now here is the point: that to whoever has once

I

learned to read history as primarily of the general movement of civilisation, and who is not a mere annalist or antiquary, indifferent or lost outside his own particular period, all centuries are interesting, all are necessary. Not only the Celtic Tower or the mediæval Palace, but the Abbot's House, so well screened from the street, and with its cautious motto, a characteristic reminder amid the turmoil of the times ; not only the old mansion with its mingling of Puritan and Cavalier spirit and memoirs, but all other buildings similarly reveal, if unconsciously so much the better, the spirit of their age to every passer-by who will take the pains to read.

Thus the extreme sternness and simplicity yet skilled proportion of Queen Anne's House, or even of Robert Adam's Stables, express the clear, cold abstract thinking yet comprehensive grasp of the eighteenth century, just as do the books of Hume or Smith themselves (see figs. 25 and 36).

To possess old buildings which illustrate the lives of eminent individuals is no doubt of interest ; but of far more value is a sufficient series to illustrate the general development of the ages, the succession of the various social formations. This is the essential historical possession, the real treasure of any city. This is not a question of individual possession or of local trusteeship—the city holds these in trust for its nation, for the larger world.

B. Historic Interest of Mills

Admitting some cogency, some attractiveness, in the idea that the real museum of a city is such an Open-Air Museum of survivals, as ignorance or torpidity, or good intentions even, may have left undestroyed, why all this bother over some ruinous, even dilapidated, little old mills ? What possible claim have they to historic consideration any more than the smithy I have proposed to abandon ?

It may again seem paradoxical (but so, be it observed, does every new point of science, historical just as physical) to say that in this old, ruinous corn mill is a historical centre, and one even more indispensable to the comprehension of Dunfermline by its own inhabitants than the Tower Hill itself. This hill, defended by its ravine and commanding the great north road and the western one alike, is of the highest significance. Yet this does not always seem so familiar to Dunfermline people as it is obvious to visitors ; while the interest in the Celtic Tower, despite its central place upon the city arms, has been too lately revived to save almost a stone above its mere foundation (fig. 2). May not, then, there be something to learn about these mills while it is not yet too late ?

Here, then, is the point : that the feudalism of the palace, the ecclesiasticism of the monastery, viewed from the contemporary economic view of history, which now takes precedence of the common romantic pictures of sword or cowl, are the two rival ways, temporal and spiritual, of exploiting the miller and his mill. In short, the economic maintenance, and therefore consciously or subconsciously the policy, of tower and abbey, of mediæval Church or State, was very largely in terms of their rival or coadjusted grips upon the corn sack coming to the mill, their dips into the flour sack going out again.

Just as the position of the Celtic "Dun" and its adjacent roads affords one of the finest object-lessons in military geography in Scotland or elsewhere, so the position of this little mill in relation first to Tower, then to abbey and palace, is the corresponding object-lesson in economic history. To destroy the mills now would thus be a less excusable vandalism than was the destruction of the Celtic tower : that was done in times of general ignorance, while the other could only nowadays be done by mere local persistence in ignorance, enough to evoke the indignation of students of history everywhere.

The importance of this mill was symbolically recognised by trustees and citizens alike in the recent admirable inaugural ceremony of infeftment ; and to destroy the ancient mill now would be to convert that admirable function from a great initiative ceremony into a mummery, a tragic farce. Whereas this ceremony of the acceptance of these great gifts involved a pledge to the future, even more than a spectacle to the present. We may thus be confident that however frequent be indifference to the value of this or that element of this great heritage, nothing is now likely to be swept away which posterity would certainly deplore.

C. The Smithy (fig. 93, Chap. XX.)

Why, then, do I propose to destroy even the old smithy, confident as I am that every historic element will be required of us by our successors ? for the position of this, again, is no mere accident, though not so definitely fixed to one precise point, like the old mill by its wheel to its lade. And, though the present building is obviously of no great antiquity, there must have been a smithy hereabouts through unnumbered centuries, historic and shadowy. It is not only that the peasant who had to cart his grain to his lord's mill might naturally have his horses shod at the same time, but for a reason wider as well as more romantic : the king's couriers from Edinburgh and the Border, the abbot's messenger from Rome, all would come up from Queensferry by Monastery Street to the Palaceyard ; and starting back they all naturally needed the services of the smith. He too was not only horseshoer and toolmaker of peace, but armourer of war. Long before heraldry was for display or pride (these are mere after developments) it was pictorial shorthand ; and as the city naturally has its initial tower, so the county has its mounted guardian and Border messenger, the " Thane of Fife " still to be seen over the door of the policeman's cottage in every village. The knight in essential origin and function was no prodigy of romance : when we think of him rationally, we see he was the mounted policeman of his time (fig. 96).

That the smith could use the sword as well as make it, we learn from Hal o' the Wynd ; but a larger view of history teaches us how, " for lack of a nail the shoe was lost," and for lack of a shoe the horse, the rider, the message, the battle, it may be the kingdom itself. So it is that, as the king's servants ever become the king's ministers, the king's horseshoer was the right man to be his marshal ; foresight growing onwards, expressed and applied here or there by individual genius. It is thus no far-fetched literary parallel, but a direct sociological development, which identifies the vast foresight of Napoleon, the precisely organised staff-office of von Moltke, as the development of the humble palace-smith's provision of shoes and nails. It is in historical education as in other matters ; thus the town child at first knows coal as a detached object and then as a word to spell, a thing to read about, by-and-by with a description of a woodcut of the mine. But we are just beginning to take the pupil to the place where it is exposed, to the mine itself. In the same way our historical studies must begin by seeing and understanding such places if they are to have educational reality. It is just because I am passing on to propose the largest scope for the literary and artistic treatment of the history of Dunfermline that I seek to put all this upon that elementary basis of everyday experience upon which science and history alike arise.

After conceding to the plan of street widening and to the due exposure of the abbey walls, the demolition of the old smithy, we noted its historic interest ; but not its everyday usefulness, nor the rare picturesqueness it shares with every smithy interior. While removing it, then, as an obstruction to our new place let us retain the public utility and renew the picturesqueness by building a new smithy (fig. 90) on the excellent site shown in plan (fig. 115) on the opposite side of the Place. This moderate outlay would be even more regularly and immediately remunerative than the refreshment rooms and Crafts Village, to which we shall come in the next chapter, and even the Carnegie Trust will soon find use for all its rent-roll. Externally, too, from every aspect, the group of mill buildings is further improved. Moreover, this old-established business is not displaced for mere æsthetic reasons ; the very idea of such a thing should surely be most uncongenial to a practical business community and its trustees, who might well have resented such an idea had it come from the æsthetic side.

I plead, then, not only for an old business and a public convenience which can cause no possible interruption or destruction to the street, since not only is this widened but space for carts and horses is provided within. I plead not merely for the historic reason above sufficiently insisted on, but for this direct one ; and next for its technical interest also.

I have no faith in the educational value of the commonplace art museum with its metal masterpieces in a glass case, and the smithy nowhere. This whole museum tradition, though still too largely in power, answers but to stamp or scalp collecting. Wherever real technical education is beginning, it centres on seeing and sharing the real work, and then applies the paper drawings and the collections of the old system to their right uses. Yet technical education begins far deeper, it begins when " the children coming home from school look in at the open door." Search our whole park from end to end and there is no better or more beautiful sight than this of the glowing forge, the flying sparks, no more elemental stuff of future music than the ringing of the anvil. Its continuity, too, with the primitive village of the Stone and Bronze Ages, by here presenting the essential workshop of the Iron Age, will again surely not be without appeal to many. But this also is the link to the present. This one more plea and I have done. Looking out from our hill-set city we see how notably our local history and civilisation centre upon the mastery of iron and steel. Nearest us the Forth Bridge, supreme in its way ; over at Bo'ness Dugald Stewart's home, where James Watt exhibited his first engine to the admiring philosophers of Edinburgh. Turning west we recall the memorial of the old girdle-smiths of Culross ; beyond glow the furnaces of Falkirk and Camelon, the forges of Carron. So that here is the very history of iron in peace and war, from the sharpening of the Roman sword, from the (only half mythical) tempering of Excalibur to the " carronades " of our old wars, for Carron was not so long ago, for Britain, for Russia even, the veritable Essen or Creuzot of the times. And now once more the war centre is returning, with its floating fortresses of steel.

Most emphatically, then, to our open-air regional museum of history and school of life the elemental forge is indispensable. Even were the preceding arguments less strong we should still regard the smithy as a no less characteristic memorial of our leading citizen and generous founder than his cottage home. Each is, in fact, the natural complement of the other, the retention of the smithy being on this ground alone almost as desirable as that of the cottage in Moodie Street.

CHAPTER XIX

THE CRAFTS VILLAGE

A. Design in Detail

As late as the last century, as old engravings show, and, indeed, the survivals of the actual buildings, there were no less than three wheels upon the lade. I propose, however, for the present to be satisfied with the restoration of one only, the uppermost and principal one. Of the history of this mill a literal time record may be seen, engraved by the revolution of successive wheels upon the old masonry of the wall. The wheel should be again an overshot one, so giving increased height to the fall below, which, as already pointed out, needs only a few days' careful work to develop it into the finest single feature of the glen ; thus I trust doing away with the suggestion of suppressing this lade altogether.

But what is to be done with this mill ? Unpractical though it may seem, it is to grind corn, and this essentially as of old. Here is, in fact, a fundamental element of the Open-Air Museum, and, still better, of that " Labour Museum " also, for which engineer, technical educationist and artist, economist and sociologist, even moralist, are increasingly looking, and which the initiative of Chicago and of Scandinavia has begun to supply to their communities.

We grind, then, our grain here, and in the repaired and improved buildings above we bake the resultant oatmeal and flour into cakes and scones for the refreshment rooms of our visitors. Here, in fact, we have at once a pleasing and an educative feature—the restoration of the fundamental domestic industry. The interior of this mill at work, supplied with the old and simple machinery of our forefathers, would be one of the most attractive sights of the whole park for many. All the more when below this, upon the course of the stream, we put in a succession of notched stones, in which boys may put their own little water mills and rig up their models of primitive forms like the Norse one.

Now to this simple installation let me add one other. For the water mill may at pleasure drive not merely its millstones but, detached from these, transmit its motion to a little room beyond, in which should stand the simplest and most primitive possible of dynamos. In this way the great steps in the utilisation of water power, from the child's toy to the modern electric developments, could be brought together, and the progress of uncounted ages thus condensed into the object-lesson of a holiday or a school visit.

Turn back to the two photographs of the mills in the previous chapter (figs. 87 and 88) and compare the present perspective sketch of them as repaired for use (figs. 89 and 90).

Looking now at the buildings above we see how the circular-ended stable has something of the lines of a little Norman church, something also of the stout simplicity of a castle tower. From its north side, on the street level, the rough wooden balcony of access to its garret gives us the needed motive. In the new design this roof is simply heightened by 5 feet, so giving a good-sized refreshment room, with ample and beautiful outlook into the den ; and its windows, seen from the glen, now give lightness and beauty to the simpler walls below. This upstairs refreshment room is next extended into the old circular malt barn, heightened again 5 feet, and crowned by a camera obscura, which would give attractive and varied pictures of the whole scene around, above and below. From this upper refreshment-room level we continue into a new building, practically represented, however, at present by an old tiled shed, and again commanding pleasing views to southward and to east and north.

On the ground floor of the present stable might be at least two main rooms of a small cottage for the miller and his wife ; or, since it is not necessary that anyone should live upon these premises, they would be better employed as the kitchen of the refreshment rooms (fig. 90).

This kitchen should be of the simple old-fashioned, hospitable type, still lingering here and there in a Scottish farmhouse or mansion, or in an English village. In its ample fireplace the oatmeal and flour from the mill below would be baked into cakes and scones upon a goodly Culross girdle, and the guests' homely tables and settles would fill up the rest of the room.

In the small room to the south should be placed a modern kitchen and scullery, with gas and all

FIG. 89.—General architectural perspective of Mill Buildings, developed as Crafts Village, with refreshment-rooms, etc., showing effect of slightly raising the present central octagon roofed kiln as camera, with roofs also of adjacent buildings to right and left, thus giving additional picturesqueness and useful refreshment-room storey. The open verandahs and stairs of the right-hand block contrast with simple, rounded apse effect of former old stables on the left. New smithy with projecting window seen to left of this. (Trees of fig. 88 left out for clearness' sake, but not to be removed.)

Below is shown the existing mill ruin repaired, with flat roof and balustrade as additional open-air refreshment-room space. The old over-shot wheel is restored. The existing second mill is also reroofed, and to the left and farther down are proposed new buildings, completing workshops of Crafts Village. Above these are faintly suggested the Tower of Pends and line of Palace wall. To the right is indicated the mill garden, with rose-arbours above, and with ample seats cut in bank, around a level oval suitable for dancing, etc.

FIG. 90.—Complementary view—*i.e.* north-east front towards Monastery Place (see fig. 91). The present buildings towards the street are removed, and their site added to the breadth of the Place. The existing small octagon Tower, with its outside stair, leading to refreshment-gallery in raised roof of old stable, and to the corresponding verandah refreshment-room on the left is again plain. The smithy is seen to right, with small court for carts and horses. The wall on each side should be lowered to a balustrade. Descending on left is seen widened out the main thoroughfare of the present Monastery Street, with proposed new road also turning down under History Building to join public thoroughfare at the Manse entrance. See general plan and fig. 115.

appliances for the rapid service of larger numbers, and from this little room would pass a service lift for communication with the floor above. Entering practically from the present descent to the malt kiln furnace would be situated the lavatories.

In these two storeys, then, we have thus comfortable accommodation for say 40 guests in the upper storey and 25 in the lower.

Note now on the south (fig. 89) in addition to this the little stair leading from the street level down to the open space above the working mill. Here, again, is room for not only a wall bench with table but for seats accommodating a good few additional persons. Again, we may extend this platform by using the flat roof of the mill itself ; this can have an awning stretched over it in summer if desired. Here, then, we have considerable refreshment-room space, with economy and picturesqueness ; our old mills are again living and working ; the park, palace, and abbey effects are notably improved without any loss of area ; and the objection of the modern spirit to these old buildings, ruinous no longer, is, I trust, completely and finally removed (figs. 87 and 88, Chap XVIII.).

What of the second ruined mill, of the ruined wall of the third, still standing at the foot of the fall ? And what of the present nettle-grown hillside within its old square wall ? (fig. 88, Chap. XVIII.).

Begin with the lowest bit of ruin (not shown in figures), and see again how this, doubtless to many a worthless fragment, is again when we view it with artistic eye a foreground element of the highest pictorial value to our whole impression of the palace ruins. Not only so, but it greatly extends the effect of these. Now looking at the whole range of ruins, from mills to palace, from every point, across, up, and down stream, we see that the former are indispensable to the extent as well as to the dignity of the latter, so that their demolition would dwarf the palace in a way which even the least observant would appreciate, though when it was too late. Photographs, however, from various points of view will show this (cf. fig. 76, Chap XIII.).

This lowest bit of ruin, then, must be left practically as it stands, at most with such slight repair, mainly of cement pointing on top and north as is necessary to guarantee its permanence. But along the wall, near the site of the vanished " King's Barns," the accompanying plan shows the proposed erection of a further group of one-storey buildings, enhancing the importance of the mills above, which thus crown a more complex composition. With the addition of these few simple and inexpensive buildings we may now complete the essentials of a further element of the whole scheme, broadly answering to the " Arts and Crafts Village " of many industrial exhibitions,

to a further development of the Labour Museum, to a very real development therefore of technical education. It would also be a rent-earning subject to the Trust and a means of legitimate industry to its tenants.

B. Crafts Village in Operation

It is but rarely that the visitor to any of our Scottish towns can get anything of any local character to take away with him : there is little choice save of picture post-cards and trifles, probably produced elsewhere. Why should the visitor not have the interest and pleasure of seeing the artist-craftsman at work and taking away something from him as a souvenir of his visit ? Why should not one or two of these new workshops, for instance, be let to weavers upon the old handloom, or some such slight adaptation of it as is now constantly being employed in that renascence of simple domestic industries which is now reappearing in so many parts of Britain and Ireland ? Beside the loom a sale counter might display characteristic examples of the many attractive possibilities of linen, hand-made and manufactured alike. The refreshment-rooms of the park might usefully help in the education of the visitor to that use of the table napkin which, were it developed to even a slight proportion of that general in Continental countries, would soon far more than double the staple industry of Dunfermline. The apparently perverse initiatives of Ruskin, and their development in the Irish village industries of Sir Horace Plunket, thus lead us on to modern Dunfermline once more.

Again, beside the weaver, why not the brass and copper-worker, with a variety of production, from the simplest napkin ring to the beaten salver and the like ? Here, in fact, would be the beginning of what, in the far smaller, less favourably-situated, and historically less art-productive community of Keswick, has spread into a large and flourishing artistic industry of wide educational usefulness and even substantial economic return. Again, in another of these booths might be the silver-worker, the jeweller, not, as too much in Edinburgh, retailing as " Scottish jewellery " South American agates cut in Bavaria and mounted in Birmingham, but the designer and executant in one. For the wood-carver there should, again, naturally be a place. Why, indeed, should there not also be a desk for the illuminator ; the germ, again, of a renewal of the historic scriptorium ?

It would be easy to multiply these suggestions still further. The point is enough if the general principle be indicated—that of forming again a little School of Crafts which would practically from the very first be self-supporting. At first sight does it seem that there is here any interference with private enterprise ? Not more than in any exhibition, of which the stalls are surely far more correctly described as extensions of private enterprise. Their products, if successful, would soon find active rivalry throughout the town, so that passing along the streets the visitor would find many things characteristic of the place and each with its own beauty or usefulness. As the scheme developed other industries would be added, or rather would add themselves. Why not, for instance, the potter with his wheel, the florist ; even the bagpipe maker, and so on ?

That an everyday village blacksmith has in his apparently homely craft-mastery a latent artistic skill only needing opportunity for its arousal is well shown by the marvellous reproduction of that Scaliger railing, which is at once one of the sights of Verona, and one of the masterpieces of the forge. A Scottish tourist, the late Mr Jenner, brought home a photograph of this, and showed it to his village smith, with the half-jesting question—Can you do anything like that ? " Let me see ! May I try ? " was the answer—and the present reproduction was the result, one well re-paying a visit to Portobello by either smith or sceptic.

Thus around the renewed industrial nucleus of mill and smithy, the finer arts would again natur-ally arise. Such a scheme is, of course, really nothing new ; it is only what has been arising once and again in many parts of these islands, following upon the incentives of Ruskin and Morris. That there is here no real clashing with the interests of the great modern machine-production is plainly evidenced by their reaction upon the improvement of machine industries themselves in character and design, and this not only in England, Ireland, or Scotland but increasingly in the United States, where the simpler art industries had so largely been lost sight of altogether.

To other towns, and even to some villages, this Crafts and Arts Village would be the most interest-ing and suggestive of all our schemes, as it is the most self-sustaining and least costly. Its reaction upon the art schools and technical schools would be a deep and increasing one. Most important of all its uses would be its reaction upon young Dunfermline. For to see good work going on, to imitate it, to help in it, was the very essence of education long before our present regime of lessons and games, and will be again when most of these are forgotten.

The presence, too, of this little hive of industries in this peaceful yet nobly picturesque and historic environment would again have its reaction upon immediate and local design, and thus upon the quality of the staple industries themselves. It would serve also as a much needed object-lesson of old-world conditions of labour upon their better side, and even for this reason alone it deserves its place in our Open-Air Museum.

Fɪɢ. 91.—View from Abbey Churchyard, looking over old Mills into Glen (Mill Dene and Manse Dene). The two main buildings to Monastery Street to be removed, and their site added to widened Monastery Place. The three old buildings seen behind are those seen in figs 87 and 88 (*q.v.*), and as improved in figs. 89 and 90.

F. HISTORY AND ART

CHAPTER XX

MONASTERY PLACE

THE general conception of the historical, because social, significance and interest of these old buildings should be thus as clear as is their possession of artistic value, and the explanation of the plan and perspective herewith submitted may now be proceeded with.

A. Improvement of Monastery Street in Detail

The removal of the unsightly portion of the mills, required also for the widening of Monastery Street, will readily be seen to disclose a picturesque view (*cf.* fig. 91), which may now be compared with the other views of previous chapters. Even in the present unimproved state the value of contrast appears. The monastery wall with its stately line of hall windows, the church spire above all, gain beyond description from the contrast of these small and irregular old buildings in front, just as the church front does from its cottages below (see frontispiece), and equally to remove these buildings would be irreparably to injure the general effect. So obvious is this that any artist or architect, anyone accustomed to pictures, would point out the necessity of reproducing this contrast by new, low, modest and irregular buildings were the present ones destroyed.

It is with architecture absolutely as it is with music or with colour : contrast is a main, indeed an indispensable, resource of effect to every composer. This principle is again illustrated on the opposite side, where it again saves an old building, otherwise comparatively unimportant. Compare the three familiar aspects of the monastery buildings (figs. 92, 93, 94). See how our impression of the finest portion taken alone is improved by the second mass, with its lower and simpler wall seen above the smithy. In the third (fig. 94) (despite discordant elements, to be removed), note how this wall appears lofty and massive by the contrast of the low crow-stepped gable. This, in fact, is the positive beginning, from which the next wall is

136

FIG. 92.—View of West end of Monastery Place, looking down and West from projection of Abbey Churchyard above, along buttressed facade of Fratry Hall towards the Tower gateway or Pend, through which the street passes; an arch and ruinous fragment of Palace kitchen seen on the left. While the main façade and ruins of this illustration are, of course, left untouched, its effect is improved by lowering the present high wall on the left to a mere balustrade, and by throwing into the street a railed-in patch of ungrouped shrubbery, thus widening the street into a place. (Shrubs might, however, with advantage be massed in the space between the buttresses.)

FIG. 93.—View taken a little farther East, and from the street level, with old smithy in foreground.

comparatively great, and the last superlative in dignity and beauty. The spectator coming up the street may not have been conscious of this source of effect, but it has helped his impression all the same. It is, in fact, the presence of this little old building which enables us artistically to dispense with a demand for some low structure in the place of the old smithy. (Compare figs. 94 and 95.)

Next, following up this consideration, we see the smithy away and this piece of graveyard wall exposed, its sternness relieved by windows which advantageously repeat those of the Fratry wall.

of death and vanished greatness above, is an equestrian statue. Here this would be no merely decorative feature, but the needed symbol of Man and Nature, of life in Joy and Power, of Youth and Energy. Mr Watts' statue of Energy, or his statue of Hugh Lupus at Eaton Hall, are here noble and suggestive precedents. The accompanying sketch of Mr Duncan's has also its own character and fitness, especially should a bas-relief be all that funds may allow (fig. 96).

From this central feature of Monastery Place we

FIG. 94.—View farther back still, showing converging perspective effect, even now largely redeem-ing its meaner elements. Note low crow-stepped gable, faintly seen to left of smithy behind wooden shed.

The ugly and careless masonry of the modern parapet is now replaced by a simple but suitable balustrade. The simple square projection, however, needs something in front to continue and complete its salience. This should be done not by a building but by a monument; and the monument appropriate here has been already practically, by our discussion of the smithy, suggested—some commemoration of smith or of knightly rider, or of both together, in bas-relief. But what would give the whole Place a new picturesqueness and an added life, a needed contrast with the associations

proceed upwards to the Pends. In the large triangular railed-in space, which I ask to be cleared of shrubs and thrown into the street, should stand a drinking fountain for man and beast, with a range of massive and simple seats under the western wall of the square projection of the graveyard above. Against this broad, plain wall the natural contrast with the statue would be a vertical line of some sort; a pillared or storeyed fountain, therefore, of some height, say at least 12 feet, or even up to the ground level above, from which the new balustrade rises. But this should be no mere stony structure—all granite, no water—but a simple spouting fountain glittering in the sun, again the ideal contrast from the stern old walls around. The view of this to anyone coming through the pends, with eyes momentarily rested and their pupils enlarged by these few seconds of passage through deep shadow, must be imagined ; it cannot be rendered by any drawing.

Now returning downhill we pass once more the equestrian statue, and then come to the little

entrance, the whole being now reorganised as its gatehouse lodge and gardener's cottage. Its little turret, again, gives contrast to the long line of wall, and leads up to the tower and spire of the abbey, but here particularly to the façade and crown of the mediæval History Building farther east, next to be described. (Chap. XXI.).

The same principle of contrast here suggests the advisability of harling this little building, in contrast with the massive masonry of the adjacent lines of wall and of the great buildings above.

FIG. 95.—The same view, but now retouched. The front buildings of the old mills on the left are thrown into the Place ; and on the right the old smithy, the sheds, and tall building also are demolished, thus giving the ample width shown on general plan (fig. 115). The crow-stepped gable now forms part of entrance lodge of Bee-Alley Garden, and this small building gives scale to the old Monastery wall above (now graveyard wall). Of this wall the old lancet windows and buttresses are disclosed by the removal of the smithy, and the present graveyard parapet above is replaced by a simple stone balustrade. A fountain is shown at angle of present shrubbery, and an equestrian statue is indicated on site of the smithy.

red-roofed building, that of the crow-stepped gable already mentioned. Its long, plain, low wall here gives again both parallel and contrast to the graveyard wall we have just passed, and serves as the east background to the statue, just as the former wall did to the fountain.

This old building is shown on fig. 95, retained yet improved, along with the ruinous little tower-like building of the present Bee-Alley Garden

B. Bee-Alley Garden

There remains now for consideration on this side only the Bee-Alley Garden, exposed by the removal of the large mill and chimney stalk. It will now be seen that this projecting gatehouse cannot be removed, since it little more than covers the projection of the Bee-Alley Garden with its retaining wall. When this present chimney stalk and large mill are removed this retaining wall of the garden will come into view. It should be simply and massively buttressed, so as to give at once the feeling of massive masonry continuously onwards to the Fratry Hall, and reappearing in the mighty buttressing of the old Abbey Church above ; this small detail thus giving increased mass and dignity to the main architectural features as we come to them.

Balustrading above this roadway wall is indispensable from the garden side, and must be of bold and simple character. Some feature to break this continuous wall, and repeat in a smaller salient feature of this garden the large square projection of the abbey graveyard above, is here desirable. This is furnished by a needed staircase to the Bee-Alley Garden, of which the existing small cloister door is not enough ; hence the spacious double stairway shown in plan and perspective (fig. 98), with the further advantage of uniting Monastery Place with Bee Alley Garden, yet of

duly limiting these. This wall and staircase still need a feature of life and contrast, and this may here be best given by the use of water. How is this to be obtained ? Another drinking fountain is unnecessary ; but the mill lade runs through the Bee-Alley Garden above, and down under the street below. To bring this out, then, from an opening in this new staircase, to let it fall into a basin, and thence disappear on its course under the street to the mill as before, is easy. This would be most effective in every aspect, and both in harmony and contrast with the fountain farther up. Of adornment this rush of troubled water needs little ; say the serpent of eternity curving round its outlet, sweeping in a second curve round its disappearance (fig. 97). Above the whole, at top of the stair, and thus recessed from this fountain by the whole breadth of its pavement, screened too from the Bee-Alley Garden by uniting masses of poet's laurel and golden yew planted to right and left, should sit enthroned a noble

Fig. 96.—Alternative suggestion of commemorative bas-relief.

figure. See, for instance, the suggestive value of such a statue as the " Sphinx " of Bistolfi, in *The Studio*.

Judge now this whole monumental scheme of the proposed Monastery Place from the existing old Pends to the new ones proposed later. Is it not evident that these improvements, with that of the Mills and of Bee-Alley Garden, may now be counted twice over, both as Park Improvement and as City Improvement ?—thus uniting these long-separated and now discordant halves as with a jewelled clasp, and, instead of costing ground to either, giving new spaciousness to both ?

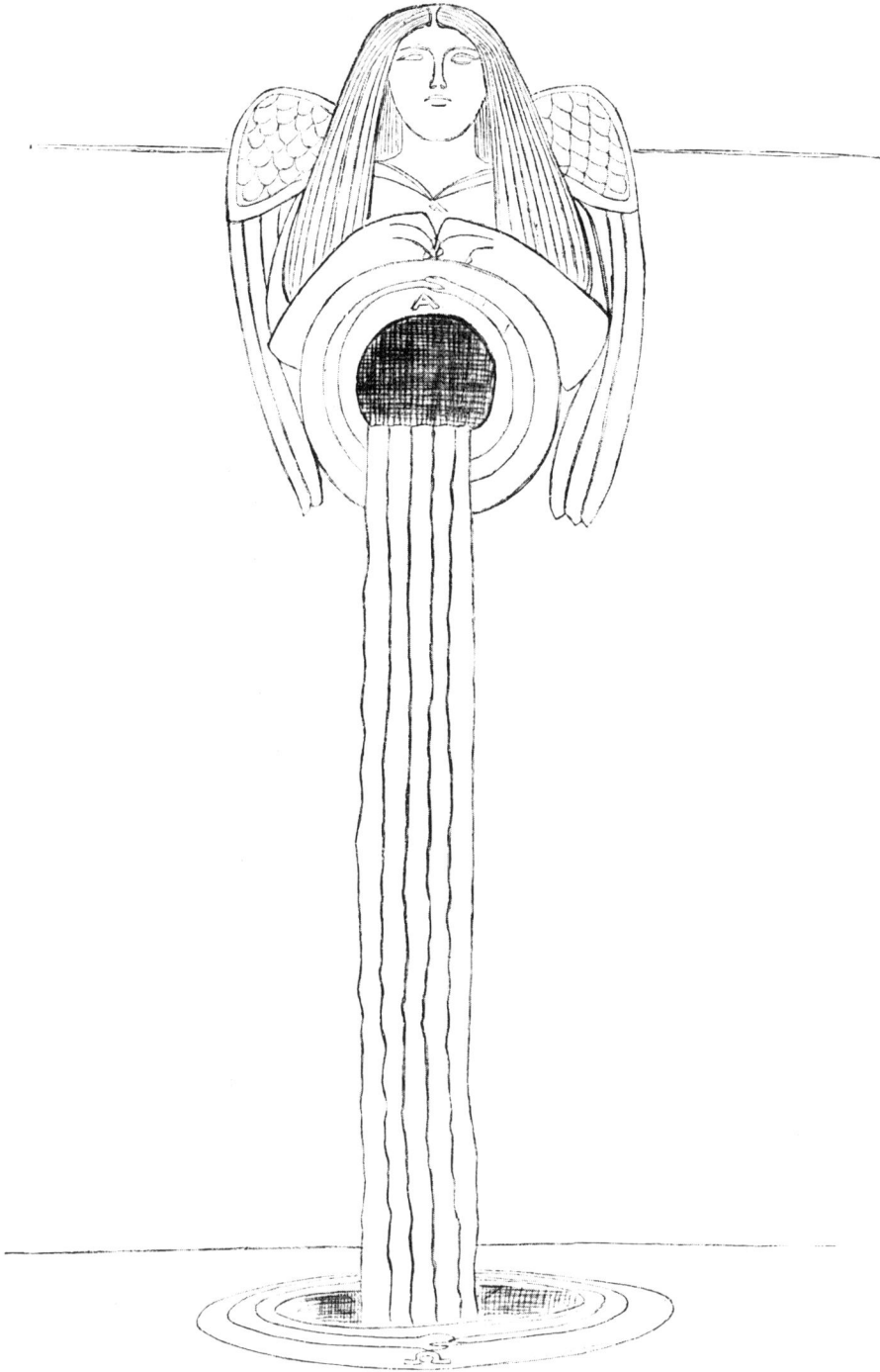

FIG. 97.—Outlet of Mill Lade under stairway to Monastery Place.   (*cf*. fig. 107, Chap. XXIII.).
Symbol of Eternity.

FIG. 98.—General view of Bee-Alley Garden, with circular pond, etc., as at present looking East from southward projection of Abbey Churchyard. The proposed cloister (fig. 102) would cover walk behind top of high retaining wall of churchyard seen on left. The main front of Mediæval History Building (fig. 105) would face spectator, thus concealing factory chimney-stalk to East, while the mill and chimney to South (right hand) would be removed, thus opening out view to Monastery Place. See plan (fig. 115).

CHAPTER XXI

INSTITUTE OF HISTORY

A. Need and Site

OUR study of nature was seen to involve at once a regional and a general survey, a study of homely details yet of vastest world aspects. Similarly our study of industry and art, beginning with the local crafts, must rise to fine art on the one hand and must descend to the simplest beginnings of human activity upon the other. This we see to admit of, in fact to require, an actual recapitulation in personal experience, from that of the Primitive Dwellings by the lake up to the Mills and Smithy, developed as a Crafts Village. Thence and later we shall come to the Art Gallery, in which this art activity and art education should blossom into subtler forms, of painting and the rest. Comparison with the best work of other places, exhibitions, and permanent collections, systematised teaching—and this of appreciation as well as of production—would all aid in raising the taste of the community, while re-establishing it upon its fundamentals. These include contact with nature and with material ; direct first-hand experience of observing and working ; and also contact with directive ideas. These have to be stated, not only as regards scientific law and artistic ideal, but as regards social ideal also ; for art is service.

That the modes of treatment here adopted for science and for art teaching are to some unfamiliar, it may be almost repellent, is possible. But, if so, I submit very seriously, as well as confidently, so much the worse for the present, or rather the declining order, deficient as it is in every one of these elements of reality just indicated, and existing far too essentially upon paper alone—paper instead of material, paper instead of nature, paper exercises and paper examinations instead of real experience, paper certificates and rewards, and paper reports to the public. I do not ask the revolutionary demolition of any existing educational machinery ; but, recognising the transition in thought and action now happily in progress, I urge the setting up by an independent body like the Trust of an equipment of real resources for contact with nature and with art such as I have been outlining. Such organisations, I do not hesitate to say, would be welcomed by all the progressive spirits of the educational world of Great Britain and of America, whether local, governmental, or general. For the fact is that, while much of the " Robert Lowe " order of education still survives in form, a new life has been arising everywhere, and in official circles no longer least of all.

It is time to outline a similar educational policy with regard to the resources of History, and those of the Modern outlook also, for the two go together. I am aware of the difficulty to many active modern spirits, that the plea for history is apt to be complicated with an undue conservatism of classical and traditional studies, and, therefore, is to be looked upon with distrust.

It is the weakness also of the historian to seem a mere antiquary of the past without adequate reference to the present, much less the future ; but is it not " the weakness of the practical man to look at the world through the single chink of the present," and so to misunderstand this in his turn, perhaps not less seriously ? Again, the mere Utopist fails also, by striving to see forward

142

without considering the present. But it is the essential advantage of the modern attitude, that gained by help of the doctrine of evolution, that we are at length learning to envisage past, present, and future together, as one continuous and unending stream, and to realise at once in the present the tremendous pressure of the heredity of the past, yet the promise and potency of the continuously varying future, of which the guidance towards degeneration, or towards true upward evolution, lies with such action as we may take.

B. History in Dunfermline

I propose, therefore, to sketch an outline of the Historic and Social Institute which is the natural complement of the Nature Institute already outlined, and the Art Institute to be considered later. For this again Dunfermline has many advantages as well as possibilities, so that here again we may reasonably carry out the founder's instructions of pioneering beyond the ordinary level of other cities.*

The immortality of the historic past is not only evidenced by the Tower Hill of Malcolm, the Cave of Margaret, by the later Abbey and its tombs, or the yet later Palace, but by the atmosphere of the city itself ; and this not only richly in literature as the recent admirable " Bibliography of Dunfermline " shows, but in the actual life and thought of its inhabitants. For seldom any soul is so completely dead as to forget the associations of his native city ; assuredly none returns without some feeling of how the heart may burn.

The tiny beginnings of an archæological and historical museum now mouldering within the Abbey Gatehouse Tower, the collection of the Public Library, or, again, the various scattered objects in private collections, are all evidences of the latency of this historic feeling : and where more appropriately than in Dunfermline can we now consider the adequate development of this—that is, upon a scale worthy of at once an ancient and historic capital, and of its present rejuvenescence ?

But historical education, I may be told, is attended to in the schools and universities ; it is represented in the greater libraries, in some measure, no doubt, in the local one ; while in Edinburgh the National Portrait Gallery and Antiquarian Museum should be sufficient for our higher requirements. I regret to traverse all

* Here I may refer to programmes of Edinburgh Summer Meeting sociological and nature teaching of former years, with their excursions to Dunfermline—of course long before the present benefactions to Dunfermline were heard of—as evidence that not only the historic interest of the city but its present significance, and even its latent reawakening, have long been matters of social prevision and educational expression.

these propositions as far as to affirm that these furnish but the materials, the suggestions, the incentives towards a new creation. This must be one utilising the advantages of all these, but transcending them, so as to furnish at once a civic and local centre of historic studies and social outlook, but a practically metropolitan institution also, befitting its central and accessible position among the cities and the universities of Scotland. I ask, then, full and frank consideration of the project and plans I now submit, the more since I make no impatient demand for their immediate realisation, but rather recognise that this should be a matter of gradual development, extending it may be over a not inconsiderable term of years, though also realisable block by block within a decade, or even less if desired.

What, then, is the problem before us ? It is to express the eventful history of our little city through its long past, to follow this onwards throughout its many vicissitudes of greatness and decline up to its present world-wide outlook and initiative, its consequent influence and example. This city is not merely a regional or provincial capital but of old a national one, and, therefore, of international significance also. Even in the everyday manufacturing present this national and this international significance are in their way no less important than ever ; while in the opening future these relations are becoming broader and more complex. Assigning, then, a historic gallery to Dunfermline and its history we see that this must be based upon a lower storey—that of Scotland as a whole—and this in turn upon a storey in which we must lodge some corresponding indication of the movement of the larger world of civilisation in all its wider aspects. For as we have seen that in geography we can only understand the world when we have a clear conception of our own region, so in history we can only understand our own city or nation in terms of that larger current of western civilisation of which it is their glory to have formed a part.

C. History in Scotland

The low average state of historical education and interest in Scotland, despite its own intensely dramatic history and its wealth of individual historic genius, has to be recognised and accounted for. The vague sentiment of Burns Clubs and Scott dinners and of boyish enthusiasm generally nowadays gives place at school to the getting up of " periods " such as that of the Norman Conquest of England, the policy of Henry VIII. or some other period of English history less influential upon ourselves. But Scotland is neither a self-sufficient nationality, as she once thought, not the mere " mutton bone of England," as is too often now supposed on both sides of Tweed ; she needs a third historical interpretation distinct from these, customary though they be to the patriotic historians of the respective countries. The interest of her history, which has made it better known in its main features and personalities to the whole world than that of any other small country since classical and biblical times, has to be accounted for ; and the explanation in a word is this, that here we are neither in Scotland merely, nor in the larger England merely, but that we are north-western Europe. It is at the tide mark that the great waves break most strongly and cast up their flotsam, even from the farthest seas. We know that the Border is on the whole the oldest, longest, and most fiercely contested of the national frontiers of Europe, but we forget that the immediate scene upon which our city towers look down is a greater and older frontier still. The Firth of Forth was not so long ago " the Scottish Sea " ; it once separated rival kingdoms just as it now unites friendly counties, and it is but ten short generations since the pirates of the opposite side harried the nearest town to our own. Within sight, too, though little visited by the exponents of that classical education which pretends to teach us of Rome—but so seldom gets us much nearer it than the decay of the Renaissance —stands what is on the whole its most notable monument outside Rome itself—the northmost Roman wall, so long the tidemark of conquest. Along the same line run prehistoric and post-Roman forts and memories almost without number. Thus, if these limits permitted the elaboration of even a single instance we should find here an indispensable link, as to north of us a starting-point, of that Arthurian cycle of legend and history, of poem and symbol, which has gone so deep and counted for so much in the literature and the idealism of Christendom, of which in our own days Tennyson, and still more Wagner, have proved the undying appeal, yet which still remains for some new poet and romancer, some true successor of Scott here in Scotland, to work out the full significance. For as Mr Stuart-Glennie and others have so fully shown, and as obvious geography and common-sense alike indicate, it was clearly upon Scotland that the Northman invasion broke before conquering its way southwards through England and Wales, Cornwall and Brittany. The heroic Arthur of all these legends is thus no mythic figure, but the composite portrait of each successive Celtic hero-king, as, despite gallant defence and hard-won victory, he fell at length, like Wallace in later days, at once betrayed and overpowered, yet leaving behind him not only memory and example, but hope, with its unconquerable renewals of strife and victory. No Scottish historic Arthur !—the dry-as-dust historian of mere records tells us, as if history were not written deep in geography first, in place, name,

memory and legend next, and read in records only afterwards, if made or preserved at all ; whereas the real truth is that Scottish history beyond all others is of this ever-recurrent cycle of victory and tragedy. Arthur follows Arthur in procession as long as Banquo's ; then Wallace with his quartered limbs, a veritable Arthur ; then Bruce, with his far-thrown heart, a Lancelot and an Arthur in one. The Douglases, desperate lords of battle, yet tender and true, are of the same stuff ; the poet-Stuarts, first and fourth alike, with their gallant reigns, their tragic ends—each in his way is a returning, a departing Arthur. In Mary is a new Guinevere ; in Charles I., in Prince Charlie, despite all imperfections and failures, something of the Arthurian spirit and fascination returns. Even now it but sleeps, awaiting call. No wonder, then, that this grey landscape south and west of our windows should have had beyond its local chroniclers and bards a veritable later Homer, a true Merlin, reawakening the dulled world to the spell of romance, ballad, and history—for Scott's romance is no idle fancying, but ballad and history in one. Only dull miseducation can make any think that magic and romance are over ; modern science, modern art alike, know that these are but beginning ; wherever man gains power over nature there is magic ; wherever he conceives an ideal, and carries it out into life, there is romance. Where, then, were more of either than are opening to us in these very times, in this very city to-day ? It is time, therefore, to be planning our buildings as homes worthy of each.

D. The Procession of History

Sitting down, then, to the actual historic materials we compile our lists of notable persons and events in chronologic order. But instead of such a table being a mere dry-as-dust burden for schoolboy memory it is the plan of a pageant, the literal order of a procession. Pending the redemption of our vast modern theatrical and musical resources from their transitory degradations, their temporary extravagances, their too common fooling or worse, to what should be—will be before long—recognised as one of their highest possible tasks, the vivid presentment to and in each city of all that is most notable and educative in its own and in the world's great past, we may at least realise this in picture. And here, as befits the frequent initiative of Scotland in history and romance, we have one of the most comprehensive examples yet executed for any nation's history—the bold design of Mr W. G. Burn Murdoch, his " Procession of Scottish History " for seven hundred years, from Duncan and Macbeth, Malcolm and Margaret, to Prince Charlie—a sketch now accessible for school or private decoration, or for library reference in a compact roll, and so awaiting fitting realisation in sculpture, in colour, and in actual periodic pageant. The historic frieze lately executed by Mr W. G. Hole for the National Portrait Gallery in Edinburgh is a

or the series of panels by Mr John Duncan in University Hall. The utility of such historic resources and of such latent leadership in

FIG. 99.—Time and the Fates; the Dial of History.

similar example, with which may be taken his historic frescoes in the same building. The decorative panels of the history of Glasgow, executed for its Municipal Buildings by four of its most eminent artists, may also be cited;

brightening " the auld grey toun " with pageant and festival anew surely needs no lengthy exposition. Such noble pleasures, such memorable holidays, would soon become protective against coarser ones.

E. Site and Approach

Where shall we place our historic building ? I need not spend time arguing out all the reasons which have determined my selection of the ancient garden of the monastery, the quaintly-named " Bee-Alley Garden," below the Abbey Graveyard, as the convenient centre and starting-point of this, since this choice may be best justified as we proceed (fig. 98). See also plan (fig. 115).

Let us enter, then, by the doorway of its ancient cloister, plainly indicated, though long demolished (fig. 102). We consider and work out designs for the reconstruction of this cloister ; and then upon maturer judgment reject and drop them. For

FIG. 100.—Statue of Sorrow, within old cloister entrance of History Garden.

beside the natural objection to renew what is long past repair, and so would be a mere " restoration " in the worst sense, and for no particular useful purpose, we see that what we need is some effective

outline of the historic whole, some clear reminder of its events and persons, some interpretation of their results and services, some memorial of its glory, its ever-returning appeal to the present.

First of all we need a worthy symbol of Time. For as in our Nature Building the everyday atmosphere of collecting, describing, and analysing was raised to the highest level of science by its vivid central reminder of the unity of the world in the Great Globe, its reminder, too, of the sublime infinitudes of space by appropriate astronomic devices around it, so now here we need a corresponding symbol, to give due scale of thought and atmosphere and feeling to our historic building. For if these are to have the educative value we seek, each must strike its characteristic note of idealism, each must awaken imagination and feeling, even before it can impart real knowledge.

What, then, is this needed initial Time symbol, and where shall we place it ? What symbol better than that of the waters of a fountain, seeming to stand, yet ever in flow ? What better than the sundial, with its passing shadow, yet its immemorial years ? Here, then, in the old garden the massively-built circular reservoir of the mills needs but little modification to suit this purpose. To renew its waters and raise the bottom to dangerless depth is, of course, easy. Next in the centre we set up a pillar pedestal, and on this the statue of Time, with his traditional scythe and hour-glass, it may be the greater symbol of the astronomic circles also, but above all the stern, high uplifted finger. Let us now pave in broad surrounding pathways the lines of the dial, and at this long distance the solemn shadow of this gnomon will travel with obvious, rapid sweep, the passing of the hours made visible (fig. 99).

Round the pillar base let us set the Three Fates —her of birth towards the morning, of life-maintenance to the midday sun, and her of the shears to the sunset, the thin golden thread of life drawn between. On the fourth face, to the north, may be carved the stern traditional motto, well fitted for such a dial : " *Pereant et imputantur* "—" Perishing, yet reckoned." Or this might be sunk between the hour-lines starting from the fountain edge, so making room for another symbolic sculpture—either that of Sphinx and Babe, which would fitly precede the series of the Fates ; or that which naturally sums up the whole place and purpose—the Muse of History in meditation.

From this symbol of Life and Time in its garden court the approach to our Palace of History may be made with the right feeling. Upon the wall let us clear the old walled-up bee niches and house the hives anew ; again in their midst setting upon the wall a simpler dial, this time with vertical noonward face, and legend : " Work while it is Day." So history, above its obvious lesson of transient life, sets the practical one, of strenuous life, of patient labour—the assurance that the good of life lies in the working for social ends more than in its results.

Yet toil and striving soon end, and all history, our Scots history surely more than most, is full of sorrow. Her statue, then, our historic garden needs ; so Sorrow sits by its very door, with a path of grass, a lane of yews, leading straight up to that unknown passage within the ancient graveyard wall, whose portal so strangely stands open yet

unexplored. Beside this silent path of sorrow and death, yet beyond it and with back turned to the place of sepulture, stands one more statue, this time fully in the garden, with head and harp up-lifted—the bardic, Ossianic figure of ever-fading historic glory, yet ever-renewing Song.*

* For the accompanying sketches (figs. 96, 97, 99, 100, and 101), expressing the designs above suggested for the monuments, I am indebted to my friend Mr John Duncan.

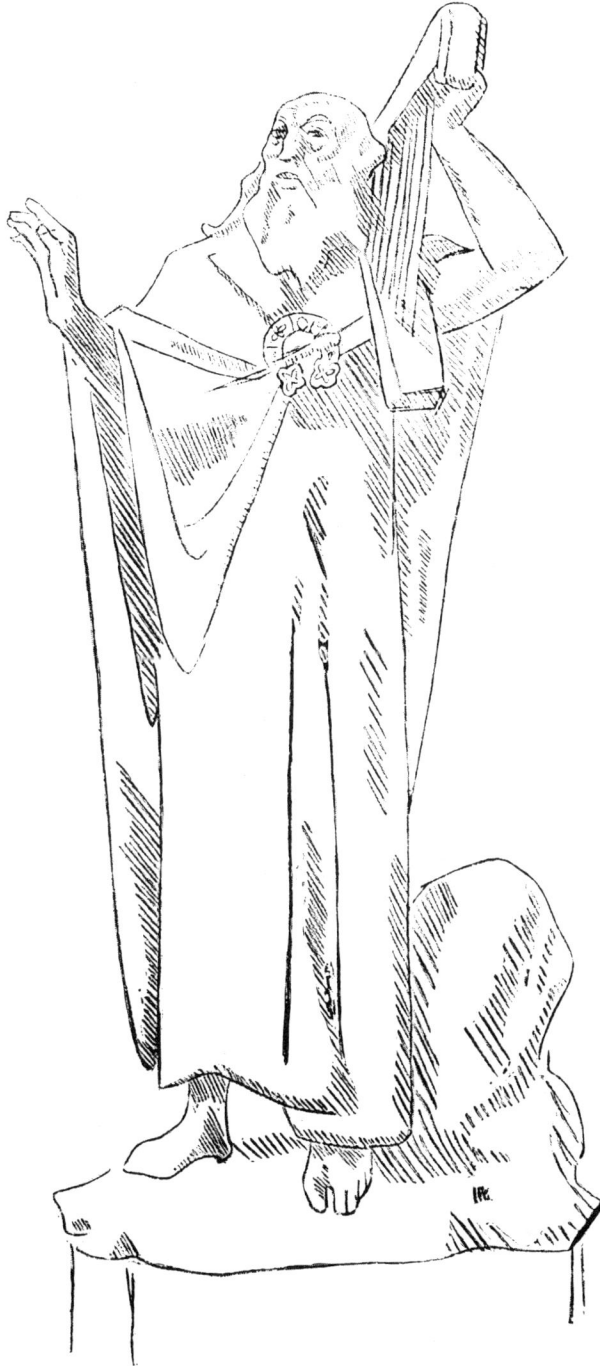

FIG. 101.—Sketch for statue of Ossian—type of Fame through Heroic song.

CHAPTER XXII

DUNFERMLINE HISTORY PALACE (ANCIENT AND MEDIÆVAL)

A. Ancient Scotland

TIME and Toil, Sorrow and Song, what now can these show us of the generations which have passed away before us ? First of all, let us set up against the cloister entrance wall a single massive unhewn boulder such as may be found not far away, and may, indeed, have actually served for ages as part of some now dismembered and forgotten sun-circle. To this we may add a stone with cup markings, an Ogham stone it may be also.

So much by way of memorials of the remote

the awakening Cuchullin ? And, midway up the staircase, the mighty Fingal with his hounds ? He would stand well near Ossian, his son and singer.

At top of this stair, recalling, though in simpler way, the famous staircase of Canterbury, let us ask permission to erect a Cloister, at right angles to this, along the existing pathway above the Bee-Alley wall, a construction easily practicable without disturbing the graves in the grass beside it (fig. 103). Allotting to saints and to heroes the sides

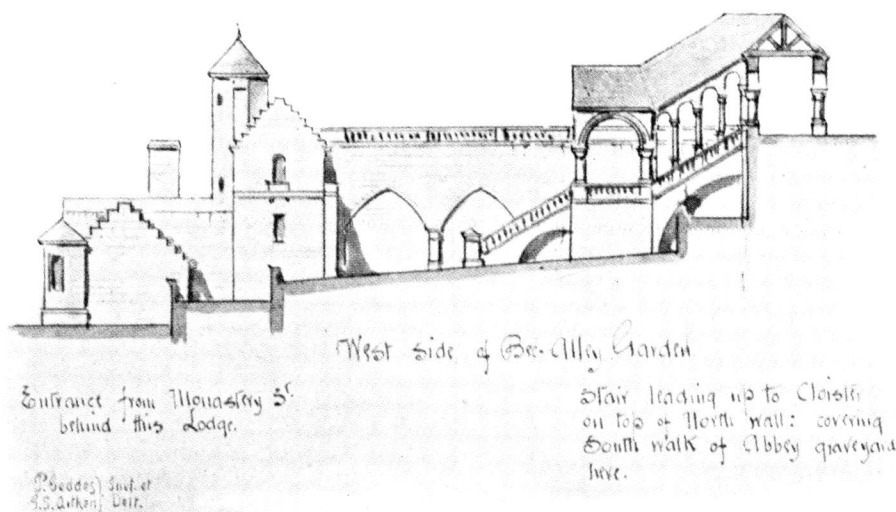

FIG. 102.—Elevation of West side of Bee-Alley Garden, shewing existing trace of two arches of ancient cloister. On left stands proposed gardener's cottage and entrance lodge, incorporating present low buildings on left. Stairway up to Abbey cloister. This would roof in the present South walk of Abbey graveyard, as shown in section, (cf. also fig. 103).

yet authentic past, the pagan Britain of pre-history and legend. Now begins the ascent towards modern civilisation which may be fitly expressed by an actual Stairway up towards the abbey precincts (fig. 102). At its foot let us carve in statue or bas-relief the Roman soldier—legionary or general, it now matters little—say, the sentinel, best of all. Confronting this we naturally need some heroic figure of ancient Britain. Who should this be ? Galgacus, the gallant adversary of Agricola ? Or, since synchronism need not here be strict,

of this which face towards church and world respectively, Columba will naturally stand first upon the northern side, Arthur upon the other, and so on through a double series, which might be nobly and picturesquely filled (fig. 104).

With " the gracious Duncan " this cloister of Celtic history—which we see is more closely connected with Dunfermline than is commonly realised—may draw to its end. It enters a Round Tower of the type represented in our neighbourhood at Abernethy, but more gracefully at Brechin : the

148

lines of this latter, consequently, have been more nearly followed here. This contains a staircase, leading not only down to the garden below but connecting with the three storeys of a new building —that now proposed for the commemoration of that larger, at least better-known period of Dunfermline, Scottish, and General History which now begins. Near the doorway, between the Celtic Cloister and this Mediæval Building, stands, naturally, the statue of Malcolm Canmore, under whom

roof pierced with an adequate series of small garret windows in triple tier, so as to keep the wall space for decoration and give vertical lighting without the resort to roof lighting of an ordinary picture-gallery, which, besides being too ample for our purpose, is incompatible with the style in keeping with this. At the north end, or rather in a recess at its north-east corner, the plan shows the statue of St Margaret. We next space out the walls into four or five large spaces on each side

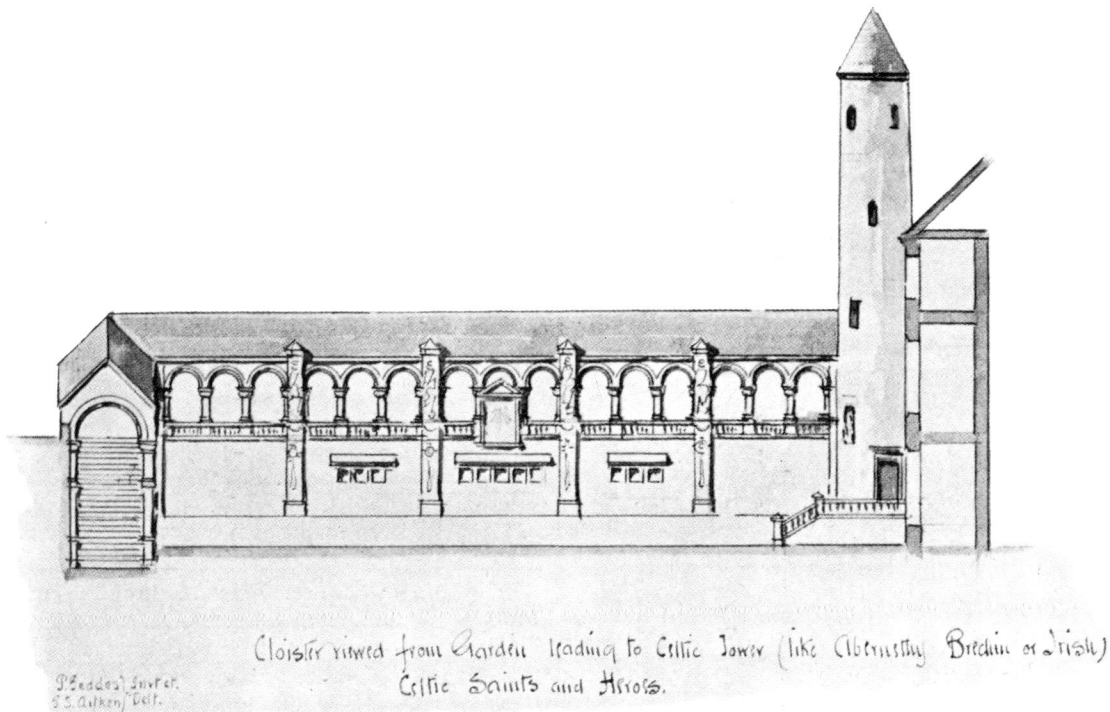

Cloister viewed from Garden leading to Celtic Tower (like Abernethy Brechin or Irish)
Celtic Saints and Heroes.

FIG. 103.—North side of Bee-Alley Garden wall, with staircase to left. Cloister above garden wall leads to Round Tower, thus completing commemoration of Celtic Periods, and this serves as entrance and staircase to main History Building, indicated in partial section. On garden wall note old bee-hive niches, again opened and filled with their bee-hives; a sun-dial surmounts the central group of hives (with its appropriate design and motto, thus completing preceding series of symbols by that of labour). Statues of Celtic heroes (Arthur, etc.) to stand in niches of buttresses; and in the (six) corresponding niches on opposite side, towards the church, the leading Celtic saints from Columba onwards.

this transition took place. Enthroned within sits his consort, to whom history has ascribed so predominant a share in it.

B. Hall of Mediæval History

(See figs. 105, 106, 107, 114.)

Here, then, leaving the simple yet fitly-adorned cloister which commemorates the Celtic centuries, we enter the larger building needed to give due expression to mediæval Dunfermline and Scotland. We may first enter its Great Gallery, a long hall, partly lit from the north by a large round-arched window, recalling those of the ruined abbey and of its kindred cathedral of Durham; its timbered

for permanent decorative panels, each representing some characteristic scene, at once of Dunfermline and Scottish history, with pedestals between, on which statues (or it may be suits of armour) may be placed. The two sides may, again, be allotted to the spiritual and the temporal powers— the material and ideal events which have made or marked our history. Leaving for a moment the allocation of these panels, save to note that these may suffice for the two centuries from Malcolm and Margaret to Wallace, this gallery opens between paired columns into a smaller central hall, with two main recesses upon its northeastern side for our two national heroes of the successive Wars of Independence—Wallace and

Bruce. These may be represented by separate statues merely, or by groups, say, of three—Wallace with Douglas and Sir John the Graeme ;

FIG. 104.—Sketch for statue of St Columba (pedestalled upon his isle).

and Bruce with Randolph and his brother Edward, or his own queen. Above them stands fitly the Central Tower. Its Crown, so charac-

teristic of our Scottish architecture, is surely doubly appropriate here.

From this Hall of Independence the gallery again runs on, with its panels and pedestals, till, at the southern end, on either side of the large rose window which should here fill and adorn its high-pitched gable, should stand in dramatic contrast the two figures with whom mediæval Scotland ended : Queen Mary on one side, Knox on the other. The former statue (or group) may be recessed, more or less as was Queen Margaret's, the latter placed just beyond the gallery in the recess of the South Tower shown in the main elevation (fig. 105) thus architecturally balancing the Culdee Tower at the opposite end of the building, and both in their simplicity contrasting with the richer Central Tower and Crown, which, as we have seen, are appropriate to that culmination of national and architectural individuality with which the fourteenth century opened in Scotland no less than in other lands.

The return from more ornate architecture to severity appropriate to the Reformation, its renewal of Culdee simplicity, as also that especial contact with the French rather than with the German or English reformers which the very name of Calvinism commemorates, are also expressed in the architecture of this Reformation Tower, since at this period the long French alliance of Scotland culminates with Mary, and comes to an end with the Reformation.

From tower to tower along the front of this mediæval building, and on the same level as the triple hall we have just described, runs an open Cloister walk, its columns more ornate than that above the Bee-Alley wall, since in keeping with the richer architecture of the abbey itself, once and again so great, as chronicles and surviving ruin alike proclaim. This twofold range of cloister walk would thus afford in itself a beautiful and attractive ambulatory, with shelter in all weathers—a changing succession of views, also, of garden and buildings, abbey and park beyond, each well framed within its cloister columns. The capitals of each cloister arch would, again, afford admirable scope for varied and appropriate design, and for working out more fitly the historic succession of architectural and decorative styles, of events, and of symbolisms. And if any fear that in thus affording a (too rare) field and opportunity for designer and carver excessive expense may be incurred, it may be well to recall here the fact that in the construction of the Oxford Museum—and of later buildings, in which such freedom has been allowed the artist and workman —the actual expense of carving has positively fallen below that customary for the mechanical repetition of a single design throughout an arcade ! For the carver can only put spirit and energy into work which interests him, and which puts him on his mettle—in short, which treats him as an artist working for a result, and not as a copying machine for wages.

Viewing now more in detail this great Hall of Mediæval History, we must now consider the pictures it should include, say rather the main events it should commemorate—first, from Malcolm

acknowledge the invaluable collaboration and creative pencil of my friend Mr John Duncan, and I reluctantly omit the results of our studies since these exceed the present compass.

In this way we should have a Gallery of Scottish History such as scarcely as yet exists in or for any city or country. For though noble commemorative halls, nobly decorated also, might be named—

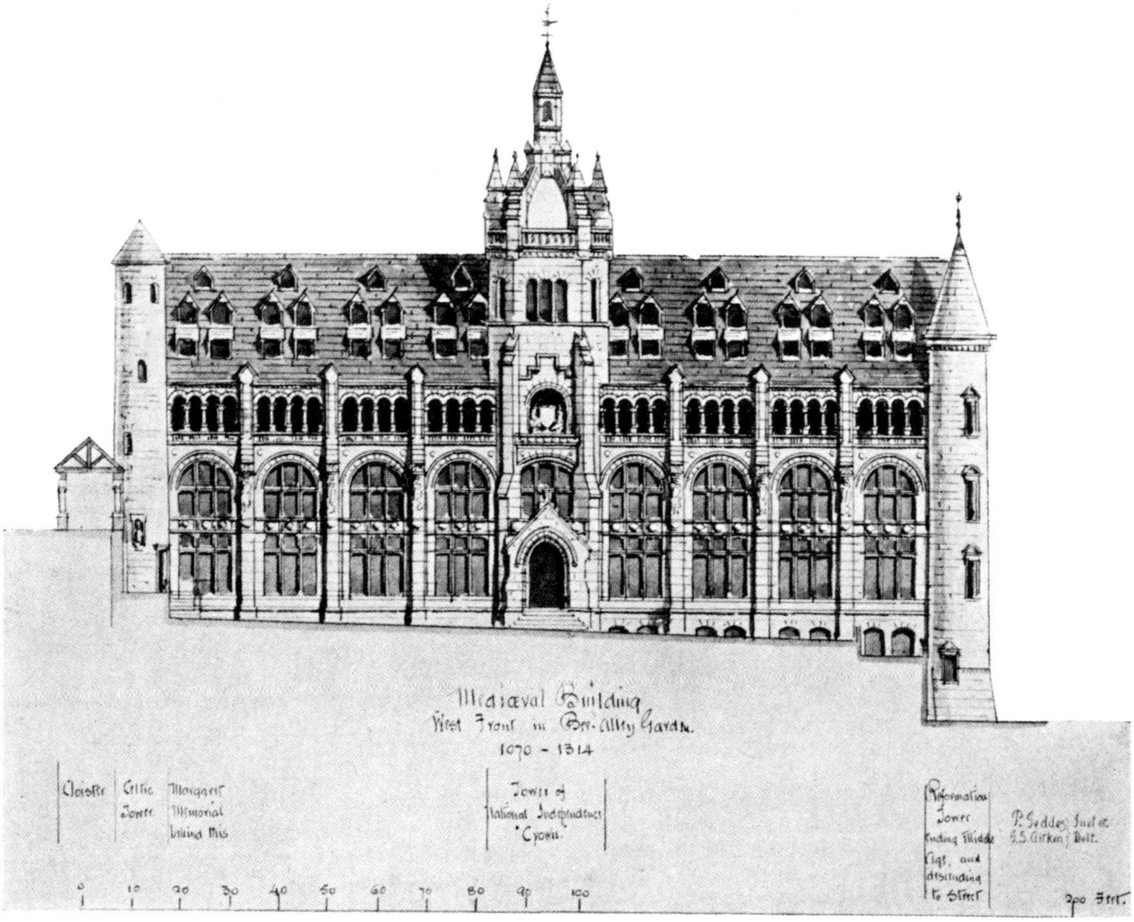

FIG. 105.—Mediæval History Building. Entrance from cloister, shown in section on left beside Celtic (staircase) tower. An open cloister of richer design is shown on higher level below eaves, thus giving a promenade of commanding views, towards Abbey Church and Fratry Hall, and over Palace and Mills to Park and beyond. Behind this runs through the whole building the gallery of Dunfermline history as shown in plan, its lofty roof lit by the many groups of small windows. An additional larger central group on opposite side could give a fuller light to the statues of Wallace and Bruce, in the Hall of Independence, behind the Crown. It will be noted that this crown is on a hexagon base, a departure from precedents.

The two main storeys below cloister include series of rooms respectively allotted to collections illustrative of the phases of Scottish and of General History. In the basement to the right are seen the tops of windows of Lecture Room and South Entrance hall from level of Monastery Place.

and Margaret to the Wars of Independence, and then from these to the Reformation. Broadly allotting, as in the Celtic cloister, opposite sides to the temporal and the spiritual evolution of our country, as far as these may be distinguished, a worthy series of scenes may readily be suggested In the study of this problem I have especially to

notably, for instance, the Coronation Hall of the ancient German Empire at Aachen—no such continuous outline of any national history, on both its temporal and its spiritual side at once, has as yet been attempted. This deficiency of precedent might, of course, be regarded as a drawback in more ordinary circumstances, but in view of the instructions and purposes of this Trust, this is, of course, to the advantage of the project, if worthy upon its own merits.

Can any doubt the inspiring value of such a scheme, and this primarily to the people and to the young, for whom, as I am not for one moment forgetting, this Trust primarily exists ? The inspiring value of our existing monuments, even of the modern Abbey Tower with its colossal modern inscription, despite its more than questionable art, is not to be denied ; but greater, of course, is that of the patriotic monuments of Stirling and of Edinburgh ; and greater still would be the appeal of the present edifice, with its statues and pictures gradually worked out, as they would be, at that higher level of painting and sculpture which so many Scottish artists have fully attained, and to express which they only need such opportunity and encouragement, such place and scope as I am here proposing.

The Trust would fulfil one of its highest possibilities in thus concentrating upon its city and population those highest powers of living Scotsmen for which at present London galleries, and still more foreign ones, are almost alone offering any adequate appreciation, yet less worthy and congenial opportunity.

To bring together such a group of artists and art workmen in and for Dunfermline would react upon the general culture, and even the industrial production, of the city. Still more obvious, surely, is the immediate effect which such a group and work would have upon education and upon the formation of ideals. That incentive to other cities, that stimulus to public spirit, to popular culture, and to private generosity alike, which it has been laid upon the Trust to afford and to organise, could surely in no way be more vividly awakened or more widely diffused.

C. Historic Reference Museum

Below this main Hall of Mediæval History two storeys are indicated. That immediately below would be the general Museum of Scottish Archæology and History from the earliest times to the Reformation. Here should be gradually accumulated a collection, not confined to originals, nor, indeed, specially aiming at these, save in so far as opportunity may naturally arise, but aiming rather at educational completeness, and hence very largely composed of good reproductions of all kinds—photographs, casts, etc. The essential value would lie in the educational arrangement. Casts of the main treasures of Edinburgh, London, and other collections are, for all practical purposes, as good as the originals. Moreover such a series selected from the great collections, which are all so incomplete, and here arranged so as to be studied in historic order, would really be of far

greater educational value than any extant collection ; and from its completeness of representation it would at once attract and instruct the public and the specialists.

An idea of the Stone, Bronze, and Iron Ages— that is, of their essential characteristics of primitive civilisation—should be attempted here ; indeed, why not with some of the same panoramic completeness as that indicated for the geographical imagery of the Nature Building ? The educative value of assembling such collections, in which especially the developments of the arts of life, from their rude beginnings up to those marvellous refinements to which ancient stones or jewels or illuminations bear witness, should all be illustrated by well-chosen types of reproductions and photographs from the great originals of London, Dublin, and Edinburgh, of Vienna, Paris, etc., so as not only to fit the Dunfermline student to profit by visiting any of these, yet for practical purposes to dispense with them also.

Of the mediæval period the same may be said ; indeed, with still greater force. Thus, though it would have been gratifying in every way to place upon the pedestals of our great hall such a collection of armour as that of Sir Noel Paton, not only an essentially identical effect, but a still more representative educational series for all ordinary purposes, historical, educational, and artistic, can be obtained by frankly contenting ourselves with the perfect electrotyped facsimiles now readily obtainable, thus saving a great outlay, and leaving the originals to the wider public of the national collections in Edinburgh.

In the same way, were photographs and colour prints of such pictures as we possess of the historic personages of Scotland, of each epoch, placed each in one room with those of the buildings and places associated with them, with facsimiles of the books and documents of the time, and so on, each of these inexpensive little museums would have a cumulative effect far exceeding that of ordinary collections of originals, in which pictures, books, documents, and museum objects are all kept apart ; in fact, in different collections, private and public, and when public in different buildings and management altogether, and this in an arrangement usually not chronological at all. Little wonder, then, that though many go to and fro, and knowledge is increased, though many would gladly learn and many gladly teach, we yet know so little. Give us here, give history anywhere, one such collection ; and we shall learn and teach to some purpose.

D. Historic Exhibitions and their Uses

I appeal, then, not only to all who are interested in Dunfermline, or even Scotland, but in art, in literature, in education, to consider this project, in confidence of their cordial general approval and support. Let me put a single example to the last named. Imagine the stimulating value even of a single visit, in which we should see, what is nowhere at present attainable, the facsimile (and when need be transcription and translation) of such a series of Scottish documents as would include, say, first of all that immortal reply of Scotland to the Pope upon the claims of Edward I.—which is the principal, yet practically unknown, treasure of the Register House — which should show such contemporary documents as we have of Wallace and of Bruce, such memorials of the early Stuarts as we can gather. Show some of the letters of Mary, which have so long perplexed historians; show, too, a letter of Knox, a copy of the Solemn League and Covenant; to which many would add as no mean climax the manifesto of Ebenezer Erskine and the Dissent and Protest of the Disruption. Place, too, among these in due order the open pages of Blind Harry and of Barbour and those of Sir David Lindsay; show, too, the characteristic early documents of Scottish song, up to those of Lady Nairne, of Burns and Scott, and see how these would gain in cumulative effect, especially when we bear in mind the associated wealth ot accompaniments and surroundings we are outlining.

Of Scottish Historic Exhibitions of various kinds there have been not a few within the last twenty years or so, and each has had its interest and its value. Recall, for instance, beside the establishment of permanent collections, of pictures, furniture, and objects of personal associations, the various loan collections of which the Stuart Exhibition was the chief, and of which Mr Foster's noble volume is doubtless partly an outcome. Recall, too, the services of various international exhibitions in this regard, from the admirable " Old Edinburgh " of the Edinburgh Exhibition of 1886, or the " Bishop's Palace " and its collections in Glasgow in 1888, to the great show of Glasgow in 1901—an exhibition which owed much of its value and interest to that free use of reproductions recommended here.

What I propose, in fact, is that we now utilise the very catalogues, the commemorative volumes, the reproductions of all these exhibitions and collections, which collectively make up a very large proportion of the total obtainable inventory of Scottish resources, and which would be now easily extended, for most practical purposes in fact completed. From this series it would then be simply a matter of some patience and intelligence to prepare a more truly representative series and exhibition than has yet existed. This is

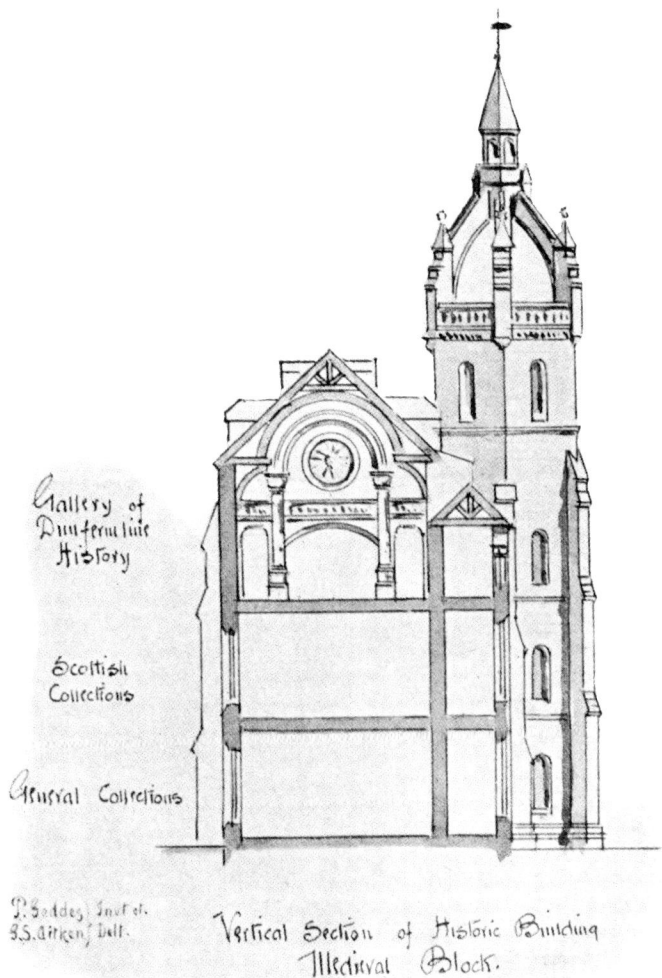

FIG. 106.—Section of Mediæval History Building, taken immediately to North of central tower; showing gallery of Dunfermline history with cloister in front, and rooms for Scottish and general collections below. The separation of the cloister above is not to be understood as continued through the lower storeys save by the necessary supporting pillars at intervals, as here emphasised.

especially obvious if due note be taken of the great examples which are now afforded us by other small nationalities, like the Scandinavian ones, like those of the Low Countries, and some of those of Germany—witness, for instance, the magnificent National Museum of Saxony, of which the educational arrangement and the artistic effect so incomparably excel the confused and confusing displays of the vaster collections of South Kensington.

While the commemorative historic gallery would depend for its effect upon its long, almost cathedral-like perspective, here upon the lower floors the abandonment of the large museum-gallery method, far too persistent in this country, in favour of the succession of smaller rooms, each devoted to a minor period, is strongly recommended. A visit to the South Kensington or Edinburgh museums, and then to any of the Continental museums arranged on the latter principle, will fully confirm this.

By the judicious introduction of old furniture, the natural variation in size and decoration, and of the still necessary museum cases, etc., with skilful and sympathetic treatment generally, much of the effect of the Musée Cluny itself might be realised—that is, an atmosphere in which history emphasises art, and art history.

The effect of the creation of such a Scottish Historical Museum as this upon young Dunfermline, upon Scotland, upon "Magna Scotia" throughout the world, would be speedy, yet enduring. Taken with the reproduction of the commemorative works of art of the gallery above, the publication of one noble volume after another would naturally result, which, again, might be popularised in widely accessible forms. The rise of other Scottish collections in Scottish cities and even beyond, the attraction to this Dunfermline museum of loans, gifts, and bequests, would all naturally follow ; while the teaching of Scottish history and Scottish literature would gain from this old and natural, yet new and active, centre a fresh stimulus, let us hope a henceforth enduring life.

The curator and assistant curator of such a collection would thus practically become the most accessible, and, therefore, most widely useful, of Scottish historical workers and teachers, and this position, in the hands of a succession of men such as we have had, have still among us however little recognised, and shall have again, would be of the widest national usefulness. Such work is needed to complete the renascence of Dunfermline by carrying it into the needed detail ; and it would aid to extend this to other cities, conserving and deepening all that is best in Scottish national feeling, relieving it of all crudeness and exaggeration, yet displaying its true bases, and strengthening these.

Our suite of Scottish historical rooms having thus completed and complemented the great gallery above, the ground floor remains for consideration. Here we have to work out the idea already suggested, that of Scotland neither complete in itself nor yet a mere province of England, late and reluctantly united, though now satisfactorily absorbed, submissively centralised ; but of Scotland as the microcosm of North-Western Europe, filled with its survivals, yet rich in its initiatives, receiving, albeit sometimes tardily, all the great waves which echo round the world, continuing them long, and carrying them far, into her deep firths and valleys, yet also sending back new waves, new forces, which have in their turn modified mankind.

Why does the history of Scotland show a share alike in European politics and culture, so greatly beyond that to which its " area, wealth, and population," as our modern method of calculation goes, would seem to entitle it ? Does it not indicate that excellent, necessary even, though that system of calculation may be, it remains not only morally feeble but intellectually fatuous until we go further and interpret more deeply ? The larger European fact which explains the mediæval importance of Scotland, just as the advantages of her military geography throw much light upon her long maintained independence, is, of course, the long Franco-Scottish alliance, which is the precise historic equivalent of the Dual Alliance of yesterday ; while her culture importance, largely inherited from the ancient, broad, and deep culture of Ireland and Iona, was continually renewed and advanced by a fuller and more sympathetic contact with Continental peoples than was that of her larger neighbour, whose misfortune it has been to be reinsularised in each century by fresh hostile contracts with them, of course with disastrous reaction upon Scotland also.

Hence, then, the need in our historical museum to express our past relation with the culture of other countries, and to recognise the increasing possibility of renewing them ; so that Scotland may once more recover her place, as the small Continental countries have already done, among the European Powers—of Culture. In this movement our Dunfermline Hall of History would play a worthy part.

FIG. 107.—General perspective, indicating view from windows of Modern History Building, looking North-West over Monastery Place towards Abbey Church. Note History Garden, with staircase to Place in middle, and with gardener's lodge at cloister entrance in South-West corner. The stairway up to Celtic cloister is in centre of picture, and the cloister itself for more than half its course. The laying out of History Garden is slightly indicated. Near the Time Fountain, towards right, is restoration of an old well as drinking-fountain, with a wrought-iron canopy.

CHAPTER XXIII

HISTORY GARDEN AND ABBEY PRECINCTS

A. The History Garden

BEFORE leaving this building one other point remains. With its design and uses fully before us now is the time to set out the scheme of its garden, not before ; to illustrate, too, the whole standpoint in gardening which this report maintains.

Starting from the entrance (Chap. XXI. E.) and its path to the staircase, with its parallel path of Sorrow, its line of yews on either hand, we pass out into the garden beside the statue of song, whose pedestal should rise from a mound of heaths, chosen for ample flower both in spring and autumn, through which should rise in summer a forest of lilies—golden, orange, and scarlet. The main walks should be paved with bold mosaic devices in coloured pebbles, regularly varying as we proceed—the marguerite and forget-me-not, the Douglas heart, the Bruce's crest, the Stuart chequer.

The old apple-trees may mainly remain, and before long will become venerable ones ; but the formal character of the garden should be maintained, and its spirit clearly expressed, by the planting of regular masses of bays ; of course the true bay, the poets' fragrant laurel, not its coarser substitute of the Roman triumph and the modern shrubbery.

In addition to these large dark masses there should be introduced in regular position along the terrace lines and the main front a series of bays in pots or boxes of architectural design, and kept trimmed in the usual formal fashion. In the shelter of this garden, especially at its warm southward lines of wall and terrace, the myrtle would grow with little protection, and even flower in exceptional summers ; while lavender, rosemary, and thyme, with rue, too, and dittany, would flourish in ample beds, their permanent shade of the soil below again providing the right conditions for the growth of lilies, in the seasonal display of many forms of which this garden should excel. Two of the old wall apple-trees would remain upon two wall panels outside the beehives ; and roses, with fine ivies and jessamine, would climb the buttresses (fig. 107).

Alternating with the bays, there should come in serial masses round the whole garden groups of giant thistles, through and around whose thorny mass should grow white lilies, bordered by dwarf thistles. In the smaller central beds would be alternately beds of marguerites and of white Jacobite roses, alike set about with blue masses of forget-me-not, masses of irises, too, with pansies, and so on. Minor details, too numerous for mention, and sometimes changing with the seasons and years, would further emphasise these effects of form, colour, and fragrance, and complete these expressions of historic and symbolic feeling. Thus the reader, say of Dunbar's " The Thrissel and the Rose " would find here carried out the very imagery of the poem ; and beside these stately flowers of poetic association the monks' herbary, the queens' simples, would find their modest place.

B. Abbey Churchyard

Ascending now to the church itself, may we not do something here ? See what noble possibilities ! —what poor use made of them !—for the historic trees, once the pride of Dunfermline, have fallen, and their successors are but of haphazard planting.

Here, however, is the ideal spot in all Dunfermline for developing those increasingly stately and solemn effects which the judicious use of the

FIG. 108.—View in Abbey Park Place looking towards West end of modern Abbey Church : St Margaret's Halls seen to right.

yew affords, and this monumental plant therefore should preponderate in several of its best varieties, chiefly the spreading and the pillared, the latter golden as well as sombre green.

One such avenue would naturally connect the new stairway opening with the south door of the Abbey Church. The weedy poplar-trees towards the south-east should be removed, and the limes of the main approach from Abbey Park Place moved into more regular position and alignment. Still better, they should be lifted, as is still quite practicable, large though they are, and planted outside the abbey graveyard altogether, upon the gravelled roadway outside, continuous with the street ; while within the gates should then be planted an avenue of the largest spreading yews up to St Margaret's tomb within the ruins of the

Lady Chapel, from which the present unsightly and useless railing should be removed. This whole approach would thus align with Abbey Park Place, which, as the accompanying photograph shows, makes one of the best street pictures in Dunfermline (fig. 108).

The main walk, running east and west on the south side of the church, should also be yew-bordered, but with smaller golden pyramids, as also the walk running due south from this to the east end of the Fratry Hall. On the north side of the church the graveyard is monotonous and neglected looking ; the ugly cement-topped wall to the east should be both ivied and screened by shrubbery, including a few spreading yews, connected by more cheerful evergreens, and brightened by flowering hawthorns above and masses of white rose below.

A similar treatment would satisfactorily screen the northern wall. The perspectives (figs. 109, 110) indicate how easily this whole view might be improved by the picturesque rebuilding of a single block, as shown, and the improving of the ugly modern block of warehouses by balconies and creepers or the screening it by trees. For this purpose one or more of the easily removed limes and poplars might also be employed, thus improving the various pictures afforded by the churchyard, and emphasising its solemn dignity in the strictest appropriate way—an old style, of course, not the modern cemetery excess of Californian conifers. Yet this is somewhat too sombre, and, as already suggested, I should relieve its pessimism of death by flowering shrubs and climbers, adding especially those of joyous and sacred associations —the rose, the almond especially, the smaller shrubs also ; daphnes, for instance, especially the white mezereon and its congeners ; the honey-suckle also. One or two of the smaller flowering willows might also find place, and close to one or two of the entrances a weeping willow.

It may, no doubt, be asked : Why do I venture to propose these improvements by the Trustees of what is not their property ? First, because this is a part of Dunfermline, and the very best, the most sacred part ; and second, because it needs improvement. The heritors, the congregation, the public, are all advantaged by this improvement without expense to themselves ; the already proposed stairway through Bee-Alley Garden to Monastery Place, for instance, would be a useful and agreeable access and exit on Sundays and week-days alike ; while the Trustees, even from the narrowest possible standpoint of their own park interest alone, are still more advantaged. For these proposals, if carried out, would practically enlarge the park and its gardens, by including, within their general treatment and perspective, the noblest feature of the whole city, the park thus practically beginning at and with the abbey.

Conversely, the abbey, which had once as its park the large area eastward now built over, would thus be truly restored, since now within a park again. The escape from the mutual exclusiveness of separate ownerships to this proposed co-operation for common amenity is surely not beyond public-spirited bodies such as those here con-

C. Associated Improvements

I next submit elevation and perspective showing the improvement of St Catherine's Wynd down to the Pends. First of all, the present north-west gateway entrance to the abbey graveyard, near Maygate, is shown set back just so far as the

FIG. 109.--View from North side of Old Abbey nave over churchyard. Note to left old cottages of St Catherine's Wynd leading up to the Town House with its spire. To right of this runs the Maygate, showing backs of its buildings, a modern warehouse in middle. Note Abbot's House to right : the picturesque tower of this has unfortunately been partly effaced in reproduction.

FIG. 110.--Proposed improvement of Eastern portion (right half) of preceding view. A new building is inserted, and the warehouse improved. Trees and shrubbery also to be planted, more thickly than is here shown.

cerned ; the civic example is also in the right line of development.

I continue, then, to suggest that the whole west side of the graveyard be next improved ; of course, as everywhere, without interference with a single grave, though even tree planting does not go nearly so deep.

principle of non-interference with graves allows, thus giving the much-needed effect of a small public place outside, below the Municipal Buildings, a space useful, moreover, as we shall see later, to the proposed Music Hall.

Descending to the main west entrance of the old Abbey Church, we note that its modern gateway, by its very daintiness and refinement, is not adequate for the situation. But this cannot, and need not, be interfered with. It only needs the addition of the two massive piers to north and south, which are accordingly shown in perspective, and which, as will be seen, harmonise and compose with the pinnacle north of the great window of the Fratry Hall, as with the proposed treatment of the park entrance and Tower Hill Road (fig. 111).

The small enclosure of carelessly planted evergreens, south of this abbey entrance, which is

of wall to St Catherine's Wynd on either hand, while this is finished by the simplest pierced masonry balustrade throughout its length, the whole being then planted with cotoneaster and ivy. On the northern half especially, where sun has access, I would add white Jacobite and Ayrshire roses and honeysuckle.

This brings us back to the north-west entrance of the graveyard at Maygate, which I should now propose to treat with new gateway piers of simple character, harmonising with the architecture and massive buttressing of the church

FIG. 111.—Bird's-eye Perspective, showing proposed return to the original disposition of the ancient roadway, from the Tower Hill—i.e. straight to the West door of the Abbey. Note advantage of widening of St Catherine's Wynd and of Palace Yard ; also the suggested massive piers and groups of evergreens on each side of the existing abbey entrance, its delicate modern carving and iron work thus set within an outer frame more harmonious with the massive simplicity of the Abbey Tower and the Fratry pinnacle to right.

actually a feu in the hands of the city, not the church, should be thrown into the street and paved, and its plants brought together on either side of the main west gateway, between this and the new piers, north and south, so as to furnish two large evergreen masses, framing the entrance on either hand. The improved effect to the abbey, seen from the street and from the park, will easily be realised.

A series of simple pilaster buttresses, much as along the Tower Hill Road within the park, are shown breaking the monotony of the long range

and with the new piers on either side of the existing western gateway already mentioned (fig. 111).

By next setting back the " Port gate " of the park, and bringing this into its ancient and natural line with the church door (as shown upon plan and elevation), we recover the effect of the ancient Palace Yard and almost its extent ; while this may be completed by obtaining the necessary permission from the Crown authorities to set back their boundary also.

Passing through the Pends, we require similar permission to remove or lower 8 feet of the wall on the left, belonging to the Crown ; and, there coming to the Trust property, I advise razing the present wall completely to the ground, demolishing the present mill barn and the front buildings of the mill. This affords the opportunity of widening the street considerably, as shown in the general plan (fig. 115).

This widening I next ask to be carried still farther, and may here recapitulate the proposal already made (Chap. XX.) for the enlargement of Monastery Street into a spacious " Monastery Place." For this purpose I advise the recent enclosure and railing-in of the poorly planted triangular space between the street and the monastery building to be undone, and this whole space up to the buttresses to be paved (fig. 92), a simple railing-bar at most being placed to protect a couple of feet of green turf edging, or a single mass of shrubs between each buttress. I of course assume the increasing respect of the public for these improvements, and the natural prevention of any natural cause for their injury

by adjacent conveniences to be supplied under mills.

The removal of the smithy I recommend, for reasons partly obvious here, partly given (page 130), so that with the demolition of the present large mill building and chimney stalk Monastery Place will have the spacious proportions shown on plan, especially when we complete this by levelling up and paving the requisite space at present forming the north edge of the small garden south-east of the Mills.

The value of restoring and improving these two ancient open spaces, Palace Yard and Monastery Place respectively, will, I trust, be recognised at once to park and city improvements. Plainly this new place would be greatly improved by closing in, by means of another archway pend, such as was once the gate farther down at the manse, of which a vestige remains. This I propose to supply, and in a very natural way, by the continuation of the History Buildings over the street. To these then we now return.

CHAPTER XXIV

HISTORY PALACE: RENAISSANCE AND MODERN

REFERRING to the plan (fig. 115), it will be seen that the back of the Mediæval Building here projects eastwards to meet the adjacent factory gable. Here is the main staircase leading from all its storeys down to the level of the street, with also a lecture hall on the street level conveniently situated for public access.

A. Renaissance Building

To resume our historical plan of exposition we ascend by this staircase and enter the Great Hall once more. From this the thorough revolution in religion and culture, politics and economic life, in art therefore also, which is marked by the succession to Mary of James VI. and I., is naturally indicated by the change of character of the buildings, from Mediæval to Renaissance. The motive of design adopted here is given by various memorials of Old Edinburgh, etc., but best of all by the type most nearly followed, that of Glasgow College, demolished scarce a generation ago (fig. 113).

The style of this Renaissance Building lends itself well both to the general purpose and to this particular situation, and when viewed in perspective, in which it is shown as it actually will be seen from the street, it will be seen to compose well with the gable of the Mediæval Building, behind which it is recessed. Also in its historic significance the design will be seen to hold. King James's departure over the border is, it will be noticed, quite at the appropriate place upon our plan, that over the crossing over the northern pavement of the street; while the last notable connections of Dunfermline with his dynasty, through the birth of Charles I. and the Restoration of Charles II., may be commemorated in the space assigned to these two reigns under the spire, either by the busts of these two kings without, or by portraits or pictures within the Tower and Spire Chamber, which continues upon a similar scale the great gallery. With these we must not forget some corresponding memorial of the great Oliver, whose general's victory at Pitreavie Dunfermline still remembers.

Giving little space to the Restoration and to the brief and wretched reign that followed it, the southmost portion on this side (fig. 112) belongs to the period of William and Mary, and to the unsuccessful, yet all the more heroic, "Fifteen" and "Forty-five," really, of course, the belated ending of the Seventeenth Century, since the last efforts of the Scottish Cavaliers.

B. Eighteenth Century Proper

Behind this the building should again recede a step eastwards, assuming, of course, that the site can be in due time acquired. Here our next historic Gallery, that of the later Eighteenth Century, faces north, and looks out only to the mill opposite. But here is surely the right position for the clear but prosaic outlook of the post-Jacobite half-century, that characterised for Scotland and the world alike by David Hume, yet more by another name no less immortal—in fact, that of the most world-transforming man of genius whom Fife has ever produced—Adam Smith of the "Wealth of Nations." Beside him, our Scottish minor worthies of the period would naturally be commemorated.

C. Nineteenth Century

From this runs southward again, and in elevation once more recessed so as to retain its own distinctive character while composing all the better with its predecessor, the large building devoted to the historic commemoration of the Nineteenth Century. It will be noted in plan how it continues on the line of the later Eighteenth-Century Hall, yet opens also from that of the earlier Jacobite age, so clearly expressing the influence yet strife of rival elements, utilitarian and romantic, which have so deeply marked the century's history, and in which our Scottish romancer has as fully led the world as did our great utilitarian (figs. 112 and 114).

The three representative generations of the nineteenth century are hence commemorated by distinctive changes of style. First comes the "Scottish Baronial" of Abbotsford, so suggestive ot all it stood for. This leads, second, to the large central feature of revived Perpendicular, fitly expressing first of all the Church movement, which did actually adopt this style in Scotland as in England — witness the new Abbey Church behind, or in Edinburgh the Free Church College — but also that advancing anglicising of the Scot, of which Mr Gladstone was but the most obvious example. The third block, in contemporary bank or office style, expresses the architecture of the current periods of Finance and Empire. Yet despite the apparent incongruity of styles in detail, intentionally recalling our nineteenth-century street effects, it will be seen that a certain unity not only of alignment but of composition has been preserved.

Throughout the upper storey of this block the Dunfermline Gallery runs on, but it is now naturally still further deprived of its former magnificence, and reduced from monumental gallery to the modest scale of the ordinary museum garret; yet this would not be without a wealth of interesting memorials, and these particularly of its working people, many of whom are well worthy of remembrance through an individuality of the rarest kind. It would include models, too, of their looms and inventions; a record of the rise from isolated looms to collective factory, assuredly one of the mightiest changes in the history of civilisation, and one for which it is not too late to compile a record which would be of inestimable value to the future; some memorials, too, of the ecclesiastic and scholastic life, of the literary production of Dunfermline also — in short, the fullest possible record of the century which has so lately closed. In this way the actual contrasts of treatment of our long Gallery of Dunfermline brings out the vicissitudes of the town, which had by the nineteenth century practically forgotten its once high estate, its Palace fallen, its Abbey mostly quarried away.

D. Twentieth-Century Building

But now from this modest museum garret of homely modern life and labour we come out upon our Modern Outlook, that of this city with the opening century. This is expressed architecturally by the spacious open gallery of a circular tower (fig. 114), from which we may look back to the old historic city and forward into its future, widening as this is on every side.

The lofty arcade of this Outlook Gallery will also afford, arch by arch, the space for at least the symbol, indeed often for the actual instrument, of each and every one of all the arts and sciences; it expresses, too, their social possibilities most of all. From the ground to this level rises

another Staircase Tower — and, for the time, the concluding one — its ascending sweep of spiral from base to pinnacle fitly again expressing the

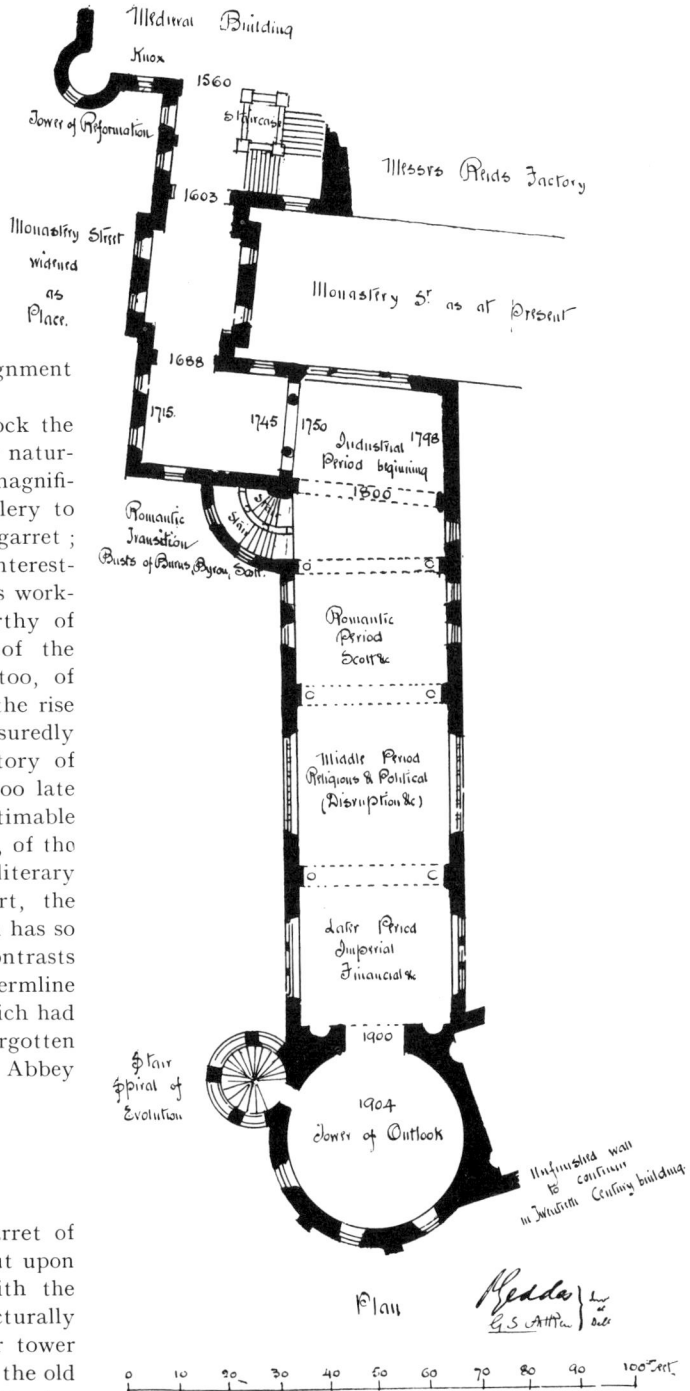

FIG. 112.—Plan of Renaissance and Modern portion of History Palace, continuing preceding Mediæval building southwards.

spiral of evolution, and in detail intentionally reminiscent of a master work of Leonardo da Vinci; since our age of modern science is but the renaissance of the Renaissance.

L

Bee-Alley Garden | Monastery. Street widened to Monastery Place |

Mediæval Period | Tower | Tower | Dutch |
Ends with | of | of | Gable | Tower
Reformation | Reformation | Renaissance | | of
| | learning. | | Processional
| | Via Sacra down through | | Way
	History building to Nature	
	building and Nether Town	
	later	

Fig. 113.—Perspective view of Renaissance Building, recessed from Mediæval Building (fig. 105), and giving a new central archway Pend for vehicles corresponding to that already existing at North-West between Abbey and Palace (fig. 92), with addition of passages on each side for foot passengers also. Below level of Monastery Place is seen a drive (or Processional Way) through another archway (descending thereafter towards Manse Entrance as shown on general plan). Note also descending staircase to Mill Garden, with rose-arbours, etc.

E. Review of History Buildings

Review now the whole elevation once more from first to last, and note how as its style building requires three storeys—for Dunfermline, for Scotland, and for Europe, in which England was too often the most foreign of nations.

With the union of the English and Scottish

Culminating Outlooks of the Dunfermline Gallery, this continuous with the Entrance in Monastery Street, and Bee-Alley Garden with the Cloister of Abbey groveyard and the monumental Gallery of Mediæval Building.

Mill Garden

Nineteenth Century Building heterogeneous in Styles, changed in its Three main generations (see Plan)

Stair Spiral of Evolution See Leonardo da Vinci's Spiral Stairs

Tower of Outlook Transitional to Twentieth Century

unfinished Wall to bond into future buildings of Twentieth Century for which site is left.

FIG. 114.—West Front of Nineteenth-Century History Building and of Tower beginning Twentieth-Century Buildings, as explained on block and in text.

expresses the change, so its height, the increasing complexity of the world. The comparative isolation and unity of the Celtic world is represented by its simple cloister, but our Mediæval crowns, indicated at the beginning of our Renaissance building, a new storey is introduced— that of English history, henceforth fundamental to Scottish, at any rate far more important to us henceforth than the general whole of Europe remaining upon the storey below.

With the eighteenth century a new storey appears, that of general World-policy and even politics, which not only the broader philosophic outlook of Scotland expressed, but even her economic expansion, her far-sighted though ill-fated Darien policy.

With the nineteenth century a new storey is again introduced—that of Empire ; while in the tower with which the nineteenth century ends, the twentieth begins, yet another storey is inserted—that one devoted to the United States, with which our fortunes, Imperial, British, Scottish, and even Civic, are henceforth so indissolubly associated. Compare figs. 113 and 114.

It will not be difficult to find suitable material to fill all these storeys, and thus to give the range of rooms on each level a unique educational value and effect, and even, as we shall increasingly see, a notably artistic character.

But, before leaving the question of elevations, note that, as such an architectural composition reasonably demands, the great Round Tower seems to conclude the buildings, as it brings us fully up to date, and even beyond. For this Twentieth Century Tower may well serve as a home and centre for our best thought and work, individual and civic, Scottish and other, in the period now opening ; as a stimulating thinking-house, which our rising generation would increasingly value and learn to use, their mental perspective widening from the noble landscape around, through an ever-deepening consciousness of an enlarging world of intelligent interest and social action, expressed storey by storey, from personal outlook to City, and thence to Scotland and Britain, to Empire and Language, to Europe and World.

Such an actual laboratory of thought, in the hands of even a single intelligent observer and indexer, would soon become a centre of reference and inquiry of real and ever-increasing value to the city and its visitors, and of still wider suggestiveness. Nor has any university or college, any school of social or political science, yet hitherto supplied so definite, yet so intelligible, a centre of preparation for whoever would conscientiously fit himself, through social inquiry and interpretation, to take up that personal responsibility for a share in the direction of social evolution on every level which is the increasing birthright of every man and woman, but which our political developments so far fail adequately to educate, or even awaken.

Is not this outlook one from which we may both educate and prepare for the man for whom Emerson calls :

> " Who to his native centre fast,
> Shall into Future fuse the Past,
> And the world's flowing fates
> In his own mould recast."

Note finally how the whole range of building, though apparently now finished, is yet also suggestively left unfinished. For this whole scheme would be incomplete were it completed ; it is of its very essence that it should be capable of continuance by successive generations, for whom we may, we must, prepare, yet to whom we cannot in any wise dictate.

Two things at least we now clearly foresee : that the future will need space, and will have a style of its own ; hence from our round tower there projects eastward an unfinished edge of wall with which the next building can be bonded, its upward projection, a practical corbelling, leaving space at the top for the one symbol we may fairly project upon the future—a symbol of Progress— say as a bas-relief winged child-figure taking flight —a symbol which optimist and pessimist will, of course, each read in his own way.

So far then the general scheme of our historic building ; and were it executed might we not again fairly say for things historic and social, as we did for those geographic, that whoever would see the world should now come to Dunfermline ?

F. Relation of History and Art Museum

But here is not yet the whole social world ? It is suggested, in outline, of course, upon our various floors, and always within the moderate, and thus all the more educative, scope of a provincial museum ; and here, too, is the explanation why this Historic Building is relatively large, and why the Art Building is comparatively small. For an art building is, or at least should be, essentially for masterpieces of the art of all time, in their reproductions, of course, when not in originals. But the vast majority of the ordinary objects of art museums, from the Assyrian brick and the Egyptian scarabæus to the Greek pot or the Roman carving, or, again, to the antique weapon, the mediæval picture of devotion, the Dutch interior or sea piece, are like the conventional academy landscape or portrait or other respectable piece of furniture or decoration—that is, each is primarily so much historical material. It is not really of much sensuous beauty, or much emotional value ; it is primarily an object of instructiveness, of informational or illustrative interest. What we use in our so-called Art Museums to teach the " history of ornament " or the like, is thus, avowedly, history first and beauty afterwards, if at all. Whereas, though the Art Gallery must and should contain examples of all times, it should only admit those examples which transcend their time, those of which the beauty is an enduring one. The application of this criterion to our art museums, great and small, is not only what is needed to relieve their congestion,

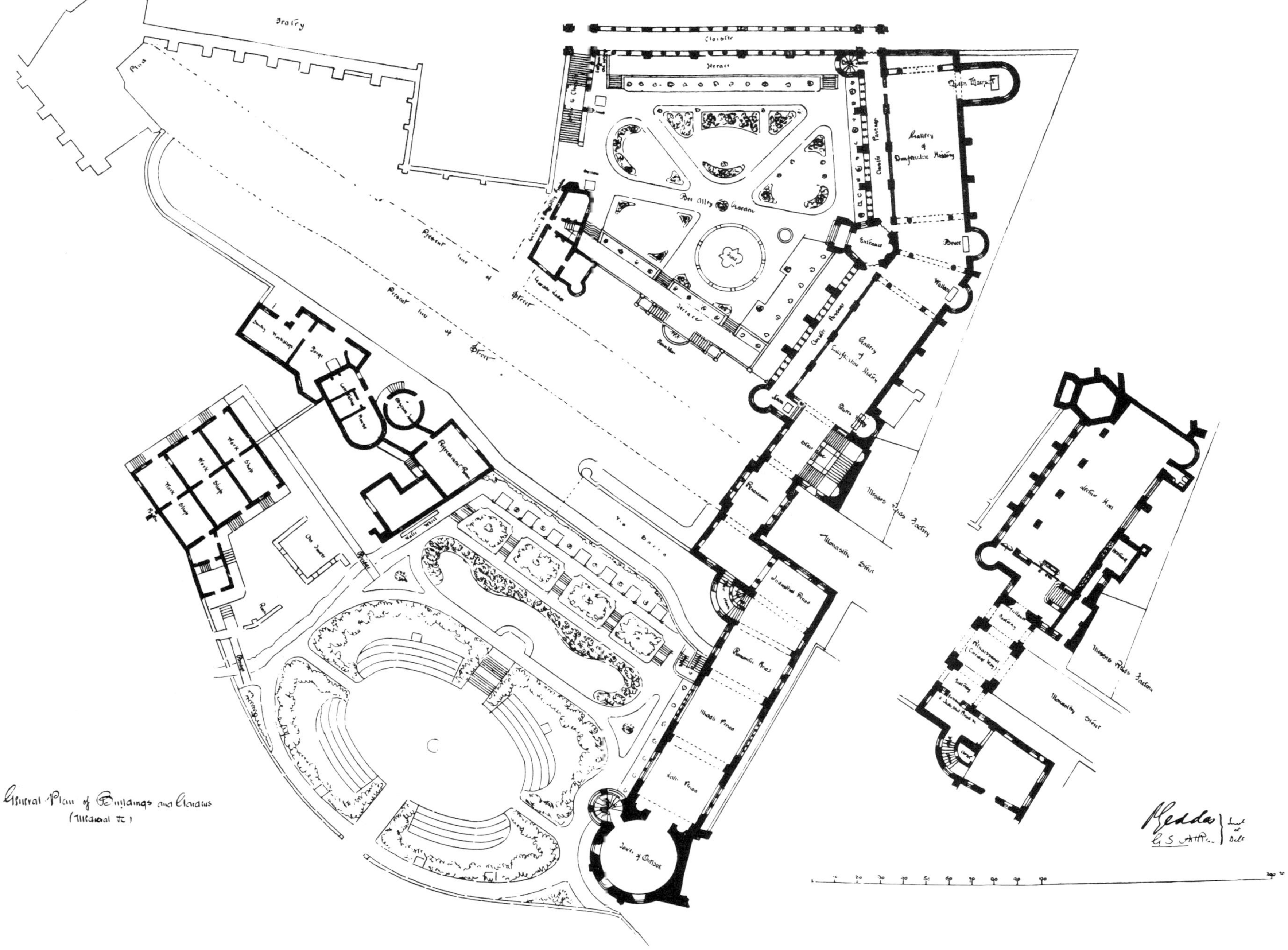

FIG. 115.—Plan of Monastery Place with buildings around it, old and new. To this may now be related all the previous photographs, elevations, and perspectives from 86 onwards. The general position of the whole—e.g. to Abbey Churchyard on North to Park on West and South—will be at once understood by reference to General Plan.

but is indispensable to relieve the public ignorance of both art and history together. Were three-fourths of South Kensington frankly looked at as a Historical Museum, and so arranged ; were its numberless duplicates distributed to the minor national and provincial ones ; then the remaining quarter would furnish a far better Museum of Art proper. We should thus have two first-rate central museums, each in its own way educational, instead of one vast and confusing pantechnicon.

The principle of selecting masterpieces only is, of course, to a very large extent applied both in the National Gallery of London and in the Luxembourg—though not yet sufficiently in the British Museum and the Louvre ; nor is it as yet sufficiently extended beyond pictures.

G. Open-Air Museum again

Are we now done with our historic proposals ? Yes and No. For as all things exist in space and place, so all things exist in time, and the education of a sane and strong intelligence requires the continuous grasp of both.

This historic Museum is, after all, but a catalogue, a type-collection, a beginning from which the student may go out to understand his ever-enlarging world. First of all, he will appreciate his own city and country ; he will see the whole park and city as one great Open-Air Museum. Its primitive dwellings, its renewed old mills and their simple yet artistic workshops, onwards to the great modern factory industry of our own time, are one continuous historic development, in which past and present and future are henceforth a continuous and living whole.

From the primitive dwellings we pass readily to the thatched cottage, thence to the quaint old red-tiled cottages, which are the main surviving beauty of Dunfermline ; thence to the dull or meretricious modern dwellings of a happily passing style (may we not hope a practically obsolete one) and to those more joyous and healthful dwellings to which we may now look forward. Why not then at Rosyth, to an initiative and representative Garden City for the world, so that again he who would study, or take part in, the better housing of the people should come to Dunfermline ?

Or, beginning once more, and this time with statelier homes, have we not the Abbot's House, which at some future time may fall into the hands of the Trust, then to be doubtless kept in repair and furnished with what can be got together of the historic furniture and decoration of its own time, as the Musée Cluny of Dunfermline ?

May not the same be said of old Pittencrieff House, so representative of the Puritan and Cavalier period ? And again of the eighteenth-century house by the Port Gate, near the Abbey, with its sternly simple exterior, its pleasant spacious rooms ? Each of these is an element, then, of the great Open-Air Museum so often argued for, and to this it will be the pleasing duty of the Trust, and of independent citizens, to carry on a generous rivalry in civic development, so that houses of each period, of each decade even, in the period of rapid housing progress now opening, may be thought worthy of preservation by our successors. Here, then, is a fuller development of the thesis of Chapter XVII. C.

H. The Opening Future

Will this complete our historic museum ? Not yet. History is no mere study of the past, as unveiling the origin and development of the present, it increasingly also foresees the future as continuing that development, be it for better or for worse. Thus I understand the improvement of the Abbey Church is at present being seriously considered ; and at some time, if not now, the rebuilding of the Lady Chapel over Queen Margaret's tomb will replace the present miserable erection against the east wall of the Church, thus lengthening out the whole perspective and largely recomposing the present too incongruous masses of the ancient and modern halves of the church building, while the natural weathering of time, to which should be added the judicious planting of ivy, will largely do the rest, thus again restoring harmony to the whole edifice.

But this is not all. This union of the historic and the modern spirit, of reverence for the past yet of practical reorganisation in the present, will not only clear out the basement of the Monastery of the rubbish pitched in two generations ago by the misrestorer of the abbey, but will some day rebuild the destroyed north and east walls of the great Fratry Hall, and roof this anew.

Yet more : some day also the Palace itself will be rebuilt ; though all this will be neither for monk nor priest, for king nor noble, but as a Hall and Palace of the Commons, as a Fratry Hall indeed. In Scotland of old, there were plain folk who knew themselves " nobles by right of an earlier creation, priests by the imposition of a mightier hand." Only as we work towards such definite reorganisation of the noblest survivals of the past into a yet nobler future can our plans and labours have real value to our city, or to that larger world whose best thought and work we have to share, and, if it may be, here to stimulate and lead.

Here then is a scheme of policy stretching beyond our time, our opportunity, our capacity, and for that very reason a Culture-Policy indeed. That the beginnings at any rate are practicable will not be denied ; and if any do not think this of its ultimate ones, of roofing of palace and hall, he may see all this and more in progress from Edinburgh Castle, with its restored Parliament

House and King David's Tower, to St Giles' ; as by-and-by he may see it at Holyrood. A further study of Edinburgh or of less frost-bitten Continental cities, more fully awakened American ones, will show that a civic renascence is begun on many sides, which may before long develop into culture-policies more ambitious than anything I venture to sketch for Dunfermline.

Past cities have had their Acropolis and Forum, their Abbey and Cathedral ; why should not we also renew, even surpass, these ? Life and the world may be on as high or as low a level as we choose to make them ; hence the cities of the world, like nature's simpler forms of life, have each and all at times adapted themselves to express every level of ideal and every route of progress upward or downward. The warmth and swiftness and world-freedom of the swallow are all as congruent with the realities of everyday environment as is the well-fortified torpor and coldness of the tortoise or the snail ; and there is no real evidence of the common impression in civic matters that such lowest and slowest creepings are the only possible or desirable examples of progress for cities, these highest manifestations of life. Let us, then, at this time of reflection shape out the highest ideals for our city that we are capable of devising : to shape any lower ideal is to ensure the realising of a lower still.

CHAPTER XXV

THE ART INSTITUTE

A. The Problem

PROBABLY in no subject with which we have here to deal is the incubus of dead history so heavy. In no educational subject, moreover, are the British public and their educational machinery, more retarded by the ideas of previous generations—first those which collected Old Masters, and which introduced from the Court of France the doubtful blessing of a Royal Academy, and then that which was aroused by the premonition of shrinking markets afforded by the great Exposition of '51. The old-fashioned connoisseur, with his picture gallery of real or supposed masterpieces, his real or spurious historic collection, hereafter no longer exclusively dominated the art progress of a city, but shared his leadership with a much less artistic development—that which long made the very name of South Kensington a byword and a reproach. And though it is but fair to recognise much recent improvement in our official art teaching, it may be gravely questioned whether even this is keeping pace with the progress of art outside official circles ; for though in exceptional art schools, like that of Glasgow, the artist has come into power, we still elsewhere commonly find points of view and educational proposals which are far behind the art progress of the times. This progress is no doubt less generally appreciated than is that of industry or science, perhaps because it has been outrunning even these. Now, if we are not simply to set up another traditional picture gallery with unthinking generosity on the one hand ; nor, with bureaucracy on the other, to go on multiplying " freehand and model drawing, perspective and shading from the cast," what sort of Art Institute do we need ? Let us by all means recognise the soul of goodness in the old miscellaneous collection, for this at least aimed at appreciation ; and admit this in the traditional drawing schools also, since these at any rate have sought to aid in art-production ; but surely here is the place and time to ask : Can we not improve our methods, both as regards appreciation in the general public, and as regards productivity of the gifted individual ?

B. Art Appreciation

As regards general appreciation, we have plainly first of all to communicate the Art of Seeing, even before the Seeing of Art. Here our park excursions and longer regional ones, our stimulus of photography, of sketching, of nature study of all kinds, our camera obscura also, are notable helps ; insufficient from the developed artistic point of view, yet surely desirable so far as they go. Such observation is the raw material which art may develop ; it is the accumulating of that wealth of impressions which it is for the developing powers of imagination and expression to re-arrange.

After and along with this art of observation, of healthy and joyous seeing, comes also the Seeing of Art. This should plainly begin (as not always at present) by teaching the student to see, not as the Mediæval or Renaissance artists saw, but as he can see for himself. The child in sunshine sees the violet shadows upon the dusty road just as the impressionist paints them : it is only the miseducated grown-up, who has been trained from old pictures, or perhaps still more from printed descriptions of them, who persuades himself that the same shadow is brown. To escape from common literary epithets and to be encouraged to observe how often earth is purple, grass gold, and the sea all possible colours by turns, is a training which most of the older generation have missed, and which the younger are not yet by any means sufficiently receiving.

Our art of seeing, and our seeing of art, are thus but different modes of that appreciation of beauty which is as organic an interest of the mind as is the naturalist's delight in life and growth. Look at any beautiful thing—say a shell : its simple colour and form interest us even before we investigate its architecture or seek the law of its development. But this is to say that the feeling of fresh wonder which it arouses in us is mingled of admiration and curiosity, and that it is the former of these which comes first. The latter more intellectual attitude is what develops into the questioning and answering of science—good and desirable in itself, but too often involving our fall out of the brief paradise of innocent joy in beauty. Far too often repressed, at any rate too seldom encouraged, is the emotional state which art-appreciation cultivates. So far from this being unpractical, it is this which prepares for action, so soon as imagination rearranges these impressions into something new. Returning to the example of the beautiful shell taken above, this may now suggest a new creation, depending upon the powers of the artist, from the child's bit of twisted clay to that architectural masterpiece of Leonardo da Vinci, of which a recent writer has traced back the suggestion and principle to a spiral shell. This man, by general consent the most representative genius of the Renaissance, reconciling the culture of art and science, of poet and engineer, of archæologist and inventor, into eminent productive achievement, in all these fields and more, is the very type of high productivity based on true education ; that education at once of appreciative senses and of active and disciplined hand, that culture of intellect yet of feeling, of imagination yet of executive power, which is again coming into sight and even reach for our children.

Let me not be caricatured as promising to grow a young Leonardo in Dunfermline, though this would be far less absurd than the more usual despair of finding any such. What I maintain for art, as above for nature-studies generally (Chap. XIII. C.), is that it is now becoming possible to arrest and redress that waste of life, that stunting of powers and possibilities which goes on daily amidst our crude educational machinery, so compact of tradition in the higher schools, as of bureaucracy in the lower. By this return to nature, and to human nature, we may, we shall, produce again that higher level of average and popular culture from which the full blossom of talent, the wonder-blossom of genius, may oftener arise, and without which these come to comparatively imperfect fruit. It was Athens that made the Greeks, more than they Athens ; so Rome the Roman, Florence the Florentine ; and so it must ever be with our little land, also in her turn so rich in genius, however less successful in her rearing of it.

Such an art of seeing is, of course, to many instinctive ; but it may be cultivated, and is often learned by child and naturalist, best of all by those who have the good fortune to number artist or art-lover among their companions and friends. My point is that it is now possible to generalise these methods, and to initiate or recall " everyday inartistic people " to a real appreciation both of the beauty of the world and of the artistic rendering of it. This can and should be done, just as with skilled popularising people are constantly being put at the point of view of this or that previously unfamiliar science. Everybody knows by this time that to walk out with a geologist or a botanist, a bird-lover or a forester, is to have his eyes opened to things he never saw before. Yet the average sightseer seldom suspects that in landscape he has still no less to learn from more trained eyes. In this connection I venture to speak with a good deal of experimental certitude, alike as learner and as teacher—in fact, from experience as definite as with scientific nature-teaching, and of the same kind, alike as guide in the open field and in the great collections.* Here also come in the camera obscura, the convex mirror, and other simple optical devices, which are of notable aid to seeing to the beginner and even to the artist. Precisely

* " Every Man his own Art-Critic." Manchester Exhibition, 1886 ; Glasgow Exhibition, 1888.

as people take a course of nature-study, of swimming lessons or of gymnastics, so they should be able, with the same moderate aptitude and good will, to obtain a course of art-appreciation ; and this, though, of course, differing in result and degree with every individual, would give all a substantial new pleasure, an increase of power and even of sanity of observation, thought, and life. For true seeing is healthy seeing ; and healthy seeing is one of the first conditions of brain health.

C. Art Education in its General Bearings

Before me lies a collection of pamphlets, of which the titles will better express this later trend of art-education, far beyond those of connoisseurship, or immediate craft-design, with which older teachings have started. For instance, Horsfall : " The Use of Pictures in Education," and, by the same author, " The Relation of Drawing to Healthy Life " (Manchester : K. Cornish). Or, again, Zeublin : " Art in Life " (University of Chicago, 1900). Literature of this kind should be before everybody, at any rate everybody seriously concerned with the problem of raising the art standard of the community. For here we are free of the jargon of past or present art fashions, as also of the sordid economist's prostitution of art into a mere means of alluring customers. Each of these writers is fully at the civic point of view, and sees art as a vital part of that ministry of social betterment and culture which is our problem here. It is when we have appreciated such points of view that we shall see better, for instance, how to treat our besetting national vice, so largely the resort of the starved artistic nature ; indeed, well-nigh the only one our phase of civilisation as yet amply provides for the people.

D. Art for Art's Sake—Technical Schools and Museums

It will be plain, then, that the present point of view is not merely that of " Art for Art's Sake " : it is with art for education's sake that we began, and with art for the city's sake that we would continue. Yet there is in this much abused maxim of " Art for Art's Sake " an element of truth which needs now to be recognised. This element is that of technical qualities, and may be approached from various sides. Traditionally the method has been that of beginning with the fine arts ; hence our usual instruction in drawing and painting. But the reaction against this has now fully begun, and the rise of arts from crafts is now in progress. Thus, instead of teaching everybody to draw more or less badly, and producing innumerable inferior draughtsmen, to whom craftsmanship then seems a descent in the social and artistic scale, we begin to supply a general basis of craft-education, from which special artistic talents will far more readily arise. Hence again the justification of our Primitive Village, our Crafts Village. To this recapitulation of the simpler craft-experience the more developed activities of a Technical School proper would naturally be linked. As such schools develop, their student will be less and less content without producing a good job as journeyman, and graduating with a masterpiece, as of old : no mere drawings or exercises will content him.

Into this matter of Technical Schools I do not think it relevant here to enter—not but that a great development of both schools and museums, etc., in connection with the leading industries of the City and neighbourhood may be expected. It appears to me, however, that such improved resources, in so far as directly bearing upon the staple industries of the city and neighbourhood, may quite fairly be left by the Trust to the ordinary course of educational development, such as would have been natural and necessary in the city without any Trust at all ; otherwise, if the Trust step in to supply these, shall we not merely have a case of that indirect relief of rates which has been so expressly provided against ? Local technical developments are to be expected in connection with the educational changes now pending ; and even if these do not fully satisfy local industrial needs, it is not the Trust which need be first called upon. Would not this be overlooking the natural organisers of such advances—the local captains of industry ? If anything whatever is to be left to their special knowledge and enlightened self-interest, it is surely such technical developments, as of Textile Museums, Schools, and the like.

I refrain, therefore, from indicating any purely technical museum. If my point of view be not approved, and the Trust see it desirable to establish or to aid strictly technical museums, these would doubtless be situated at or near the present Technical School, and need not therefore, be considered upon the present site.

E. Exhibitions—Studios—Art Library

I return, then, to these possibilities of general art furtherance, which are the main problem before us here. The true way to foster the highest possible development even of purely technical excellence in our industries is, there can be no doubt, that which also takes part in the larger art movement of the world. Hence the indirect but truly educative value of such an Art Exhibition as that recently held, presumably only one of many exhibitions to come.

May I plead that these Exhibitions should be frequent, small, and of specialised purpose, rather than annual, large, and general, like the too miscellaneous exhibitions of other towns ? Exhibitions at best are but museums of the moment, and need to be vitalised by relation to the real work of the world. Hence, then, another characteristic feature of our Art Institute beyond its exhibiting and its teaching work becomes clear. It should contain at least one studio, if possible a group of several ; and in these should be continually in progress this or that piece of decorative work for a building of the Trust, a school, or the like. Here, in fact, would be the true continuation and culmination of the workshops of the Crafts Village.

With the painter at work, why not the sculptor also ? Why should not an artist, instead of receiving a commission for a picture, be rather engaged by time-salary for specific tasks ? This principle, which applies so obviously for decorative painting, and which has been once and again found to be satisfactory to all concerned, might also fairly be applied to the elaboration of other undertakings of the Trust, at any rate to the fitting detail of their execution, as in wood-carving, mosaic work, etc. In this way the fullest possible contact of arts with crafts, as of smith, weaver, embroiderer, would be effected, and the artistic impulse deepened in the community. The existence of such a living art school would not only interest the designers and amateurs but through them stimulate the whole town ; while it would aid in keeping up the artistic quality of the panoramic creations I have already indicated for the Nature Buildings (Chap. XV.). In this way we see, as a main function of the Art Institute, the carrying on of the task of the present volume, the development of park, gardens, and culture institutes ; in fact, the improvement of Dunfermline in all its æsthetic and technical aspects. Of the material advances of civilisation through Primitive Village, Crafts Village, History Buildings, and Museum of Masterpieces, here, in fact, is the planning-room, the studio, and the school.

As already suggested, a small but well-chosen Art Library might conveniently here be centred ; at any rate an art Bibliography : this should include guidance to the art books not only of Dunfermline but of Edinburgh and Glasgow, so as to save time to all concerned. A table with Art Journals and Magazines would be also greatly appreciated, and would relieve that pressure upon the ordinary library reading-rooms which may be reasonably expected to arise as soon as these become adequate. One of the offices indicated on the accompanying plan would naturally be that of business administration ; the other would serve for meetings and deliberations connected with art

—whether those of the Trust or its staff, or those of the artistic groups and associations which exist, or may be reasonably expected to develop.

All these suggestions will be seen to converge towards that fuller idea of culture, which not only seeks, as in Matthew Arnold's definition, to " know the best that has been thought or done in the world," but which also seeks to go on with the best, and this not only in imagining it, but in producing it. In short, here is another case of the education of experiences replacing that of exercises.

F. Collections

Do I provoke my reader by delaying to come to what is commonly considered the essential matter of an Art Institute—its collections ? I must once more refer to the position taken up in preceding chapters (XXII. C. and XXIV. F. G.), which is practically this—that the art objects of most ordinary collections should be distributed into three series— one that of History, for which we have liberally provided ; secondly, that of the Pathology of Art, which we should not here provide at all for ; and thirdly, that of the Masterpieces ; and it is for these masterpieces that I would fain plead that our gallery space should be reserved. The distinction of masterpieces from historical specimens is, of course, not always easy, yet often quite practicable. Thus, for instance, it is obvious that a collection of Cyprus art is of notable historic interest but of little artistic merit ; while conversely, a selection of Tanagra figures, a good Greek vase or two, are masterpieces indispensable to the smallest collection. The masterpiece should be approached with admiration—that is, emotionally ; the historic illustrative specimen is approached with interest and curiosity—that is, intellectually ; and to use the one for the other, as is too commonly done, in our museums — South Kensington and its minor institutions for choice—is to combine two evils : on one hand a training in admiration of the merely curious—that is, the unbeautiful ; with, on the other, a merely informational—that is, inartistic—use of things beautiful. It is this use of science to spoil art, which is at the root of the comparative uselessness of what should be our greatest educational treasure-houses. Thus each museum, begun as a paradise of beauty, lets in its serpent, and prepares its ruin.

Just after designing a temple to the muse of history, such as she has never in this world possessed, I may be pardoned for refusing to surrender to her impartial serial presentment the masterpieces of beauty also ; these need surely a no less distinct temple of their own, smaller yet not inconsiderable, and not necessarily neglectful of historic grouping, though kept apart from ordinary presentment of it. Am I thereby neglecting the claims of education ? Not at all ; I am defending these, by distinguishing the enjoyment of beauty from the pursuit of knowledge, and seeking to give due place and prominence to each. I shall not here enter into what in my view would be the masterpieces ; of course, largely accessible in reproductions. But as regards a further use of reproductions, I may here simply outline my view of a lending museum of art—that is, of few originals, but many well-chosen reproductions, photographs, and books.

G. Lending Museums

Besides the permanent decoration of schools, a notable resource of interest and of educational stimulus is afforded by the plan of circulating specimens which prevails in many museums. The best example on a great scale is, of course, the circulating system established by South Kensington, soon, it is hoped, to spread to other museums. Dunfermline children cannot often go to Edinburgh or Glasgow, and even if they do it will not be to see this or that class of museum objects in detail. Hence the desirability of arranging as far as possible to borrow specimens from larger centres, though I am aware that in many cases parliamentary powers would first have to be granted to these. In the meantime it would be easy to work out in Dunfermline the practical argument for such circulation of art objects, natural history specimens, etc., by lending out the duplicates of the Dunfermline museums, as they accumulate, to the schools of the city, and I trust also to such surrounding towns and villages as might desire to participate.

In this good work the Liverpool Museum has long had a well-earned pre-eminence, its late curator, Mr Higgins, making a special point of the beauty of the collections which he was accustomed to circulate, since the better the specimens the more impression they create. He was wont to maintain, and with great justice, that the inferior specimen was good enough for the specialist, whose knowledge enabled him to supply the rest, but nothing could be too good for the important task of awakening the interest of the beginner. It is very largely because a less generous if not opposite view has been too common that the educational importance of travelling collections has not already been more fully established.

American training colleges also carry this system of lending to great perfection, alike as regards natural history and art museum specimens—both originals and reproductions—photographs, engravings, and so on, to which may be added music, pianola scores, or anything else— the machinery once set agoing being, of course, adaptable to all sorts of requirements. Great examples of this educational use of museums are afforded by the Natural History Museum of New

York, where Professor Bickmore is able to boast an audience of 800,000 for his teaching! His magnificently illustrated lectures at the central museum, sometimes to as many as a thousand teachers, are stenographed and printed, the lantern slides are reproduced to many copies, and the edition is sent round the schools of the

from which in earlier times first the constitution of the University of France, and from this indirectly, in turn, that of the University of London was appropriated, and which is again a centre of widespreading initiative. Professor Dewey is bringing his library and university work together into an extending system of University Extension,

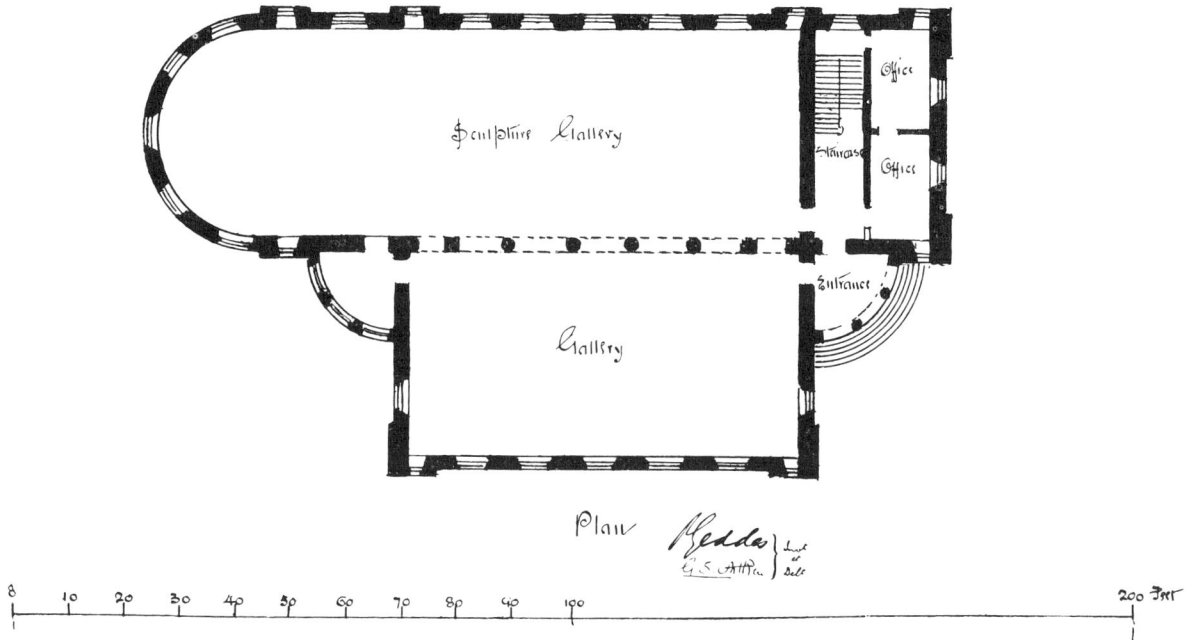

FIG. 116.—Plan of Art Building, ground floor.

FIG. 117.—Sketch for main South elevation of Art Institute. (For perspective see fig. 132 Chap. XXXI.)

entire State, and such other states as are gradually coming into co-operation. Sets of museum specimens are circulated also, until in the course of years they have made the complete round.

An even more extraordinary organisation, a veritable staff-office of this aggressive culture, is that of Professor Melvil Dewey, the well-known bibliographer, who appropriately and successfully unites the functions of heading a library—which aspires to surpass the British Museum and French National Library put together—with the Principalship of that remarkable University of New York

and looks forward to pumping the best books and courses of reading from his central reservoir into every one of the million households of the State. This, again, we may associate with the atmosphere of Chautauqua and its kindred movements, which, however, may be more conveniently discussed elsewhere.

I press this principle of circulation for a reason obvious to all, yet constantly forgotten—that an element of change is constantly needed to reawaken interest. Even occasionally to alter the hanging of pictures in the same room gives them a new freshness. It is largely by the fuller use of this plan in the Japanese household that the exquisite sensitiveness to nature and art alike, which is so fully diffused through all classes of the people, is developed and maintained. The new book from the library is more likely to be read than that upon our shelves, and so the small consignment of fresh specimens from the large museum will be looked more keenly at by teachers and pupils alike than any permanent treasure. I have lately visited the finest school museum I have ever seen, one full of objects of which any greater collection might be proud, yet practically un-visited by either boys or masters, who, feeling they

education in art I mean the increasingly general participation, both active and passive, both appreciative and productive, in the best art movements of the time and of the world. Art is not an isolated interest ; beauty is universal like truth itself ; and throughout human life, as in nature, there is a continual struggle of beauty to realise itself over inferiority or ugliness. This is in its way no less legitimate and important than is the strife of truth with error in the world of science ; the one is perhaps no less intimately connected with the perpetual strife of good and evil than is the other. A well-known hero of comedy discovered that he talked prose without

FIG. 118.—Indication of the method recommended for the further working out of requirements and arrangements of each and every museum building before completion of plans—i.e. by means of an actual model, with blocks, sketches, etc., to indicate cases, objects, etc. (Photograph kindly lent by Mr R. Quick, Curator of Horniman Museum.)

can see them at any time, hardly look at them at all. The same is true of university and even national collections. Let Dunfermline, then, begin to act more and more fully, as the regional culture-capital she is again becoming, and brighten up her surrounding towns and villages by generous and regular circulation of her ever more abounding best—so pioneering at once in cultural advance and educational helpfulness.

H. Higher Art Education

" Higher art education." What is to be under-stood by this ? Not, of course, more grades, examinations, and certificates. Not alone the encouragement of individuals of more developed skill, more genuine productivity. By higher

knowing it ; so, whether we notice it or no, we are each and all expressing our preferences and giving our influence—that is, taking our part—in this or that evolution of art : we are realists or conventionalists, idealists or symbolists. These are different attitudes of mind which appear on each and every level of culture—nay, are already latent to everyone who has been aroused to observe them—in the play of children, in reverie, or even conversation, and in current literature most plainly of all.

Let no one think that these artistic attitudes may be all very well in Paris, or even in Glasgow, but are not necessary for Dunfermline. Surely no culture problems or interests are foreign to us here, least of all one so utilitarian, practical, industrial. It is a national affectation at present not to take art seriously ; hence, even at its rare public appearance, an Academy dinner, the guests are wont to lecture the artist upon politics, instead of learning from him to see.

Only a generation ago, then, in the Salon of Paris, only a decade ago in the Academy Exhibition of Edinburgh, only last year in that of London, to be a living and modern painter, not a traditional one, was to be rejected and despised. But though many thus attained martyrdom, many also escaped into the open air, with all its wealth of impressions, to enjoy and to express its light and atmosphere, its colour and movement, and mirror the life of all the changing world. Thus in these hard conditions was developed a new art—that of impressionist realism—of " painting the thing as we see it, for the god of things as they are."

But after thus " seeing the thing as it is " arises a new art, a new inspiration ; not only to see the thing as it is, but to make it as it might be, as it should be. With this selective skill we now get the more developed artist, the designer, the truly decorative artist. Yet, if this be all, his art, and still more his successors', hardens from a style into a convention ; and so we land in the dead conventionalism which has ever been the end of art movements and the character of the official teaching of them to this day. But instead of this, there may arise another development behind the sense-mirror of the realist ; beyond the selective intention of the decorator comes a deeper and more emotional development. Our artist observer and craftsman now has his work again transformed by the rise of the poet within ; he sees beyond the things as they seem to stand in the present, and discerns them in their birth and change and tendency—that is, he discerns and expresses more and more of their ideal. But these ideals, which men of old believed in as absolute and unchanging, and which many, thus discouraged, have too often come to reject altogether, are now reappearing, and this in a new sense. For the old ideals are neither fixed nor yet shattered ; they are such expressions of the trend of evolution as we can discern, and hence they must again grow ever clearer with the personal and social progress of thought. Finally, our artist begins to feel the fuller and more complex inter-relations of things and their ideals to the spirit of man ; and now his art takes its highest yet most individual form : he is at length a symbolist. Apply this outline now to the works and the biographies of artists, and see if these be not the various periods and manners through which they pass. And is not our own higher art education measured by the degree in which we appreciate or share these stages of development ? Here, in short, is the outline explanation of the various schools of art—now falling from vital, through traditional, to academic, and thence to the lowest official dulness of bureaucracy ; again with science becoming realist, with invention decorative ; then with thinker and poet becoming idealist and symbolist, and, of course, these with all possible varieties and combinations. The interest and the relevance of this interpretation is twofold. First, it is necessarily to be kept in view in the development of our art-teaching and art-treasuring ; and it throws fuller light, for instance, upon that sharp distinction of the Art Museum proper—that of enduring Masterpieces, from the Historic Museum, to which the greater part of most collections should be relegated. This sympathy with the best movements of our own time will enable us to reinterpret the historic phases of art, and even our own traditional academic or scholastic adversaries, with a new charity—as owing their persistence to the greatness with which past ages and schools have expressed in their own way our present phases and ideals—the Mediæval painter, for instance, more idealist and symbolist ; the Renaissance painter more decorative, and so on. Such a conception will help us in many ways, as notably with the choice and arrangement of our exhibitions, and with their interpretation to their

visitors. And thus we reach once more the essential problem, that of helping a larger proportion of our fellow-citizens of all ages to appreciate, and so far to share in, the great movements of art.

The same mode of criticism thus does not end with schools of art : it will help us equally in the library ; for art is not a mere special education, as pedants think, it is a general education also, and one often deeper, as well as truer, than that of books. Among the current romancers, among the recent poets, we find the same great schools ; and as we next return through modern, Renaissance, and Mediæval classics to Roman, Greek, or Hebrew ones, we find the same developments making up each turn of the spiral. Turning to the study of philosophy, we see that our painters, little though they may have read, have been unconsciously imaging all the schools, "each an Aristotelian or a Platonist." Thus from art we come into the very heart of the education problem, both past and present, in literature and learning, philosophy or science. We naturalist observers, reporting the facts of nature or life as we find them—whether for the scientific journals or the daily press matters little—are like the realist painters of thirty years ago ; while, in so far as we seek to arrange our knowledge, we begin to reach the level of the designers. Beyond this again, as we begin to discover the trend of evolution, we necessarily become in so far idealists, optimistic or pessimistic ; and then as we discern more fully the complex inter-relation and unity of things, and their significance in terms of personal or social life, we become so far symbolists.

Hence such difficulty as may be reproached to the present volume ; since its treatment of its theme is by turns from each of these points of view ; not only that of photographic realism, or next of constructive design, with its technical detail and grouping ; but also essaying the expression of evolutionary ideals, and the suggestion of corresponding symbols. And if any reader be still perplexed by this departure from the traditional fashion of unthinkingly establishing another collection or setting up another art school, let him glance at some contemporary art-treatise ; say some book of Santayana, Bosanquet, or Hirn, to name only writers in English. Even such a title as Hirn's—"The Origin of Art : a Psychological and Sociological Inquiry " (Macmillan, 1900)—will indicate that the present approach is not so unconventional as it may appear.

I. Final View of Art Institute

Leave now art for science, which is commonly taken more seriously. No one any longer doubts that the current social evolution is one which science is slowly but surely transforming, alike in war and peace. But what of the details of this ? Must it not soon become obvious that just as the stone age is divisible into two very well-marked and distinguishable periods—the " Palæolithic," with its coarsely-chipped implements, and the later " Neolithic," with its finely polished ones—so two such phases are becoming recognisable in our modern technical civilisation ?

In our Primitive Village we should see and show how the rude stone age with its rough-chipped flints became replaced not only by the culture of a finer age but by the man—one not only of advanced knowledge, but of higher industry, of more developed art. In this wondrous technical age, which is again transforming the world and history, do we not recall with pride that we here in this island, indeed in this particular central region of it, have been the initiators par excellence ? But if so, is it not of the older and lower developments that we have been historically the masters—those of coal and steam rather than those of electricity and art ? Must we not, therefore, call this earlier and crude mechanical civilisation which still predominates among us the " Palæotechnic " stage, and recognise that the formerly less prominent industrial peoples, who now increasingly dispute our mastery in markets, because in taste no less than in science they are excelling us, are passing more quickly than we into the " Neotechnic " stage—that of industrial civilisation proper ? And if this be so, as so it surely is, may not the raising of our art-level be as truly important an aspect of our whole development, even of our racial and national continuance, as are forms, or institutions, or policies at present more prominent ?

I have not minimised the claims of natural science, of history, or of social science ; yet I cannot refrain from expressing the conviction that even more urgent still to our educational and even our social betterment is the problem of a real national advance in our appreciation and our ideals of art. " To teach taste is to form character," as Ruskin showed long ago : yet the social reformer, specialising upon intemperance or ignorance, degeneracy or dirt, is too slow to recognise that these are each and all practically congruent with our dominant yet declining Palæotechnical order, but incongruent with the incipient Neotechnic one ; and hence that he may even best serve his special cause by helping forward this larger movement of the age.

Amid the various Ministries of Culture, of which the Trust is the central Cabinet, that of Art is assuredly not the least important. It is not so exceptional as it may seem that social forces so influential as Ruskin and Morris have come to general questions from the side of art ; everywhere in the younger generation the artist is seeking to escape from the amusing of the rich to the service of the people. Soon his task in the Neotechnic Transition before us will be no less recognised than are those of science and invention, of wealth, and of organising power. Some many-sided and deeply socialised artist, then, as Art Director—now decorating, now organising, now teaching old and young—is thus the needful leader of our Art movement.

G. LIFE AND CITIZENSHIP

CHAPTER XXVI

SOME EDUCATIONAL BEARINGS OF THE SCHEME

THOUGH no scheme of schools nor explicit treatment of Education is offered above—albeit whole chapters withheld—the subject in one respect or another is implicit in every chapter. Teacher and pupil from kindergarten to higher schools may here find something towards their concrete needs, their abstract problems—at any rate some freshening suggestions alike for work and play.

Nature studies and humanities have alike been considered, even technical studies also—from the strenuous muscular effort of gymnasium or running track, of primitive cave-digging and the rest, to the refined draughtsmanship of the studio and the scriptorium, and from the primitive lever to the electrician's work bench, or from the simple to the complex loom.

The world of classical studies may be, as I for one believe, only too much with us late and soon ; yet even so our Historic Institute, with its periodically associated excursions to the Roman Wall, its classic art treasures, will protect our children from mere bookishness. The " modern side " of education—that concerning nation and empire, the whole English-speaking world, and our brethren of the foreign tongues we increasingly need as well—is all presented more fully than ever to scholar before.

Here particularly I appeal to the teachers who know how their profession is at length escaping— and this more thoroughly in America, France, and other countries than as yet in our own—from the bureaucratic and memorising period of codes and cram. Surely all see that education is becoming once more treated as the birth-helping of the spirit, the fostering of mental evolution, not as a matter of mere academic exercises and official status. Yet we are but escaping from this age of bondage ; there is a generation of hard yet invigorating pilgrimage before that promised land of education, now foreseen by all our leading spirits, can be attained.

In these developments university extension and such movements play their part, and the opportunities for it are here. Our new museums or renewed library, our historic and scientific resources, will be doubled in value if we arrest on their north and southward journeys the best teachers from the great university cities around us ; we shall get from them teaching fresher and better, because freer, than they could give us from their own chairs.

A. Summer Schools

Most important of all, we teachers, as we transcend the formalist order and see education, our own and others, as a vitalist progress, should make Dunfermline the centre of a great Summer School ; and with even a beginning of such resources as I am suggesting above we could and would do so. Why not of a veritable Chautauqua, to name that source from which all our Summer Meetings have been historically suggested, and which still continues an ever-increasing, ever-vitalising work ? Long experience of a small and early beginning of this kind has accustomed me to the initial criticism of the weary teacher that there is no time nor strength left in the summer vacation for more work. But those who venture to try it soon appreciate the new spirit, and understand with a new freshness how the ancient, the true and perpetual meaning of the word school—" *schola* "—is simply Leisure. For true culture is recreative, as all true recreation is cultural, developing not only the body or mind or feelings separately, as has been too much the case in our own time, but uniting all together in ever-varying measures into that happy and expanding unity of function, which is Life.

Such a Vacation Gathering is thus, however, not so much for the body of the teachers of Dunfermline. Change is needed, and to them the Vacation Summer Schools of Edinburgh or Cambridge, Paris or Jena would be naturally the more refreshing ones ; its first appeal would be to the teachers of Scotland and beyond. In this new Chautauqua we should thus be renewing the traditions of the Abbey at its best, its open hospitality, its perpetual freshening of learning and interchange of thought. Yet with our Nature Survey from sea to hills, our study in the glen, our laboratory in the gardens, our archæology in the Primitive Village, our technical instruction in the gardens and at the mills, our history in pageant and drama ; even the Dunfermline teacher would soon find this truly recreative, and carry back its spirit into regular work, henceforth less wearisome since with freshened initiative. For as our park and culture-institutes constitute one vast Open-Air Museum, so the whole contemporary transformation of culture is leading us to the Open-Air Education. All very good for natural science, for history also, it may be said ; but how can one speak of Open-Air Education in other subjects ? Is a definite illustration needed ? Assuming in our Summer School the usual lectures and conferences on education, the usual review of its ideals from Socrates and Plato to Rousseau, or from Froebel and Pestalozzi to our own leaders or contemporaries — James, Stanley Hall, and Dewey, Sadler or Struthers, Reddie or Rein—we might also imagine and work out, in jest and earnest, in masque and play, a veritable procession of the history of education—surely one of the strangest in all the chequered history of mankind. Strange primitive folk and sublime world-teachers, philosophers and scholars of all schools and centuries should defile before us, up to the present with its disputing factions, each by turns affording a subject worthy of an Aristophanes or a Molière. The pessimist would show us the teacher as a Laocoon with his children, struggling vainly amid red tape convolutions ; and the optimist of child-study reply, with his infant Hercules breaking such coils. One actor would popularise the art of alternate swallowing and disgorging of all various objects of information in its simpler conjuring form, and another solemnly award certificates and diplomas for proficiency in this with all the solemnity of older sales of indulgences. One, again, greatly daring, would show us anew some rare youth aspiring beyond such philatelic accumulations, such paper securities, and so lead us on through the windings of our studious groves to our renewed Acropolis—there to show forth a higher imagery than I dare outline here.

B. Relation to the Universities

It is one of the best signs of educational progress that we need no longer hesitate to speak of the Higher Education of the People, and now in a way beyond that of University Extension, which twenty years ago or more was successfully tested in this city. It is for a renascent city—for Dunfermline then, first of all—to make her return for all the services of the universities to her in the past by helping to vitalise these anew, by working out for them, even ahead of them for a season, this and that element of that Educational Revolution which is in progress throughout the world, and which the weight of insular traditions, of present responsibilities, makes so peculiarly different for them.

Instead, therefore, of indicating a mere sixth university centre in Dunfermline these plans set forth a group of culture-resources, not only adapted to the city and the occasion, but of value to the larger cause of education in Scotland and beyond.

To our own local founder our Scottish universities recently owe the greatest of material endeavours towards renewing their historic accessibility to the people—checked though this be for the time in the instinctive interest of the prosperous classes by the heightening of the traditional and formal barriers at their entrance. To the same generosity they also owe the substantial top-dressing of many of their various specialist fields, which are now showing not a few improvements, though naturally of those kinds which least obviously threaten the traditional curricula.

But the main result of these improvements will no doubt be to make more obvious to the public, and to the universities themselves, the need of a far fuller modernisation, and that in the best sense. This is not, as some still fear, a sweeping out of old books once classic to make room for the dry bones of a no less formalised science, or the routine views of a narrow commercialism— but the vitalising of all studies, humanist and naturalist, their unification also—of course in no mere dogma, system, or classification, though increasingly capable of clearer restatement—but in a fuller seeing, a more efficient sharing of that social duty and progress which is at once the true labour and the high pleasure of life.

With our schools and universities thus again in evolution there is room not only for all pioneers, speculative or practical, but even for the specialists of the old order, who will soon become reconciled to the new order as they understand that all that was vital in their subject has been conserved. Instead of the string they have so long toiled in solitude to spin or stretch being rudely broken or cast away, its characteristic note is sought for and welcomed in the reopening orchestra.* For evolution does not lie in destruction of the past but in its fulfilment.

It now lies with the people and their representatives, led no doubt by pioneering initiative, and therefore particularly by such bodies as that which I am here privileged to address, to assure the recovery of that popular usefulness and accessibility of the Scottish University, that full contact with Continental and general thought which have been its best features in the past. Such reformers will, of course, guard themselves against that cry of "lowering the standard," which has ever been the temporary safeguard of an outworn yet well-established order against its assailants. It is for these to have a higher

* The reader who cares to pursue this idea further may find a noteworthy expression of it in a recent essay by Mr Branford. See "Ideals of Science and Faith," edited by J. E. Hand. (Allen, 1904.)

standard of their own, and this in every subject. I trust such a standard is plainly indicated for not a few subjects in the preceding pages. It is surely where the raising of local culture is being attended to that the modernisation of entrance examinations and of curricula may also most fairly be demanded.

Into the details of the educational revolution now so manifestly begun on all sides I cannot, of course, go fully here, but without fear of disapproval from any progressive teacher, academic, secondary, or primary, I may define this as a change from the formal view of things, considered and analysed separately, and statically thought of as at rest or dead, towards the vital or kinetic view—the synthetic correlation of all studies, henceforth thought of within the moving drama of evolution. Till comparatively recently the practical problem to which universities have devoted themselves has been to attend to the spinning and fixing of the needful warp-threads, the filling by each specialist of his particular spool. But now the time is approaching—nay, has already come—for making some use of all this enormous capital, this still dormant potentiality, and of now throwing athwart the warp of specialism, the flying shuttle of synthesis, so creating a solid fabric both of warp and woof.

Thus our universities have now got or are getting, with whatever difficulty, most of their needed specialist institutes of astronomy and geology, of botany and zoology, of chemistry and physics, of anatomy and physiology. No doubt all these need fuller development ; yet it is also time to organise and to unify them—that is, by the corresponding development of these more comprehensive and synthetic studies, those unifying disciplines, which are at present throughout our universities conspicuous by their absence. To wit—Meteorology, which assumes and unifies knowledge from the whole group of physical subjects ; still more organic Nature-Studies, not only in a comprehensive whole of Biology, but beyond this again in the vast whole of Geography. Similarly the many specialisms of history and languages have now to be completed by a comprehensive Institute of Social Studies, which, again, is complementary to the Institute of Geography.

Now, one of these synthetic institutes is our Nature Palace, the other our History Palace and Museum, with its Social outlook. Such institutions, then, do not compete with the existing university, they prepare for these, and yet pioneer beyond them. First, they furnish the introduction to university studies, so that our youth of Dunfermline, who should here grow up within an atmosphere of nature and of history continued into social progress, would be most able, most willing to profit by the analytic resources of the special sciences as developed in the various univer-

sities ; yet they would also return to their native city with a fuller appreciation of its characteristic culture-institutions, and profit by these far more fully than before.

C. Further Significance of Proposed Culture-Institute in Education

Our History Palace, our Nature Palace, are thus no mere personal dreams. They are presented as approximate solutions, open, therefore, to every possible improvement, but still solutions for the time being of the twofold problem of at once furnishing a better introduction to higher studies and yet of completing their outlook by a larger and more modern evolutionary culture—that is, one at once more philosophic, yet more directly human and social also. That such an education appeals to both sexes is evident ; but this also peculiarly to women, for whom the too purely analytic studies of the universities are increasingly insufficient. As woman for her housekeeping must combine the results of many arts and industries, so her culture-interests touch all specialisms. The university, it is true, offers its synthesis under the title of philosophy, but this is as yet too abstract for most minds, and the problem of presenting some reasonably complete image and view of the evolution of nature and of humanity has, therefore, to be dealt with. Hence it is that I press the serious and thoughtful consideration of the present group of institutes as the approximate solutions required.

The intellectual justification of this group of institutions is thus far more full and thorough than may appear at first sight ; yet it must be put more clearly still. Broadly speaking, the educational developments of the nineteenth century may be expressed in two or three main movements. Of these the first, and as yet the greatest, is the magnificent development of the German Universities from about 1810 onwards, in their adoption of the encyclopædic movement, exiled from France, and its development into a generous recognition of all specialisms, the free opening of the fields of learning, and of teaching and investigating in every direction. This German University movement has since been gradually rejuvenating the education of the world, and this is the predominant aspect of progress in America and this country to-day—e.g. that for which our own founder and his contemporaries have especially displayed their munificence.

Especially retarding and antagonising this, there has been, and I fear I must say in Great Britain especially, the survival of mere pre-encyclopædic Renaissance learning, and this, indeed, too often relapsing into mere monkish traditionalism, as of grammar by rote. Besides this, but fully profiting by it, there has gone on the development of a vast modern quasi-educational system, originally that of Napoleonic bureaucracy : this our current educational codes, our worship of machinery and of examinations, our official departments still substantially represent ; and from this they are derived, with as yet but quite inadequate infusions of German specialisms, still ·less of German liberalism.

But beyond this yet another movement has risen, and this time in later France—that stimulated by the magnificent revival of education and industry, of art and literature after the Franco-German war, with regard to which it has till lately been the misfortune of our country to remain substantially ignorant, when not positively prejudiced. For the vital idea of the renewing University of Paris, and of her provincial sisters, is now a development beyond current German or even American progress ; it contains besides a full adoption of the German methods, with their analytic progress of research, higher elements also. First of these is the idea of a synthetic reconstruction of knowledge towards a scientific and unified whole, an evolutionary philosophy, and, further, the application of all this to the general social and human weal ; hence, too, instead of ·losing beauty, as ever in the analytic search of knowledge, it strives towards the comprehensive carrying of art into all the resources of education, all the aspects and activities of life.

Far too little is known of this renascence of French education in this country or indeed in America. All our senior educators, still in power, had completed not only their ordinary college course at home but their " wander-year " in Germany also before this had fairly begun, still but twenty-five years ago, so that I believe I am the oldest British university teacher who has come into contact with this renascence of the French universities—say, rather, renascence of the University in France—during his formative years. Even among younger teachers such an experience is still far too uncommon, although, thanks largely to the Franco-Scottish Society and other endeavours, our students are beginning to realise the advantages of adding experience of France to that of Germany.

This newer movement is, of course, far from complete anywhere ; and it is hence open for us here to take active and useful initiative in it, and so advance the cause not only of the Higher Education of the People but of higher education for all.

Nowhere more than in the universities, however apparently tradition-bound, are men working and waiting for such things. I make bold to say that the establishment of such vital institutions for which I have been pleading would be felt attractive and found helpful by the most progressive spirits in every university in Scotland ; indeed, in every university in these islands, and in many beyond. It is an old teaching of the philosophic historian that " the esoteric must become the exoteric"—that " the mysteries have to be revealed." In plainer words, it is in proportion as the problem is solved of bringing the people the most comprehensive thought of their time, the highest ideals also, that every constructive period in history has begun. The same is coming true once more ; such a constructive period is assuredly beginning, and it is for us here to share in it, and even to pioneer.

I am thus not entering here upon the thorny questions of "university reform." Yet I submit that one not indirect way towards their solution, apart from the political and administrative reforms which have so long occupied and delayed us, lies in a refunctioning of education—civic, historic, and social, hygienic and naturalistic, technical and artistic—higher, therefore, in almost every sense of the word, such as is here not only generally proposed but materially planned for.

D. Youth in Dunfermline

Enough, then, of the most general view of these proposals and designs from the standpoint of the present education movement in the world. A word now of their appeal to the individual, the Dunfermline youth and child.

That the immediate surroundings of home and playground, garden and field, the nature contacts of air, earth, and water set a deep and enduring mark upon childhood is surely plain ; so that, in proportion as our source of democratic inspiration passes from orator to hygienist and eugenist, the realisation of the abstract rights of man, or of woman, is seen to require a fuller recognition of the concrete rights of childhood to the best attainable environment. Hence the weighty argument and appeal of fig. 56 from amidst its neighbouring ones.

The individual type and stamp, the measure of educability and productive power seem predominantly a resultant of the particular family stock and of its home and immediate conditions ; but we still largely forget the importance of that new tide of life which sets in with adolescence. The view is becoming prevalent among some of our foremost educationists that it is to our general ignorance and neglect, if not tragic mismanagement of this critical phase of human development, that the manufacture of our vast criminal, diseased, and defective classes is more largely due than to any faults of parentage or of early home-upbringing. But enough here if we recognise that defects of nature may at this phase be largely corrected or redressed by the awakening of the corresponding qualities.

That appeal to the moral and social instincts of youth which is furnished by the games and discipline of the average English public school, albeit to my mind too crude and too exclusive, has yet been extraordinarily rewarded in developing the present type of governing Englishman—one to which the governing Scotsman has also for the time conformed. It remains now for the truly democratic reformer who would redress the pre sent class preponderance which has been so largely determined by this class education to organise a better education for the children of the people. Is this possible ? Assuredly yes. Although for a time our Scottish schools have been overwhelmed by the English traditions, and often forced into more or less poor imitations of them, we may now and here develop in Dunfermline a school system which, while retaining its elements of intellectual advantage, shall give in fuller degree that stamp of personal dignity, of corporate life, and social feeling in which hitherto the strength and the measure of superiority of the English schoolboy and university man has lain.

With the improvement of housing, and the corresponding rise in culture upon which we are entering, the home need have much less to fear from the competition of any artificial orphan institutions, however these may be strengthened by the devotion of occasional foster-parents of talent, or even genius, such as the best masters of our great public schools. For the parents, with their home or day-school education, should also be able to demand the services of specialists no less eminent, and more willing to co-operate with them than have been the leaders of the dominant school systems.

Yet education undoubtedly needs something more than home. Great though be the importance of immediate home surroundings, we constantly see that children, and especially gifted ones, are more sensitive to the larger influences of nature, and even to the associations of history from tender years than we customarily imagine. How young may not this lovely glen, these tombs of hero and of saint, begin their appeal to the awakening spirit ?

But in such scenes, such associations, lies the best strength of a great English school, still more of the English Universities, not in their official studies with their intellectual appeal, so often poorer than our own, but in their noble wealth of impressions of architectural and natural beauty, of " ordered parks and gardens great." The High Street of Oxford, the " Backs of the Colleges " at Cambridge are thus two of the supreme assets not only of England but of Education, of Humanity ; and beside the encyclopædic analysis of Germany, the synthetic and artistic and social genius of France, our conception of Higher Education must also recognise and include this pre-eminent element of education in England, this charm of noble historic association, this environment of ever-present beauty. Here, then, is a real need of our Scottish Universities : a collegiate High Street of Edinburgh, a yet nobler Acropolis of Glasgow, a conserved yet developed Old Aberdeen and St Andrews, even a bonnier Dundee.

Here, too, is the value and significance of the elaboration and completion of our design, which would furnish here, in some respects no less than does St Andrews or Old Aberdeen, that beauty and harmony of surroundings which are needed to carry out the full idea of evolutionary education—as ennoblement. For as in our Labour Museum we have pleaded for the necessity of completing the student through the vital reality of labour as man, so on the other it needs this rich environment of beauty and culture in all its aspects to make our man and scholar a gentleman in the true sense also.

In this larger sense, then, our city, with its manifold culture institutes, its veritable modern cathedral, must appear as in principle and germ not only a northern Bayreuth but as much of a northern Oxford also. Our suggested Institutes, our Summer School and Assembly, have thus more possibilities than we at first assumed, and make more appeal even to the universities than they yet know.

Let me conclude by now inviting the very criticism which I sought to bar at the outset (Introduction, page 14), the question of where have such things been done before—for now there is the simplest of answers : here in this very Dunfermline. This abbey had the unique historic distinction amid all other culture-centres of the direct parentage of the two metropolitan culture-capitals of the north—Iona and Canterbury ; and in its time it had a corresponding influence also ; so that, in now pitching high our ideal and our pioneering, to the utilisation of the best culture movements around us, to the establishment of a group of Synthetic Institutes, to a policy of education at once naturalist and humanist such as philosophers have dreamed from Comenius to Spencer, and such as the Universities, even the greatest and most progressive, have not yet fully realised—we shall but be returning to the early past upon our modern spiral.

CHAPTER XXVII

THE QUEENS' GARDEN—THE ARENA

A. Queens' Garden

THE old garden below Queen Anne's House may, perhaps, have been more or less shared in by the old Convent of St Catherine, whose magnificently ivied chapel ruin makes now so delightful a feature (fig. 26): it is obviously the ancient garden of the tower and, doubtless, of the palace also. Almost from time immemorial, in fact, this must have been the garden of each successive queen, and only since the unfortunate filling up of the glen and the covering of both sides of Bridge Street has the ancient path of connection with St Margaret's Cave and beyond become effaced. " Queens' Garden," therefore, we may fairly call it, especially since its special name seems to have lapsed.

From every point within and without this garden is worthy of the most careful study ; it has hence been the subject of a peculiarly careful photographic survey, of which some results are given (figs. 120, 122, and 124).

All possibility of splendour in treatment befitting a palace garden is, however, excluded by the deep shade under which this lies ; while the palace garden proper is now represented by the sunny gardens of the park, the terraced formal gardens especially.

Another possibility is that of a quiet cloister garden, one of snowdrop and narcissus, lilies and marguerites, befitting the tradition of St Margaret ; but this I have suggested more appropriately near her Cave, and something akin also at the History Garden. The herbs and simples of the old nuns' garden next suggest themselves, but these are for various reasons unsuitable. Yet another alternative would be to accept the shady situation, to plant it up and intensify its sombreness, but this would merely be continuing what nature already offers us in all the rest of the glen below. Nor is a formal treatment suitable, the more so since we can obtain this far more impressively by the improvement of the Abbey Churchyard, as suggested above.

Another idea, only partially suggested above, is to make this a bulb garden for early spring, but this is also provided on far greater scale and with better effect in the glen below ; while after spring such a bulb garden would become too desolate.

Better than any of these alternatives seems to me the use of this spot in further developing that " open-air treatment " to which I would fain increasingly tempt the citizens.

B. Arena

Here in this peculiarly sheltered and accessible spot is one of the best places to be found anywhere for a great open-air arena. I say anywhere in the fullest sense, and this advisedly, not simply because of its shelter, its splendidly picturesque environment, or its easily arranged accesses and exits, but because of its extraordinarily perfect acoustics. I have experimentally proved this, not only by placing both actor and singer where the stage would naturally be, and satisfying myself as to their perfect audibility at every point, even at the comparatively distant entrance drive from Abbey to Tower Hill, but also by ascertaining that even weak voice and indistinct articulation can be heard at unexpected distances and with positively surprising clearness.

C. Proposed Damming of Stream: Effect of Lake and Waterfall

Hence, then, the present design of this arena, which ranges from below the existing terrace of the old buildings nearly to the present edge of the burn. I say nearly, because here I propose to raise the stream (at present running unseen at the bottom of what is practically a high-walled ditch) so as to flow out upon the lower edge of this garden, now arena, thus producing the effect, if not of a small lake, at any rate of a moderate and placid stream, giving beauty of aspect similar to that already suggested at the Nethertown, but also the additional charm of reflections of the buildings and trees around from ever-changing points of view.

This proposed damming of the stream must not be misunderstood. It has, of course, been carefully planned, so as not in the slightest degree to interfere with the present waterway under Bridge Street, the area of the proposed water being

FIG. 119.—North half of panoramic view, looking East from hilly slope of Park over gardens and backs of houses of Bridge Street to Municipal Buildings, etc.   The exit of stream from culvert under Bridge Street is in deep hollow on right.

ample, though kept not an inch higher than that of the present outlet of the culvert to the south of Bridge Street.   For it is easy somewhat to lower the level of the foot of the Arena.

To avoid danger the deep ditch should, of course, be filled up.   A further advantage of this damming is that it does away with the one disturbance of the perfect acoustics already referred to—the noise of the stream at this point ; while yet another is that it gives us the opportunity of creating not only here the beautiful reflection mirror, which is all that is needed to make this little valley an exceedingly perfect one, but also an opportunity of affording a real climax to the naturalistic beauty of the winding dell below.   For, thanks to this dam and its long pool above, we can now arrange a waterfall over its top, of some 16 or even 18 feet in height—in short, with the effect of a lakelet above we should also obtain a fall below, thoroughly comparable to that which is the climax of Jesmond Dene.   While this dam is, of course, first of all a bit of substantial engineering, though not by any means an expensive one, it need have none of the usual engineering baldness, but, as the accompanying illustration shows (fig. 123), can be easily converted into a picturesque waterfall.   The passage desirable here, from one side of the stream to the other, may be given better than by a mere path along the top of the dam by a single-span stone bridge, as, again, at Jesmond Dene * (fig. 84).

* I am, of course, aware of the regrettable presence of the drain, which runs down concealed in the bed of the stream,

D. Interior of Arena: Aspects and Accesses

To complete the Arena we balustrade the terrace below the houses, thus affording a main access and promenade, from which would descend the low-stepped passages to the tiers of seats.   This terrace might be extended, not only without loss to accommodation, but giving a row of boxes below.   Three other larger boxes are also easily provided behind, next the old buildings ; say, one for the Municipality to the north, one for the Trust to the south, on each side of a middle one for the Donor and his immediate guests.

To the south the needed spacious main entrance and exit staircase connects with the Tower Hill drive ; while the widening of this drive upon open arches gives a new set of picturesque shadows, recalling those of the old arches under the palace kitchens, though, of course, less lofty and well sunned.   To the east the effect of the old buildings looking towards the abbey (see Frontispiece once more) is so fine that little need be done beyond the necessary repair and reharling of these.   No doubt even this involves for the moment a certain loss of picturesqueness, but one necessary in itself, and which weathering will soon make up for.   On

but if at any time this needs to be opened it would be easy to supply an unseen sluice exit below the waterfall and thus run off our lake altogether, and, excavating at any required point the mud with which the present deep ditch would be filled, thus permit access and repair to the deep drain without difficulty or expense.   But some day, it is to be hoped, this drain will be given up altogether.

FIG. 120.—The same panorama continued southwards. Compare Frontispiece, and note again value of old buildings of Queens' House in composition below Abbey Spire. The Queens' Garden and retaining wall of Port Gate entrance drive faintly seen through trees.

FIG. 121.—Perspective sketch of the proposed Arena in Queens' Garden. By somewhat extending present terrace in front of houses a row of boxes is obtained, while the arches seen under Church and Abbey to right are furnished by the underbuilding for widening the park roadway above. Stream raised for lake and fall.

Fig. 122.—Photograph from Tower Dene, looking Eastward, showing Queens' House, Abbey Church, and old retaining wall of Park Drive, as at present.

the western side the amphitheatre has its present background of ivied and ferny slope and tree-crowned hill, with paths somewhat overgrown at present but easily restored. On the north the cloistered façade of the Music balustraded edge of the public place, occupying its roof above, would serve as a gallery above this dress circle. Another practical gallery, somewhat distant, no doubt, but not out of hearing, is afforded by the widened edge of the old entrance

FIG. 123.—The Details of Arena, more precisely sketched into this photograph ; with effect of waterfall produced by damming of stream at foot of Arena.

Hall and its balustraded Place above enclose our view.

This arena should seat between three and four thousand, and also give accommodation upon its spacious promenade, east and south, for at least a thousand more. The southward cloister of the new Music Hall (Chap. XXVIII.) would be the best of situations, for hearing especially, while the drive from Abbey to Tower. In such way very large assemblages can be held ; and open-air functions, oratorical and musical, historic and dramatic, may thus again become common, especially as the current exaggerated terror of the climate disappears with a generation reinvigorated by that open-air treatment, which, as already repeatedly urged, is no mere resource of medicine in desperate cases but an incipient general revolution of our recent way of life.*

The advantage of having, besides this Arena, a spacious Hall, to which even normally open-air functions can be transferred on bad days, will be obvious ; and this luxury, it will be seen, is provided in the next chapter.

E. Stage

But where is the stage, the platform, of this arena, it will be asked, especially since a lake is shown where this should be ? This difficulty is, however, again an opportunity : the stage is a floating one, moored to the western side. I need not discuss any doubts as to the structural possibility and safety of this, since, if a floating stage suffices to support the immense passenger traffic of Liverpool, it may fairly be constructed here to carry the largest of orchestras, to bear the weigh

tiest of orators.† This stage could be drawn up out of sight, if need be even between acts, into the arched exit of the stream from below Bridge Street, and might thus descend with its actors ready.

F. Garden Details, etc.

Along the main passages of our arena something of the feeling and tradition of the ancient garden would be preserved by the use of decorative plants, the larger in movable tubs or vases, as also by leaving narrow earth borders filled with lines of turf, in which bulbs would be planted for spring. This would be green throughout the year, and so at all times would give a pleasing contrast to the stone construction. Again, the coldness of the stone seats would be provided against by the supply of a series of light wood-framed or trellis seats in 8-foot lengths or so ; these could be kept in the ample storage accommodation of the ivied ruin, or that of the ground and first floor of the easterly group of buildings, and brought out and taken in as required.

---

* Little though we realise it, it is to the unlucky proximity of the date which practically determines our national holiday season, that of the coming of age of grouse, to that of the Lammas floods, that we must ascribe the current exaggeration of distrust of our climate. Our Park functions would be at their best from Whitsunday to St Swithin's Day, and again in later August and September.

† I had supposed this idea to be without a precedent, but have since learned that it is in actual use at a village in the State of New York for an annual performance of " Hiawatha."

FIG. 124.—View from Park Road between Abbey Church and Tower Hill, looking North over Queens' Garden. Note Park Hill on left, backs of houses in Bridge Street, and Town House on right.

CHAPTER XXVIII

MUSIC HALL

A. Accommodation, Site, and Plan

WE have now provided most, yet not all, the buildings required by the work of the Trust. At least one, and that in some ways the most important of all, still remains—the great Music Hall. It is peculiarly difficult to determine the proper size and dimensions for such a hall, since here authorities differ. After prolonged and varied inquiries there is little doubt on my mind that from 3000 to 3500 is the maximum size compatible with full enjoyment of the best music, since beyond this magnitude the subtler effects both of voice and instrumentation begin to be lost.

Where in Dunfermline we can find a site for so large a building without cutting up a quarter of the park has been no easy matter to answer. But, again, after very full consideration I believe that the following proposal will not only be found workable but will gradually overpower the various objections which may at first sight be urged against it.

While regretting the great injury both to the glen and town of the building up of Bridge Street I frankly regard this as irreparable. Even had the Trust the enormous sum which would be necessary now to remove these buildings, to re-open the glen, and provide a suitable bridge, the money might be more usefully employed in other ways. The southward view this would yield is undoubtedly of the greatest beauty, far excelling almost all else in Dunfermline, hence chosen as my frontispiece ; but I venture to say that this can be fully displayed, and at its best, at far less expense than that of the wholesale demolition which at first sight one feels tempted to wish for.

The startling beauty of this view to no small extent depends upon its unexpectedness and upon the contrast which the present commonplace little street affords. Here, then, is one of those artistic disasters and present difficulties which offer opportunity to the designer. We study and photograph this view from the three best stand-

187

points—from the west, middle, and east of the back windows, etc., of Bridge Street. We then see we can possess the public of all these views by simply acquiring the derelict gardens below and running out a terrace on these. The fine view shown in frontispiece is thus made fully accessible, and will remain uninjured, at least so long as we do not make our new terrace too broad.

To open this terrace upon the street, all we absolutely need is to remove even a single building, conveniently the middle one. Thus we now have recovered the lost effect, restored the southward view, with a mere fraction of the expense which at first sight it seemed desirable to incur.

But what of the opposite view upwards, from the Arena below and from the Tower avenue northwards ? What of the present south backs of the Bridge Street buildings, so irregular and unbeautiful ? How tempting to demolish these—and show the hotel and other buildings of the opposite side ! Again this alteration disappears on second thoughts. For even were the south side of the street demolished, and the north side rebuilt to-morrow, the effect would only be that of Princes Street with its hotels—that is to say, if not mostly bad in detail, in any case a simple street alignment. Whereas, not only to harmonise with the picturesque old buildings of the east side of the arena but to group around the spire of the Municipal Buildings, the present irregular buildings of Bridge Street are really less unsatisfactory. Next, these can be improved : thus the tall block, that next but one to the Municipal Buildings, might be treated with oriel windows, gabled above, thus relieving their baldness as I have done with the old buildings of Ramsay Garden or Blackie House, both obvious features of the high ridge of Old Edinburgh (fig. 125).

This, then, would be no mere makeshift improvement. I maintain this as giving not only a relatively less expensive solution, but artistically a better and more picturesque result, than would the at first sight more obvious ones of large and costly clearance. Even were the street demolished to-morrow we should still need to widen it by constructing the proposed terrace as a public place, with which the High Street should end.

The view of the glen to the north I am not forgetting, and, of course, at any time a similar terrace might be thrown out upon this side also ; but I have already amply suggested better use of any available expenditure in restoring the stream and carrying open spaces and walks along its course northward (Chap. XI.).

Our proposed terrace must be substantially supported, and this needs a massive wall front to the Queens' Garden Arena below. In so doing we have now enclosed a vast internal space, for since our terrace corresponds broadly to that extension of East Princes Street in Edinburgh which is afforded by the roof of the Waverley Market we have a corresponding interior to consider. What use now shall we make of the vast space ?

Here is our Music Hall. A crowd of objections of course immediately raise themselves. Not structural, of course, since the Waverley Market shows what can be done, but practical on one hand, artistic on the other.

Taking the practical matters, here is the needed space, not, indeed, upon the property of the Trust, but upon mostly disused gardens, surely far more cheaply obtainable than where buildings have to be demolished. A large portion of the proposed site, for instance, is actually at present municipal property, at present put only to the humblest uses, or practically not used at all. While the plans (in which I have peculiarly to acknowledge the assistance of Mr G. S. Aitken) show accommodation for about 3500 it is evident that this can be to some extent increased, if required, both in length and breadth. I particularly press, however, that the breadth be not exceeded more than is possible, since the further we encroach upon the arena and the nearer we come to the abbey the more we begin to lose the fine effect shown in the frontispiece.

It is possible somewhat to lengthen the hall, if required, beyond the dimensions indicated. To reduce its size for more ordinary occasions the top gallery can be completely shut off by iron shutters and curtains, thus reducing the accommodation to 2800 or so. The same process can, if necessary, be applied below the gallery, so using only the body of the hall and the main gallery behind, but shutting off that portion of the pit under the gallery.

Acting on the advice of musical experts I have abandoned the idea of combining a theatre or opera stage with the Music Hall, which remains a Music Hall simply. But if stage accommodation be decided on by the Trust there is ample room to supply this by building farther west upon the proposed site, assuming the needful garden space to be acquired.

B. Accesses and Exits

The question of accesses and exits has, of course, presented considerable difficulties, but that it has been substantially got over an inspection of the plan will show. Thus the new oblique drive from Bridge Street to St Catherine's Wynd (fig. 126) would be found of great service. I need hardly say that the deafening of the roof of the hall is an easy matter, its perfect central lighting and ventilation also.

I am well aware that people do not easily think of entering a hall from above and of coming out at top, and that such associations are nowadays with underground buildings, though this was very generally the custom of classic theatres and arenas.

Fig. 125.—Perspective taken from the same point, showing effect of removing central block of Bridge Street and bringing forward a new public Place ("Carnegie Place"). The large tenement to right is shown somewhat improved; those to the left beside the Campanile of main entrance as rebuilt. Central in front of entrance of the new Place stands the Restored City Cross. Under the large space thus enclosed is the proposed Music Hall, the perspective shows its ample South front well adapted for monumental treatment with open cloisters and lateral staircase towers, with archway opening of the stream into widened reflection mirror below. This archway would be deeper than is indicated in sketch, therefore more effective. The foreground is occupied by the Arena, with its small lake widened at foot.

Yet does it matter much after all whether we descend at the beginning of the evening and ascend at the close, rather than the opposite ? Only in one respect, and that not a trifling one—that of public safety—for the frightful panic accidents of modern times are constantly associated with the rushing of crowds to downward street accesses. If the same people had to hurry up, this frightful overcrowding would be physically impossible, and safe exit far more easily assured. On practical

C. Façade

Upon the one façade of this hall some architectural richness is surely permissible. Of this whole scheme of buildings along the east side of the glen this frontage is, as we ascend, the culminating one, though itself in turn a pedestal to the buildings above, themselves leading up to the Town House spire. This I would improve, restoring its original design by removing the present

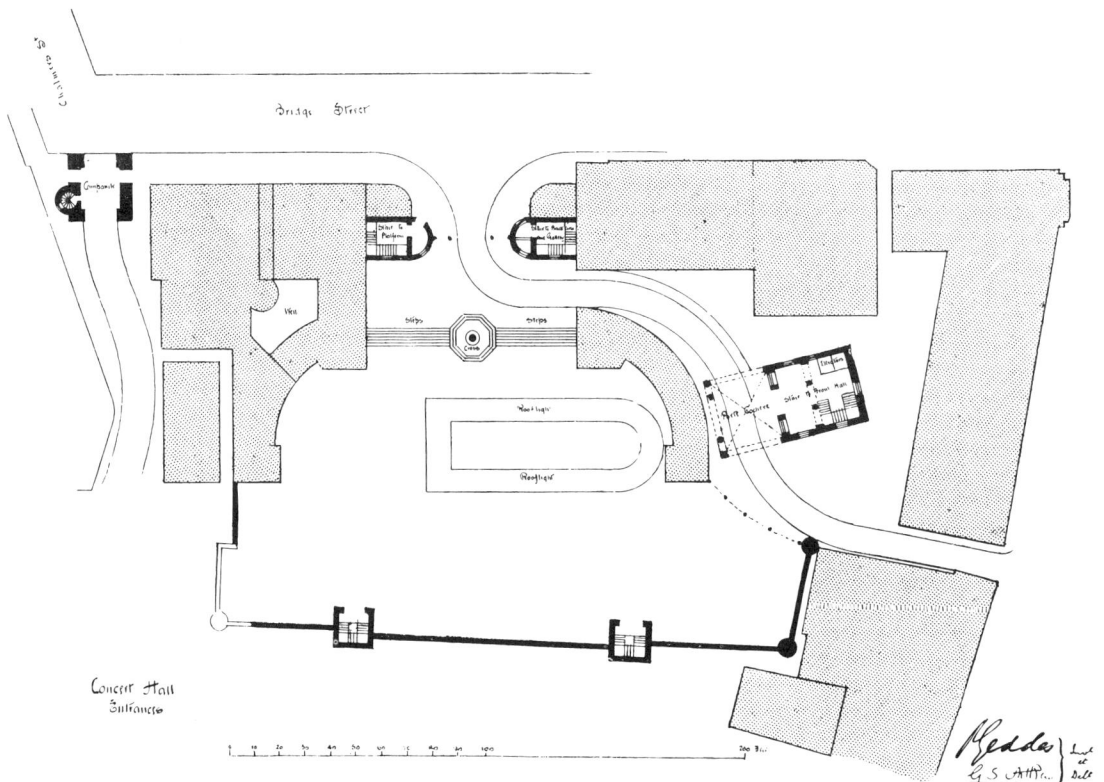

FIG. 126.— General plan of Bridge Street and new Carnegie Place. Note on right City buildings, and West of these the two existing tenements. West again comes new entrance to Place, obtained by removal of central tenement. Note entrance drive over Place, with exit to Kirkgate, Maygate, and St Catherine's Wynd, with carriage entrance for Hall below. Remainder of Carnegie Place reserved as Promenade, with City Cross (also Bandstand, and shops if desired). A pair of staircases descend to all levels of Hall at Bridge Street entrance, and a pair also from the towers of South front, thus connecting all levels of Hall (and their open cloisters or loggia) with the place above and the Arena below. An additional staircase can be added at any side or angle if required. Returning to Bridge Street, note the suggested rebuilding of West blocks, with corresponding widening of street, as also Campanile, completing perspective of Bridge Street, and still more of Chalmers Street.

grounds of safety, then, this plan has a notable advantage ; and for this reason alone I do not hesitate to predict a large return to this classic tradition in future hall constructions. It will be observed also that there are exits not only (1) upon the large public place of the roof ; (2) upon the vast arena below ; but (3) upon the spacious open-air cloister promenade between these levels ; hence, despite the initial difficulties, few halls can be named with more ample or rapid exits.

Town clock to a new Campanile shown at the western side, completing the triangle of which the other points are the Town House and Abbey spires. The Hall front thus requires massive and monumental simplicity as a whole, as well as due enrichment. Both effects might be gained by building it in rose-coloured granite, with its colonnade pillars in green serpentine, their capitals touched with gold, and with the open cloister paved with mosaic, walled with marble, and medallioned in bronze. This cloister would be at once the *entr'acte* promenade of the great Hall and an everyday passage for park visitors between the Arena and the hill above ; while it would furnish one of the best view-points also for all functions in the arena. Architecturally, it is to be regarded as repeating on a finer scale the cloisters of the History Buildings and garden. The view of this from the Entrance Drive of the Park, as well as from the Arena itself, is indicated in fig. 125.

the Library and St Margaret's Halls as Central Institute ; Queen Anne's House and its neighbours as a Hall of Residence ; and so on. Here remains one of the very best of all these correlations. For besides its use for music this Great Hall would be the principal one of the city. Hence it can conveniently be entered from the Civic Buildings, to which this, with its adjacent Arena, would respectively furnish, in fact, a vast additional indoor and outdoor apartment.

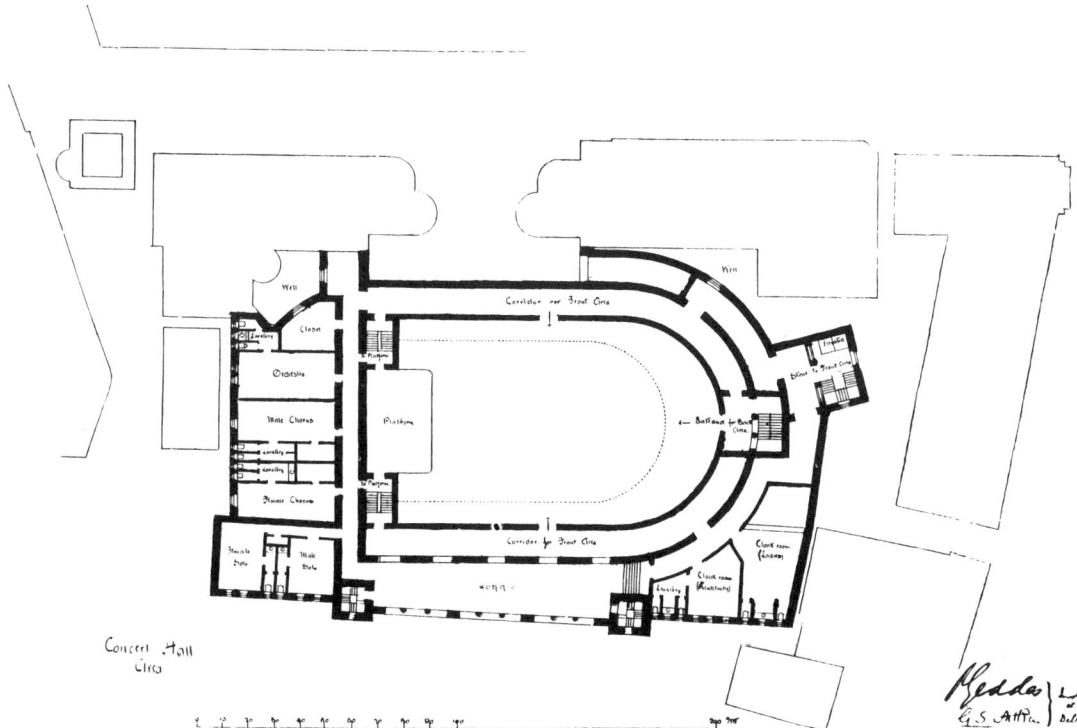

FIG. 127. Main plan of Music Hall.

On either side of the main open spaces of this cloister are shown tower staircases, connecting the arena below and the place above with all the levels of the hall. Central between these is the deep-arched issue of the stream, which would be loftier than is shown in the perspective. Into this would be towed out of sight, under the floor of the hall, the movable floating stage of the arena, so leaving its central lakelet upon the stream open and unencumbered under ordinary circumstances.

D. City Hall

One other advantage of this situation appears to me to justify a request for the most openminded consideration by its critics. Instead of erecting new buildings apart from all the existing ones we have at each point reinforced the old ones, and this for both artistic and practical purposes— witness the Mills as Labour Museum ; the Abbey and Palace Buildings with the History Buildings ;

For the city, entering as it is upon new, unprecedentedly vast, and generously democratic developments, these two additions would make the present Municipal Building, already an unusually palatial one, one of the vastest and completest centres for public life in the country, if not even in the world. To have these Municipal Buildings with their existing Council Chamber and Court House practically continuous with Hall and Arena, would be not only a symbol but a very substantial and practical aid towards the formation of the largest public spirit, the whole scheme thus becoming understood, not merely as providing an additional hall of amusement, but a Forum, a Civic Cathedral. Within such an environment, such a growing centre of civic activity and modern aspiration, of noble and historic associations also, the musician should surely surpass himself.

This union, then, at once material and moral, practical and educative, needs next to be frankly symbolic in its supreme adornment. What symbol shall we use, deep enough for any, simple enough for all ?   Take the old Cross, now standing half forgotten behind a railing at the County Buildings; re-erect this, like the Cross of Edinburgh or Aberdeen, upon our new " Carnegie Place." With this simple civic monument, one comparatively costless, yet supreme, since at once historic, actual, and predictive, our constructive tasks would here be ended ; while from its reinauguration a new civic era might fitly begin.

E. Music and Drama

As regards the question of musical development, I can but hand on the suggestive letters I have received from musicians both in Dunfermline and beyond. As regards drama, I have also been favoured with letters from eminent experts—deserving the highest consideration of the Trust—pointing out the way in which the dramatic culture of a German city might here be gradually developed.

Beyond the small Open-Air Theatre of the Park, and the great Open-Air Arena, I have not, however, ventured to allot any site to the construction of a theatre, the more so since I am informed that the present theatre is not only of recent construction but of not inadequate design. If my personal impression be worth offering, it is that some

gradual progress towards more ideal dramatic developments is all that we in this generation are capable of ; and I would seek to aid this, not only by encouraging selected performances of special interest and merit, not otherwise likely to be remunerative, but indirectly also through dramatic appeals to the historic and to the moral sense—interests which are stronger among us than are those of pure drama.   Just as in the Middle Ages, a modern Scottish audience is deeply moved by a morality play like " Everyman " ;   while the modest experiments of Summer Meetings also afford evidence of the stirring appeal of the dramatisation of historic events and personages. It is, I believe, by such co-operation of our musical, historic, and educational developments that the preparation for the adequate renascence or naturalisation of the best drama may be increasingly possible.

I return briefly to this point later in its appropriate connection (Chap. XXXI. H.) ; meantime here we should acquaint ourselves with the best that is being thought and done in this regard in the more advanced of foreign cities of moderate size, such as Weimar, Meiningen, Sondershausen, and Bergen. The example of Stratford-upon-Avon may also be suggestive despite our local disadvantage.

CHAPTER XXIX

THE GRAND ENTRANCE

A. Bridge Street

LET us now assume the acquirement of an entrance from Bridge Street. This gateway should, of course, be designed as a monumental feature of the city, concluding the perspective of High Street. For this entrance, though the designs would be as manifold in detail as the minds of architects, they must all, notwithstanding, fall into the two main classes which we find everywhere—the more formal and the more naturalistic—the architects of the former class conceiving this entrance primarily as an opportunity of stately architectural completion to the perspective of the High Street, the latter primarily as an opportunity of opening out a crowded street view into a pleasant mass of foliage, a promise of the park behind. Of course, all designs must have something of both, but the proportions will vary greatly.

B. Buildings in Park: Pros and Cons

Before discussing these, however, we must decide on the interior treatment. The very first suggestion offered me when beginning this work in October last was to continue Bridge Street right through the park to the Coal Road, and the next was to use this north-west section of the park as the site of the museums and other buildings.

But after the fullest consideration I have no hesitation in maintaining that the series of sites I have selected along the town side of the park ravine are greatly preferable, and this on many grounds. The suggestion of a street I of course entirely disapprove. One can make a new street anywhere else, but not a new park. As regards buildings, there is no doubt that a magnificent group could be erected on this site, and the economies and advantages of centralisation make this policy worthy of consideration. On this subject I have consulted not a few leading authorities, and am relieved to find that (with a single exception, that of an administrator, not an architect) they all decide against unification, and this for very varied reasons.

Besides all their arguments, a knowledge of the ten university buildings in which I have taught, the twenty in which I have studied, the fifty or more I have attentively visited, as of the plans I have more than once drawn, leaves no shadow of doubt on my mind that the centralisation of different institutes, each of distinct purpose, into one architectural whole, however impressive at the moment, is in the long run a mistake, often a disastrous one. For each building sooner or later requires alteration or extension, and this in its own way and at its own rate of growth.

Already, for instance, the magnificent School of Medicine of Edinburgh is cramped and crowded, despite frequent alterations ; while the Glasgow University building, unsuccessful from the first, has undergone many costly alterations and additions. There, in fact, is now being practically adopted in all the recent extensions the modern plan of separate and independent institutes. This plan characterises the great majority of the new American institutions, where efficiency is so greatly sought, and is at length prevailing in French universities, although in France the monumental and centralising tradition is so extraordinarily strong. It would be a pity, then, if the method which has been so fully tried, and which is being abandoned elsewhere, should be repeated anew here ; yet this is a constant danger of smaller cities everywhere—to repeat the earlier experiments of the great centres instead of profiting by them.

The real reason of the attractiveness of the idea of a monumental pile in the line of Bridge Street is the architectural craving, not any utilitarian purpose. This, again, analyses into two points—one the general architectural improvement of the city, to which these new buildings, if they were all carried into the interior of the park, would no longer contribute save in this one view, since we should have no buildings left to beautify the town with. Beyond the monumental gateway these new buildings would practically remain unseen, save to park visitors, and this even though trees were greatly sacrificed, so spoiling its present secluded character, in contrast with the busy street.

Moreover, is the park so very large that we can afford to give up this quarter of it, and this one of the most beautiful, to buildings however magnificent in themselves ? The reposeful character of the park, with its rolling, unbroken landscape of grass and trees, is surely, after all, its main use and advantage. Yet here, as at so many points already, can we not reconcile the existing with the desired advantage ?—keep our park practically unbroken and yet get a monumental perspective from Bridge Street.

C. Harmony of Advantage: Gateway and Fountain

Here let me ask the reader to make a simple experiment. Looking from a moderate distance at the nearest church spire, surely higher than any of our buildings would be, let him simply

Fig. 128.—A perspective sketch for Entrance Gateway from Bridge Street ; base of Campanile to left.

hold up his thumb or forefinger erect at arm's-length against it ; and thus realise, first, how small a distant building is, and, second, how large a near object may be. Standing at the highest point of the High Street, and looking down to the Town House spire, let us next observe the same effect. Notice, again, how at the distance of Bridge Street the present houses, where this new entrance would be, are again still further reduced in perspective, and how small are even the trees behind them.

We are thus prepared for the proposition I now make, that a sufficiently monumental gateway at Bridge Street is the main thing upon which the proposed effect of great buildings would practically depend. So that in so far as the view from the town is concerned, there is no such great advantage to be got by monumental buildings as at first one is tempted to think.

But now suppose we have our gateway, and enter it—should we not then see the monumental buildings ? Not immediately, for their site would only begin 100 yards farther in, with their centre, say, 100 feet farther. Here, again, perspective would greatly reduce their magnitude. But now upon my general plan it will be observed that at about 120 feet—i.e. a third of this distance from

the entrance, and completing its short but spacious avenue, or rather place—I show a large gravelled square, from which drives and paths run both north and south, and from which a flight of steps descends to the park in front. This square is surrounded by a monumental balustrade, and bears upon its entrant angles a vase or statue, each of which would contribute to that feeling of architectural stateliness which is here so desirable.

But this is not sufficient ? No, not yet ; a central mass is required. This is now given by a large monumental fountain, its basin, say 36 feet in diameter, answering broadly to the fine fountain of West Princes Street Gardens, Edinburgh. With this fountain in play an architectural effect not inferior to that of a group of buildings at a greater distance, in some ways positively superior to this, would be obtained, and all this practically without encroaching upon the park at all.

Again, is this site, after all, such a fine one to display a monumental group of buildings ? From where would it be seen ? From this, the principal approach, we should only see the east side of the proposed group—but this is in shadow after mid-day ; while for its southern and western view, as the park paths and levels show, we have no adequate view points at all. No doubt a fine terrace effect could be obtained from below, but only for a distance of a couple of hundred feet ; while the access to this low drive is necessarily a somewhat steep and inconvenient one.

Could the buildings be adequately seen from the ravine ? No ; it is too deep, while the Tower Hill would cut off the view of them from the other side. From above one would only see their north side, which is completely sunless, and from the main avenue from Pittencrieff Street the contours interfere.

On every ground, then, this apparently attractive project does not survive a critical examination. Whereas, less attractive though my proposed sites for buildings may appear at first sight, I submit that the more and the longer they are critically examined the better they will appear, and this from every point of view, monumental and practical. This is especially the case when we keep in view not only the approaching addition of a new town but the reaction of all these changes upon the improvement of the old one.

Plans and perspectives show that we have met the requirements of improving not only High Street and Bridge Street but many others, by the adoption of the marginal sites—those " along the edge of the park," as the donor's letter expresses it. The photographs of the existing good views surviving and the elevations and perspectives of the proposed buildings show a far more varied range of effects than could be possibly obtained from any single central mass, nobly designed though this might be.

D. Conclusion as regards Sites of Buildings

But I am told—you are practically working out this whole scheme of a park without putting into it any important buildings at all! Precisely so : that is the essential result of those many months of planning—the essential merit of and claim for the present scheme—that it improves the park as park, the town as town. The park, though now filled throughout its range with new and varied defects, its domestic architecture so poor and crowded, its monuments in all the melancholy of their ruin. Whereas, the supreme argument in favour of the marginal sites over the park ones is that we thus solve, instead of neglect, the essential problem of preserving the rare combination of naturalistic and historic charm of this wonderful glen by reinforcing and enhancing its marginal buildings. The Tower Hill, the Abbey Church, the Monastery, the Palace, and the

FIG. 129.—View from within Park, looking towards Municipal Buildings ; the Piazza, with Fountain, approached from short avenue from main entrance, would project somewhat in front of present dwelling-house seen midway between Town House spire and left side of figure.

interests and beauties, has yet the same restful expanses of grass and trees as ever, the same shady and sequestered dell, and this although all reasonable monumental demands, as of a stately approach from the High Street, of an elaborate formal garden within, have been fully met. But this is very different from cutting up the park for buildings, and thus also practically leaving the town unimproved by them ; in fact, bringing out by this sharp contrast all its present Mills, decayed though they all are, still constitute one of the most remarkable groups of culture assets to be found in Scotland or elsewhere ; upon the present plan each and all of these are preserved, supported, displayed, developed ; whereas to abandon all these and set up our new culture apparatus practically in a new quarter out of sight, for the sake of a little greater proximity to the business street or the like, would be a tragic misunderstanding, an irreparable disaster.

CHAPTER XXX

MANSION-HOUSE AND QUEENS' HOUSE

A. Mansion-House: its possible Utilisation

SINCE my previous references to the Mansion-House in Chapter V. were written I have become aware of that final act of generosity which rounds off this magnificent property.

What now from the public point of view is the best use we can make of this central and notable building ? A museum is but of limited appeal, though such use might be temporary. It is not large enough, nor accessible enough at night and in all weathers, to become a Central Institute, even if we had not found that elsewhere (Chap. III. *B.*).

After the fullest consideration, must we not come back to the idea that the Mansion-House had best remain a Mansion-House still ? But whose ? Follow once more that method of historic retrospect which, as no mere annal-reading but as the review of the stages of social development, has been of service in previous chapters. Here, as the buildings of our open-air museum remind us, are many successive centres of power and social leadership. This has passed from the Celtic and early Saxon Tower to the mediæval Abbey, from this to the Renaissance Palace. With the demolition of the royal power by the Commonwealth and the re-establishment of squirearchy at the Restoration this Laird's House became the natural apex of Dunfermline society ; while with the industrial revolution of the late eighteenth and nineteenth centuries the prosperous burgess succeeds the ancient families, to establish a more closely walled-in exclusiveness in turn. Here, then, are, as it were stratified before us, all the main formations of the social past, just as are the geologic ones in the glen or in our proposed rock garden.

Nor are the recent proposals for its use any less historic in their regular succession. First the acquirement by the captain of industry to whom we are here so peculiarly indebted ; then the idea of using this as a temporary home, of which the position and surroundings unite noble traditions and civic sympathies. Next came the proposal that this should become the Mansion-House in the civic sense no longer the rustic one, and, as the official dwelling of the chief magistrate express the utmost civic dignity, the utmost popular accessibility also. Later suggestions have been from the standpoint of the technical and scientific order of things, as for temporary museum accommodation Yet the last word cannot be with arts and sciences ; a house must be a house. To living, not to learning, let us dedicate this building.

Looking at life, then, as simply and generally as we can, at our own lives and ambitions along with others, what do we work for beyond the mere continuance of existence ?—towards a success of some sort. And on whatever plane of success, it is the simple fact that however high the goal of our ambition, even concluding the grandest perspectives, we think of a little time of pleasant retirement within a home more restful and spacious than our present one, and commonly with garden, grass, and tree, with kindly bird-note, and, if it may be, a sound of running water.*

Hence that mansion-house magnificence which has so specially dominated the three kingdoms for centuries ; hence that growth of suburban villas, each with its miniature park and wood and garden. Indeed, as Mr Wells has specially pointed out, the poorest fragment of iron railing upon the steps of a town house represents alike in history and in imagination the park boundaries of that rustic home, to realise which is the ambition and instinct even of the city-born. And that rightly, for, more than rich food and good clothing, a home with some rustic conditions is the first organic need of healthy individual life and upbringing. The contemporary Park movement, and the incipient Garden City one, are recognitions of this, which must before long transform the map of cities anew.

In Dunfermline, as in Edinburgh, I would fain

---

* We have sympathised too long with the ordinary criticism of Sir Walter Scott's ambitions as laird and planter as if Scott's ruin had been due to this instead of his imaginative anticipation of our present era of city speculation. To his country life as child we owe the material and the awakening of his great imagination, and to his later rustic life and activities the breezy realities of his best creations. Despite all the moralisings of Carlyle, might it not have been better for the latter's work and teaching had he laboured in his summer home at Craigenputtock instead of too continuously encouraging dyspepsia at Cheyne Row ?

conserve all we can of our ancient cities, and am thus no over-sentimental advocate of a garden city, least of all as a new kind of gourd beneath whose shade we may inveigh against the larger community we have left. But it is exactly here and now in Dunfermline, with its many approaching improvements and extensions, that this wholesome and healthy ideal of life may be best renewed and democratised.

So that the return towards the essentials of country life which we all have in holiday time, or in convalescence, should fully re-enter the conception of success in life—success in living, a foothold in country conditions as well as in town ones—a country house, in short.*

B. Specific Uses recommended

For this one country house, which is our present problem, my proposal is that not only the common use of our park and culture buildings but the occasional individual enjoyment which goes with the ordinary idea of property, be centred here in this house, henceforth every man's, still more, therefore, every woman's. It is with the actual possession and enjoyment of his house that the heir truly and fully comes into his estate and the fortune which accompanies it. Here is the very centre of all this wealth of recreations and of culture resources, with their bettering of health, bodily and mental, moral and social. After the dignity of king, abbot, and lord, of laird and millionaire, of provost and Trust, there thus not only arrives the day by which all these have to be judged, in proportion as they have helped or hindered the development of the people, their completeness, efficiency, and culture, but even the day when their personal dignity passes to the people in their turn.

With this ideal clear we are now, and only now, in a position to come down to plans, to enter the house and see how it can be best adapted to subserve this widest popular, yet highest individual, usefulness. No plan could well be simpler. Upon the ground and first floor is a single moderate-sized apartment to east and west, the latter with a room opening from it

* Not many even of our most aspiring working-class leaders are aware that there are already many cities where the ordinarily prosperous working man has his country house as well as his town one, and thinks of these as his standard of comfort as naturally as does laird or Member of Parliament at present. But a photograph of the environs of not a few continental cities, large and small — say Marseilles for a smaller Glasgow, or Nîmes for a larger Dunfermline — would show him the landscape not only dotted, but for miles composed, of small but real country houses and vineyards, which are not only the possessions but the regular summer or autumn homes of the working families of the town. Is not this a fair example of the need of concrete and geographical knowledge to give reality and encouragement even to our would-be most forward ambitions of social betterment?

beyond. On the ground floor to the east the kitchen with little change would become a picturesque old-fashioned kitchen once more, with two alternatives for use—a playroom for girls, with their instinctive and acquired interests in domestic economy; or, with its side door opened to the east, it would make a smoking-room for men.

The old dining-room would be the general retiring-room, the withdrawing-room beyond, again with separate door, being reserved for women.

Upon the first floor we have on the west side the drawing-rooms proper, and these two thrown into one would give a long room for entertainments, the floor being strong enough to bear even dancing. The panelled walls should be painted with decorative pictures, such as they once probably possessed, or at any rate were intended for. With such decoration little furniture is required, chiefly wall sofas and light chairs; a large table being at any time extemporised upon trestles kept in the adjacent hall store. The room to the east would be rearranged as kitchen and pantry, etc., with gas and sink, food being easily sent in from town.

While the ground-floor rooms would be constantly open, and this drawing-room also on ordinary occasions, it should be permitted to any and every citizen, on the simplest conditions of application to the Trust, to be able to obtain the use of this for a short period of hours, morning, afternoon, or night, there to entertain at her or his own pleasure, and in their own way, instead of in their own homes. And for the hours concerned, with the same privacy for themselves and their invited guests, simply for the time shutting off this first floor by its hall door, with a label " Engaged till   o'clock "—the entertainer thus becoming for the moment the tenant of a private flat upon the common staircase.

Ascending this staircase we come to the bedroom and garret floors. As suggested in a recent excellent paper (H. F. Kerr, *Glasgow Archæological Society* 1904) the whole set of partitions and intervening floor should here be demolished, thus furnishing one long and stately gallery, its lofty roof adorned with that magnificent plaster-work, so characteristic of our best old Scottish mansions and town houses, of this period especially, and which is being successfully revived. The use of this gallery in a way worthy of its central and culminating position in the whole park may be discussed more fitly in the following chapter.

C. External Improvements

The corresponding external improvement would restore the lost seventeenth-century window pediments, and, perhaps, open out the stair turret-room into a belvedere more sightly without and more agreeable within.

Lime-washing and verduring have been already suggested (Chap. V.), so there remains only the back to be considered. Since on the proposed plan new cloakrooms for both sexes are required on the ground and first floor, we have to build these out to the north, while continued upwards these would become external towers, and afford excellent little side rooms or wide bays to the main gallery. Were this done with the simplicity yet sense of proportion of our old Scottish architecture, and again of its recovery by living designers, who are happily not far to seek, this at present blank and grim back wall would suddenly become the picturesque and attractive north front of a little castle overlooking its ravine (see fig. 75).

For, as an additional resource towards this effect, note what the present poor and ragged hedge conceals—a massive retaining wall upon the steeply descending bank. Regularise and balustrade this, buttress it below the two new towers: our old building thus not only becomes loftier and statelier, but is seen as a pendant and contrast to the striking and massive double bridge opposite. By now continuing the fine mass of ancient hollies west of the house, and by the slight improvement of walks shown on plan, the house will have been at once conserved, yet transformed and improved, I trust to the permanent reconciliation of all parties, both conservatives and whilom iconoclasts.

The present reproaches of the exterior and interior, thus alike transformed, their qualities retained, we re-enter the house with the feeling of an ancient yet improved home. Are we in everyday mood ?—the comfortable rooms of the ground floor will suffice us. Are we sociably inclined to make merry with our friends ?—let us secure our innings of the drawing-room. Or as, after all, it would often be vacant, we may rest there among its outdoor views and indoor pictures, alone or in the freedom of a club.

D. Theory underlying proposed Use

Upon the uses of this room may I be permitted yet fuller insistence ?—for, as a thoughtful friend expresses it, "just as the park and glen provide the people with the outdoor elements of an ideal country home and life upon a larger scale, so should they be provided with the indoor elements of a home life upon a similar measure of largeness and beauty."

The regulations for the temporary lending of these as guest-rooms must depend upon the view we take of contemporary social evolution. Here is a matter apparently too small and domestic to be recognised by the politician or the social reformer, yet largely, I believe, explaining the continual failure of their theories, since of the action and effort founded upon them. What is the explanation of this perpetual failure of democratic ideals and aspirations, from the

earliest Greek city to the modern American one ? Why is it that in spite of the painful conquest of free institutions, of equality before the law or Church, of equality of economic opportunity and of intellectual education, our work is constantly being undone? For is not every society practically restratified upon lines of group domination, and, therefore, ultimately of class privilege ? Here and there, indeed, some disillusioned democrat seizes the real reason, and states it in terms of the perpetually rearistocratising agency of women, into whose hands is coming almost as completely the rule of modern and democratic America as of old monarchical France.

Putting most briefly what would require a whole volume for its analysis, we have to face the facts, to recognise that women do and will ask from life more than democratic politicians or social reformers, educationists, abstract economists or moralists have ever offered them. Their social demands are more concrete and personal, more emotional, more ideal also. They seek more of home beauty and of social intercourse, and this selected on grounds of personal sympathy and admiration, not of doctrine or party.

Thus, however men may assert themselves as lords of action, they have sooner or later to learn that women are queens of life. Hence it is that in America practically the old class distinctions are reconstructing themselves anew—it may be more seriously than ever. And is it not largely some perception of this truth which discourages the democratic idealist, or excludes him from politics altogether ?

Here, then, is no mere academic dissertation but a needed social analysis ; one of those investigations which we begin to see are increasingly needed for every stage of our journey into the social future ; still more, when, as at each point of a social study like the present, we have to fit our homeliest action to the highest ideal—"to hitch our waggon to a star."

Our political reforms, our democratic ambitions, are commonly stated as the attempt to redress the continually recurring evils of class aristocracy in the sense of class privilege. We are coming to see this is a too generalised and abstract statement ; a more concrete view is enabling us to restate it as our modern phase of the long insurrection of men against the abuses of the social rule of women, with which history well-nigh opens and of which tradition is so full. This understood, a new social development becomes possible with corresponding social ideas and different political issues ; for we now see that we have to reconcile the two apparently contrasted ideals of democracy and aristocracy, by uniting them into the true democracy of true aristocracy. But this implies culture and selection in every sense, from organic to spiritual. Thus we should reach an ideal of democracy which levels up not down, and so becomes an aristo-democracy, in which the old vices of both parties should increasingly diminish, if also diminishingly reappear.

So far the theory. In other words, without forgetting that "a man's a man for a' that," we have to recognise that a woman has not only henceforth to count as a man in the political sense, but must continue to win as a woman in the social one. In future politics, as in the past, it must be the side she sides with that wins. Our next statement of the ideal of democracy must thus be no mere restatement of the rights of man, as with the French Revolution, nor of the rights of woman with later reformers—not even of duties with the moralist—it involves an increasing satisfaction of the ideals of woman, and these both on temporal and spiritual planes. Has not her instinctive inevitable struggle towards realising one or other of these continually wrought tragedy in the world—from that of Troy, through innumerable Helens to our own Queen Mary, or to those of the day's newspaper ?

In social, as in natural science, we are but becoming conscious of everyday facts, of laws long in operation ;

FIG. 130.—Reproduction of sketch in colour for a decorative mural painting for Wedding-room of Mansion-House; "The marriage of Malcolm and Margaret," by Mr John Duncan.

truths always latent become patent. But thus Science becomes ready for Action ; she begins to claim the adaptation of her freshly-stated or recovered idea into the arts of life. So after all this social philosophising I come to what, be it at first sight pleasing or no, I believe to be the most vital and useful of the various synthetic inventions, the social symbols, of this report, perhaps the farthest-reaching of all its pioneering, scientific or social. For the whole conception of this park, with its homely and stately gardens, its leisure and pleasure grounds, its learned museums, its palaces of art, its halls of music and drama, its civic campus and forum, and all as the theatre of an ennobled civic and social life, has had its practical starting-point, from the humble everyday home and home-maker (Chap. II.), and now returns to find its climax in the same conceptions, though now upon a higher spiral.

It is for Parliament, and so but indirectly for us, to give to or withhold from woman her political status and vote ; but, taking the political and the social order as we find them, we can at once give her what, as we have seen, she values even more— something of her social and ideal status.

E. Use in further Detail

Each plain working woman in Dunfermline who chooses to claim her turn of this drawing-room and organise her little social function, thus for the time being, takes for it social precedence of all else in Dunfermline. She thereby becomes for the time being the Lady of the Mansion-House, the first lady of the city, representing not only trustees and donor but her own long line of predecessors to queen and saint.

That before long the demand might exceed the limited accommodation is no objection to these proposals, but the recognition of their expediency. The Mansion-House will bear such enlargements and developments as have been proposed for it by various architects, and even where such new wings are daily and nightly overcrowded by their happy circles there is room, on the lawn or hard by, for a new mansion altogether, such as has, indeed, been planned already.

Here, too, is a use for the gardens and garden-houses and for the many and stately open-air apartments of our formal gardens, for our woodland nooks. Each may have its *fête champêtre*, and each of these should reconcile the qualities of old aristocracy and new democracy, and thus avoid their defects, so uniting courtesy and grace with the hospitalities of home. Each such bright experience of true merry-making would thus be an education in bettered social living.

Of the common-sense regulations which would naturally arise for all this—the possible trifling registration or cleaning fee, the order of priority of application or ballot, and so on—I need not here speak. Let me in conclusion plead that special preference be here given for wedding applications, since in no respect is the spaciousness and beauty of the Mansion-House more at advantage over the ordinarily too narrow and small-roomed home. To make the old Mansion-House a wedding-house is also surely specially fitting in a city whose essential history dates from a happy wedding (fig. 131).

F. Queens' House

Though the Mansion-House thus becomes of more value and significance to these schemes than at first appeared, such use by anyone must, after all, be but occasional and temporary. It is the everyday home which is the true centre, in which woman centralises the arts into that of living, and thus, beside our people's mansion, we need a correspondingly ideal and representative home. Once more our open-air museum of history is equal to the occasion. A mansion-house to entertain in is much for any lady, but a queen's house to live in would be more ; and this is now actually available between Tower and Abbey, Queen Anne's House replacing Queen Annabella's. Below us, too, is the Queens' Garden, its arena paved and terraced, yet no longer flowerless.

Within this precinct is the ivied Chapel-ruin of St Catherine, herself no mere shadowy or plaster saint, but a noble memory, an immortal symbol.

Where now in any city, even the greatest, the sacredest, should we find a home more rich in associations, more environed with beauty, more simply practical and homely as well ? Here, then, let woman worker, nurse, student, teacher come together and renew for themselves, in and from and around this recovered historic centre, the sisterly fellowship, the queenly service, of old.

For and with one such group, which would soon grow and divide, as with all active life, Dunfermline would be again in this respect of the culture and career of women no longer a mere provincial city, far from the resources of Edinburgh and London, of Girton or Newnham, of Boston or Paris. Here is an available home and centre of which any one of these greater cities might well be proud—one readily in full communion with all their characteristic advantages.

The intimate life of such a community cannot, and need not, be planned out here, any more than the detail of its furnishing or decoration. Its many-sided interests, its social learning, would gradually adjust themselves, and find their varied expression both in a widening corporate life and in individual developments.

The establishment and spread of such residences for women and for men is one of the most encouraging and educative features of our time. I have been too long and intimately connected with this movement from its earliest years to share all its illusions : and am fully aware, for instance, that the main result of most endeavours of " sending out university men to educate the people " is that the people are sometimes not without influence in educating them. I submit, however, that even this numerically modest educative result is not found to be valueless. Moreover, in Dunfermline the university element would not be too strong, especially with houses of women. In fact, the unfortunately named " settlement " need not arise, but something of more ordinary and democratic type.

Into the furnishing of such houses it is unnecessary for me here to go into detail ; enough if I refer to what has been said in earlier chapters (II and III) of Housing improvement and of Social Institutes and Central Institutes, and to the suggestion of a Civic Union in Chapter XXXIV. In these respects, moreover, the condition which must ever precede the adoption of any scheme of pioneering, as of its detailed development, is the right person, who, with an adequate culture, unites the knowledge, experience, and energy required with the capacity of inspiring yet tactful leadership.

G. The Working Women of Dunfermline

For the unmarried workers of the social hive, here proportionally so many, there are also great problems to be worked out, nowhere easy, yet here less difficult than elsewhere. For without disrespect to the humbler industries of cotton and jute, it is no flattery to claim for this more refined linen industry a more refined quality of worker also ; one more ready, therefore, for all that an enriching culture can afford.

Of all contemporary progress and pioneering in Dunfermline may not this turn out to be one of the most vital possibilities, as obviously one of the largest ones ? Without presuming to enter upon the development of an industry to which I am a stranger, I may yet recall one or two examples of kindred rise or transformation of whole occupations within our own lifetimes. First, that of Nursing. If fifty years ago Sairey Gamp had not been a common portrait, or at any rate a fair caricature, her name would not have become a household word, much less lasted to this day. Yet about that very time arose Florence Nightingale ; and now we have a whole profession many thousands strong, whose representative type is Sister Dora.

Again recall the dame's school, the " accomplishments " of the " Finishing Academy," or the immortal Mrs Squeers, these types and bywords of popular illiteracy, of genteel futility, of debased commercialism. Next see how, within the same period, the women teachers were beginning to de-

velop what are now at this moment the leading branches of the teaching profession, primary and secondary, not only more sympathetic and conscientious, but more awakened and skilful — in short, more efficient—than are we of the historic schools, or of the universities either.

Now, if changes such as these be matters of common knowledge for us of the older or middle generation, why may not similar changes take place within the younger opening one ? If so, why not here, first and most of all, in Dunfermline, this representative British centre of the working aristocracy of the textile industries ? For here the misery and squalor, the intemperance and demoralisation, too common stains upon other textile centres, are comparatively rare ; purity of life and dignity of character are constantly maintained ; why not, therefore, especially at this time of opening and extending culture-resources, a further movement of practical idealism ?—that is, of life practical in larger ways than before.

The past generation has afforded more examples than does the present or opening one of " industrial success," understood as emergence from the ranks of labour ; and there are weighty reasons for thinking the difficulty to be an ever-increasing one. But, if so, there is also fuller opportunity and hope for the utilisation of the special talents which formerly removed their possessor into a wealthier class, towards the help and betterment of the working community as a whole.

Of the development of this idealistic yet practical view of the possible progress of the workers of our staple industry I offer no suggestions in detail, but leave this subject with a final symbol —that of the History Fountain, with thread ever spinning around the pedestal of Time. For the thread of history is ever beginning anew ; and here is a new movement in our history. In this literal everyday thread of working hands, there lies a renewed possibility of future developments, individual and social, civic and national, indeed international as labour and capital themselves. For, in the opening future, as in the early past, the future of civilisation lies not with the destroying sword, but with the patient, the unremembered detail of life-maintaining toil. Once more, then, the refrain of so many of these proposals towards pioneering, that who would see or share or aid the progress of labour may also come to Dunfermline. For though much obviously remains to be done, here surely is the place, here the people, to do it.

CHAPTER XXXI

THE GENERAL VIEW: ITS ASPECTS AND INTERPRETATIONS

A. General Perspective Views

THE accompanying small and large bird's-eye or balloon perspectives of the whole range of buildings along the east margin of the glen, for which I must again specially acknowledge the skilful collaboration of my friend Mr G. S. Aitken, were at first intended to be left to speak for themselves. Yet so complex a group of buildings necessarily demands consideration from many distinct individual points of view; and their critic must, therefore, place himself at each of these in turn. For by the elaboration of this whole design upon the present scale, far exceeding that of an ordinary preliminary report, and, in fact, carried at every point up to the level of assured practicability and often of detailed planning, needing only large scale plans for execution, the richness of detail and the variety of appeal may readily obscure the underlying unity of conception. The principle here adopted, of elaborating each department of horticulture, each great period of history, each essential demand of archæology of art, and so on, up to the standpoint and general standard of the progressive specialists in each department, carries with it a corresponding risk of seeming to overload the design—at any rate for readers not specially interested in this and that subject. See then figs. 131, 132, and 137.

Yet it is with a design of this kind, as with the building of a ship—unless each and every legitimate specialist's demands be adequately met the resultant whole will not be seaworthy.

Leaving, however, gardener and architect, technician and specialist to judge for themselves, let me now act as guide through this labyrinth to representatives of the various classes of the more general public, so as, if possible, to satisfy them that in elaborating the requirements of others their particular demands and point of view have also been considered.

More generally, any comprehensive park design, such as the present, has to satisfy as far as may be not only all sorts and conditions of men, all occupations also, but all phases of life—childhood, youth, maturity, age; childhood in its innocence and play, in that admiration and that questioning, too, which are its true self-education; youth in its hope and aspiration, its ambition and energy; maturity in its strenuous life of labour and service, and in its need of rest, refreshment, and repose; age in its power and influence, its calmer and broader outlook.

B. The Processional Ways

Let us accompany representatives of each of these in turn. Yet a quiet and conversational ramble is not in itself sufficient; in almost all ages of the past, perhaps before long in the opening future, we see the larger social view, the civic and the occupational interest dominating the individual one. Hence our designs must be adapted to the largest public and processional use as well as to the everyday individual rambler. For as the modern park is becoming the Cathedral of the People it must express, as this did in its various chapels and their altars, the various ideals to which individuals and classes are devoted; must be adapted to their group interests and activities as to their general collective and civic functions. In short, then, our laying out of roads and paths is also one of routes for visitors, and these not only practical and convenient but suggestive and educative, and even individually emotional and collectively dramatic: it rises to the designing of the courses and the stations of the individual meditative pilgrimage, and even beyond this to the renewal of that greatest and noblest of all the features of an ancient city—its routes of symbol, festival, and triumph, its Processional Road, its Sacred Way.

C. The Child and the Naturalist

With whom, then, shall we begin? Surely first of all with the little children. Large and dramatic child-functions, the teacher, musician, play-leader will need but a little encouragement to organise. Or, left to themselves, the children will naturally hurry past all our great buildings and prefer the gardens. They soon leave these for the open park and playgrounds, next to be tempted down their little dell into the stupendous and mysterious glen below, and once there will seek above all things to paddle in the stream.

The same course will be instinctively followed by those children of a larger growth—the Naturalists. Rambling together, as child-naturalist and naturalist-child should ever do, they may explore in fuller detail the gardens, tame and wild, the lakes and pool and stream and Zoo—yet both always instinctively working up-stream, out of the park altogether, into the open country.

Here, then, is a justification of the order and treatment broadly adopted in these pages. After such nature explorations, widening into regional survey, the need of laboratory, library, and museum appears. Thence this whole wealth of concrete educational resources develops towards that larger conception of the natural world, that of Lyell and Darwin, of Humboldt and Reclus, which is expressed in the Nature Palace, its Museums and Great Globe.

D. Youth and Labour

With developing youth the play instinct demands that larger athletic outlet not illiberally provided for both sexes, but next also some initiation into the dawning responsibilities, the opening work, of life. Here, then, is a main justification of the Primitive Village and the Crafts Village, of Girls' Play-houses too. Just as child and naturalist went naturally roaming together, so now may Youth and Labour.

Let them start sometimes from the building, decorating, or gardening operations in actual progress, sometimes with the masterpieces of the Art Museum, and thence pass through the workshops of the Crafts Village to a fuller understanding and share in the developed activities of the industrial city and the corresponding studies of its technical schools.

At times, too, they will work back together to the earliest beginnings of all these industries in that simpler contact with nature which the Primitive Village commemorates and affords ; and thus, like the naturalist in his way, having here touched bottom—that is, returned to contact with the elemental facts of life—they are in the true position to renew their ascent to the masterpieces of modern art or invention. I cannot too strongly emphasise the reminder that it is precisely the practical and inventive spirit of Chicago which heads this pioneering of a truer technical education by this recovery of its elemental industrial basis. And not only is it the child-gardener who becomes the horticulturist, the child-builder the architect, the child-mechanic the inventor ; such early technical experience offers also a real means of moralising and socialising industry, one far in advance of

that too abstract " moral and civic instruction " which is now threatening to sterilise the void created by the shrinkage of the older methods of moral and religious instruction.

For in the Primitive Village everyone understands his large and responsible part in the small division of labour, and this feeling of responsibility must be early gained if it is to be maintained in the almost unintelligibly complex subdivision of modern life and interests. As already urged, it is at least a beginning of that " Trial School " for the work of life which is still so urgent a necessity of our education ; that trial school for which Ruskin pleaded thirty years ago, and which is still and increasingly a need of our educational resources. With all this arises instinctively that sense of the dignity of labour which depends not upon the rhetoric of the past but upon the perception of its social responsibility and usefulness. For we begin to treat the poorest scavenger with a new courtesy, not because of his vote, but as a lay brother of that order of St Pasteur whose cleansing tasks are not only steadily driving back disease, but, with their more than ritual purification, preparing the advent of a new personal and social idealism.

So on for every craft. We have to express in terms of its scientific and technical realities elements of a new dignity exceeding that of ancient guilds ; indeed, of a new poetry at least rivalling that which commemorates the actual culture-heroes and civilisation-founders of antiquity.

For miller and blacksmith especially, the same line of thought has been worked out above, and for weaver and others at least suggested. Hence the normal scheme of decoration for the refreshment-rooms of our Crafts Village would be afforded by the characteristic symbols of the crafts themselves.

The Primitive Village, Crafts Village, and Art Museum are thus main interests for youth and worker, but the detailed progress of their respective arts will be found expressed with increasing fulness in the long and ample galleries of the Historic Museum. Here, then, we have at least a glimpse of the developing craft processions of the future, with their ceremonies of initiation, their graduation days of mastership, as already of those exhibitions of their masterpieces which are already the most magnificent of civic functions, and even of international ones. Our Park Roads, then, to and through these various centres are the processional routes of future festivals—the *Via Sacra* and *Via Triumphalis* of Labour.

E. The Historian

With the Archæologist and Antiquary, still more with the Historian, we have already had whole chapters. Suffice it, then, to recall him as a guide of all whom we have as yet considered—child and naturalist, youth and worker, towards a completer conception of man, from his emergence from nature to his highest developments, with their present confusion of promise and decay. We leave him to communicate his magic of evocation for every phase of the long procession of the past, his deeper spirit of interpretation of its inward forces, both spiritual and temporal. We thus appreciate more fully his conception of our goodly environment—the park, the city, the world itself—as a vast open-air museum of social development. Thus emancipated from our petty modern insistence upon the present, and with minds thus opened to the vast perspectives of the past, we may look with new hope and courage to that opening perspective of the future to which "the specious present" leaves its devotees so blind.

For it is in great things as in small: it is not the child to whom to-day is as yet all, who can make much use even of his tiny garden, but only that older one who has learned from the experience of past seasons to prepare for coming ones. It is the lover of ancient trees who is most ready to plant the new ones whose fruit he may never eat, whose full expansion he can never see. So any who may have feared a too academic conservatism in my pleadings to preserve our despised fragments of antiquity may surely now admit that I have not hesitated to develop them, nor to meet what I believe to be the fresh needs of the present upon a new and sometimes unprecedented scale.

F. The Citizen

But it is time to leave the historian for the Citizen, or rather to pass with the historian into the citizen, present though his interests rightly and primarily are. Of bettered housing even beyond his average demands, witness a repeated insistence upon open-air treatment, which he may as yet too commonly consider exaggerated; though of suggestions for the brightening of family life some, I trust, may be found not uncongenial. Suggestions towards technical as well as general education have been pushed beyond the secondary education resources of a minor city or those of university extension. His fundamental requirements as regards Town and School have thus not been forgotten. Even if our institutes of wider ambition do not so strongly appeal, he may let them pass, as offering, in their modern way, some reconstitution of the ancient Abbey, some cloisters of the meditative life, in which, apart from his ordinary range of life and thought, he may some day also find retreat, and even now some fruitful suggestion or friendly counsel. His natural distrust of the speculative life, with its cultured weakness, its shrinking from action, may be abated as he sees the increasing wealth of practical application to life which comes forth from each true cloistering of thought. But without detaining him amid our museums and studies, our paradise of nature and art, its wealth of literal blossom in the present, let us set upon his restored City Cross (Chap. XXVIII.) what may serve as a simple signpost and map to all these labyrinths of thought and action. The mason at least will bear with this; I trust even approve its renewal of his ancient symbolism.

On one of the six sides of its arcaded base, from which its pillar shaft should rise, let us carve the symbols of the Mechanical Industries, yet mark unobtrusively behind, the symbols of the Physical Sciences on which these industries increasingly depend. On the next side let us carve in full daylight the plough and spade of Agriculture, the mortar and pestle of Medicine, yet its winged serpent-rod as well. The broom of homely and public Hygiene must have due place of honour; yet behind all these, in shadow, must be set the seal of Biologic science, the scarabæus with all its manifold significance, Egyptian to evolutionary. Upon the third side, that of Government, and appropriately turned towards its buildings, city and county, we set the Burgh Seal, the Scottish Arms, the British Standard, the scales and sword of Justice. Behind this, again, would be the open book of Economics and Law. So far the three sides towards the street; not all citizens see so many; comparatively few look for more.

Yet some will note upon the side towards the Abbey the crosier and crook of antique and modern guidance, and in the shadow behind these the Celtic cross renascent, with its union of spiritual and cosmic symbolism.

Southward, towards the Arena, we carve the symbols of Education—the historic rod and the present three R's—and, it may be hoped, newer and better ones. For again, behind these, comes the winged Psyche of psychologic science; and with this, her geometric symbol.

Finally, upon the sixth side, towards theatre and garden, we carve the symbols of the Fine Arts—the palette and chisel, with square and compasses above. Over all these the radiant lyre; behind, less seen, the notation of music, the symbol of Æsthetics.

From the side of Art we thus come round to Industry again; it may be with a fuller suggestion of their kinship, a fuller perception of this whole unity of meaning. Our civic decoration is thus civic indeed, since a view of all its forms of work and thought, a Classification of the Arts and their related Sciences, is thus plainly popularised. The interconnection of all the activities of the city, of all its divisions of labour, is simply set forth; and with this also that intimate reaction of theory and practice, which it is the foolish fashion of the moment to decry, is reaffirmed to the simplest bystander.

From this central hexagon a corresponding sixfold pavement design (renewing, therefore, the ancient star-pattern of intersecting equilateral triangles) radiates over the whole Place. The Pillar of the cross is now seen as the gnomon of a colossal dial, and as its whole structure stands for the renascent and ideal city, so its travelling shadow is the fitting symbol of such individual life. Hence this travels from the side of beauty and art at dawn, through that of labour with morning, towards citizenship and rule as the day wears late, and finally lengthens eastward towards the ancient spire of loftier contemplation with the falling night.

Our new Place is thus no mere return to the picturesque view-point of our frontispiece, but one at which to recover and to express that civic feeling which is our noblest and most enduring inheritance from the past. Here, then, our civic processions will sometimes muster, sometimes disperse, and from this point of view the developed City Buildings, with their great Hall below, their vast Arena beside, will all be needed for that reviving sense of citizenship " of no mean city," which even the most cosmopolitan of teachers was proud to affirm.

G. The Politician

Our great Hall and open Arena, our Public Place and City Cross, our Campus and Parkways are now surely a very paradise for the Politician, who cannot henceforth grudge us historic treasure or naturalistic paradise, since his field of action has been so fully recognised, his expression so fully provided for.

Upon every plane the schemes above suggested can but widen his appeal and usefulness—civic, regional, national, international, all are considered. So our history building culminated with no retrospective survey, but with an outlook over the widening world.

Conservative and Radical may thus meet here no less amicably than behind the scenes at Westminster. Indeed more so, for the respect of all that is vital in the past, the burial of what is dead or evil in it, has been more fully accomplished. The chivalrous memories, the joy in life and nature, which are the strength and life of the Cavalier party, are all represented here, but no less are the stern and abstract intellectuality, the faith in ideals, which have characterised the Puritan. For these are still our two great parties, however degenerate they may seem to each other, towards potman or huckster respectively ; and that reconciliation of order and progress, towards which the best spirits of both parties ever look, must surely be some such synthesis of these as is materialised in these designs. Hence the deeper meaning of the two statues proposed in Chap. V.

H. Woman

We may now come to Woman. Of her special interests within this scheme I have already spoken, first and last (Chaps. II. and XXIX.), from the bettered homes of the neighbouring street and city to the mansion-house, with its expression of that levelling up both of her sex and the other, in which the ideals of democracy and aristocracy reunite. Yet for her also other ways in this labyrinthine design will be seen to open. What park-maker can forget that not the least real, if tacit, of his instructions—in

fact, one of his most practical civic responsibilities —is to lay out better surroundings than are offered by the streets alone, or by most places of amusement, for the meeting and resort of young men and maidens ? Here, again, as ever, his task is to combine the too long separated standpoint of the poetry and the romance of life with that of its deeper issues, and use both again to ennoble that of the everyday world. Here least of all can we forget this where the very boundaries of our historic glen and park run, like the refrain of a ballad, " from Wooers' Alley to Lovers' Loan." Here, surely, we have justification and worthy use for our purified stream, our romantic waterfalls and restful glades, our flowery field-paths and blossomed seasons, our merry tennis courts and rose-hung bowers ; for stately old wedding-house also, for whitest lilies and for bridal orangery, for evergreen foliage and golden fruit.

For the many unmarried women of the city there is the Women's Pavilion, not only as everyday Rest-House but as that Woman's Club, which would still remain one of the most vital and truly progressive of American institutions, even were we to grant all the criticisms so customary from the inferior standpoint of men's clubs generally. Hence, too, our Mansion-House and Queens' House (Chap. XXIX.). Hence, best of all, in health and pleasure, in play, in dignity, and in beauty alike, is the assignment, primarily, to her uses of the lawns and terraces of our central Palace Garden, and, in deeper significance, of the Memorial Garden of St Margaret.

I. The Artist

Let us now call in the Artist to aid. He is no longer, as through his nineteenth-century career, in the main the amuser of wealth. Again, he begins to see, that, as a worker of skill, touched with imagination and emotion, his place is again with the people, his work again for them. Here, indeed, is the interpretation of any good there may be in these designs of park and gardens. Such designs but prepare the ground for greater artistic constructions, lay out the paths of more than floral processions, prepare the theatres of a drama greater than the seasonal one. Among the spectators of the recent opening procession and " infeftment ceremony " were artists who might have doubled its artistic effect, and this not by imposing their own knowledge, their own fancies and dreams, but by aiding this and that particular craft to improve the part it felt its due in the whole social procession. Craft-idealism, craft-symbolism were conspicuous at almost every point in this, sometimes in the forms of old art no longer living, sometimes in forms fresh but still crude. These are what the artist is now especially ready to express and to refine, thus setting out for each craft its social purpose, its dignity, and its brightening future.

Of the endless, the infinite detail of all this art service from the social child-games of our play leader to the Crusoe-like isolation, the barbaric recapitulation of our Primitive Village, or, again,

emotional spirit and aspiration of the whole in Music.

Let no one think this spacious Arena too great, these Processional Ways too long. All will soon be needed for the opening future. We are not laying out and prettifying this or that garden for a nine days' wonder, not setting up this or that museum

FIG. 131.—Bird's-Eye Perspective to explain Building Scheme. This is taken from above East side of Park, and is looking eastward over the main range of new buildings along the left bank of the ravine, and thus at once forming the West border of the city and the East margin of the park. Central to this picture is the open area of Palace Yard and Monastery Place, with its main group of historic buildings—Palace, Pends, Monastery ruins, and Abbey Church—to left. Note also Queens' House to left of church, with corner of Arena seen below. The slightly widened St Catherine's Wynd is further enlarged at Maygate; of this the improved buildings run obliquely to the group of Library, Central Institute, Trust offices, and St Margaret's Halls, faintly indicated above the Tower of the modern Abbey Church.

To right (South) of Abbey Church is suggested the improvement of the Abbey Church yard by formal planting of yews, etc.

The development of Monastery Place as a central feature, uniting Park, New Buildings, and City, will be clearly understood, as also the general proportions of Crafts Village, Mill Garden, and History Garden; and the development of the entire range of History Buildings through Entrance, Stairway, and Cloister, through Mediæval, Renaissance, and Modern Buildings to the Twentieth-Century Tower and outlook.

to the improvement of garden beauty, I need not speak: with all such tasks the work of our artist-leader as educationist again begins. His problem reappears for adolescence, in attuning the energy of athletic youth towards a more than knightly ideal. His, too, to brighten the wedding festival, to organise on greater holidays his pageant and drama. Beyond all this, to express in fullest wealth of sense impression, in most strenuous intensity of meaning, in fullest depth of significance, the whole possibilities of culture, and thence, when word and imagery fail, to express the

as a new sarcophagus. We are here preparing the material stage and scene for that dramatic evocation of past history, for that vital criticism and re-interpretation of the present, for that symbol-drama of social redemption and evolution in the opening future which are the true divisions of the trilogy of twentieth-century art. Within some division of this general scheme all true artists are already labouring; scenic beauty, musical subtlety and intensity, dramatic passion are all to be found in their works. What these need is but the occasion, one of social purpose, of popular aspiration, of civic unity, and it is now for this city to offer all these, to evoke a development of public art worthy of the occasion and of the opportunity, one of pioneering truly ahead.

In such ways, then, our ancient capital, our modern industrial town, reappears in the future not only more historic than ever, but in its char-

new fire is not ended though the flint seems cold. So that, without the political power which makes the capital, without the vast resources of a modern university, there may yet arise here, first in Scotland—indeed, in the English-speaking, the Anglo-Celtic world, a characteristic and individual culture-city—a new and needed Bayreuth of the North.

FIG. 132.—The same perspective continued southward ; for the sake of clearness it repeats a portion of the preceding, from the South-East end of Monastery Place. East, and somewhat South, of the Twentieth-Century Tower stand the Art Institute. Opposite this, farther South, stand the large Nature Palace and Museums (Chap. XIV. to XVI.), with small Campanile rising behind. The Children's Garden (Chap. VII.) is faintly indicated behind this again. South of Nature Museums the smaller building is the Lion-house, etc., of the "Zoo." Across stream at foot will be noted proposed West Bridge (Chap. XIII., fig. 79). Relations of Manse Entrance to Streets and Park will be readily understood.

acteristic and individual way a centre of renascent art. The contemporary Irish Renascence has now passed the preliminary stages of solitary study and experiment ; it is already passing forth into artistic and social expression. Where better can we initiate the analogous, the latent Scottish, development than here ? I am well aware how such suggestions delight and invigorate the scoffer, but as social faith acquires scientific grounds it is not shaken by sneers. Said a foreign sociologist lately, sweeping his finger over the Scottish map by Glasgow and Edinburgh, St Andrews and Dundee to Aberdeen : " Strange so many great universities in this little land ! Yet no ; these are but the sparks struck from the contact of the Celtic and the Saxon genius along their racial frontier." Where more in the past have such sparks been kindled than here ? The possibility of

In Chapters XXVII. and XXVIII. we have discussed the material possibilities of an Arena and Music Hall, each of worthy dimensions, adapted to great public functions ; while in Chapter IV. we laid out a small Open-Air Theatre, suitable to the use of schools or small dramatic associations. The fuller development of these resources is alike beyond my task and powers, but it is plain that at few points can our provision for a bettering future be more legitimate or more desirable. The method of wholesale discouragement and repression of the dramatic and musical instincts has been too long tried in this country, and its twofold results have long been plain—on one hand, stunting the lives which have submitted to the regimen ; and on the other, of provoking the most violent reaction towards debased and debasing pleasures in those who have revolted from such control. It is in drama as in painting ; the mirroring of life, the idealising and symbolising of it, are to be wisely guided, then generously encouraged, and here in this opening co-operation of cultural and social agencies is surely the opportunity of worthy initiative. This city and its noble associations and evolving future, this History Palace with its wealth of wider suggestions, these Processional Ways, are all surely resources which cannot but be increasingly utilised. Composer, dramatist, critic, each is ready with his creation or his counsel.

K. Thought-Ways and Thinking-House

In Jena, and, if I mistake not, in other German University towns, there is a " Philosophenweg," a quiet path traditionally associated with the daily " constitutional " by which some noted brain-worker was wont to renew his forces, and now more or less well worn by later students. For our thoughtful ramblers there is here ample choice ; for our young Teufelsdroeckhs, too, there are lofty outlooks, each with its vivid intellectual stimulus, its notable objective aid at once to the informing and the inspiring, the calming and the broadening of the inner vision. This secret of education, literally upon the heights, the old world knew well, with its sacred mounts of meditation or vision, to the " high places " of old paganisms, or from our own fire-crowned hill-tops to our church and castle towers. Everywhere and all at times the governing spirits, spiritual and temporal, in peace as in war, have climbed the heights and raised themselves towers. No doubt this idea is nowadays largely forgotten, or even popularly discredited ; this is but natural to a period more marked by the progress of detail than of synthesis in science, and by division of labour in invention as in everyday industry ; yet the matter, like most others, is open to experiment. Whoever seeks at times, intellectually or normally, to rise above what he rightly calls his " everyday plane " may well ascend each available hill-top, or seek for himself some congenial outlook tower. For each way of thought what better symbol than its lofty stair ?

Business offices and workshops upon the level are, of course, needful, and it is the service of our passing age to have worked out so many forms of these ; but let no one think that social or individual evolution ends with these. Here and now, as of old, our resources of material and of immaterial culture cannot be completed without such architectural expression, uniting the needs of popular culture and of private meditation ; and this not only in cathedral and in cloistered retreat but in pealing belfry and in lofty tower. Hence the many constructions of these pages end, not even with this comprehensive perspective, but with its contribution to the City's sky-line (fig. 136), and by this it will in every sense be judged, first and last.

But before reaching this generalised civic standpoint, which needs its own chapter (XXXII.) for due expression, the more purely intellectual aspect of the present scheme may now be briefly outlined. The main threefold grouping of these buildings, their expression of naturalistic, historic, and civic culture will be plain after inspection of this panoramic sketch, or even the reading of its brief explanation ; and the further development and expression of these may now be thought out, each in turn from the standpoint of its own particular edifices and towers—respectively the naturalist's, the historian's and sociologist's, and the citizen's. But we need in conclusion to find and to establish some central and unifying standpoint, some simple yet comprehensive summary of thought. The problem thus, as already so often, becomes that of expressing and embodying a usually merely intellectual conception in a fitting plan, in a visible structure, and a practical use. Is any such unified view of things in our day possible? it will be asked ; and even if so, how can such high philosophic synthesis be put before the people — and this in their park, their place of recreation and enjoyment? Yet the answer is also plain. In the high recreative arts of old neither priest nor singer, neither artist-builder nor planter forgot that upon the joyous note of L'Allegro the graver one of Il Penseroso must surely follow, were it even for the deepening of joy.

Hence the old Abbey Church arose above its spacious park, its solemn acre, as our initial and still supreme culture-institute, since the perpetual reminder of the mystery from which we come, of the contrasted ideals towards which we go ; for towards one or other the resultant of every thought and action tends. Next, there followed those more personal treatments of the great questions which make up literature ; and with this the successive libraries of the city, so notably historical, because each in its day a forerunner—once that of the monks of Iona and of Canterbury, then of the scholars and poets of the Renaissance, and now of that more democratic type our founder has so generously broadcast over the world.

Beyond the church with its many general questions and answers, beyond the libraries with their many individual ones—in short, beyond the Religion and Learning of the past—there has come the questioning and answering of Science, and hence we need its museums and its schools. Partly following this, partly anticipating it, have come also the urgent questions of Industry, and this both in its simpler and technical developments, and in its highest forms, as Art. Yet once more there press forward other questions, other answers. From the interrogation of nature we return to the history of Humanity as the supreme problem of evolution, and, correspondingly, from industry controlling nature we rise to Policy guiding man. Here the lower stages of personal ambitions and of party struggles at first obscure all the preceding outlooks, but also (and where more than here and now?) the outlook of local polity begins to recover these, and to pioneer in co-ordinating them all into Culture-Policy. But any such practical co-ordination of our public life and aims must rise or fall with such general thought of the times as may accompany it ; hence, instead of this being an academic dissertation, foreign to the practical problem of this volume, as a weary or a timid reader may fear, we now reach the very heart or crux of it. We need thus concretely to construct some central thinking-house, chart room, and conning-tower, in which intellectual clearness of conception and practical efficiency in execution must meet. An actual chamber or hall, then, I ask to be set aside for this definite purpose, this ultimate and highest Council-room of the Trust—one outside its ordinary meeting-place, its everyday business offices and committee rooms, yet the periodic meeting-place of its broadest executive policy with its most general investigating and pioneering functions.

CHAPTER XXXII

CITIES AND CIVIC PROBLEMS

So far, the preceding chapters have dealt with the specific problem and situation—that of improvements to Dunfermline so far as directly related to the new park and its associated buildings. These proposals have, it is true, been related to more general ideas, and this necessarily, just as the corresponding plans are related to the points of the compass. Now, however, it is time that the general conception of civic development and culture policy, within which all these proposals fall, should be briefly indicated, the more since some of the proposals above made depart from conventional lines.

Hitherto I have mainly been endeavouring to apply the practical experience acquired during Edinburgh, London, and other constructive improvements, urban and rustic. Let me now briefly speak from the standpoint of a student of social science, to whom the observation and interpretation of the growth and development, the progress and decay of human societies—and these especially as presented in historic and contemporary cities—constitute the central problem to which all the sciences lead up, to which all the arts converge, and to which all the problems of the individual are related.

A. Significance of Historic Cities

In the development of social science itself now philosophy and now history has predominated, at other times politics, at other times industry. Institutions and laws, manners and customs have been scrutinised; now the individual or the nation has been in the focus of attention, at other times the race or the language. But of late there are signs that the City must again occupy a central place in our thought, as of old, an immediate place in our attention, even a foremost one in our activities.

The city was foremost in Hebrew and Greek civilisation, though in different ways, and central also in the Roman one; it fell into ruin and neglect in barbarian times, but revived in opposition and complement to the feudal order in the mediæval cities, which we are now learning again to understand, after a long period in which we have too much judged them by the mere products of their subsequent decay.

Here in Dunfermline we have sufficient relics and memories of this past not wholly to accept this still too common misunderstanding of it. But it is not too much to say that whoever would efficiently take part, still more pioneer, in this incipient civic renascence will find not only

general encouragement and warning but specific suggestion and even guidance by refreshing and extending his knowledge not only of the classical cities but of the great mediæval communes—particularly those of Northern Italy and France, of Germany and of the Low Countries. He should know something, if possible, from observation, and at any rate from records, not only of Jerusalem, Athens, and Rome, but of Bruges and Nuremburg, of Florence and Paris.

Such history is no doubt often studied and appreciated from the point of view of monumental public buildings or picturesque domestic ones, but not yet sufficiently from the standpoint of its civic organisation and democratic life. It is far more than a Scottish misfortune that our great romancer, who reopened to the world the picturesque and dramatic interest of the feudal age, should have been comparatively ignorant of the simultaneous but contrasted burgher civilisation of its great industrial towns. He has thus proportionally deepened for many, rather than removed, the long prevailing ignorance or misunderstanding of the mediæval city. It is one of the most notable results of the science of the later nineteenth century to have recovered this great tradition, yet we still await the popularisation of these great facts —that not only have many of the noblest ideals of democracy been expressed, but their as yet fullest practical realisation has been once and again attained, and this by the old citizens of Florence, by the guildsmen of the mediæval communes, of the Netherlands, of France and Germany, and in some not despicable measure even by our own forefathers, more fully than by the heirs of the French or the American Revolution, or by our own modern selves.

An eminent American writer on municipal questions, Dr Albert Shaw, has chosen as the Old-World types most instructive for the development of American cities, on the one hand Paris, as the example of the developed culture-capital; on the other hand Glasgow, as of late the most progressive of the great industrial towns. Yet it is not too much to say that when one has learned the best that is being done and thought in America, in Glasgow, or in Paris, one is but the better prepared to understand the civic ideal of ancient Athens or Rome on the one hand, of Mediæval Europe at its best on the other. Alike for the Birmingham or the Glasgow Town Councillor with his public ambitions, for the American citizen struggling with abuses on one hand, and carrying out ideals with vast wealth upon the other, there is probably nothing at this time within the range of experience which would be more practically useful, and more inspiring, than an intelligent visit to the market-place of Brussels, the Hotel de Ville of Ghent, the Belfry of Bruges—to name only spots accessible in the shortest continental holiday. It is not surprising, therefore, that the last named has had its best singer in an American poet, although even he was far from realising its full civic significance.

As I trust the preceding pages sufficiently show, there is

here nothing proposed for the sake of merely archæological interest, still less of mere artistic romanticism. What is urged is the scientific recognition that in such places we obtain a better comprehension of past blossomings of civic greatness, which must give us more hope, it may be even more skill, in dealing with much of what is with ourselves again in the bud. I am no more seeking to return to the Mediæval or the Roman past than to the Hebraic or the Hellenic order of things. On the contrary, I maintain return to the past to be impossible, its imitation to be undesirable ; simply that the conservation of the memorials of the past and the interpretation of its development are of encouragement and of service to that opening future which, with our greater resources, it should be possible to assure. It has been the achievement of the past century to obtain a knowledge of nature, a command of natural resources far exceeding that of the past, and it now behoves us no less completely to aspire to a corresponding evolution in all the higher arts, in the completest social art of city building, therefore, most of all.

As we have seen, in connection with the furthering of natural knowledge and of technical education, that the individual cannot too fully begin by recapitulating the simple and direct nature experience, the correspondingly simple and direct technical experience, from the very dawn of civilisation, so it must be in matters social and civic. Neither a moral nor an intellectual evolution can be imagined which would not profit from the examples which have been preserved to us in the literature of Judea and of Greece ; nay, it is this very advance of science which, to many timid souls, has threatened to sweep away one or another of these, which must now most fully profit by their spirit, whatever its emancipation from the letter.

In no department of human activity has progress been more active, or the utilisation of new resources more eager, than in the art of war ; none, therefore, in which the mere slavish imitation of the past can be more completely futile, more necessarily disastrous. Yet while it may be enough for the ordinary soldier in the ranks to manage his modern weapon, and while it is plain that a mistaken historic loyalty to ancestral weapons or tactics can but diminish his efficiency, the fact remains that it has been precisely the greatest modern commanders who have most fully recognised the suggestiveness of their historic predecessors.

B. The Civic Problem : its Various Statements

As suggestive to the fuller study and more effective grasp of our problems, it may be of service here to append a few examples of treatments of the city from representative points of view. First, then, I select a clear and orderly statement, not only studious but practical, as befits its writer, an advanced municipal worker of one of our greatest cities, and head of its most effective university settlement.

Municipalities at Work :
An introduction to the study of Municipal Administration

By T. R. Marr
Warden of the Art Museum and University Settlement

In this class the aim will be to explain simply local government. So far as possible illustrations

will be drawn from Manchester, Salford, and district.

1. Town government. The relations of local and central government. The limitations of each. The problem of town administration.
2. Roads, Streets, Canals, and Waterways. How the town controls these. Means of transit : railways, tramways, and other services. Street construction.
3. Town markets. Control of the food supply. Market rights. Food inspection. Milk supply.
4. Public health. The prevention of disease. The sanitary code. Life statistics. Notification and isolation of infectious diseases. Hospitals.
5. Cleansing work. The drainage system. Sewage works. The disposal of refuse and dirt. The supply of water. The atmosphere and smoke prevention.
6. The growth of a town. New buildings. Building byelaws. Incorporation of outlying districts. The housing of the working classes.
7. Public art ; municipal buildings, parks ; libraries ; the provision of means of recreation. The police and the licensing system.
8. Public utilities. Gas and electric light undertakings. The provision of power. Baths and washhouses. Fire prevention and salvage.
9. Education : primary, secondary, and higher. Technical education. Special schools.
10. The Poor Law. The Board of Guardians. Out relief. The Workhouse and Casual Wards. The problems of poverty and pauperism.
11. Municipal finance. How the income of the town is raised. The Overseers. Rates. Subventions from the central government. Municipal loans. The control of municipal finance.
12. The citizen in relation to his city. His rights. His responsibilities.

In the preceding summary of civics it will be seen that the problems essentially considered in the preceding report occupy a very modest share of attention—mainly that of a portion of its section 7—and in this the majority of civic treatises broadly agree, the standpoint of British municipalities also.

I therefore select a very different statement of the essential civic problems for my second citation, the chapter headings of Mr C. W. Robinson's " Modern Civic Art ; or, The City Made Beautiful " (Putnam, 1901), a representative expression of a more ambitious civic point of view now rapidly spreading through American cities. Here the standpoint of material betterment is maintained as in this country, but also awakened to the standpoint of civic art by contact with Paris, Berlin, and other monumental cities of the Continent, the class to which Washington, of course, also belonged in its very inception, and seeks to rival or surpass in its magnificent renewal.* To quote them :

Introduction : A New Day for Cities. What Civic Art is.
1. *The City's Local Points* : The Water Approach. The Land Approach. The Administrative Centre.
2. *In the Business District* : The Street Plan of the Business District. Architecture in the Business District. The

---

* Park Report, District of Columbia, 1900.

Furnishings of the Street. Adorning with Fountains and Sculpture.
3. *In the Residential Sections*: Street Plotting among the Homes. On Great Avenues. On Main Residential Streets. Among the Tenements.
4. *The City at Large*: Comprehensive Planning. Open Spaces. Pathways. Distribution and Location of Parks. Park Development. Temporary and Occasional Decoration.

Here we have the architect as again the literal " chief workman " his name implies. Long left aside in the rush of industrial expansion, and with his opportunities so rare as to make his success with them still rarer, he is here claiming, and justifying his claim, to the high office of civic edile, charged with the gradual redress and transformation of the disorder of the past, and with the immediate better regulation of the expansion of the future. Such American civic improvers " are not asking the town to help art but art to help the town ; the artists not to glorify their art but by their art to glorify the city." From this outline, and still more from the inspiring volume itself, it will be plain that such associated city improvements as I have ventured to suggest from the sides of park approaches or of stream purification are but modest anticipations of that largeness and vigour with which Dunfermline, as henceforth the cynosure for American as well as British cities, may be expected soon to grapple with its various improvement problems.

Finally, the third statement of the civic problem I select is that more general and comparative treatment suitable to the initial course of applied sociology in the University of London which I have lately been privileged to deliver. This is submitted here, partly as indicating the lines of a fuller comparison of towns and cities, great and small ; as stating in general lines those universal problems and tasks of culture development towards which the plans and proposals of the preceding pages offer particular and local solutions ; and, further, as indicating more fully the high significance of Dunfermline in the past of civic history, its typical interest in the present, and now in the opening future its renewing culture-initiative, its extending example and influence among the cities of the world.

Introductory Course in Sociology
University of London. Lent Term, 1904

Cities and their Culture-Resources Actual and Incipient

A Study in Civic Development

1. (*a*) LONDON.
Continental cities and their resources ; American cities and their ambitions. Great but less developed resources and less awakened ideals of London, and of most, if not all, Britannic (British and Colonial) cities. Symptoms of awakening.

How may we arrange our general impression of cities, derived from home, travel, or reading, so as to be of scientific (" sociological ") value? Need of orderly description, comparison, etc., for interpretation : rational action then becomes more possible.

Need and results of observation—*e.g.* Booth's " London " and kindred works. Further surveys needed, extensive and intensive.

(*b*) SMALLER CITIES—*e.g.* EDINBURGH AND GLASGOW.
Smaller national or provincial capitals, with their associated culture-developments, afford convenient preparation

FIG . 134.—Spire of Town House from Park, near East entrance to Tower Hill.

for study of London and Westminster. Examples : Edinburgh, Dunfermline, Winchester.

Similarly, less enormous commercial and industrial cities are more convenient to begin with than London, the City and the East—*e.g.* Glasgow and kindred cities. Simpler are minor ports and burghs—*e.g.* of Fife, Devon, etc. In short, we must study towns from their geographical origins onwards.

Comparison of Edinburgh and Glasgow in contemporary and historic development : suggestiveness of this.

2. SMALL TYPE-CITIES—*e.g.* DUNFERMLINE.
The smallest type needed, in which historic, actual, and incipient developments more easily traceable. A most convenient type at present Dunfermline : mediæval capital and abbey, and modern manufacturing town—now beginning new expansion as naval base, and also as culture-centre (*cf.* Mr Carnegie's initiative).

3. THE CIVIC PROBLEM.

This is now capable of explicit statement, alike on material and on intellectual and moral sides.

Beyond and above discussion of traditional or current political problems, Liberal, Imperial, and Financial, is urgency of culture-problems and culture-policy; since expansion or development of institutions, of empire, and of wealth are all dependent upon development of civilisation and race. In short, quantity depends upon quality, not conversely.

Attempted outline of this culture-development: (*a*) Scientific and Technic; (*b*) Geotechnic and Synthetic; (*c*) Evolutionist.

4. CULTURE DEVELOPMENT IN DETAIL: NATURE RESOURCES.

Return to nature; this a moral and intellectual as well as hygienic need. Travel. Parks and Gardens. Museums and Science-schools, etc.

Problem of development and co-ordination of these.

5. SCIENCE AND ART RESOURCES AND TEACHING, continued.

Criticism of these: need of continuing and unifying the Educational Revolution (Formal to Vital—Static to Kinetic).

Technical Education and constructive reality. Arts and Crafts. More elemental solution needed: outlines towards this.

6. RESOURCES FOR HISTORICAL CULTURE AND SOCIAL GUIDANCE.

Historic heritage of the city: suggestions towards utilising and developing this: a Historic Institute and its uses.

The need of contemporary guidance, moral and political: the news-room as a familiar beginning towards this: possibilities of development—*e.g.* "Current Events Clubs" and their records. Libraries, public and academic: immediate need of Bibliography as the Public Intelligence Department.

Need and possibilities of Sociological education. Beginnings of this in various cities.

7. RESOURCES OF THE FINE ARTS.

These no longer viewed as of simply technical achievement but as concretely synthetic (geotechnic, etc.), as expressing civic development, and as furthering it.

Corresponding need of fuller and truer art-education of public; how to organise this?

Literature and Music.

Painting, Sculpture, Architecture, and Gardening.

Drama and Pageant. "Melodrame." Civic Festival.

Resultant of all the preceding individual and social culture-developments in the characteristic culture, regional, civic, individual.

The development of each City at any given place and time may thus be conveniently compared with that of any other, both as regards material environment and moral and intellectual atmosphere.

Civic needs, and personal possibilities and responsibilities accordingly.

8. CULTURE DEVELOPMENT IN THEORY AND POLICY.

Further comparison of towns and cities; classic, mediæval, and modern. Of the various culture-centres of the past—*e.g.* Acropolis and Forum, Abbey and Cathedral, what are the modern or incipient analogues? How promote and develop these?

Varying policy needed with local history, circumstances, and outlook. Era of civic development fully beginning—*e.g.* Glasgow, Dunfermline, American cities.

London and its Boroughs? Provincial Cities?

Colonial Capitals?

That other and higher statements of the civic problem are possible, more distinctively social and ethical, more truly religious, I gladly recognise; the best function of such a discussion as the present is to provoke the superseding of it. For the present, however, it may serve as a summarised indication of the standpoint of the present volume, and as an introduction to the concluding chapters devoted to our particular civic development.

CHAPTER XXXIII

DUNFERMLINE AS TOWN AND AS CITY

A. The Town

So far, then, the study of the city in general. Suppose the concrete suggestions of the preceding report discussed and improved upon as fully as may be, and the Trust then to carry out a scheme of civic improvements satisfactory alike to themselves, the city, and the world, fully expressing the best attainment of our time, even the highest it has been able to foresee. Were all this accomplished we should have legitimate cause for a day of civic festivity, such as that which recently marked the public opening of the scheme.

What then ? Not only the larger world but our own city would thereafter live on in its accustomed way, leaving our series of new institutions, once completed, to " settle down," which too commonly means to freeze or degenerate. Only an aim and conception of ever - extending, ever - expanding individual and social culture can protect them and us from this.

Why at this day is our Mediæval Abbey ruined, our Renaissance Palace fallen in ? Because from these the great stream of national and of world life which once animated them moved away, leaving their dignified exteriors, at first apparently unchanged, to fall steadily and inevitably into ruin.

How, then, shall we safeguard these new beginnings ? Though civic renascence seems fully begun, who can protect our schemes and institutions and buildings from falling into decay in their turn—it may not be into picturesque ruin, as of old, but with that far subtler dry rot which has befallen so many of our lately most hopeful modern constructions, educational and other ?

How are Dunfermline and its Trust—presumably at this moment the most eagerly progressive community and body in Scotland—to escape sinking in time, albeit distant, to the frozen conventionality of Edinburgh, the hopeless paralysis of its happily disappearing Board of Manufactures ? For when such things have befallen our national capital —still with all its frosts one of the greater culture cities of Europe—what is to be hoped for this little Dunfermline ? Has it any future beyond that of provincial mediocrity at best ? Must not its young ability be creamed for larger centres— each " lad o' pairts " leaving us just as we have reared him ? Must not the universities, as they revive, search out more and more keenly each individual of intellectual gift or moral glow ? Must not the larger world—Glasgow, London, America— more and more call away our vigorous youth to ever-enlarging but increasingly distant careers ? Develop local and civic patriotism as we may, the larger call of nation and empire can but the more largely predominate. We have seen this in our own generation ; we see, too, that the next will be yet more open to the call of the common language —nay, of the larger humanity beyond. And must we not loyally accept this ? The little grey old mother city will still take pride in the sons whom she has sent out, well schooled and nobly inspired, to battle in the larger world ; ever and anon may welcome one who returns, as in our own day her most successful child has done, to rise up and call her blessed.

But all this does not wholly content us. It cannot, it need not. Let us consider, then, what larger possibilities of civic life may also lie before us here. But what principle is there to guide us in this vast question, what clue ?

Here, as in all true progress, we must not only comprehend and transform the environment without but develop our life within. Our inevitable and permanent provincialism must be accepted as one of the facts of life. Dunfermline will and may enlarge and develop, but it cannot become a Glasgow or Edinburgh. What is the vital element which must complement our provincialism ? In a single word, it is Regionalism—an idea and movement which is already producing in other countries great and valuable effects. It begins by recognising that while centralisation to the great capitals was inevitable, and is in some measure permanent, this is no longer so completely necessary as when they practically alone possessed a monopoly of the resources of justice and of administration, a practical monopoly also of the resources of culture in almost all its higher forms. The increasing complexity of human affairs, with railway, telegraph, and business organisation, has enabled the great centres to increase and retain their control ; yet their continued advance is also rendering decentralisation, with local government of all kinds, increasingly possible. Similarly for culture institutions : the development of the local press has long been in progress ; the history of the city library movement is in no small measure identified with that of this very town ; while the adequate institution among us of other forms of higher culture is just what has been discussed in the preceding pages. We see, then, that the small city is thus in some measure escaping from the exclusive intellectual domination of the greater ones, and is tending to redevelop, not, indeed, independence, but culture individuality.

There are more immediate reasons for the development of smaller cities. They lie in the hygienic, the intellectual and æsthetic, the moral and practical advantages of country life over city life, particularly for the young. The environs of every large city show how willingly paterfamilias faces a long and fatiguing double journey in addition to his daily work in order to give his children even a tincture of rustic upbringing ; and the same principle is still more manifestly at work in the Garden City movement.

As personally a strong conservative in this matter—that is, as long more actively interested in the renascence of our ancient and historic cities than in the creation of new ones, however delightful—my own testimony must yet be given to the side with which I personally least sympathise. Having had the exceptional freedom among busy men of choosing and varying my home for four-fifths of each of the last five and twenty years, I have made large use of this to familiarise myself practically with the special and regional advantages of city and of country life, both in northern and southern Europe, and, indeed, from the East to America. And hoping that the present frightful inferiority of town vitality to that of country might be adequately treated by help of open spaces, better atmosphere, and so on, I experimentally built my city home on a spot scarcely surpassable in any modern city in combining the convenience of central position with that of adjacent vast open spaces and almost of hill air—the lofty and open Castle Esplanade of Edinburgh. But even in this quite exceptionally healthy urban environment it needed but little observation of one's own or neighbouring families to see that vitality still droops, and that, to ensure the full vital development which is the main essential to the adequate upbringing of children, a far fuller contact with rustic conditions is necessary. Still more when, with the advance of biological thought, we increasingly take into account not only our immediate children but theirs, and, in fact, the future of our breed and race, henceforward no longer to be thoughtlessly sacrificed in the immediate struggle for wealth or daily bread, but to be considered with that long and more than statesmanlike patience with which we select and plant the forest, with which we tend, select, and improve the humbler animal breeds. These things now being matters of scientific certitude,[*] as of everyday fact, are now beginning to be popularised ; witness the vivid and stimulating work of writers like Mr Wells or Mr Bernard Shaw, which are as obviously, again, but the prologue of new discussions deeper than current political or social ones.

Looking, then, at the position of Dunfermline upon the map, so conveniently situated upon great lines of communication also, we see that it may readily combine the advantages of an ancient and revived Culture City with those of a modern Garden City, and these independently even of the new maritime city and garden city projected in the immediate neighbourhood.

Here, in fact, at Dunfermline (especially assuming some future lowering of railway fares, of which the Hungarian zone system and other improvements give promise) we have the most convenient residential centre within easy reach of Edinburgh. For the large class of retired people, and for those whose main concern it is to educate their children, Dunfermline, especially in view of the progress and initiative of its schools now being provided for, should be able to exercise a permanent attraction.

The Park is but the centre from which must increasingly radiate the lines of an enlarging web of civic improvement, not only extending town into country but fully diffusing country into town. With its charming and sheltered walks, and those afforded by the natural extension of the park, through and beyond St Margaret's Glen, and gradually for miles beyond, we have ideal conditions for the invalid, the convalescent, as well as for the tourist and holiday-seeker, with substantial economic import to the city.

* Francis Galton, " Eugenics : its Definition and Scope." Sociological Society. May 1904.

Beyond the increased efficiency of the staple industry due to the bettered health, intelligence, and happiness of worker and employer alike, new industries will become increasingly possible. Thus the prominence of Edinburgh in printing is very largely a consequence of the present higher education of the Scottish workman, as among greater centres. The proposed renewal of a scriptorium side by side with the encouragement of the local press has more and deeper reasons than may at first appear. Good printing, good writing, and good drawing can best progress together.

The development of the local textile industries,

FIG. 136.—Sketch indicating new sky-line of Dunfermline Towers from South, a view necessarily changing in every perspective. In the present ordering and numbering from left to right comes first the great Campanile, then the Town House spire, the Abbey Church with its old West spire and modern square tower, the History Palace with its five towers, large and small; and finally, the small Campanile of the Nature Palace. The needed complementary effect to these many towers and spires would be afforded by the large low dome of the Nature Palace, with its four smaller domes around it. In many groupings these monumental effects would be substantially aided by minor buildings—as notably by those of Queens' House and of Crafts Village, by the lodge of History Garden, etc.—while the gradual improvement of domestic architecture in the city itself would constantly yield new combinations, fresh pictures in endless variety—in short, an increasingly picturesque Dunfermline.

well as of the past activity of Scottish writers, and enterprise of publishers. There is no reason why Dunfermline should not obtain some substantial share of this. The city which in the early middle age united the scriptorium of Iona with that of Canterbury, which at the Renaissance sent Erasmus to Italy, and where the modern Library Movement has in such large measure begun, cannot think itself to have ended its history and possibilities, in producing books as well as using them, at the very moment when its culture facilities are being revived, and when it is re-entering upon civic rivalry, even leadership, and this not only in quantity but in artistic quality also, is an obvious progress; and when this is taken with the gradual transformation of the city, in private homes as well as through public buildings, it should give us here some distinctive individuality and productiveness in art industries of all kinds. And, as has already been urged, the erection of the Trust's buildings and the decoration of the existing ones, such as schools, should foster the development of a local school of architecture, sculpture, and painting as well as of decoration and ornamentation in some, perhaps many, of its branches.

With the bettering of homes, as of the larger environment, there are here all the conditions, and these in unusual and ever-increasing proportion, for those conditions of bodily and mental health which are needed for full industrial and commercial efficiency and artistic performance, and, perhaps, especially for that mental alertness in the application of science to industry upon which the opening future of our country so largely depends. As a single specific instance, it is a very small German city, not half the size of Dunfermline, that has developed what is at once the best and the greatest scientific instrument-making business in the world : and with this it has taken a no less notable lead in all that concerns the conditions of housing, insurance, and general well-being of the workers, in technical and higher education, in city and university improvements also.* There is surely reason and incentive here for analogous initiatives to be possible and fruitful.

Such are many ways, therefore, in which a minor city like Dunfermline may open new careers for its more gifted children, in which, indeed, it may not only retain many of its best, but attract high ability from other places, with all the mutual advantage, the perpetual fertilisation which such interchange involves.

In this respect, as in so many others, the strangely chequered history of our own little country is of no small significance. It has been fixed in our minds, chiefly by the tradition of school geography books, that every country, every kingdom, for that matter every county, has its "capital." Yet we do not here very seriously feel the governmental yoke of Cupar-Fife, nor even bow exclusively to the educational authority of the ancient and once metropolitan university of St Andrews. We hope freely to utilise not only this but the academic resources of Edinburgh, Glasgow, and Aberdeen, as well as remoter ones if need be. Edinburgh was only created the capital in 1437, and, of course, largely ceased to be so in 1603, and for most purposes in 1707 ; while in earlier times we find Perth, Stirling, and Dunfermline all rivalling, indeed sometimes exceeding, Edinburgh in importance.

Beyond these again we find a network of smaller regional capitals ; witness the traditional glories of Scone, or of the Tower of Abernethy, still more that wealth of folk-lore and tradition which pious memory has preserved from among the ruins of Iona. Around the almost forgotten yet long independent capital of the Lord of the Isles, Finlagan in Islay, the researches of Mr Campbell of Islay and others have disclosed a wealth of tradition even surpassing those disclosed by German folk-lorists and philologists, a level of culture almost Icelandic.

* Müller, "Das Zeisswerk in Jena." Jena, 1900.

But it is not necessary to go back to this remote and shadowy antiquity. One has only to go north to the thriving regional metropolis of Aberdeen to find the city which best, perhaps, in all the British Isles combines an ever-widening development of manufactures and commerce, national, imperial, and international, with intense local life and progressive culture, popular and academic alike. It is this intensive individual and regional development which presents for us the truest type and forecast of our Scottish cities ; and particularly in Fife, where Scottish individuality has always notoriously been pushed to its very furthest, and which has produced such world representatives of individualism in philosophy, in personal life, and in practical affairs as Adam Smith, Robinson Crusoe, and Andrew Carnegie, we have evidently little to learn even from the Aberdonian.

We have thus reviewed not only the regional development of this place but the corresponding and extending possibilities of its regional work, with a glance at the corresponding development of the life and conditions of family, and even with that improving "social selection," not only as regards industry but family, which is increasingly seen to be a vital condition of all human progress. For the romantic tales, of which our too serious critics of libraries are apt insufficiently to appreciate the popular use, even those of Edwin and Angelina, of Cinderella and her Prince, or of rustic lad transformed by fairy Princess, are now reappearing, as per Mr Galton's and other works cited above, in the very forefront of twentieth-century science, which has now to popularise eugenics, as the last decade has diffused the idea of hygiene.

Place, work, family—region, occupation, life—geographic, industrial, and social well-being—these are but varied wordings of the threefold unity of life, work, and surroundings—organism, function, and environment—which we are seeking to realise in this our own good town.

B. The City: its Schools

But this idea of the Town, its Place, its Work, its Families, is as yet too purely material and objective ; we must more and more fully take into account its deeper and subjective developments. To rise from the conception of Town to that of City we need far more than better laying out, better organisation of industrial and residential conditions, fuller access to nature and so on, needful though all these are. We must first now complement material "Town," even "Garden Town" though it thus become, by the no less indispensable developments of its non-material life. First in this would be the idea of its associated " Schools," these in a sense not only including the everyday one, yet with all the older and wider senses of the word—the School as place of culture leisure, the School as a recognisable brand of art, as a local colour in literature, and so on. For to be really conscious of our where-abouts, to appreciate our Place, we need an ever-expanding mental life in sense, in intellect, and in feeling. Here comes the naturalist with all his resources of regional survey ; the artist with his light and colour. Hence the ever-continued, ever-vital usefulness of those natur-alistic and artistic resources which we have above outlined.

Again coming to the next great conception of Work, here the development of the individual must recapitulate the essential development of the race if it is ever healthily to continue and to surpass it. Hence the need of that perpetual renewal of primitive occupations, that village of primitive life which we have pleaded that the children should have the opportunity of actually constructing, of maintaining, reconstructing also, generation after generation.

Here, too, is the plea for the forge, the mill ; and here again the argument for recapitulating the whole development of the loom, and this from its most primitive beginnings, even for the very sake of mastering its complexity and advanc-ing this.

In the same way the claims of rustic labour, in every form from the simplest ploughing to the most complex gardening or most skilful fruit-grow-ing, have their place and their corresponding scientific disciplines. The technical school thus escapes from the mechanical bondage of art to science, and utilises a living and progressive experimental science in the actual pursuit of industry and art. The current Education of Exercises too tardily applied in practice, thus gives place to an invigorating Education of Ex-perience, a discipline of widening responsibility, in which scientific reflection and investigation are combined. At present a boy often learns geometry for years before he comes to land-surveying ; whereas, starting anew with the primitive rope-stretching of the Egyptian, his practical efficiency and his mathematical power swiftly increase together.

Scientific research has nothing to fear from this intimate relation with practice : the great chemical factories of Germany surpass in their research activities the university laboratories ; while that extraordinary focus of medical pro-gress, the Pasteur Institute, is at the same time a centre of advance of many other kinds, from pure chemistry to social science.

Social science and the corresponding efficiency of social service thus begin essentially with the study of place and of work, with geographer and economist. Hence our progressive schools begin with nature and handicraft in the Kinder-garten, and go on to scientific instruction with the Secondary and Technical Schools already familiar to us ; but it has thus still to be com-pleted by a Social School, without which a com-munity or city cannot attain to full consciousness or developed efficiency.

For it is the development of the past, inter-preted as above from the standpoint of the present ; it is social education as regards the present, the opening future also, which is now needed to com-plete alike the everyday education of the citizen by awaking within him an ever-growing con-sciousness of his city. Is it not upon the poor and imperfect development of this high element of education that we must explain the weakness of the modern city in these respects as compared with the great historic cities, not Rome only, but others before and since ? Our cities lack their forums ; but this, again, our Parks, our arena, may increasingly supply, the renewed city cross at any rate stand as a centre.

In this way we see developing from the place, the work, the family of our Town, not only the web of occupation and the organisation of industry, the volume of aggregate industry, the state of well-being and health, the various institutions, but also the School—*i.e.* the set of ideas connected with each of these, and needful for their efficient exercise. From elementary geography and other primary knowledge, from technical instruction of the simpler sort, we may thus rise to higher and higher schools, and in special cities to institutions of higher education, even to college faculties of the old professions, such as medicine or law, as well as to the new professions of engineering, agricul-ture, fine art, or most lately, in Birmingham, of commerce. Here, in fact, we have the usual idea of a university, or at any rate of a university college. This type of development, however, Dunfermline does not require to follow to the full, since to her completion of her own school system by utilisation of the five neighbouring University Cities, as to her useful reaction upon these, there is evidently no limit.

C. The City: its Cloister

But in addition to such a school, or group of schools, a new development may arise, that which retires from the practical everyday life of a city, or even its everyday educational duties, into the meditative life—in antique phrase, therefore, into " the cloister," the " Abbey "—in later phrase into " intellectual retirement " ; while in more modern times this mental attitude is largely re-placed by that of " original research." The common character of all these cloistered orders, as I may call them, is that their members are no longer mainly concerned with the town's working life or even its educational service—though, at their best, they have always taken a not inconsiderable part in these. It is that their essential relation and responsibility are now with the highest aspects of truth, as they understand it, and with the deepening of their own contact and that of others with this. Abbey-founding, as I may call all furtherance of institutions devoted to the contemplative life, whether of religious ideals in the mediæval past, of philosophic systems in Greek or in recent times —for the Academy of Plato, the Lyceum of Aristotle were the cloisters of Athens in their day, or nowadays of the scientific order of the universe— has of late years been liberally advanced, indeed, in this latest form, by our own founder; but, obviously and rightly, in our university cities, in Washington and the like, not here. It is this union of School and Research Cloister which in our day makes up the ideal of the University proper; and we see that present conditions do not favour this—in short, that no such renascence of the abbey is to be expected upon any great scale here. An occasional speculative hermit may generally suffice, even for occasions like the present.*

D. The City: its Cathedral

Yet another type of civic development remains —and this the highest; again in antique phrase it is the Cathedral, even more than the University, the Cloister, or the School, which raises the conception of the Town into that of the City. What, then, was the Cathedral? What was its contrast

* In such ways, above and beyond the scope and purpose of the faculties and schools, are arising in these years, here and there, in Paris, in Edinburgh, in London, some small and as yet extra-mural schools of sociology, as yet unrecognised, if not disapproved, by the universities, because transcending, alike in scientific level, in intellectual range, and in social and moral ambitions, their traditional faculties. Yet, none the less are these preparing an educational revolution throughout the university system no less important than that which has been wrought once and again by extra-mural agencies, as of Renaissance learning in the sixteenth and seventeenth centuries, or of Encyclopædic philosophy and science in the eighteenth and nineteenth. In this evolution of social consciousness our city must now for a season lead—its Trust being thus increasingly a group of sociological observers and inquirers (that is, of investigators) no less than of practical pioneers, their "library, hall, and offices" in modern phrase becoming thus an "abbot's house and bishop's palace" in antique phrase, or, say, a "chapter-house" of the most comprehensive kind. Or, if we prefer a phrasing in incipient use, these become a social observatory and laboratory, a centre at once of social survey and social service, a school and example of civic life and duty.

with the Abbey? Obviously this: that while the abbot and his monks were a "regular clergy"— whose whole principle and reason of existence was to be concerned primarily with what they believed to be the highest attainable theory of the Universe, its highest order and law—the bishop and priests were a "secular clergy," less highly learned, as a rule, but more practical, their principle and avowed task being to bring the highest attainable measure of truth, of beauty, of moral and social order into the everyday life of the citizens. For this purpose they gradually evolved the marvellous art synthesis of the Cathedral, in its way the vastest of historic educational endeavours, the veritable popular encyclopædia of its times. Hence its astronomic symbolism, its naturalistic detail, its presentment of the creation, of the origin and fall of man, of national history also, with its kings and heroes, of civic history and interests also—even to the freest criticism or caricature of the citizens of the time. Within, too, the same encyclopædic presentment appears; from its many chapels of the crafts and arts, symbolised by their various patrons, to its presentment of the unity of these within the larger plan. In such ways it offered not only a religious and a philosophic system, but a correspondingly provisional, social and scientific explanation of things also. That this was sufficient is far from suggested; it has long been generally recognised that it was, above all things, the inadequacy of this which led to the downfall of the Cathedral from its once so important place in the regulation and the development of civic and regional life. But what is nowadays important is not to reiterate with the iconoclast a criticism which has become a commonplace, but to recognise with historian and socialiser that just as we have seen Town and School and Cloister of thoughtful retirement to be in principle permanent, so, above all, must the Cathedral be again considered. In principle, in ideal, this was the highest agency of the times towards the bringing to bear upon the community the best cultural resources, the synthesis of ideals and of knowledge, in their working theories, the orchestration of all the arts—painting, sculpture, and architecture, music and symbol-drama. The incorporation of the whole body of citizens, was here an essential idea, primarily, in their personal capacity, irrespective of age, sex, rank, or wealth, but offering "to each man all that is human," yet secondarily in their social capacity also, from the craft guild to civic council, often even a more or less independent city-state. From this high view of life it is little wonder that the town took a new aspect—place architecturally transfigured, occupations developed and ennobled, individual and family guided and moralised, education developed on all levels, even universities founded—in short, the whole cycle of developments, material and ideal, temporal and spiritual,

of Town, School, Cloister, and Cathedral developing anew.

Am I, therefore, proposing to restore the pre- or
post-reformation " Prelacy " which our forefathers
broke with so decidedly ? Such literal misunderstanding is impossible ; the understanding, however, of the city of the opening future is none too
easy for any of us. Enough for the present if
we see that as industries and aspects of Town
change, and families, institutions, and the corresponding technical and theoretic schools have
changed with the times, and ever need to be
brought abreast of them anew, so the true Cloister
of thought and meditation, of observation and
experimental labour must ever be restored in
appropriate form ; and so, finally, the true Cathedral established. Where shall this be ? Where
better shall we find our modern Civic Cathedral
Close than in the People's Park—with its vast
places of assembly, its halls of music, its expressions
of symbol ? The presentment of nature in its beauty
and its variety, its sublimity and its unity are
again here. The presentment of history and its
unfolding meaning are again set forth to be plainly
understood of the people, and this on every level,
from the local drama with its saints and heroes to
that of the larger world—contemporary and civilised—indeed, to that of human origins. If the
old emphatic doctrine of human destiny be in
some respects less clearly expressed, there is at
any rate reappearing the conception of life and
labour towards the fuller realisation of the noblest
ideals which, in our time and our phase of evolution, we can discern, even if never fully attain.
The processional ways of our park and city Cathedral thus fully open into as many pilgrimages.

E. Summary

Putting this more concretely, and bringing it to
particulars, it is, I trust, apparent that the purpose of the present volume has been more than to
supply a succession of suggestions more or less
attractive, or simply for criticism piecemeal.
Through all these concrete plans and perspectives,
these generalised discussions of their respective
purposes, there runs a unity of thought and
of design, be this successful or no. It is not only
that of meeting general needs, more or less felt
everywhere at present, but also of expressing the
character and individuality of the city before us,
of conserving all that is essential or worthily representative in its past and present development,
yet of boldly continuing this into the enlarging
future. This conception of the City is as a
necessarily unique social personality, a definite
regional and racial development, yet one capable
of increasingly conscious evolution, and this

through a cycle of culture-phases potentially
common to all cities, and broadly outlined here
as of Town, School, Cloister, and Cathedral, will
be found increasingly useful and applicable as it is
reflected upon—increasingly incompatible also
with either the merely dull or the merely Utopian
view of life. Yet to claim for this civic conception unity and order, no less than for the design
of its appropriate culture-palaces, its parks and
gardens, is to leave them not less varied and
open—nay, more living and more free.

Social science is thus no mere abstract study,
apart from practical problems such as those
which have been before us ; it arises from active
life, and it returns thither with fresh suggestiveness, new invention. What mechanics is to
engineering, biology to medicine, electricity to
telegraphy, chemistry to agriculture, physiology
to medicine, bacteriology to hygiene, that is
sociology to civic life and well-being. That this
relation of theory to practice, of science to application, is more complex than any of the preceding
is no doubt true ; yet here also is an element of
hope, since with fuller knowledge we may feel
assured of bolder applications in the future than
any I have here ventured to propound.

The study of the body not animated by the
mind is a post-mortem examination ; and this has
been too much the case with the old economics
and politics, which are ever seeking to eliminate
most of that which makes society living. Our
returning idealism is thus no mere abstraction, no
mere affair of sentiment, it is the recovery, in
new and evolutionary form, of that greatest of all
traditions—that recognition of the comprehensive
intellectual and moral order which ever underlies
and conditions any high level of social action.

Again, the various proposals of park and city
improvement, which I have above submitted, may
now be seen to conform to the various stages of
art. First came that of description, of simple
realism. Next came that of improving technical
details ; this rises to arrangement and organisation,
and thence passes to a yet higher phase—that in
which the process and direction of things again
begin to be discerned as part of an orderly
universe in evolution. The wider inter-relations
of social life and of natural law thus admit of
being expressed in concrete forms, and in comprehensive symbols, so that to the religious spirit
these modern scientific institutes may again be
expressed in his terminology no less than in their
own.*

Starting, then, with the fundamental problem
of purifying our stream and cultivating our
garden, we naturally and necessarily progressed
towards the idea, first of bettered dwellings of the

* Cf. "A Gardener's View of Science, Old and New."
Monthly Review, May 1904.

body, and then to that of higher palaces of the spirit. The whole scheme, material and intellectual, domestic and civic, scientific and artistic, is thus thoroughly one ; whereas without such fundamental basis of natural and industrial reality much of our present-day idealism but flutters in the void ; while our would-be practical world, as yet too much without this evolutionary idealism, is continually sinking into material failure or stagnation, moral discouragement, or decay.

Let us, then, unite both elements, and, in the immortal phrase of Socrates, at once " labour and make music." For even modest practical effort, then, a high note must be struck from the very outset. " Except the Ideal build the house, they labour in vain that build it."

CHAPTER XXXIV

THE CIVIC UNION

A. Introductory

A WORD may be permitted of and to the Citizen. The mercenary view of the Trust as something to be exploited is easily disclaimed or protested against ; but with false ideas, as with bad institutions, " we can only destroy what we replace." I now submit, then, as the essential suggestion—one taking precedence even of park and buildings, recreation or education, " sweetness or light," this social and moral proposal—that, as the city is only to be elevated in proportion as the citizens elevate themselves, it is for them to work in and with the interests of the Trust rather than for their own. To plead for the setting up of definite and well-organised agencies towards this is thus in principle my initial recommendation, as here actually my final one.

Putting this matter yet more concretely, is not the truster too often considered as an exceptional and isolated individual on one side, with all Dunfermline on the other ? Yet, despite the unparalleled magnitude of his gifts, and the rare elevation of his purpose, he is avowedly and truly but the foremost of his fellow-citizens ; in taking an unparalleled initiative he is yet setting a civic example. He calls upon others to follow this ; and though no other may contribute dollars by millions, nor acres by scores, a substantial increment to the Trust, or at any rate to its purposes and their accomplishment, as contemplated in the truster's letter, may thus be increasingly hoped for. Still more may we be assured of this when the people themselves awake to this participation, and surpass the generosity of the rich with their added mites, renewing that principle of voluntary taxation for culture purposes so notable in the history of Scotland.

For though some have spoken as if the available sum were much, even too much, for Dunfermline, the answer may be simply expressed, that after all even this large income averages but £1 per annum per inhabitant, and most people's experience shows that one's culture and recreation expenditure is not in any great danger of extravagance at 4½d. per week. Again, it is only the shallow observer of Scottish character and temperament who thinks it mean and narrow ; the most critical of all peoples, founding upon six centuries of political and economic alliance more intimate than modern ones, crystallised its judgments into proverbial phrase, not only " proud as a Scot," " hospitable as a Scot," but even " généreux comme un écossais." That some of us still remember how our fathers went through the Disruption or the Chartist movement ; that we know the tale of their grandfathers through the '45, and so back through the generations, is answer enough also to any not oblivious of mental and social heredity. Or, returning to the present, the columns of the Press regularly show that the Scottish subscriptions to social and national objects are in notable proportional excess even of those of the City of London itself, focus of wealth though it be.

As the present Trust adequately grapples with this second great object of its founder, that beyond its immediate duty of administration of his gifts, and passes on the task of awakening and guiding individual sacrifice to civic ends, there need be no fear but that the Scottish cities may again rise, it may be even lead ; as Edinburgh, for instance, was wont to do in architecture, or as Glasgow now does in some other respects. Here, then, in our own city—in some respects even more richly endowed than either by nature and by traditions, as well as by larger proportional " common good," and now again by generous citizenship —a new tide of civic initiative may and must be evoked, unless all concerned are to fall lamentably short of their initiative impulse.

In making a report of this kind, which to be useful must be definite, and to be definite must advise specific properties for acquirement, and suggest operations which tend to enhance the value of others, I venture to hope that such negotiations be approached as far as possible by all parties from the standpoint primarily not of the interest of the private citizen expecting advantage or generosity from the Trust, but from that of the Trust, which, as representing the common weal, has a right to expect always reasonable and, when possible, generous treatment from the ordinary citizen. I am glad to have found distinct encouragement in such very tentative inquiries as I have ventured to make at several specific points ; the owner sometimes freely promising to value his property, if required, as a willing seller—i.e. at no more than ordinary market rates—and in several cases even generously offering the ground or access required without payment altogether.

I take upon me to make this appeal in assured

confidence that it will often and increasingly be responded to by the private citizen, who, remembering that he is of the same stuff as the founder and trustees themselves, must also increasingly become an active sharer in their civic feelings and their practical generosity of means, or time.

Again, it must be asked, how is each new culture-agency, such as the present, to escape gradually yielding to the too common fate of human institutions—the gradual oncome of routine and senility, if not death and fossilisation ? How is each community, for its part, to protect itself from multi-corporate degeneracy ; indeed, from a measure of individual pauperisation ? How are such easy descents of good intentions to be prevented ?

Obviously in one way only : by defining the direction of " progress," by organising it into an active and resolute ascent. But this involves the recognition, the definition, of some goal to be ascended to ; it implies some well-matured and clearly maintained policy and principle, albeit adaptive in detail ; and this on the part of the citizens as well as their representatives and leaders. What we thus first of all require is some clear conception of general policy by which to select among the many deserving existing agencies, and the almost innumerable desirable new projects which are put forward on all hands. In such ways, then, Trust and citizens must increasingly find themselves committed to comprehensive and continuous inquiry on the one hand, to no less maintained economic and moral endeavour on the other.

Having discussed many recreative, educational, and other problems, their treatment in working institutions, their needed buildings, appropriate situation, aspect, and final setting of gardens, etc., I may now be permitted to sum up that conception of the Trust and its purpose which I have kept in view—that of the City, and citizens also.

Starting with the initial clauses of the deed, and with the admirable letter which accompanies it, I note in each the emphasis upon experimental purpose, and the injunction of " continuously pioneering endeavour." I note the donor's insistence upon not relieving Dunfermline of any responsibilities already municipal, but rather of initiating her to new responsibilities which may thereafter be municipally adopted. I note that the agency is for the higher benefit of the whole people, rich and poor moving onwards together in mutual touch—" all pioneers, always ahead."

In these times, when not only minor Scottish corporations have appropriated sums recently granted towards education for the relief of rates, but are in this only following the example of Edinburgh, once an educational metropolis, it will be greatly to the credit of Dunfermline if no attempt be made to transfer rateable burdens to the shoulders of the Trust.

B. Potential Auxiliaries of Trust: the Civic Union

A word now of the working of schemes and organisations. Since our park and gardens and buildings are but a stage on which the men and women are the players, what is to be their part ? Mere passive receptivity, whether of immaterial or material dole, is of no value ; it is apt, indeed, to be directly pernicious. It is as yet far too little recognised that the conditions commonly regarded as those of " perfect material well-being " —rest, security, warmth, food, abundance—are also the organic conditions for degeneration far more than for progress. They are only realised in nature by the most degraded forms of life, the parasites, so that, " plunged in an ocean of nectar and ambrosia, men would come not only to multiply as fast as the parasite but to degenerate as far."

It is the perception of this truth which explains and largely justifies even the surlier aspects of our Scottish independence. Yet we would here gratefully accept all that generous and initiative pioneering can do for us, guarding against all these dangers by acting on the simple reflection that the better the pioneering the more surely the main body may advance. But how secure the advance ? Some organisation is required for this general advance, no less than for the pioneering Trust and its administration. What form should this more popular organisation take ?

This is, of course, a matter for the most full and anxious consideration. Yet partly it is solving itself in practice. The various culture activities of the town, the institutions of learning, like the schools and libraries, the associations and societies naturalistic, horticultural, artistic, musical, and dramatic, are all stirring to renewed activity ; and the public are increasingly learning to appreciate their contribution towards the progressive whole.

The naturalists, the musicians, and the like are thus, so to speak, practically so many organs of the Trust, carrying out its cultural aims more intimately than its central body could possibly do, and developing their own organisations, from the best members of which, in the natural course of events, the Trust will recruit itself. In the meantime, may not the Trust consider the expediency of creating a body or bodies of Associates who would, each in their own department, become increasingly helpful to the Trust, and who might usefully at times be invited to give evidence to it, even to join deliberations of its special Committees, though not, of course, trespassing upon its powers ? In this way the Trust would have an opportunity of judging potential members before election, and its own recruitment be more than ever assured.

Even without going so far as this at the outset, this democratic principle is worth diffusing. Every person who is willing to aid in the general work of the Trust on every side thereby becomes for practical purposes its associate. In a very true sense, every giver of a mite in money or kind to the common good, still more the giver of time and pains, is so far a true co-operator with the founder himself, and with those whom he has directly associated, and is fulfilling and extending the highest objects of the foundation.

In the Social Union of Edinburgh the card of membership bears, or used to bear, a design for the donor's subscription in four columns; not, as usual, in one—the first marked, indeed, with the purse, for a money column; the next with a plan of the city for gifts of houses or lands; the next with a bale of goods for gifts in kind; the last with an hour-glass, for what may at once be the easiest, yet the most precious gift of all—time generously applied. Might not one of our designers work out this plan afresh in his own way for the membership card of these proposed Associates?

Such a group would be worthy of a yet more distinguished and ambitious title; they would practically constitute a Civic Union. Such a Union would naturally have many and increasing branches, which cannot be fully anticipated here. The principle, in fact, of immensely increasing the culture staff, and, therefore, the culture resources and culture efficiency of the Trust, by organising the voluntary labour, and developing the varied aptitudes of an increasing number of associates from among the ordinary citizens is no doubt difficult, but is practicable. Such work, more-over, is not less educative to its voluntary leaders and its officers of all ranks than to its youngest members.

A fuller conception of the Civic Union may be stated by recalling the treatment I have suggested for the City Cross, with its side towards each great group of practical interests, with its group of occupations, its corresponding sciences. Another presentment, yet more synthetic in its way, is that above suggested for the disposition of the Council Gallery in the Mansion-House; while a third is suggested in that interpretation of the four phases of the evolution of the city set forth in the previous chapter. At the initial meeting of the Civic Union, with its representatives of all its component organisations, let us place on the table our architectural model of the City Cross, with its graphic reminder of the claims and duties of the division of labour within the civic whole—the naturalists with their surveys, the physicians with their health pro-gramme, the horticulturists, no less ambitious, with theirs of "Flowers Unlimited," and so on— the educationist, no doubt, most active of all.

These respective organisations, each active in its own field, would meet periodically in general committee or general meeting, and might there-after bring their resultant ideas before the Trust, which would accept one proposal, reject another, modify or co-operate with a third, as it found practicable or expedient.

The fresh ideas and suggestions which arise—such, for instance, as those which, as already mentioned in the Intro-duction (page 18), I have received from many esteemed cor-respondents—would thus be fully and profitably discussed. To such suggestions from fresh eyes and different experience civic progress must always be indebted, and there is already evidence that as a city becomes increasingly fertile within herself she also becomes more open to ideas from every quarter. Hence an additional reason for not at present printing the correspondence and other material which lie before me. Yet fuller inquiries and more thorough discus-sion than even the vastest appendix could afford are desir-able; while such unity of treatment as the present volume possesses, harmonising in its various points of view, may be best appreciated apart from further detail.

Obviously adapted to co-operation in this way are on one side the Naturalists' Society, on the other the Archæologists, on a third the Horti-culturists, on a fourth the Photographic Society, and so on.

C. City Improvement Associations

As an example of such combined activities, do we not require in Dunfermline some analogue to those " Improvement Societies " which are now springing up through towns and villages, of the United States especially, but which have been in active work in German cities, especially for a generation, with the largest results upon their towns?

Thus the remarkable natural and historic at-tractiveness of Freiburg, alike as university and residential city, has been very greatly increased within the past generation by the labours of its " Verschönerungsverein " or Improvement Asso-ciation. This, for instance, has laid out probably not less than a hundred miles of paths, with the necessary seats, throughout the magnificent city forest which stretches from the cathedral place to the mountain tops. Besides all this, it has carried out many improvements in the town, as well as exercised a most useful conservative influence over its historic buildings. If a narrower patriotism be wounded by the comparison of this glorious Freiburg forest with the piteous Townhill wood, all the more need for a larger patriotism which admits the lesson and applies it.

Our Edinburgh Cockburn Association has not been without similar aims, though the critical rather than the constructive atmosphere of modern Edinburgh culture has for the most part paralysed its usefulness. Of late years a more vital initiative has also been given through our " National Trust," yet it is rather to German and American examples that we must still mainly rely for example and practical incentive. That the Dresden Towns Exhibition of last summer, the Paris Exhibition of Housing also, should have been practically ignored in this country is a vivid evidence of how much pioneering educational endeavour lies before the Trust. From their Exhibition of 1904 and its presumable successors much leavening influence may be hoped for.

In this work of improvement the photographer and sketcher may take an active share, the method suggested in some preceding pages, of putting side by side the actual and possible, being capable of far greater development than that which I have here given.

In this way this Civic Union, this reorganised or independent group of associates, as an Improvement Association, would be actively co-operating towards the continual improvement of the city and organising in their periodic exhibitions suggestions from which the Trust and its landscape-gardeners might alike profit—and not these alone. The services of such an association in developing love of beauty and love of city, and in raising the general interest above the merely personal one, could not but soon react upon the whole life of the city, and spread to others also.

With such mainly outdoor · activities those educative and constructive arts would naturally co-operate. With all these the directly social and human activities would be increasingly prepared for. The musician and teacher, amateur as well as official, have here also a limitless field. For dramatic associations there arise openings at once for keen criticism and ideal incentive.

D. Teachers and Clergy

The place of the teacher, as that of an Education Club, uniting all seriously interested in educational work and progress, in such a Civic Union, is too obvious to need any elaboration here ; a word, however, may be permitted of the share of the most kindred profession.

Writers on civics or education sometimes forget that every city, every county town is a centre of a group of men whose time is essentially divided between private studies and public application of them—in short, that in each of the various presbyteries, using the term in the wider sense, we have an analogue of the abbey of old, with its learning and its ministrations. Neither in the advance of

knowledge nor in the conduct of practical affairs have the clergy been leading so fully as of old ; but the readjustment of their attitude towards evolution, natural and social, has been in progress, and there are many indications of a renewal of the higher educational activity of the churches, as of their social and civic impulse. Not only, therefore, to the general body of the churches, but to the individual clergy, the idea of a Civic Union must strongly appeal, with its actively moralising possibilities, its courageous recognition of ideals, as of their expression in education and in social life. To them of all men, as to their predecessors of old, such a plea as that for material purification will carry its fullest symbolism also, and their idealism may thus be strengthened by fuller contact with everyday fact. For it is with the city group of to-day, as of old with the individual ; the needed cleansing and healing, enlightenment and awakening, are all best advanced together.

Sociology has been slow of developing, because the social being, the Family, the City, the Nation, must first come into existence, and even develop towards maturity, before attaining to that adequate self-consciousness. Least of all the sciences can this be learned in books. Every science has its real initiation in practical work, so that what the laboratory and the works are to the chemist, the hospital and practice to the physician, that the participation in occupational experience and in social endeavour is to the sociologist. The secret, then, of attaining to a grasp of this new science, this sharing of the dawning self-consciousness of the social being, is to " become oneself a socius." This, of course, is but a recent technical way of expressing the old statement that he must live the life who would know the doctrine. The historic services of members of the clergy to many sciences are not to be denied ; seldom, however, is it yet recognised that their share in the prosecution and advancement of the social sciences must soon become an increasing one, and still more their participation in the application of social knowledge and social ideals to the actual bettering of life.

At present many of the most moral and active individual forces of every community have been awakened to the particular line of helpfulness they follow through having lacked it in youth themselves. Our successors, however, will be increasingly fortunate—freely having received, they may also more freely give.

ENVOY

In studying the possibilities of this new park for the people, and assigning to " the admirable sites upon its edge " the needed structures, these, whether successfully or no, have been considered and treated with at least a sincere endeavour to keep in view the ideals laid down by the donor in his deed of trust and accompanying letter, and maintained in the chairman's inaugural address, which fitly accepts and develops the intention of the Trust.

However inadequate, the present report is thus a systematic endeavour to think out into the needful details the general principles laid down in the three documents referred to—an organised attempt to outline a comprehensive treatment of the material elements of park and buildings, and of their uses—and all this upon a scale sufficiently large to occupy the available resources and the activity of years to come, yet elastic enough to foster and stimulate, not limit, further development.

I am fully prepared for some of the preceding proposals being considered at first sight too simple, too democratic, too juvenile in their purpose, character, and point of view ; while others, again, will to many at first sight seem too ambitious, Utopian, since certainly " seeking to introduce into the lives of the people pleasures and enjoyments at present beyond their reach."

If so, I have only one request to make—that is, that the three initial documents above referred to be reread before my proposals are rejected. For since the keynotes there given forth are not those of our everyday practical life, but express ideals of exceptionally bold initiative, struck out at moments of highest insight and enthusiasm, the practical policy of the Trust and the proposals of the present report must aim at, must be attuned to, the corresponding height. It is not simply in his everyday business mood that the reader must judge of them, but in his highest moments of hope and resolve. It is for him to surpass the tide-mark of these chapters, not to judge it from everyday average, much less from the low water-mark of discouragement, of critical pessimism. The higher line once taken, its practicability may become clearer. For " tasks in hours of insight willed may be through hours of gloom fulfilled."

The members of this Trust, then, are no mere body of executors or almoners. They are, or should be, for the time the world's foremost council of sociological and social pioneers, and their present deliberations upon map, plan of campaign, and war chest are preliminary of campaign pledged to the boldest initiative. Thus viewed, the creation of this Trust may be considered as a move of the highest importance in that civic evolution of the world which claims hearing amid the political clamour of the times—it may be ere long precedence of this. Here then, once more in Scotland, as in the stirring times of old, we see opening before us " actions of a very high nature, leading to untrodden paths."

Floruit.   **Floreat!**

227

INDEX

229

*" You say life seems a struggle after nothing
in particular. But you are wrong. It is a
struggle after the peaceful home of the soul in a
natural and loving state of life. Men are
mostly unconscious of the object of their struggle,
but it is always connected in some way with
this."*

*" Give to barrows, trays, and pans
Grace and glimmer of romance ;
Bring the moonlight into noon
Hid in gleaming piles of stone ;
On the city's paved street
Plant gardens lined with lilacs sweet ;
Let spouting fountains cool the air
Singing in the sun-baked square ;
Let statue, picture, park, and hall,
Ballad, flag, and festival,
The past restore, the day adorn,
And make to-morrow a new morn."*

.   .   .   .   *" Paradise, and groves
Elysian, Fortunate Fields—like those of old
Sought in the Atlantic main, why should they be
A history only of departed things,
Or a mere fiction of what never was?
For the discerning intellect of man,
When wedded to this goodly Universe
In love and holy passion, shall find these
A simple produce of the common day."*

" Hitch your waggon to a star."

THE RIVERSIDE PRESS LIMITED, EDINBURGH